Conditio Judaica 43
Studien und Quellen zur deutsch-jüdischen Literatur- und Kulturgeschichte

Herausgegeben von Hans Otto Horch
in Verbindung mit Alfred Bodenheimer, Mark H. Gelber und Jakob Hessing

Placeless Topographies

Jewish Perspectives
on the Literature of Exile

Edited by Bernhard Greiner

Max Niemeyer Verlag
Tübingen 2003

Veröffentlicht mit Unterstützung des Deutschen Akademischen Austauschdienstes (DAAD), Bonn

Die Deutsche Bibliothek – CIP-Einheitsaufnahme

Die Deutsche Bibliothek verzeichnet diese Publikation in der Deutschen Nationalbibliografie;
detaillierte bibliografische Daten sind im Internet über *http://dnb.ddb.de* abrufbar.

ISBN 3-484-65143-1   ISSN 0941-5866

© Max Niemeyer Verlag GmbH, Tübingen 2003
http://www.niemeyer.de
Das Werk einschließlich aller seiner Teile ist urheberrechtlich geschützt. Jede Verwertung außerhalb der engen Grenzen des Urheberrechtsgesetzes ist ohne Zustimmung des Verlages unzulässig und strafbar. Das gilt insbesondere für Vervielfältigungen, Übersetzungen, Mikroverfilmungen und die Einspeicherung und Verarbeitung in elektronischen Systemen. Printed in Germany.
Gedruckt auf alterungsbeständigem Papier.
Druck: AZ Druck und Datentechnik GmbH, Kempten
Einband: Nädele Verlags- und Industriebuchbinderei, Nehren

Inhalt

Vorwort
   Exil und Exilliteratur im jüdischen Horizont 1

Guy Stern
   From Exile Experience to Exile Studies 21

Sidra DeKoven Ezrahi
   When Exiles Return: Jerusalem as Topos of the Mind and Soil 39

Jakob Hessing
   Heinrich Heine's *Reisebilder* as Images of Exile 53

Philipp Theisohn
   Erde / Papier. Kafka, Literatur und Landnahme 61

Pierre Bouretz
   Yichuv as *Teshuvah*: Gershom Scholem's Settlement in Jerusalem
   as Return from Assimilation 89

Mark H. Gelber
   Stefan Zweig's Conceptions of Exile 103

Christoph Schmidt
   Deus sive natura. The Transformation of the Jewish Apocalyptic
   Version of History into a Natural History in Jizchak Fritz Baer's
   Treatise of »Galut« (Exile) 115

Doerte Bischoff
   Exile, Trauma and the Modern Jewish Experience: The Example
   of Else Lasker-Schüler 127

Adi Gordon
   German Exiles in the ›Orient‹. The German-language Weekly *Orient*
   (Haifa, 1942–1943) between German Exile and Zionist Aliya 149

Bernhard Greiner
Re-Präsentation: Exil als Zeichenpraxis bei Anna Seghers 161

Rochelle Tobias
The Homecoming of a Word: Mystical Language Philosophy
in Celan's »Mit allen Gedanken« 175

Carola Hilfrich
»The Land of Others«. Geographies of Exile in Hélène Cixous's
writings 187

Frank Stern
The Two-Way Ticket to Hollywood and the Master-Images
of 20th Century Modernism 203

Philipp Theisohn
Nach Jerusalem 217

Autoren des Bandes 223

Personenregister 227

Vorwort

Exil und Exilliteratur im jüdischen Horizont

Der vorliegende Band geht auf eine Konferenz über jüdische Perspektiven der Exilliteratur zurück, die im Mai 2001 an der Hebräischen Universität in Jerusalem stattgefunden hat. Die Konzentration auf jüdische Aspekte der Exilliteratur und die Wahl des Konferenzortes waren ein Programm und wurden von den Teilnehmern auch als ein solches aufgegriffen: der Erwartung folgend, daß zum einen gerade durch die ›Einschränkung‹ auf jüdische Erfahrungen und Traditionen der Horizont der Exilliteratur-Forschung entschieden erweitert werde, und daß zum andern das Ins-Spiel-Bringen des Ortes Jerusalem grundlegende Paradoxien von Exilliteratur schärfer hervortreten lasse.

Das babylonische Exil der Juden ist die erste uns bekannte Exilerfahrung eines Volkes und schon diese zeigt die charakteristische Strategie der Literarisierung des Exils, d. i. den Versuch, durch Narration aus der Erfahrung des Verlusts Identität neu zu begründen. Seit 2.500 Jahren ist in der jüdischen Tradition die Erfahrung des Exils präsent und ist eine Vielfalt von Strategien ausgebildet worden, diese Erfahrung zu bewältigen, theoretisch und praktisch u. a. auf den Feldern der Theologie, der Philosophie (Gedächtniskultur), der Geschichte wie der Literatur. Gleichwohl konnte ein Experte wie Yosef Hayim Yerushalmi auf das Paradox verweisen, daß einerseits aufgrund der konstitutiven jüdischen Erfahrung des Exils »jede umfassende Geschichte der Juden letztlich auch eine Geschichte des jüdischen Exils sein müßte«, andererseits aber »die eigentliche historische Analyse des Exils wohl erst noch geleistet werden« müsse.[1] Als Wegweisungen zu dieser noch ausstehenden Arbeit verweist Yerushalmi auf den Band *Golah venekhar* (»Exil und Entfremdung«, 1929/30) von Yehezkel Kaufmann und auf die Studie *Galut* von Yitzhak Baer; letztere preist er um ihrer Kürze und Prägnanz willen. Es ist erstaunlich, daß dieses Buch 1936 in Nazi-Deutschland erscheinen konnte. Christoph Schmidt untersucht im vorliegenden Band den Umschlag im jüdischen Geschichtsdenken, den diese Studie vollzieht und zugleich reflektiert.

Die jüdische Tradition legt eine anthropologische Universalisierung des Exilgedankens nahe, derart, daß es das Wesen der menschlichen Existenz ausmache, aus der dem Menschen ursprünglich zugehörigen Welt vertrieben zu sein:

---

[1] Yosef Hayim Yerushalmi: Exil und Vertreibung in der jüdischen Geschichte. In: ders., Ein Feld in Anatot. Versuche über jüdische Geschichte. Aus dem Amerikanischen von Wolfgang Heuss und Bruni Röhm. Berlin: Wagenbach 1993 (Kleine kulturwissenschaftliche Bibliothek; 44), S. 21–38, hier S. 21.

theologisch-geschichtsphilosophisch im Gedanken der Vertreibung aus dem Paradies, psychologisch im Konzept des Geburtstraumas resp. der Ablösung aus dem Stadium der Mutter-Kind Dyade (des ›primären Narzißmus‹), sprachphilosophisch-poetologisch im Gedanken, aus der magisch-mythischen Sprachwelt, in der Wort und Sache eins sind, in diesem Sinne aus der Welt der ›heiligen Sprache‹, herausgefallen zu sein.[2] Gegenüber solch universalgeschichtlicher Fassung des Exilgedankens auf der Grundlage einer scharfen Opposition von Heimat und Fremde, Bei-Sich-Sein und Außer-Sich-Sein bringt die jüdische Geschichte im engeren Sinn, die mit Gottes Bund mit Abraham einsetzt, eben diese Opposition ins Gleiten. Die Geschichte des von Gott auserwählten Volkes setzt damit ein, daß Gott Abraham gebietet, seine Heimat zu verlassen, um einer ihm versprochenen neuen Heimat willen. Die Geburt des jüdischen Volkes, die Offenbarung und der Bund am Sinai, findet in einem Zwischenraum statt, das Land der Knechtschaft ist verlassen, die Ankunft im gelobten Land steht aber noch aus; für das Nichtbefolgen der auferlegten Gebote wird als Strafe Exil in fürchterlicher Weise angedroht (Deut. 28,63 und 64–67, Lev. 26). So ist Exil in jüdischer Tradition integraler Bestandteil von Gemeinschaftsbildung und Landnahme.[3] Das theologische Konzept hat sodann seit dem babylonischen Exil auch historische Entsprechungen, zuerst, nach dem Ende des babylonischen Exils und in den folgenden Jahrhunderten, als Effekt jüdischer Migration, im Spannungsfeld von Heimat und Diaspora, seit der Zerstörung des zweiten Tempels und der Vertreibung dann unter der Bedingung, daß der Identität begründende Bezugsort des Exils absolut entzogen ist.

Die Konzentration auf jüdische Perspektiven des Exils gibt der Auseinandersetzung mit Exilliteratur eine umfassende historische Tiefe, zugleich erweitert sie diese Auseinandersetzung literarisch, da sich in diesem Horizont jede Beschränkung auf eine Nationalliteratur von vornherein verbietet. In diesem weiten jüdischen Erfahrungshorizont von Exil und Exilliteratur sind auch neue, produktive Zugänge zu dem literarischen Corpus zu erwarten, das in der deutschen Literaturgeschichte unter dem Begriff ›Exilliteratur‹ zusammengefaßt wird, d. i. »eine Literatur, deren Autoren durch Verbannung, Vertreibung oder Flucht von ihrem Wirkungsfeld und damit auch von ihrer angestammten sprachlich-kulturellen Lebenswelt getrennt wurden, ohne jedoch die emotionale bzw. intentionale Beziehung zu ihrem Herkunftsland gänzlich aufzukündigen oder einzubüßen«.[4] Diese Definition bleibt allgemein, so daß sie z. B. auch Ovids *Tristia ex Ponto* umfaßt oder Autoren, die im Zuge der europäischen Revolutionen oder der auf diese folgenden Epochen repressiver Restauration ihre geographische, politische und sprachliche Heimat verlassen haben (etwa Heine und Börne in Paris, Marx in London). In der deutschsprachigen Literaturgeschichte wird ›Exilliteratur‹

---

[2] Zu dieser Universalisierung des Exilgedankens: Elisabeth Bronfen: Exil in der Literatur: Zwischen Metapher und Realität. In: Arcadia 28 (1993), S. 167–183.
[3] Ausführlicher hierzu in der Einleitung zum eigenen Beitrag im vorliegenden Band.
[4] Bernhard Spies: Exilliteratur. In: Reallexikon der deutschen Literaturwissenschaft. Berlin, New York: de Gruyter 1997, Bd 2, S. 537–540, hier S. 537.

gleichwohl auf Werke eingeschränkt, die zwischen 1933 und 1945 von Flüchtlingen aus dem Machtbereich von Nazi-Deutschland verfaßt worden sind. Guy Stern zeichnet in seinem Beitrag – als Betroffener – den Übergang von der Erfahrung des Exils zur Konstitution des Genres ›Exilliteratur‹ im genannten engeren Sinn und der auf diese bezogenen Exilliteraturforschung nach.

Die Auseinandersetzung mit Exilliteratur, die der vorliegende Band dokumentiert, hat im Rahmen der Konzentration auf die jüdische Erfahrung des Exils einen weiteren Akzent darin, daß sie den Ort Jerusalem systematisch einbezieht. Jerusalem ist zum einen der Ort, auf den in der jüdischen Tradition seit der Vernichtung des Tempels und der Vertreibung nur als entzogener Ort – A-Topos – Bezug genommen werden kann, was die produktive Kraft hervorbringt, das Entzogene mit Bedeutung aufzuladen: neben dem historisch realen der topologische, allegorische und anagogische Sinn von ›Jerusalem‹, die Transformation mithin von Jerusalem zur Idee. So steht Jerusalem im Spannungsfeld von real-historischer und ideeller Stadt, seit Begründung der zionistischen Bewegung aber auch im Spannungsfeld von Exil und Heimkehr, das semiologisch die Frage heraufführt, wie Präsenz im Raum der Repräsentation geleistet werden kann,[5] theologisch ist diese Frage in der Opposition von messianischer und geschichtlicher Existenz impliziert. Die messianische Idee im Judentum, das Leben in der Hoffnung, was auch besagt: im Aufschub, so hat Gershom Scholem betont, hat den Preis »der unendlichen Schwäche der jüdischen Geschichte, die im Exil zum Einsatz auf der geschichtlichen Ebene nicht bereit war. Sie hat die Schwäche des Vorläufigen, des Provisorischen, das sich nicht ausgibt. Denn die messianische Idee ist nicht nur Trost und Hoffnung. In jedem Versuch ihres Vollzuges brechen die Abgründe auf, die jede ihrer Gestalten ad absurdum führen.«[6] Jerusalem als Bezugsort von Exilliteratur treibt die Widersprüchlichkeit dieser Atopie mit besonderer Schärfe heraus. Zur Idee aufgeladen transzendiert dieser ›Ort‹ jede Konkretisierung, um doch zugleich als der Antipode schlechthin von Exil zu firmieren.

Kompliziert wird der Raumgedanke im Konzept ›Exilliteratur‹, konzentriert man sich auf die jüdische Perspektive, weiter dadurch, daß auch der genuine Ort des Exils selbst, Babylon, in jüdischer Tradition in abgründiger Widersprüchlichkeit gedacht ist. Babylon ist nicht nur der erste historische Ort des jüdischen Exils, sondern auch der Ort der Sprachverwirrung, des Verlustes mithin der Heimat in ›einer‹ Sprache (vgl. Gen. 11,1: »Es hatte aber alle Welt einerlei Zungen und Sprache«). Nach der Sintflut hatte Gott seinen Bund mit den Menschen (Noah) erneuert und dies mit dem Gebot verbunden, sich in der Welt zu zerstreuen, was die Bibelerzählung dann auch festhält im Aufzählen der Nachkommen Noahs, der diesen entspringenden Völker und Sprachen. Danach aber setzt Gen. 11 mit der Aussage ein, daß alle Welt eine Sprache hatte, daß die Men-

---

[5] Hierzu ausführlicher der Beitrag von Philipp Theisohn in diesem Band.
[6] Gershom Scholem: Zum Verständnis der messianischen Idee im Judentum. In: ders., Über einige Grundbegriffe des Judentums. Frankfurt a. M.: Suhrkamp 1970 (Suhrkamp-Taschenbuch; 414), S. 121–167, hier S. 166f.

schen in der Ebene von Sinear eine Gemeinschaft werden und bleiben wollten, als Volks- und Sprachgemeinschaft, und daß sie dies wollten aus Furcht vor Zerstreuung. Sie wollten eines bleiben und zum Zeichen dieser Einheit einen Turm bauen. Die Menschen wollten identifizieren, totalisieren, d. h. das Vielerlei von Einem, vom eigenen Zentrum her denken, was besagt, das ›Andere‹, Fremde als das Andere des Eigenen zu fassen und es sich so zu unterwerfen.

Gott hatte den Noachitischen Menschen geboten, »seid fruchtbar und mehret euch und füllet die Erde« (Gen. 9,1). Daß dies besagte, sich zu zerstreuen, hält der Bibeltext positiv im Aufzählen der verschiedenen Völker und Sprachen fest, die aus Noahs Nachkommen hervorgegangen sind, negativ in der Furcht der Menschen von Sinear, zerstreut zu werden, sowie im Effekt der von Gott geschaffenen Sprachverwirrung: »so zerstreute sie der HERR von dort in alle Länder« (Gen. 11,8). Zerstreuung als Gebot Gottes ist allerdings unerfüllbar. Zerstreuen die Menschen sich, bleiben sie darin zurückbezogen auf das Gebot des Herrn als einheitsstiftenden Grund, bleibt das Vielerlei von einer ursprünglichen Einheit her gedacht, hat wirkliche Zerstreuung mithin nicht stattgefunden. Zerstreuen die Menschen sich aber nicht, schaffen sie eine Gemeinschaft mit dem Erbauen von Stadt und Turm, haben sie sich zwar von ihrem ursprünglichen Bezugspunkt, Gottes Gebot, losgesagt, aber sich eben auch nicht zerstreut, bilden sie vielmehr eine vom Ursprung unabhängige Einheit. Gottes Niederfahren und Verwirren der Sprache, abstrakt formuliert: die Negation der Nicht-Zerstreuung, leistet erst eine Zerstreuung, die keinen einheitsstiftenden Grund mehr hat; denn nun gibt es weder einen positiven Rückbezug zu Gottes Gebot, noch eine vom Ursprung unabhängige Einheit. Mit der Verwirrung der Sprache schafft Gott die Bedingung für die Unmöglichkeit des Vollendens. Die Nicht-Vollendung des Turms, das nicht vollendete Zeichen, wird zum Ort der Öffnung für eine Vielfalt, für ein Fremdes, das nicht auf eine vorgängige Einheit (als das Eigene) zurückbezogen werden kann.

Babylon, der paradigmatische Ort des Exils, ist widersprüchlich. Das Erbauen von Stadt und Turm steht für Totalisierung, d. i. für ein Denken, das das Andere der Logik der Identität unterwirft. Zugleich steht Babylon für Zerstreuung, für Vertrieben-Werden aus einem identifizierenden Denken, was auch besagt: für die Chance des Hinübergehens zum Anderen als Anderem. Wenn man das konstitutive Anliegen und die konstitutive Leistung von Exilliteratur darin erkennen kann, Identität aus einer Narration zu begründen, die zwei Orte in Beziehung setzt, den Ort des Schreibens und den Ort der Zugehörigkeit, d. h. der Heimat als dem Bezugspunkt des Schreibens, so sind in der jüdischen Tradition diese beiden Orte – Babylon und Jerusalem – als in sich widersprüchlich bestimmt. Babylon ist der Ort des Exils, aber als Ort von Gemeinschaftsbildung durch Identifizieren und Totalisieren, in der jedoch eine abgründige Zerstreuung schon immer am Werke ist. Umgekehrt führt Jerusalem als das geistige und reale Zentrum des Judentums dessen Paradox mit sich, daß in die jüdische Gemeinschaftsbildung von jeher das Exil einbeschlossen ist. Das jüdische Schreiben des Exils findet in ›Babylon‹ statt, das als Ort abgrün-

Exil und Exilliteratur im jüdischen Horizont 5

diger Zerstreuung ein Nicht-Ort ist; und dieses Schreiben ist auf ›Jerusalem‹ bezogen, das entweder entzogen ist oder Exil in seinem Zentrum enthält und insofern gleichfalls ein Nicht-Ort ist. Als Schreiben an einem Nicht-Ort, das gespannt ist auf einen Nicht-Ort, ist jüdisches Schreiben des Exils so in einem umfassenden Sinne ›Topo-Graphie ohne Ort‹. Die hier versammelten Studien zeigen, wie diese doppelte Paradoxie im jüdischen Schreiben des Exils in unterschiedlichsten literarischen Strategien entfaltet und reflektiert wird. In den Untersuchungen zu Heine, Kafka, Scholem und Stefan Zweig, ebenso zur Zeitschrift *Orient* wie zur neueren Hebräischen Literatur hat der Aspekt des Raums, verbunden mit der Frage der Begründung von Identität, besonderes Gewicht. Im Schaffen von Else Lasker-Schüler, Anna Seghers und Paul Celan erscheint die erläuterte Paradoxie semiologisch akzentuiert, während das Schreiben von Hélène Cixous das in dieser Paradoxie enthaltene Alteritätskonzept in beispielhafter Weise produktiv macht.

Es versteht sich von selbst, daß Auseinandersetzung mit Exilliteratur in Jerusalem selbstreflexiv wird. So wird diese Konsequenz hier auch nicht zum ersten Mal vermerkt. Ein anregendes früheres Beispiel hat Jürgen Nieraad gegeben, dem die hier referierte Konferenz gewidmet war. Im Mai 1989 hat gleichfalls an der Hebräischen Universität in Jerusalem eine Konferenz über ›Deutsch-jüdische Exil- und Emigrationsliteratur im 20. Jahrhundert‹ stattgefunden, die in einem 1993 im gleichen Verlag erschienenen Band dokumentiert ist.[7] Die Planung und Organisation der früheren Konferenz war wesentlich das Werk von Jürgen Nieraad, der zwar keinen Vortrag gehalten, wohl aber im erwähnten Band eine Zusammenfassung des Symposions gegeben hat, die er aus grundlegenden Überlegungen zur Exilliteratur-Forschung entwickelt.[8] Die hier dokumentierte Konferenz zur Exilliteratur ist, trotz der anderen Akzentuierung ihres Themas, eine Weise, den Dialog mit Jürgen Nieraad fortzusetzen, mit unserem Kollegen am German Department der Hebräischen Universität, der hier seit Mitte der achtziger Jahre bis zu seinem Tod im November 2000 gelehrt hat. Die hier vorgetragenen Gedanken über das Thema und den spezifischen Akzent des neuerlichen Symposions zur Exilliteratur sind in mancher Hinsicht eine Antwort auf Jürgen Nieraads Fragen und Forderungen, eine Antwort, in die selbstverständlich die Perspektiven, das Interesse und das Wissen, wie es zehn Jahre später gegeben ist, mit eingegangen ist. Aber unterschiedliche Positionen und Ansichten zu formulieren und gegenseitig zu konturieren, war für Jürgen Nieraad nie eine Hindernis wissenschaftlicher Diskussion, vielmehr deren Voraussetzung.

---

[7] Deutsch-jüdische Exil- und Emigrationsliteratur im 20. Jahrhundert. Hg. von Itta Shedletzky und Hans Otto Horch. Tübingen: Max Niemeyer Verlag 1993 (Conditio Judaica. Studien und Quellen zur deutsch-jüdischen Literatur- und Kulturgeschichte; 5)

[8] Jürgen Nieraad: Deutsch-jüdische Exil- und Emigrationsliteratur im 20. Jahrhundert. Nachgedanken zu einer Konferenz. In: Deutsch-jüdische Exil- und Emigrationsliteratur im 20. Jahrhundert (wie Anm. 7), S. 271–280.

Damit es nicht nur eine Behauptung bleibt, daß das hier dokumentierte Symposion den wissenschaftlichen Dialog mit Jürgen Nieraad fortsetze, seien dessen leitende Thesen und Fragen zur Exilliteratur und deren Erforschung in Erinnerung gerufen, die er in der erwähnten Zusammenfassung entwickelt hat.

Jürgen Nieraad arbeitet drei zentrale Fragefelder der Auseinandersetzung mit Exilliteratur heraus. Das erste Fragefeld betrifft selbstverständlich die Konstitution des Gegenstandes dieser Forschung. Nach welchen Kriterien ist Zugehörigkeit zu Exilliteratur zu bestimmen? Von den Kriterien, die Jürgen Nieraad auflistet – geographische, ideologische, literatur-soziologische, pragmatische und literarisch-ästhetische – sei die Aufmerksamkeit auf das letzte gerichtet. Wenn Literatur als ästhetisches Phänomen wahrgenommen werden soll, da sie dann erst in dem ihr wesentlichen Aspekt im Blick ist, kann dies nur im Fragen nach ihren jeweils spezifischen ästhetischen Strategien, Formationen und Orientierungen und nach deren Grundlage geschehen. Mithin haben wir Exilliteratur vor allem anderen von spezifisch ästhetischen Konzepten her zu bestimmen, die diese Literatur ausgebildet und angewendet hat.

Das zweite große Fragefeld der Exilliteratur-Forschung, das Jürgen Nieraad herausarbeitet, betrifft die Frage nach dem jüdischen Anteil insbesondere in der deutschsprachigen Exilliteratur und nach dessen Status. Wenn Jürgen Nieraad vor zehn Jahren festzustellen hatte, das dieser Komplex in der Forschung zur deutschsprachigen Exilliteratur noch nicht systematisch bearbeitet ist, so haben wir heute einzuräumen, daß dies – cum grano salis – immer noch zutrifft. Jürgen Nieraad entwickelt diese Fragestellung in phänomenologischer Perspektive, d. h. er stellt die Frage ins Zentrum, worin die Besonderheit der deutsch-jüdischen Exilliteratur zu erkennen sei. Die Antwort sucht er im Status einer potenzierten Besonderung der Autorengruppe (als Minderheit einer Minderheit) und in deren prekärem Bezug zur deutschen Kultur. Letzteres erkennt er vor allem in einer größeren Bereitschaft zur Distanznahme und entsprechend einer größeren Bereitschaft und Fähigkeit, die Grenzen einer Nationalliteratur zu überschreiten (im Vergleich mit anderen Gruppen deutschsprachiger Exilliteratur). Dem sind allerdings die hohen Erwartungen entgegenzuhalten, die gerade in der deutsch-jüdischen Tradition mit der Kulturidee verbunden werden, insofern in dieser zum einen die universale Idee der Freiheit akzentuiert ist, zum andern aber – als ihrer ästhetischen Komponente – das Insistieren auf dem Besonderen als Besonderen, so daß in der Kulturidee der Anspruch jüdischer Emanzipation und Gleichstellung verfolgt werden kann, ohne daß dies als Preis die Aufgabe der jüdischen Besonderheit einschließt. Die größere Bereitschaft, auf Distanz zu gehen zur deutschen Kultur, hat derart in der deutsch-jüdischen Tradition ein starkes Gegengewicht in einem besonderen Nahverhältnis zu dieser Kultur. Gegenüber Jürgen Nieraads phänomenologischem Zugang zur Frage nach dem jüdischen Anteil in der deutschsprachigen Exilliteratur weisen die hier vorgetragenen allgemeinen Überlegungen zur jüdischen Tradition der Exilliteratur auf einen theologisch-hermeneutischen und einen allgemein historischen Zugang zu dieser Problemstellung: in der Frage nach dem biblischen Konzept von Gemeinschaftsbildung und Exil und nach deren Relation zu den historischen Erfahrungen, die die jüdische Geschichte bereithält. Erwartet wird, daß sich im Horizont dieser Fragen neue produktive Auseinandersetzungen auch mit der deutschsprachigen Exilliteratur ergeben werden.

Ein drittes zentrales Fragefeld der Exilliteraturforschung erkennt Jürgen Nieraad im Problem des Diskursmodus dieses Forschungsfeldes. Das Forschen hat gerade in diesem Bereich in besonderer Weise dessen inne zu sein, daß der wissenschaftliche Gestus des Strukturierens, des Fragens nach Regeln, die die gegebenen Phänomene erklären, des Verstehens, indem etwas einem Verstehenskonzept zugeordnet wird: daß dieser wissenschaftliche Gestus all die erneut verletzen muß, die eben die leidvolle Erfahrung des Exils gemacht haben, mit der sich die zu analysierende Literatur auseinandersetzt. Dieses Problem betrifft die Exilliteratur selbst wie deren Erforschung: findet sich hier Offenheit für das Besondere, das Spezifische, für das, was nicht zum Fall einer Regel gemacht werden kann und darf? Ist die Forschung über Exilliteratur im Besitz einer Sprache für dieses Besondere der Erfahrung, wobei sie doch eine Sprache der Wahrnehmung und Erkenntnis bleiben muß (was immer verlangt, eine Vorstellung mit einem Begriff zu verbinden)? Man kann Jürgen Nieraads Forderung nur unterstreichen, daß Forschung über Exil und Exilliteratur – und dies gerade auch im jüdischen Kontext – in einer besonderen Weise aufgefordert ist, auf ihre eigene Sprache zu achten. Eine Strategie, mit dem dargelegten Dilemma produktiv umzugehen, ist, Exilliteratur vor allem und grundlegend als ästhetisches Phänomen zu erkennen und zu erforschen, da damit wesensmäßig gefordert ist, das Besondere als Besonderes anzuerkennen, bei ihm zu verweilen, es nicht zum Fall einer Regel zu machen, ohne daß dies besagen würde, daß auf Konzeptualisierung der Phänomene verzichtet werden müsse, mithin anzuerkennen, daß eine Verknüpfung des Besonderen mit (immer generalisierenden) Konzepten des Verstehens erreicht werden muß, aber nie erreicht werden kann. Gewiß würde diese Art Rekurs auf Kants Bestimmung des ›Schönen‹ in der *Kritik der Urteilskraft* im Zusammenhang der Auseinandersetzung mit Exilliteratur zu einer intensiven Debatte mit Jürgen Nieraad führen. Wenn nachfolgend sehr unterschiedliche Zugänge zu Exilliteratur und deren Erforschung vorgetragen und begründet werden, wird dies als solch eine weiterhin lebendige Debatte mit Jürgen Nieraad verstanden, was das Aufgreifen und Erwägen seiner Positionen einschließt, aber ebenso das Akzentuieren eigener.

* * *

Mit *Guy Stern* eröffnet diesen Band einer der Geburtshelfer der ›Exile Studies‹, der sie in ihrem Werden und ihren Verschiebungen, vor allem aber auch in den ihr konstitutiven und keineswegs unproblematischen Übergängen von Zeugenschaft zu Theoriebildung, vom Erleben zum Erzählen stets kritisch begleitet hat. Auf einem Forschungsfeld, dessen Ursprungsaufgabe nicht nur darin bestand, dasjenige zu bewahren, das um seinen Ort gebracht worden war (und ihm in der archivalen Zusammenführung des Zerstreuten gleichsam wieder einen Ort zu geben), sondern das diese ›Ent Ortung‹ selbst gerade faßbar machen sollte und sie zunächst dort aufsuchte, wo sie sich am offensichtlichsten eingeschrieben hatte – in der Biographie –: auf ebenjenem Forschungsfeld stellt das Eindringen (literatur-)wissenschaftlicher Paradigmata und Fragestellungen eine immer wiederkehrende Herausforderung an die Erfahrung ›Exil‹ dar. Ist bereits die Frage nach der territorialen Begrenzung von Ortlosigkeit, also etwa nach der Möglichkeit einer »inneren Emigration«, als leichte Erschütterung eines positivistisch fundierten Begriffs von ›Exil‹ zu verzeichnen, so stoßen wir mit der Frage nach dem Verhältnis von Vertreibung und Rückkehr in weit komplexere Dimensionen vor. Ist ein Exilschriftsteller, dem die Rückkehr in sein Heimatland wieder offen steht, der von dieser Möglichkeit aber keinen Gebrauch macht, immer noch ein Exilschriftsteller? Gibt es überhaupt eine Rückkehr vom Exil? Und schließlich (womit wir bereits im Herzen der Konferenzdiskussion angelangt wären): was geschieht, wenn wir Vertreibung *als* Rückkehr denken? Es ist unstrittig, daß all diese Überlegungen für die Exile Studies nicht nur deswegen von zentraler Bedeutung waren und sind, weil sich je nach Definition in der Folge ihr Korpus und Kanon einschränken, verschieben oder ins Unermeßliche erweitern, sondern weil mit jeder dieser Fragen auch immer wieder der Zweifel bewältigt werden muß, ob sich Textwissenschaft und Entortungs-Erfahrung wirklich sinnvoll vermitteln lassen. So droht auf der einen Seite mit dem Aufkommen des Postkolonialismus die Rede vom ›Exil‹ in eine universale Rede überzugehen, welche der Spezifik der Exilerfahrung nur bedingt gerecht werden kann; auf der anderen Seite birgt jedes Klammern an der Authentizität ›erlebter‹ Vertreibung, zumal an der Vertreibung aus Hitlers Deutschland, die beunruhigende Vermutung, daß mit dem Versiegen dieser Erfahrung auch die Wissenschaft von ihr schnell an ein Ende gelangen könnte. Im Angesicht dieses Zwiespalts skizziert Stern die Aufgaben einer zukünftigen Exilforschung, die zum einen in der kulturwissenschaftlichen Öffnung, dem Überschreiten der Grenze von ›literarischen‹ und ›außerliterarischen‹ Exilvertextungen, zum anderen in der komparatistischen, das Schreiben jenseits der Nationen nun auch jenseits der Nationalliteraturen aufsuchenden Vernetzung des Exils, schließlich aber auch in der Beobachtung der Interaktionen zwischen Exilschaffen und dem es umgebenden Kulturkreis (nicht zuletzt auch dem Nachleben der Exilanten in der nicht- bzw. postexilischen Literatur) begründet liegen.

Insofern sich die jüdische Vorstellungskraft für Jahrtausende dem Exil ›verschrieben‹ und ein Kulturkonzept begründet hatte, welches, anhebend mit der Zerstörung des zweiten Tempels, sich ganz auf die Simulation des entzogenen Kulturraumes durch den Text stützte, so steht mit dem zionistischen Projekt einer Heimkehr aus der Galut ein ungemein traditionsreiches Kreativitätsmodell in Frage. Das Wiederauftauchen des Ursprungs als einer konkreten Verräumlichung des Heiligen ist für eine Poetik, welche die Abwesenheit des Raumes immer schon als Legitimationsnachweis mit sich führt, eine ›Exilpoetik‹, von äußerster Virulenz. *Sidra DeKoven Ezrahi* erkundet vor diesem Hintergrund die Mechanismen, die den mimetischen Bezug einer diasporeischen Kunst zum abwesenden Ort regeln, die Bedingungen, unter denen eine solche Kunst im Raum des Profanen überhaupt möglich wird. In den Blickpunkt rückt hierbei zum einen die Transformation der nicht-jüdischen, tendenziell idolatrischen Welt in eine Sphäre der Neutralität, in welcher nicht nur sozialer wie kultureller Austausch, sondern in der Konsequenz auch Verhandlungen über das Ästhetische, das Ikonische, das Kultische statt haben können; zum anderen aber auch die antiidolatrische Funktion des Textes: während es der synagogalen Architektur untersagt ist, den Tempel nachzubilden, wird der Tanach selbst – etwa von Profiat Duran – als proportionsgerechte Analogiebildung, als ›Bauplan‹ des Tempels verstanden.[9] Indem Schrift immer schon das Stigma des Surrogats, der unüberwindbaren Distanz zur Stätte des ›Wirklichen‹ mit sich führt, vermag sie die Zeichen der Häresie und des Paganen aufzunehmen, versichert sie doch zugleich gegen die Idolatrie, gegen die Aufhebung der Unterscheidung zwischen Symbol und Gottheit. Der Schrift des Exils geht das Bewußtsein ihres substitutionellen Charakters nie verloren, sie bleibt immer teleologisch gespannt auf die Erinnerung einer verlorenen Vergangenheit im Namen einer zukünftigen Rückkehr und gleichzeitig doch wesenhaft gebunden an den Raum der Diaspora. Sie wird, wie die Dichtungen Yehuda Halevis eindrücklich dokumentieren, getrieben vom Verlangen nach Zion und doch geht dieser Eros stets einher mit der Angst vor dem Verlust der eigenen Existenzberechtigung, dem Versiegen vor den Toren Jerusalems. Bis auf den heutigen Tag, d. h. auch nach der staatlichen Wiederherstellung Israels, stoßen wir bei genauer Betrachtung dementsprechend immer noch auf zwei von Grund auf voneinander geschiedene Topographien: den Versuch, sich in den Ort wieder einzuschreiben, sich mit dem Heiligen zu verbinden und aus der zweiten in die dritte Dimension, von der Skizze zum Bau vorzustoßen; und den Versuch, diesen Ort wieder in die Schrift überzuführen, ihn zu diskursivieren und – um einen Gedanken Herzls aufzugreifen – Jerusalem gleichsam zu »exterritorialisieren«.[10]

Jakob Hessing beschäftigt sich in seinem Beitrag zu Heinrich Heine mit einer sich unentwegt an Auszug und Erlösung abarbeitenden Imaginationskraft, deren ironische Durchbrechung das Subjekt stets wieder an seine Vertreibung, sein Ausgeliefert-Sein, sein finales Scheitern im Kampf um Selbstbestimmung zurückverweist. Hinter den Frauenvisionen, den Paarträumen und der märchenhaften Verklärung der *Reisebilder* kommt eine Welt zum Vorschein, die keinen Messias kennt, in der die Toten niemals wieder auferstehen. Der Dichter vermag den eschatologischen Umbruch, das Ende der Verbannung nicht herbeizuführen; die ästhetischen Transformationsmodelle der Kunstperiode (konkret: etwa das Modell des Erhabenen) greifen nicht mehr, sondern obstruieren vielmehr die revolutionäre Tat. In jenem Moment, in dem die illusionäre Verkleidung des Exils durchdrungen wird, tritt die Gewalt, die ihm zugrunde liegt, augenblicklich hervor und wendet sich sogleich gegen das Ich in ihrer radikalsten Form – im Tod ohne Erweckung.

---

[9] Vgl. Kalman Bland: The Artless Jew. Medieval and Modern Affirmations and Denials of the Visual. Princeton: Princeton University Press 2000, S.84.

[10] Vgl. Herzls Tagebucheintrag vom 7. Mai 1896, in: Theodor Herzl: Tagebücher I. Gesammelte zionistische Werke II. Tel Aviv: Hozaah Ivrit 1934, S. 395f.

Die Frage nach der Möglichkeit, das Land in das ›Exil Literatur‹ wieder zurückzuholen, die Erde wieder unter dem Papier hervortreten zu lassen, steht im Zentrum des Beitrages von *Philipp Theisohn*. In Auseinandersetzung mit Deleuzes und Guattaris Bestimmungen einer ›kleinen Literatur‹ wird dabei am Beispiel Franz Kafkas der Versuch unternommen, das Verhältnis von Marginalität und Territorialität neu zu denken. Die Aufmerksamkeit gilt dabei zunächst der binären Konstruktion marginalen Schreibens als eines stetigen Prozesses von Deterritorialisierung und Reterritorialisierung, die dort fragwürdig zu werden beginnt, wo die Polis sich nicht *gegen*, sondern *durch* das Nomadentum begründet, wo ›Landnahme‹ nur aus der Verunklärung der Margo heraus möglich wird. Im Bau der chinesischen Mauer wird die Deutungsherrschaft der kartographischen Logik über die territoriale Logik desavouiert und gebrochen; zurück bleibt nicht nur eine materiell wie ideell nicht zu verknüpfende (›zu totalisierende‹) Ansammlung von Teilbauten, sondern ebenso eine narrativ geschlagene Bresche zwischen Literatur und Land. (Dabei gilt es zu beachten, daß gleichzeitig in den von Kafka rezipierten religionsgeschichtlichen und religionspolitischen Quellen[11] sich die Fragmentarisierung eines anderen Baues, der jüdischen Gesetzesmauern, vollzieht, eine Destruktion, die angetrieben wird von einer Kraft, die dem Gesetz selbst noch vorausliegt.) Im weiteren hält jenes Prinzip des ›Unvermauerten‹ Strategien zur Lösung des Konfliktes bereit, dem sich einer der berühmtesten Exilierten der modernen Literatur, der nach Amerika verschiffte Karl Rossmann, ausgesetzt sieht. Für den ›Verschollenen‹ bedeutet das Exil eine semiotische Gewalt, die Fesselung an einen Raum, dessen Maschinen dem Subjekt die Kontrolle über seinen persönlichen Signifikantenvorrat entziehen und diesen – Zeichen für Zeichen – an sich reißen, um ihn einem kaleidoskopischen Mechanismus zu überantworten, der unaufhörlich Bedeutsamkeiten kodifiziert, spatialisiert und Kommunikationsbarrieren errichtet, vor denen Karl ein ums andre Mal zurückbleiben muß. Dieser Mechanismus ist im Zweifelsfalle unbesiegbar, es gibt keine eschatologische Perspektive, in die das Exil das Schreiben wieder entlassen kann, allerdings gibt es eine eschatologische Perspektive, in der Karl sich der Zeichen wieder bemächtigt und die Schrift sich über ihren Bezug zu dem, was unter dem Papier begraben liegt, der Erde, Klarheit verschaffen kann. Theisohn liest das »Teater von Oklahoma« als Wiedergänger eines zionistischen Aliyah-Unternehmens, als Inszenierung eines Staates und damit als Fiktionalisierung einer Zeichenpraxis, mit Hilfe derer aus dem Exil urplötzlich ein Land auftaucht, das sich zwar nicht ›beschreiben‹, darin jedoch auch nicht beherrschen läßt: der Untergrund, dem sich die Literatur verdankt, den sie jedoch nicht einnehmen kann.

---

[11] Das sind (neben Graetz' *Geschichte der Juden*) zum einen die *Religionsgeschichtlichen Volksbücher für die deutsche christliche Gegenwart*, die sich nicht zuletzt auch mit der historischen Genese der ›Gesetzesreligion‹ beschäftigen, zum anderen die Abhandlungen Moriz Friedländers und Ignaz Zieglers, in denen im Rückgriff auf die Geschichte um eine aktuelle Neubestimmung und Umwertung des Judentums gerungen wird.

Mit dem Problem der Rückkehr aus der Sphäre der Galut, konkreter: mit Modellen, diese Rückkehr zu denken und zu vollziehen, beschäftigt sich auch *Pierre Bouretz'* Analyse der nationaljüdischen Konzeptionen Gershom Scholems. Vor dem Hintergrund einer radikalen Opposition gegenüber dem ›Golußjudentum‹ der Väter skizziert Scholem schon früh einen Gegenentwurf zum deutsch-jüdischen Akkulturationsprojekt, als dessen akademischen Vertreter er auch und gerade die ›Wissenschaft des Judentums‹ Zunz'scher Prägung mit ihrer Zielsetzung eines ›würdevollen Begräbnisses des Judentums‹ bekämpft. Die Wiederbelebung und Neuausrichtung des Judentums aus der Judaistik bleibt dabei nicht nur Postulat, sondern ist von vornherein Praxis und bestimmende Kraft in Scholems Vita. In der Hinwendung zur kabbalistischen Tradition, zum Zohar – einem etwa von Graetz noch als »geistige Giftquelle« titulierten Werk[12] –, stößt er auf Paradigmata, die ihm erlauben, das zuvor mit den Termini *Galut – Teshuvah* (Umkehr) – *Yishuv* (Besiedlung) umrissene zionistische Raster neu zu fassen und metaphysisch aufzuladen, weiterhin, die messianischen Bewegungen innerhalb der jüdischen Geschichte nicht mehr als Verirrungen, sondern als das eigentlich vitalisierende Ferment der Gola zu begreifen, eben als Ausweis der ›Umkehr‹, einer Dynamik, in der das jüdische Volk der Verbannung zu entkommen versucht, die jedoch noch nicht konstruktiv zu wirken vermag. *Teshuvah* muß für Scholem in der Folge *als Yishuv* gedacht werden[13], insofern jene Kräfte, die das Judentum in der Galut bisher am Leben erhalten hatten, den Assimilationsbestrebungen der ›Golußjuden‹ auf lange Sicht zum Opfer fallen würden. Erst die Rückkehr in den Staatsverband vermag die Fortexistenz einer jüdischen Tradition – und damit verbunden die messianische Hoffnung auf Erlösung – auf Dauer zu sichern. Nach seiner eigenen ›Rückkehr‹ in den Jerusalemer Haredi-Stadtteil Me'ah Shearim 1923 wird Scholem allerdings rasch von der Tatsache eingeholt, daß mit der Besiedlung, der räumlichen Neuformierung des Judentums sich zwar die größten nationalkulturellen Probleme aufgelöst zu haben scheinen (so gibt es nun wieder eine große hebräische Sprachgemeinschaft und eine ›lebendige‹, mit der Gründung der Hebräischen Universität zudem auch akademisch institutionalisierte Wissenschaft vom Judentum), für das metaphysische Projekt der ›Teshuvah‹ jedoch aus der Realisierung des ›Yishuv‹ eine weitaus größere Bedrohung erwachsen ist: die territoriale Beschränkung der ›Umkehr‹, die sich abzeich-

---

[12] Vgl. Heinrich Graetz: Geschichte der Juden von den ältesten Zeiten bis auf die Gegenwart. Leipzig: Oskar Leiner 1907, Bd IX, S. 345.
[13] Mit dieser Konzeption bleibt Scholem freilich nicht allein; so faßt der wohl für die nationalreligiöse Bewegung bedeutsamste Theoretiker des 20. Jahrhunderts, der Rav Avraham Jizchak Kook, erster Oberrabbiner Israels, im Schlußkapitel seiner 1924 verfaßten ›Lichter der Umkehr‹ (›Orot ha-Teshuvah‹) die »Wiedergeburt der Nation« als »Basis der Struktur der großen Umkehr, welche die erhebende Umkehr Israels ist und die Umkehr der ganzen Welt, welche in der Folge eintreffen wird.« Vgl. Rabbi Kook's Philosophy of Repentance. A Translation of »Orot Ha-Teshuvah« by Alter B. Z. Metzger. New York: Yeshiva University Press 1978 (Studies in Torah Judaism; 11), S. 111.

nende Profanisierung des zionistischen Unternehmens, wie sie Scholem symbolhaft im Verfall der hebräischen Sprache zu erkennen vermeint. In dieser Perspektive erscheint der Staat Israel dann nicht mehr als der Raum, in dem das Judentum zu seinem Ursprung zurückkehrt, sondern nurmehr als die perfideste Modifikation des Exils.

Mit Stefan Zweig rückt sodann ein Autor in den Blickpunkt, dessen Werk zu einem großen Teil zwar an die conditio exul gebunden war und im Grunde schon einen kanonischen Platz auf dem Feld der Exilforschung errungen hat, über dessen eigene Bestimmung des Exils jedoch bisher kaum gehandelt wurde. *Mark H. Gelber* unternimmt nun den Versuch, Zweigs Perspektivierung des Exils anhand dreier Texte – dem *Jeremias*-Drama (1917), dem *Begrabenen Leuchter* (1936) und der *Welt von Gestern* (1942) – durch die zeitgenössischen zionistischen Diskussionen um den kulturellen wie politischen Stellenwert der Diaspora zu kontextualisieren. Wenn etwa Zweigs Prophet im Auszug aus Jerusalem die spirituelle Macht, welche das Judentum als Gemeinschaft auch in der Zerstreuung am Leben erhält, über die territoriale Macht, deren Verlust er mitansehen muß, stellt und somit in der exilischen Existenz Israels Erwähltheit sich nurmehr vollständig bewahrheiten sieht, so bildet die durch die Veröffentlichung von Jakob Klatzkins »Grundlagen des Nationaljudentums« im *Juden* 1916 angestoßene Debatte um die Legitimität einer in Opposition zum wiedererrichteten jüdischen Staat fortexistierenden Galut (die Klatzkin verneint) die Folie, auf der sich dieser Argumentationsgang erst in seiner ganzen Tragweite entfalten kann. In der Folge fungiert ›Exil‹ in Zweigs Vorstellungswelt als Bedingung eines schöpferischen, kulturdurchquerenden Daseins, einhergehend mit einer Bestimmung des Judentums und seiner ›Mission‹ zum Universalismus und dem Bekenntnis zu einem ›geistigen‹ Vaterland, einem ›unendlichen Jerusalem‹. Schon bald wird diese emphatische Apologie der Galut einer doch eher nüchternen Bestandsaufnahme weichen müssen – das Exil zeigt sich Zweig fortan unmaskiert, in all seiner gewaltvollen, ›ent-setzenden‹ Bedeutung: im Angesicht der nationalsozialistischen Machtergreifung in Deutschland beschließt er Ende 1933, das Folgende vorausahnend, Salzburg zu verlassen und nach London überzusiedeln. Gleichzeitig beginnt Zweig damit, Kontakt mit der Jüdischen Nationalbibliothek in Jerusalem aufzunehmen, um dort einen Teil seiner Korrespondenz sichern zu lassen, den Zeugnissen des Exils gleichsam eine Heimat zumessend. Der *Begrabene Leuchter* entwirft dementsprechend ein unmaskiertes Bild der Diaspora, darüber hinaus artikuliert sich in diesem Text – so Gelber – ein grundsätzlicher Zweifel an der Sinnhaftigkeit der Diaspora sowie die explizite Bekundung einer Hoffnung auf ›Heimkehr‹. Scheint diese Neupositionierung allerdings noch ganz situationsgebunden, so eignet den letzten Aufzeichnungen aus Zweigs brasilianischem Exil, in dem er 1942 sich das Leben nimmt, doch der Zug grundsätzlicher Überlegungen. Im Rückblick auf *Die Welt von Gestern* gelangt Zweig schließlich doch noch zum Theorem des frühen politischen Zionismus, der ›Landlosigkeit‹ des jüdischen Volkes als dessen fatales Defizit, ein Argument, dem er zwar offensichtlich nicht widerstandslos nachgibt, geschweige sich von ihm ›bekehren‹ läßt, dem er angesichts der Shoah als äußerstem Zustand der Exilerfahrung letztendlich aber eine bestimmte Hellsichtigkeit nicht mehr absprechen kann.

Mit der zweifellos ›interessierten‹ geschichtsphilosophischen Rekonstruktion der Galut durch den Zionismus selbst beschäftigt sich im weiteren *Christoph Schmidt*. Anhand Jizchak Fritz Baers Traktat *Galut* (1936) zeigt Schmidt, daß die Galut einen zionistischen Historiker der 1930er Jahre (dessen Anliegen vor dem Hintergrund der heraufziehenden Katastrophe natürlich darin besteht, bei seinem Publikum sowohl das Mißtrauen gegenüber dem deutsch-jüdischen ›Kulturprojekt‹ zu wecken, als auch die Akzeptanz der Galut als eines von Gott auferlegten Zustandes zu brechen) vor die Aufgabe stellt, das theologische Raster, das sich mit dem Begriff unweigerlich verbindet, in ein kausales, man könnte sagen: ein naturgeschichtliches Raster zu überführen. Dieser Transfer seinerseits ist keinesfalls nur ein begrifflicher oder ideologischer, sondern er soll ›innergeschichtlich‹ erfolgen: die Tatsache der Galut, des jahrtausendelangen Überlebens einer Minderheit in der Zerstreuung unter den Völkern ist nämlich in der Tat nur unter Rückgriff auf theologische Kategorien, als Ausnahmezustand des Naturgesetzes zu erklären. Die Beendigung dieses Ausnahmezustandes, die Wiedereinsetzung des Politischen kann dementsprechend nicht über die schlichte Suspendierung dieser Kategorien erfolgen, sondern sie muß die mit ihnen verknüpfte Hoffnung auf Erlösung sich zu eigen machen, um »die letzte Konsequenz des modernen kausalgeschichtlichen Denkens mit dem letzten Schluß der alten jüdischen Geschichtsauffassung«[14] zusammentreffen zu lassen. Die zentrale Verfehlung in der Geschichte der jüdischen Diaspora sieht Baer in der Aufspaltung dieser Geschichte in eine apokalyptische Perspektivierung, die das Judentum als einen im Märtyrertum sich überhöhenden Volkskörper sieht, und eine naturgesetzliche Beschreibung, in der sich das jüdische Volk gegenüber seiner nichtjüdischen Umwelt durch politische Ohnmacht auszeichnet, in einen himmlischen, von Gott beschützten und einen irdischen, von den fremden politischen Gewalten tyrannisierten, um Zugeständnisse ringenden und über diesen die Tatsache der Galut letztendlich vergessenden Körper. (Eine zentrale Rolle bei der Ausbildung dieser Verfehlung wird dabei der Marranentheologie beigemessen.) Die Herausforderung des Zionismus besteht dementsprechend darin, unter Inanspruchnahme der theologischen Dimension der jüdischen Geschichte ihren tatsächlichen politischen ›Zustand‹ in den Vordergrund zu rücken und dabei von der jüdischen Deskription des Politischen zur politischen jüdischen Aktion zu gelangen, die religiöse Verheißung politisch zu vollenden. Indem er somit versucht, die Realisierung des göttlichen Willens in der Rückkehr des Judentums zum politischen Naturgesetz zu erkennen, rückt Baer letztendlich in die Position eines zionistischen Spinozisten, arriviert zum Vertreter eines an die Grenzen nationalpolitischer Loyalität gebunden bleibenden Pantheismus.

An der Schwelle paradigmatischer Verschiebungen jüdischer Exilerfahrung operiert das Werk Else Lasker-Schülers. Im Aufrufen einer Symbolik, die ehe-

---

[14] Jizchak Fritz Baer: Galut. Berlin: Schocken Verlag 1936 (Bücherei des Schocken Verlags; 61), S. 103.

mals die spirituelle Einheit, die ›geistige Heimat‹ der Diaspora verbürgte, in der spielerischen Konstruktion Palästinas, vollzieht sich unversehens der Umschlag von einer sich an Begrifflichkeiten wie Absenz, Erinnerung und Repräsentation orientierenden zu einer ›radikalen‹ Konzeption von Exil, in welcher die Möglichkeit einer symbolhaften Identitäts(wieder)gewinnung schon immer unterlaufen wird. Am Beispiel der Texte *Der Wunderrabbiner von Barcelona* (1921) und *Hebräerland* (1937) zeigt *Doerte Bischoff*, wie zum einen zionistische Visionen einer ›Heimkehr‹, eines Anlangens am Ort kollektiver Wirklichkeit in einen Fluß nicht-referentiellen Erzählens überführt werden, der sich kein Land erschließt, sondern dieses immer wieder nur entwirft, in dem sich Realitätssegmente, Privatmythologie und jüdische Tradition vermischen, Zeichen unaufhörlich erzeugt, widerrufen und ständig in neue Signifikationsprozesse eingebunden werden; wie zum anderen das räumliche Symbol göttlicher Präsenz, Makom, letztendlich im und für das Erzählen zerfallen muß, um einer Kraft Raum zu geben, die hinter die machtvoll errichteten Ordnungen des Einzelnen, des Selben hinausreicht und sich in der völligen Auslieferung an den ›Anderen‹ – und was kann eine stärkere Erfahrung von Exil ausmachen? – manifestiert. Damit gewinnt dieses Erzählen, insofern es das Generieren von zeichenhafter Identitätsstiftung als solches sichtbar werden läßt und mithin jenes Dem-Anderen-Ausgeliefert-Sein gerade darin kennzeichnet, daß dieses Andere sich nicht über Repräsentationssysteme fassen läßt, an verblüffender Aktualität und an Bedeutung für die sich mit den Namen von Blanchot, Kristeva, Jabès oder Levinas verbindende Bestimmung von Exil als dem Raum von Sprachlichkeit überhaupt. Vor einem totalitären Denken schützt nicht die Flucht zu einer spirituellen oder territorialen Heimstatt, sondern einzig und allein deren Diskursivierung, die Bewahrheitung seiner Symbolsysteme als Interpretamente, die dem Anderen, demjenigen, den es zu unterwerfen bestrebt ist, aufgegeben sind. Wenn im *Wunderrabbiner* schließlich von Palästina als »der Sternwarte der Heimat« die Rede ist und im Anschluß das »Ein Cheker«, die Unerforschlichkeit Gottes aufgerufen wird, so bleibt das Exil einerseits unumkehrbar und andererseits eine hermeneutische wie ethische Limitation, auf die sich das Erzählen gründet. Wo sich in den Hauptfiguren Eleasar und Amram verheerende Zerstörung und wundersame Errettung gegenüberstehen und die entgegengesetzten Enden des Narrativs bilden, dort überantwortet der Text das Unentschiedene der Deutung dem Leser und überträgt ihm damit gleichsam die Aufgabe, im exegetischen Fortschreiten zwischen den Polen das Exil auf sich zu nehmen und weiterzutragen.

Einem bisher unbeachteten und doch bedeutsamen Kapitel deutscher Exilgeschichte widmet sich *Adi Gordon* in seinem Beitrag zur Geschichte der deutschsprachigen Wochenzeitung *Orient*, die von 1942 bis 1943 unter der Herausgeberschaft von Arnold Zweig und Wolfgang Yourgrau in Haifa erschien. Im Gegensatz zur überwiegenden Mehrheit der deutschen Emigranten in Palästina fühlten sich die Mitarbeiter des *Orient* in keiner Weise irgendwelchen Aliya-Bestrebungen verpflichtet, sondern sahen sich ganz im Dienst einer deutschen Exilpresse, als Exilanten und nicht als Heimkehrer. (Dies läßt sich natürlich insbesondere für Arnold Zweig konstatieren, der bereits an seinem ersten ›Heimkehrversuch‹ 1932 gescheitert war und seine zionistischen Illusionen in seinem Roman *De Vriendt kehrt heim* begraben hatte.) Als ein Hauptanliegen der Wochenschrift läßt sich zweifellos die Repräsentation eines ›anderen‹, nicht von den Nationalsozialisten usurpierten Deutschlands ausmachen. Dementsprechend wehrt sie sich gegen die Gleichsetzung von ›Nationalsozialismus‹ und ›Deutschtum‹, wie sie den Yekke vor allem von Seiten der zionistischen, mehrheitlich aus Osteuropa stammenden Veteranengeneration, den Vatikim, vorgehalten wurde, die den deutschen Immigranten mit Mißtrauen und Feindseligkeit begegneten, wobei gerade der Aspekt der Sprachlichkeit, d. h. die Frage nach der Legitimität der deutschen Sprache in Israel, einen hohen Symbolwert zugesprochen bekam. Schon bald gerät der *Orient* in die schwelenden Auseinandersetzungen zwischen der deutschen Aliya und den Vatikim, und insofern sich die Zeitung auf der einen Seite den Yekke verbunden fühlt, auf der anderen Seite aber ein völlig eigenes, sich jedes nationaljüdischen Pathos entschlagendes Verständnis von Aliya artikuliert (das Palästina nicht als Ort der Bestimmung, sondern schlichtweg als ›Fluchtort‹ begreift), kommt es unweigerlich zum Konflikt mit den altzionistischen Vertretern unter den deutschen Immigranten, die durch den *Orient* ihr Bild innerhalb des Yishuv beschädigt sehen. Mit der scharfen Abgrenzung von Seiten der deutschen Olim sinkt die Zeitung in der Folge zu einer Randerscheinung der deutschsprachigen Immigration herab, gleichzeitig beginnt die Situation allerdings auch auf beiden Seiten zu eskalieren: während der *Orient* dazu übergeht, den Yishuv in seiner Gesamtheit zu attackieren, seinen Kulturentwurf und sein Bildungssystem ins Lächerliche zu ziehen und im Zusammenhang mit den totalitären Anwandlungen des Yishuv auch NS-Vergleiche nicht scheut, versucht die Gegenseite, die Einstellung der Zeitung zu erwirken, was ihr letztendlich auch gelingt: am 2. Februar 1943 detoniert ein Sprengsatz in der Druckerei des *Orient* und besiegelt das Schicksal der Zeitung. Die im vorliegenden Band oft doch sehr vorsichtig anvisierte Trennlinie zwischen dem Exil der Fremde und dem Exil der ›Rückkehr‹ erweist sich demnach in dem von Gordon aufgearbeiteten Fall im wahrsten Sinne des Wortes als explosiv; von ihr weist ein Weg auch in Richtung einer Neubewertung von kultureller Kontinuität innerhalb der Aliya-Bewegungen im allgemeinen wie in Richtung der Anerkennung eines spezifischen Immigrationsnarrativs der Yekke im besonderen.

Das Exil als eine spezifische semiotische Konstellation, in der das Sprechen von einem Ort einzig und allein durch dessen Abwesenheit ermöglicht wird, gleichzeitig dieser Ort aber im Sprechen wieder zurückgeholt werden soll, wirft für die sich durch diese Grunderfahrung bestimmende Literatur das poetologische Problem der Erzeugung von Präsenzmomenten auf dem Feld der Repräsentation auf. Die jüdische Tradition kann bezüglich der Bewältigung dieses Paradoxons mit verschiedenen semantischen Strategien aufwarten, die sich grob in drei Lösungsmodelle unterteilen lassen: die allegorische Antinomie, die in Benjamins Verständnis vor dem Hintergrund des erwarteten messianischen Umbruchs jedes Glied des Exilkosmos zugleich als referenzloses Provisorium abwertet wie als mögliches Gefäß der Verheißung auflädt; das Widerspiel von Assimilation und Dissimilation, Entgrenzung und Begrenzung, die Bewahrung der partikularen Identität des Judentums gerade in der Transgression zum Universalen hin, wie sie das Purim-Fest Jahr für Jahr erinnert; schließlich das sich mit der Idee eines ästhetischen Zionismus verbindende Konzept einer auf ›Verwirklichung‹ ausgerichteten Semiose, welche das Bezeichnete immer bereits im Zuge der Materialisation des es Bezeichnenden perspektiviert. Anna Seghers Erzählen, dessen sich der Beitrag von *Bernhard Greiner* annimmt, ist jenem letzten Modell zuzuschlagen, insofern dieses Erzählen sich zirkelhaft selbst begründet, die Wirklichkeit der von ihm auf der Ebene der Histoire etablierten Zeichen performativ verbürgt, so wie auch die Autorschaft ›Anna Seghers‹ zunächst eine erzählerisch produzierte Signatur darstellt, die letztendlich auf der Diskursebene anlangt und sich über die Texte stellt. Der literarische Akt selbst verkörpert, was er vorstellt. Bemerkenswert – und für die Frage ihrer exilischen Verfassung bedeutsam – erscheint dabei die zunehmende Tendenz dieser Texte, den aus der Verschränkung der Erzählebenen hervorgehenden Realisierungsprozeß an eine Negationsleistung zu knüpfen, Bedeutung zu erfüllen, indem Materialisationen ausgespart bleiben, Zeichen zu verkörpern, insofern man sie entkörpert – das »siebte Kreuz« bleibt eben leer. Im *Transit* (1940/43) greift dieses Verfahren dann letztendlich so weit, daß das Schreiben mit seinen Signifikanten sich selbst aufhebt: das Exil als transitorischer Raum, der »Transit« als Roman des Exils kann die Befestigung von Zeichen nur dort gestatten, kann sich nur dort ihrer bedienen, wo diese ihre tatsächliche Bindungslosigkeit stets mit sich führen, die auf Verwirklichung gespannte Erzählbewegung sich gänzlich vom Ziel einer von ihr zu erbringenden stabilen Semiose abgekoppelt hat und nurmehr ein Nichts tradiert, ja, nurmehr tradieren kann, *weil* sie ein Nichts tradiert. Das Transitvisum, das Eintrittsbillet des Exils, wird immer bezahlt mit einer Verfehlung, an die der Transitreisende gebunden bleibt – verkannte Liebschaften, zu früh verstorbene Dichter, zu spät geschriebene Erzählungen. Der Raum, den ›Anna Seghers‹ *mit* diesen Insignien und gleichzeitig *für* sie zu stiften vermag, kann somit in der performativen Verschränkung letztendlich nur noch dann präsentische Momente erzeugen, wenn es sein eigenes radikales Getrennt-Sein, seine Re-Präsenz jedem der ihn erfüllenden Zeichen einschreibt, diese gleichsam semiotisch exiliert.

Mit dem Aufscheinen einer kabbalistischen Verhandlung von Exil in der Lyrik des 20. Jahrhunderts beschäftigt sich *Rochelle Tobias'* Beitrag zu Paul Celan. Auf der Textgrundlage des Gedichtes »Mit allen Gedanken« skizziert Tobias die Zusammenhänge zwischen Celans Poetik und der durch Scholem reaktualisierten Lehre von den zehn Emanationen Gottes, den Sefiroth, deren unterste die ›Shechina‹ (die ›Einwohnung‹) darstellt, auch sie gemäß der Kabbala eine Versprachlichung des unaussprechlichen Gottesnamens. Gleichzeitig handelt es sich bei der Shechina um jene Sefira, die mit den Menschen aus dem Paradies vertrieben wurde, die seitdem unter ihnen wohnt und mit ihnen zieht, ohne gleichwohl den Boden zu berühren, auf dem sie wandeln.[15] Es verbindet sich mit ihr ein Sprechen, das die Wiederherstellung des Zusammenschlusses mit jenem Wort, das es geschaffen hat, die Rückkehr zur adamitischen Sprache, in der Wort und Welt eines waren, in Aussicht stellt. Celan inszeniert die lyrische Rede dergestalt als eine Vereinigung des Ichs mit der Shechina in Abkehr von der Welt, wodurch das Wort, der ›Name‹, mit dem der Dichter sich der untersten Sefira nähert, in einem Prozeß des Aufstiegs über die oberen Sefiroth an die Grenzen der ›Binah‹ (der dritten Sefira) – oberhalb derer keine Rede ist, das En-Sof (das ›Es gibt kein Ende‹) sich im Schweigen ausspricht – gelangt und von dort wieder hinabsteigend sich selbst gebiert. Das Exil der Worte wird in einem Zirkel durchbrochen, der im Vers »du empfingst uns« kulminiert: die Shechinah nimmt das Sprechen des Ichs einerseits auf, auf der anderen Seite bringt sie es aber auch allererst zur Welt. Die Zeilen, gesprochen ›aus der Welt‹, laden sich pneumatisch auf, erheben das Gedicht von seinem Ende her als Gewölk zum Anfang – reshit – und lassen es von dort als eine göttliche, erlöste, heimgekehrte ›Gestalt‹ wieder hervorgehen.

Ein ›Logbuch des Exils‹ verfaßt Hélène Cixous – *Carola Hilfrich* wird es zu entziffern versuchen. In anderer Weise als zuvor geht es dabei um Verkörperungen, um Zirkel und um Wirklichkeit; Cixous propagiert eine ›Schriftsprache der Realität‹, eine Sprache, welche die Wirklichkeit aus ›ihrem Inneren‹ zu fassen vermag, indem sie sich selbst aus ihr erzeugt und sie gleichzeitig auch reproduziert. Inwiefern aber ist dies auch eine Sprache des Exils zu nennen? Wir müssen jene Schrift als einen Akt der Entäußerung begreifen, der dort statt hat, wo es zu Verhandlungen ›zwischen den Welten‹, zwischen Menschen, zwischen Natur und Kultur, zwischen Politik und Poetik, zwischen Wirklichkeit und Imagination kommt, kurz: überall dort, wo sich jene Verschränkung zwischen Selbstproduktion und Reproduktion des ›Anderen‹ auffinden läßt. Exil ist dann bestimmt als eine Bedingung irdischer Existenz und ihre Schrift, die ›Schrift der Realität‹, ist bestimmt als dasjenige, was schreibend die eigenen Grenzen überschritten, sich ›aus-geschrieben‹ und körperhaft eingeschrieben hat. ›Exil‹ bewahrheitet sich damit als ein an Erde und Körper gebundenes Geschehen, ein sich von Interaktion zu Interaktion, Grenzüberschreitung zu Grenzüberschreitung fleischlich und territorial perpetuierender Text. In der

---

[15] Die Umdeutung der kabbalistischen Ordnung zu einem Exilgeschehen ist natürlich ein Verdienst Lurias; dass man Malchuth – das Reich (im Sinne eines Herabsteigens Gottes in die Natur) - und die Shechina in der modernen Kabbala nicht mehr streng differenziert, impliziert als vielleicht wichtigste Schöpfung Lurias das Faktum, daß die Shechina sich nicht mehr von der Welt abwenden, in die göttliche Ordnung zurückkehren kann. (Die klassische Kabbala kennt etwa noch den Mythos, daß die Shechina ursprünglich im Ersten Tempel gehaust habe und mit dessen Zerstörung 576 v. Chr. wieder in den Himmel zurückgekehrt sei.) Zur Transformation der Sefiroth von Cordovero zu Luria vergl. Harold Bloom: Kabbala. Poesie und Kritik. Aus dem amerikanischen Englisch von Angelika Schweikhart. Basel, Frankfurt a. M.: Stroemfeld/Nexus 1997, S. 60–75.

Folge entwirft Cixous genealogische Geographien, die als eine Vielzahl körperlich erstellter Kartographien von Wirklichkeit die Erde überziehen; über den Körper dokumentiert sich das Exil als eine das Kontinuum von Jahrtausenden überdauernde Erzählung, in der sich betretenes und niemals erschautes Land, Präsentes und Erinnertes vermischen. Dies hebt an bei Cixous' eigener Genealogie, die eine in Algerien geborene und in Frankreich sozialisierte Frau auf die Fährte der Vorfahren ihrer jüdisch-deutschen Mutter und ihres jüdisch-marokkanischen Vaters in alle Himmelsrichtungen und unzählige Kulturkreise führt; von hier aus multiplizieren sich dann in Cixous' poetisch-politischen Epen (in denen sie sich der Genealogien der Mandelstams und Mandelas annimmt) die Schriften der Wirklichkeit, aus denen sich die wirtschaftlichen, kulturellen, rassischen, geschlechtlichen, politischen und poetischen Formationen körperlichen Lebens ergeben. Zur Vollendung gelangt diese Sprache global-irdischen Exils dann allerdings bezeichnenderweise nicht in der epischen Fiktionalität, sondern an jenem Ort, wo Wirklichkeit mit Wirklichkeit sich ausdrückt, ein wahrhaft körperliches Narrativ entsteht: auf dem Theater. Die Bühne als das ›Land der Anderen‹ erschließt uns jene Verschiebungen, Limitationen und Delimitationen, die exilische Bedingung, der wir in unseren Verkörperungen immer schon ausgesetzt sind und die wir mit jeder unserer Handlungen neu ausschreiben. Diese Schrift lesen zu lernen, heißt, sie *ganz* lesen zu lernen, das Offenstehen der mit ihr verfaßten Texte nie aus den Augen zu verlieren und sich keinem ihrer Zeichen – auch und gerade nicht den Marginalisiertesten – zu verschließen.

Jenseits der Literatur wird sich schließlich *Frank Stern* einem ganz anderen Ort zuwenden. Hollywood, freilich kein durch das Exil generierter Topos, verkörpert gleichwohl als Schmelzpunkt exilierter, insbesondere exilierter jüdischer Produktivität in besonderem Maße den Antitypus zu einem theologisch wie semiologisch doch sehr stark aufgeladenen Atopie-Diskurs. Vor dem Hintergrund einer Fülle unterschiedlicher Biographien ersteht die Heimstatt der modernen Unterhaltungsindustrie als eine ›Black Box of Modernism‹, in welcher die Wege der aus den unterschiedlichsten Motiven ihrer europäischen Heimat entronnenen Schauspieler, Architekten, Musiker und Regisseure zusammenlaufen und aus welcher ein Kino hervorgeht, welches beständig zwischen Alter und Neuer Welt zu pendeln und ein Kulturnetzwerk von globaler Wirkungsmacht zu bilden beginnt. Obwohl dieses Projekt eines ›Exils mit Rückfahrkarte‹ schon in den 1920er Jahren seine Anfänge nimmt und sich dort natürlich vor allem mit dem Namen Ernst Lubitsch verbindet, so kann gleichwohl kein Zweifel bestehen, daß erst mit der nationalsozialistischen Machtergreifung und der damit verbundenen Flucht zahlreicher Filmschaffender aus den großen europäischen Produktionsstätten Berlin und Wien die eigentliche Blütezeit Hollywoods einsetzt. Die großen amerikanischen Lichtspielproduktionen des 20. Jahrhunderts sind im wesentlichen Schöpfungen eines ›Emigrantenkinos‹ (wobei die Unterscheidung von erzwungener und ›freiwilliger‹ Emigration nicht selten nur schwer zu vollziehen ist, als problematische Beispiele lassen sich etwa Billy Wilder oder Fritz Lang anführen) – geschaffen von Exulanten, welche die Innovationen und Errungenschaften europäischer Filmkultur in die Fremde trugen, um von dort die Fremde – ihr ›Include me out‹ – nach Europa zurückkehren zu lassen. Auch die Erfolgsgeschichte jenes Mediums, welches das 20. Jahrhundert wie kein anderes geprägt hat, bleibt somit letztendlich auf das Engste verknüpft mit dem Narrativ einer Fluchtbewegung, das sich über den Film fortschreibt und in ihm eine ortlose Gegenwelt zu errichten vermag.

Bernhard Greiner
Philipp Theisohn

Guy Stern

From Exile Experience to Exile Studies

One of the most famous modern poems about expulsion and exile, Brecht's protest declaration »About the Designation Immigrants«[1] was utterly irrelevant for the five youngsters, me included, who, under the guardian eyes of a German-Jewish social worker, made the crossing from Bremerhaven to New York in 1937. Brecht had proclaimed himself an exile, ready to return after the fall of Hitler.[2] We, all five of us, whispered to each other – because it was a German ship – that we would never return. Rejection had bred resentment and defiance. Even on the ship, as I sipped my first Coca-Cola, the donation of an American fellow passenger, I began an evolution, which I dubbed in an article published elsewhere, »The Americanisation of Günther«.[3] Once I had arrived in St. Louis I traded my allegiance from soccer (or football) to boisterous fanhood of the St. Louis baseball teams, joined the high school newspaper, talked German only to fellow exiles, swapped the memories of Gerda, my first tentative girlfriend of my home town, for ›dates‹ with a true-blue fellow American student with the improbable name of Idamae Schwartzberg. She furthered my Americanisation by calling me Guy instead of Günther. The name stuck.

And yet Günther never became a completely American guy. Two years later, in 1939, I found to my surprise that pride in my cultural heritage surged through me when on the same day two icons of my boyhood, Richard Tauber and Thomas Mann, visited St. Louis. I ran an obstacle course to garner an interview with the Nobel-Prize winning author, triumphantly published in *Scrippage*, our high school newspaper. Was that my first, if adolescent, contribution to exile studies?[4]

---

[1] See Bertolt Brecht: Über die Bezeichnung Emigranten. In: B. Brecht: Gesammelte Werke in 20 Bänden. Band 9: Gedichte 2. Hg. vom Suhrkamp Verlag in Zusammenarbeit mit Elisabeth Hauptmann. Frankfurt a. M.: Suhrkamp 1967 (Werkausgabe Edition Suhrkamp), p. 718.

[2] Various declarations of Brecht about his intentions in Klaus Schumann [commentator]: Das letzte Wort ist noch nicht gesprochen. Bertolt Brecht im Exil 1933–1948. Begleitheft zur Ausstellung in der Deutschen Bücherei Leipzig, 24. März – 20. Juni 1998. Leipzig: Die Deutsche Bibliothek 1998.

[3] Guy Stern: The Americanisation of Günther. In: The Legacy of Exile. Lives, Letters, Literature. Ed. by Deborah Viëtor-Engländer. Oxford, Malden: Blackwell 1998, p. 3.

[4] A full account of my encounter with Thomas Mann will appear in a soon to be published anthology: »Man erzählt Geschichten, formt die Wahrheit«. Thomas Mann – Weltbürger und Demokrat. Hg. von Michael Braun und Birgit Lerman Frankfurt: Peter Lang 2002.

But I think I became reconnected that day to my boyhood reading habits, when I voraciously devoured the fantasies about Ancient Rome by Felix Dahn, the no less imaginary Wild West adventures of Karl May and, yes, precocious as I was, Thomas Mann's *Buddenbrooks*. All these were part of my parents' library. In retrospect it would have been wise to read more ominously sounding texts, because it has recently become my conviction that German exile literature preceded the actual exile experience.

What could be more exilic than Ernst Blass' early poem »Ich bin in eine fremde Stadt verschlagen« or Gertrud Kolmar's poem »Ewiger Jude«[5] or, above all, a whole galaxy of stories by Franz Kafka, which inspired an American author, Philip Roth, to prolong Kafka's life in his fiction into an exile existence in New Jersey.[6] And further research will uncover a goodly number of texts that I should like to label »The Poetry of Packed Suitcases«, as exemplified by Rudolf Frank's novel of immigration, *Ahnen und Enkel*, or the eve-of-flight poems of Theodor Kramer.[7] I wish I had then read more of Feuchtwanger's Andromeda-like warnings, rather than the patriotic poems of Ernst Moritz Arndt, abounding in my parents' and in my primers.

My simmering interest in well-known exiles was fanned by my war-time encounters. My experiences as a prisoner-of-war interrogator taught me that not all Germans, especially the mangled veterans, were fervent Nazis. And I also, through sheer happenstance, met a remarkable exile woman, Marlene Dietrich, when she gave a USO show within 20 miles of our prisoner-of-war enclosure. A friend of mine and I had the good fortune to spend a few hours with her. I mention that because that encounter led to my most recent, if least academic contributions to exile studies. A documentary about her includes me as one of the »talking heads« that, satellite-fashion, swirls around the superstar.[8]

More important, the months in Normandy forged a lifelong friendship with a remarkable Viennese-born fellow soldier, Karl Frucht, somewhat older than me, who had, in collaboration with Hertha Pauli, founded a literary agency, when the first wave of refugee writers had fled Germany for Austria. Late at night, as the last interrogated prisoner had been marched back behind the barbed-wire fence of our ›cage‹, Karlie regaled us with tales of the literary prowess and personal fables of Hertha Pauli, E. B. Ashton, Walter Mehring

---

[5] Ernst Blass: In einer fremden Stadt. In: E. Blass: Die Straßen komme ich entlang geweht. Heidelberg: Weissbach 1912 (Nendeln: Kraus Reprint 1973; Bibliothek des Expressionismus), p. 56. Also see Gertrud Kolmar: Gedichte. Auswahl und Nachwort von Ulla Hahn. Frankfurt a. M.: Suhrkamp 1983 (Bibliothek Suhrkamp; 815), p. 159.

[6] Philip Roth: I always wanted you to admire my fasting or looking at Kafka. In: P. Roth: Reading myself and others. New York: Farrar, Strauss & Giroux 1975, p. 247–270.

[7] Rudolf Frank: Ahnen und Enkel. Roman in Erzählungen. Berlin: Erwin Loewe 1938 und Theodor Kramer: Wien 1938. Die grünen Kader. Gedichte. Wien: Globus Verlag 1938.

[8] The film *Marlene Dietrich. Her own song* was directed by David Riva, the grandson of Marlene Dietrich, in collaboration with Karin Kearns. A Gemini Film production, it was released in the Fall of 2001 on the occasion of Dietrich's hundredth birthday.

and Paul Frischauer – all of whom I was to meet in New York through his introduction into a loose-knit circle of exiles.[9]

As a returned veteran, I had outgrown the fostering home of my aunt and uncle in St. Louis and had moved to New York to complete my undergraduate studies at Hofstra University, supporting myself beyond the G. I. bill by applying my skills as a waiter, acquired in a St. Louis restaurant owned by an enterprising refugee from Berlin. But, how did I, at that time a college junior, enter the periphery of a New York exile circle, loosely presided over by Hertha Pauli and her husband E. B. Ashton, visited at random intervals by Walter Mehring, Paul Frischauer, Ivan Heilbut, Walter Sorel, George Grosz and once by Oskar Maria Graf? To be sure Karlie had introduced me.[10] But I would not have been invited to their interminable, coffee-sustained discussions and gabfests, if I had not brought an unusual qualification to their informal soirees. I hasten to add that they were not intellectual flights – usually I listened rather than talked – but rather my employment as an after-school waiter at the Broadway Lobster Pond, just two subway stops removed from Hertha's and Ashton's hotel. Those two and all members of their entourage were dedicated dog-owners, and appreciated that I had access to huge amounts of choice meat, collected for me for a small tip by cooperative dishwashers. My entrebillet to exile prominence was scraps of *Hundefutter*, leftovers from prime steaks and hamburgers.

In short, despite their straitened circumstances the exiles were often exclusive, if not elitarian. The quest for self-assertion, answering the implicit question once posed by Heinrich Mann in *Der Sinn dieser Emigration*[11] led inevitably to a sense of self-sustaining pride. I witnessed its manifestation again after I had entered graduate school at Columbia. Our club of German graduate students had invited Walter Mehring in 1952 for a guest lecture. During the question-and-answer period, in which Mehring explained the mythopoesis of his anti-Nazi poetry, he was suddenly upstaged by Kurt Pinthus, then a member of Columbia's theater department. Pinthus, before our club president Gustave Matthieu reined him in, tried to outdo mild-mannered Mehring in his claim of co-representing »das andere Deutschland«.

I wish I had written immediately about that fascinating group, while I still enjoyed living at its periphery in the years right after the war. But I utilized my vicarious exilic experience only once. I cleverly inserted one episode in a term paper for my music appreciation class. I had been allowed to escort Hertha Pauli in 1947 to a piano recital by her famous uncle and cousin, Arthur and Ulrich Schnabel. And I narrated my brief post-concert conversation with them in my paper, much to the joy of my with-it instructor.

---

[9] The beginnings of Karl Frucht's and my association is described in his *Wir waren ein PWI Team*. In: K. Frucht: Verlustanzeige. Ein Überlebensbericht. Wien: Kremayr & Scheriatt 1992, p. 183–202.
[10] Guy Stern: Hertha Pauli. In: G. Stern: Literatur im Exil. Gesammelte Aufsätze 1959–1989. München-Ismaning: Hueber 1989, p. 282–302.
[11] Heinrich Mann: Der Sinn dieser Emigration. Paris: Europäischer Merkur 1934.

But in writing so sparsely of those remarkable personalities at that time (e. g. as feature editor of our college newspaper) I was no exception. There was then very little so-called secondary literature written about the exiles by established or incipient scholars. The first phase of exile studies was truly dominated, in America as well, by the exiles themselves, frequently via the pages of *Aufbau*.

They were, in obvious and subtle ways, the first chroniclers of exile literature. Obviously, when they deliberately set out to survey and assess the texts of their fellow writers in books, articles and lectures, as did F. C. Weiskopf's study *Unter fremden Himmeln. Ein Abriß der deutschen Literatur im Exil 1933–1947* or Alfred Neumann's lecture in California »Literarische Bestandsaufnahme«, in which both writers consciously intended to inform a larger public of a remarkable group achievement.[12] The numerous autobiographies, which often veered from self-depiction to intellectual history – focusing on the life and works of fellow exiles – manifest a similar intent. That holds true of Klaus Mann's *Der Wendepunkt* and of Heinrich Mann's *Ein Zeitalter wird besichtigt*, or of Ludwig Marcuse's *Mein zwanzigstes Jahrhundert*.[13] It holds equally true of fictionalized autobiographies such as Hans Sahl's *Die Wenigen und die Vielen*, of Rudolf Frank's tendentious novel *Fair Play* or of some rare biographies, written by one exile about another, e. g. Lisa Tetzner's biography of her late husband, the writer Kurt Held.[14]

But in addition to these obvious contributions there is a whole set of subtle contributions to literary and cultural history by this first wave of creative writers. Their exchange of letters, eliciting and supplying information about fellow exiles, or their diaries may also be read as fragments of history. Hermann Kesten's letters laid one of the cornerstones of exile studies in the U. S., as did – as a genre unto itself – Thomas Mann's *Entstehung des Dr. Faustus*.[15] Furthermore, given their frequently isolated state, the exile writers communicated with a wider circle of admirers than they would have bothered to acknowledge in pre-exile times. A lawyer from Offenbach, Siegfried Guggenheim, became the self-appointed promulgator of Karl Wolfskehl in New York. He had managed to initiate a copious correspondence with the poet. He was, as we would say today, an average exile, but an utterly unique personality. He refused to learn English. I once entered a subway station with him near his apartment in Queens, New

---

[12] Franz Carl Weiskopf: Unter fremden Himmeln. Ein Abriß der deutschen Literatur im Exil 1933–1947. Mit einem Anhang von Textproben aus Werken exilierter Schriftsteller. Berlin: Dietz 1948 and Alfred Neumann: Literarische Bestandsaufnahme, 1945. In: Guy Stern: Alfred Neumann. Verschollene und Vergessene. Wiesbaden: Franz Steiner 1979, p. 162–169.

[13] Heinrich Mann: Ein Zeitalter wird besichtigt. Stockholm: Neuer Verlag 1946 and Ludwig Marcuse: Mein zwanzigstes Jahrhundert. Auf dem Weg zu einer Autobiographie. München: Paul List 1963.

[14] Rudolf Frank: Fair Play. New York: American Guild for German Cultural Freedom 1983 and Lisa Tetzner: Das war Kurt Held. Vierzig Jahre Leben mit ihm. Aarau: Sauerländer 1961.

[15] Thomas Mann: Die Entstehung des Dr. Faustus. Roman eines Romans. Frankfurt a. M.: S. Fischer 1949.

York. He went up to the agent and demanded subway tokens in German. The agent, preconditioned by him, complied without demurrer. Graduate students at Columbia and Princeton, I among them, became oral historians of the readings and lectures by Walter Mehring, Armin T. Wegner and David Luschnat. Long before Hans Sahl penned his famous line »Fragt uns aus, wir sind zuständig«,[16] we, the future scholars of exile, such as Gustave Matthieu writing on Brecht, asked pertinent and impertinent questions of exiles to whom we had access.

But even more important the exiles I encountered purveyed not only facts, but convictions, which, as I stated before, dominated our field without demurrer for decades. These convictions on the part of my new friends, such as the concept of »das andere Deutschland«, were born not only out of ideological and political considerations, but out of a search for self-orientation – in a different country and under radically changed circumstances. I know of few self-analyses by the exiles, regardless of the literary form, in which the writer does not reaffirm his/her self-worth and grasps for reasons to justify it. In the words of the British writer Tom Stoppard, an exile of sorts himself, »Public postures have the configurations of private derangement.« They may not always have been right in their assessment of exile culture – the Austrian expert Lutz Winckler argues that exile studies need to discard erroneous myths or premises to which they have clung[17] – but I do know that these concepts, whether tenable or not, were their oral or written legacy which they passed on to us. Most important though: What the exiles imbued in the first generation of American exile scholars was the resolve that the legacy of the exiles, literary and personal, must not be lost. They set an example, by ceaselessly if not uncritically, evoking the lives and works of their colleagues.

Elsewhere I have chronicled, in reportorial style, the beginnings of concerted exile studies in America.[18] On the initiative of John Spalek, one of the chief prime movers of the nascent field, also of Joseph Strelka and myself, we founded the Society for Exile Studies and gave impetus to annual conferences. With scholars from both Europe and American participating, early organizers such as Helmut Pfanner, Dieter Sevin, Alexander Stephan and the team of Wolfgang Elfe, Gunther Holst and James Hardin focused attention on lacunae in exile studies. Exile scholars in Europe and America learned from each other. Americans traveled to congresses in Germany, Austria and Scandinavia – specifically the one initiated in 1969 by Walter Berendsohn in Stockholm (with the help of Gustav Korlen and Helmut Müssener). Conversely Hans Albert Walter and Werner Röder traveled to the United States to acquaint themselves with our advances.

---

[16] Hans Sahl: Die Letzten. In: H. Sahl: Wir sind die Letzten. Gedichte. Heidelberg: Lambert Schneider 1976, p. 13.

[17] Tom Stoppard: The Real Thing. London, Boston: Faber and Faber 1982, p. 33. See also: Lutz Winckler: Wirkungsgeschichte. In: Handbuch der deutschsprachigen Emigration 1933–1945. Hg. von Claus-Dieter Krohn, Patrick von zur Mühlen, Gerhard Paul and Lutz Winckler. Darmstadt: Wissenschaftliche Buchgesellschaft 1998, p. 1041–1054.

[18] See my »Abriß der Exilliteraturforschung in den USA« in *Literatur im Exil* (note 10), p. 83–96.

Perhaps here, too, a personal reminiscence will reify that reportage, especially as it pertains to the participation and the indominable spirit of the exiles themselves. In mid-November 1983 during the German-American Tricentennial year, I had convened a forum on German women exiles and had secured the appearance of scholars such as Dagmar Barnouw and Martha Wallach. But as featured speaker I had invited Marta Feuchtwanger. In return for providing the funding for her appearance – all our conferences depended on piecemeal funding – Leonard Simons, a prominent Detroit businessman and an old acquaintance of hers, requested the privilege to entertain her and to pick her up at the airport.

Marta Feuchtwanger was then in her nineties. Leonard Simons, to ease her arrival, had lobbied for a curbside parking permit and for a wheelchair at the arrival gate. Marta Feuchtwanger descended from the plane, greeted her escort, but waved away his proffered help with her hand luggage and indignantly refused to get into the wheelchair. »But I have commandeered two airline staff members to wheel you to the car«, he remonstrated. »I'll lose credibility, if I send them back.« Marta Feuchtwanger pierced him with a look: »Very well, then you get in the wheelchair.« And that is exactly what happened.

The initial approach to exile studies was biographical and positivistic. Some of the harvest was systematic and professional, as when Max Kreutzberger, the first director of the New York Leo Baeck Institute, traveled through the United States, Europe and Israel in search of literary legacies, thus laying the corner stone for that magnificent LBI-Archive. But often these discoveries were random. I was invited to a party by a friend, like Karl Frucht a former army buddy. While explaining my research interest to a fellow guest, she asked: Oh, you mean letters by, for example, Jakob Wassermann and Karl Wolfskehl?« »Exactly«, I answered. »Oh well, I have several cigar boxes full upstairs. I'm the niece of Julia Wassermann.« My first article on exiles was my commentaries to hitherto unpublished letters by Karl Wolfskehl. Today such acquisitions would be priceless and complicated. In the same mood of nonchalance Lotte Lenya entrusted me with the publication of a whole set of letters by Kurt Weill – for a college textbook, no less.[19]

While this phase of gathering has subsided, in part because the stock of unpublished materials has declined, it still continues today. In Germany, Austria and Israel competent archivists are steadily on the lookout for new primary material and on any day John Spalek can be observed carrying suitcases from the domiciles of the inheritors of the erstwhile exiles.[20]

---

[19] Guy Stern: Ich friere wo im andern Ozean. Ein Bericht über Karl Wolfskehls letzte Jahre. In: Stern, Literatur im Exil (note 10), p. 239–249. Also see: Gustave Mathieu / Guy Stern: Franz Werfel, Kurt Weill and Max Reinhardt: Ein Broadwaydrama wird geboren. In: Brieflich erzählt. Ed. by G. Mathieu and G. Stern. New York: W. W. Norton & Company Inc. 1956, p. 214 – 225.

[20] John Spalek is currently an important contributor to the exile archive of the Deutsche Bibliothek in Frankfurt.

But the search for materials slowly yielded in priority to a search for defining a newly founded subdivision of German-language literature. We, the first pioneers of exile studies – many European-born, but fortified by a sprinkling of native American researchers – had found a niche on American campuses. Egon Schwarz, Dagmar Barnouw, Peter Heller, John Spalek, Joseph Strelka, Gustave Mathieu as Europeans and native American such as Erna M. Moore and Carol Paul-Merrit changed from devotees to analysts of the concept of exile literature – sometimes the almost inevitable consequence of pursuing a Ph. D.

There is a bit of exile lore in my own development. I had had a residue of reservations about becoming a Germanist and had entered graduate school with the ultimate goal of getting a Ph. D. in comparative literature. But when my professors urged me to stay with German literature because I had, they said, a flare for it, I followed their advice. If that was a talent of mine, then its amputation, I felt, would have been continuing the work of Hitler. I had made my decision. So when I got an assistant professorship at small, residential Denison University in Ohio and was soon after elected coordinator of its Liberal Arts Fair, I inundated the campus with an Expressionism Festival, which featured a preponderance of the works of exile authors and artists. The same kind of activity, while of course episodic and ephemeral, must have taken place at many other campuses.[21]

The quest of exile scholarship soon became one for nomenclature, periodisation and territorialisation. Let me give examples of each. In the early writings of our craft one will still find alternate terms such as »Emigrantenliteratur« or »Antifaschistische Literatur.« That was, of course, to be expected. Designations have shifted during various phases of German literary movements. The word »exile literature« won out and has now been adopted as well by colleagues concerned with other national literatures, e. g. by the Hispanists.[22]

The controversy about periodisation has not yet been definitely settled. Some scholars argue that the possibility of return, in 1945 to West Germany and Austria, in 1948 to the GDR, also ended the forced absence of the exiles from their homeland. Other scholars, fortified by the support of exiled authors, maintain that exiles remain exiles, sundered from their home by a different ticking of the clock and by the inevitable changes in the life and works of the »stay-at-home« contemporaries.[23] I displeased the adherents of both views

---

[21] For example as early as 1946 Vassar College became the first stop of a traveling exhibit that featured works by Marcel Duchamp, Max Ernst, André Masson, Kurt Seligmann and Yves Tanguy. See Stephanie Barron and Sabine Eckmann: Exiles & Emigrés. The Flight of European Artists from Hitler. Los Angeles: Los Angeles County Museum of Art 1997, p. 400.

[22] A recent example of interest in exile studies on the part of Hispanists is Michael Ugarte: Literatura española en el exilio. Un estudio comparativo. Madrid: Siglo XXI de España 1999.

[23] For a restriction in dates see Konrad Feilchenfeldt: Deutsche Exilliteratur 1933–1945. Kommentar zu einer Epoche. München: Winkler 1986. For an expansive view see John Spalek and Robert Bell: Exile, the writer's experience. Chapel Hill: Uni-

when I, at the first International Exile Congress in Stockholm in 1969, suggested a compromise. Let's call all literature before the possibility of return »exile literature«, all works beyond that »immigrant literature.« The Nestor of exile studies, Walter Berendsohn put me in my place. »Stern scheint das Ei des Columbus gefunden zu haben. Aber der Unterschied ist einfach nicht stichhaltig.« Today I admit defeat and profess that exile literature does not end until the last exile author has died.

Territoriality also divided scholars. I will illustrate the controversy by detailing four frequently raised questions:

1. Does oppositional literature, mostly unpublished during the Third Reich, deserve the title »inner immigration« or »internal exile«?[24]
2. Does an author, who had fled Germany, but remained relatively unmolested during the later Nazi occupation of his country of asylum, deserve inclusion under the designation »exile author«? The examples that come to mind are Hans Henny Jahnn in Denmark and Stefan Andres, living in an Italy dominated by Germany during the final phase of World War II.
3. If an author, such as Ernst Glaeser, made his treacherous peace with Nazi Germany, and returned after six years of exile in Switzerland, can he or she still be included in a roster of exiles? Still more complicated, did Irmgard Keun continue to be an exile when she returned from France and led a clandestine existence in Cologne?
4. When a Jewish writer fled to Palestine, did he go into exile or did he accomplish an alijah? I would not presume to answer that question.[25]

On a related point we asked whether there was a difference between the socalled political exiles and Jewish exiles. Of course the two categories often overlapped. And I personally found only three primary, specifically Jewish, components in exile literature: a propensity for gallow's humor, as in the somewhat surrealistic prose of Jakov Lind, an invocation of the Old Testament, and a reexamination of faith in the light of the Holocaust.[26] All these points were matters of debate during this phase of exile studies, which the Germans called »Einordnung« and we in America described as »staking out the territory«.

---

versity of North Carolina Press 1982 (University of North Carolina Studies in the Germanic Languages and Literatures; 99).

[24] The controversy is revived once more by Annette Schmollinger: Intra muros et extra. Deutsche Literatur im Exil und in der Inneren Emigration. Ein exemplarischer Vergleich. Heidelberg: Winter 1999 (Beiträge zur neueren Literaturgeschichte; 161).

[25] The title of Margarita Pazi's anthology avoids a clear position on this issue. See her Spurenlese. Deutschsprachige Autoren in Israel. Eine Anthologie. Gerlingen: Bleicher 1996.

[26] Guy Stern: March 11, 1938. After German troops march into Austria, many Austrian and German-Jewish writers flee. In: Yale Companion to Jewish Writing and Thought in German Culture 1096 – 1996. Ed. by Sander L. Gilman and Jack Zipes. New Haven, London: Yale University Press 1997, p. 544–550.

We, that first generation of exile scholars, mostly to our credit, did not remain isolated from the political or intellectual controversies that swirled around our campuses. As a fear of socialism gripped the United States I had the temerity to suggest at a meeting of our exile society that we might include a qualified scholar from the GDR on the editorial board of our exile yearbook. A colleague found the choice appellation of »Roter Stern« as a response to my meek suggestion. But exactly the opposite denunciation fell to my lot when Hilde Spiel, mistakenly thinking that I had withdrawn from a congress in Vienna because of invitations to Soviet scholars, expressed her displeasure with this American anti-Communist in the *Frankfurter Allgemeine*. But when I, ingenuously, showed up at the Wiener Kongress, she at least showed her integrity by apologizing.[27]

No, we were not isolated. During the last two decades, when literary theory invaded and often overwhelmed our departments of literature, our colleagues and, even more often our students, demanded that publications and seminars, including those on exile, demonstrate a variety of critical approaches. The exile scholar Ernst Loewy had suggested that exile studies have undergone a paradigmatic change.[28] That certainly applies to the works of many of our colleagues.

That phase of exile studies is still very much with us: It is the integrative process of bringing the latest literary theories to bear on exile literature. Obviously I do not mean the excellent application of theory to single works, say Rainer Nägele's deconstruction of Brecht's *Lehrstücke* or Egon Schwarz' structuralistic analysis of Jewish characters in the novels of Thomas Mann.[29] Rather I mean the receptionist approach that Frank Trommler applied to exile literature[30] or the feminist approach to exile studies championed by such American scholars as Dagmar Lorenz and Gabriele Weinberger and Elke Frederiksen and Martha Kaasberg Wallach.[31] The theoretical upgrading of children's literature has of late been supported by the bibliographies raisonnées published respectively by

---

[27] For a general description of the controversy surrounding the congress in Vienna see Werner Berthold: Krise der Exilforschung. In: W. Berthold: Exilliteratur und Exilforschung. Ausgewählte Aufsätze, Vorträge und Rezensionen. Hg. von Brita Eckert. Wiesbaden: Harrassowitz 1996 (Gesellschaft für das Buch; 3), p. 51 – 56.

[28] Ernst Loewy: Zwischen den Stühlen. Essays und Autobiographisches aus 50 Jahren. Hamburg: Europäische Verlagsanstalt 1995.

[29] Rainer Nägele: Brechts Theater der Grausamkeit. Lehrstücke und Stückwerke. In: Brechts Dramen. Neue Interpretationen. Hg. von Walter Hinderer. Stuttgart: Reclam 1984, p. 300–320 and Egon Schwarz: Die jüdischen Gestalten in Doktor Faustus. In: Thomas Mann Jahrbuch 2 (1989), p. 79–101.

[30] Frank Trommler: Die »wahren« und die wahren Deutschen. Zur Nicht-Rezeption der Exilliteratur. In: Das Exilerlebnis. Verhandlungen des vierten Symposiums über deutsche und österreichische Exilliteratur. Hg. von Donald G. Daviau and Ludwig M. Fischer. Columbia SC: Camden House 1982, p. 367–375.

[31] Insiders and Outsiders. Jewish and Gentile Culture in Germany and Austria. Ed. by Dagmar Lorenz and Gabriele Weinberger. Detroit: Wayne State University Press 1994 and: Facing Fascism and Confronting the Past. German Women Writers from Weimar to the Present. Ed. by Elke P. Frederiksen and Martha Kaarsberg Wallach New York: State University of New York Press 2000.

the Literaturhaus, Vienna and the Deutsche Bibliothek Leipzig, the one compiled by Ursula Seeber and Alisa Douer, the other by Andrea Thomalla and Jörg Räuber. Recent articles by Paul Michael Lützeler about Hermann Broch reveal his predilection for a post-modern approach.[32] J. M. Ritchie, concentrating on Kurt Hiller and Magnus Hirschfeld, has introduced the perspective of Gay Theory into the field.[33] Research-in-progress shows that younger colleagues-to-be are beating out new applications of theory to exile studies. Research-in-progress in my own department by Kausi Krishnamorthi, a doctoral candidate, examines the writings of exiles in India from the vantage point of Postcolonialism.[34]

I personally have delved once more into my past and have looked, as a dyed-in-the-latest wool post-modernist, at the ordinary exiles I encountered or continue to encounter. After sixty years I was reunited with my best friend in elementary school and high school in Hildesheim, Fritz Dagobert Palmbaum or rather Fred Palmer. Three years ago we were sitting opposite each other in a restaurant in Zurich after he had discovered my whereabouts through my entry in the Golden Book of our hometown. He told his story. Australia had made 600 emergency visas available to Jewish youngsters. Fifteen times that number applied. He was chosen, a happy circumstance, because he became his family's sole survivor. A week after his arrival in Sydney an older, more established refugee accepted him as an apprentice in his watchmaker shop. He married his employee's daughter, established his own shop, sold it to start a jewelry business, sold that at the peak of its success, began a wholesale trade in parts of jewelry and settings, his most rewarding venture of all. Now in retirement he lives in one of the most desirable suburbs of Sydney. In the future I wish to write this postmodern story of the exiles-in-the-average, some highly successful, some frustrated despite their ingenuity. As an example of the latter I have already told the story of Johnny who wanted to bring, in 1940, an unpropitious time, a European-style restaurant to St. Louis, in which I performed my first dubious artistry as a waiter considerably prior to the post-war dog food gatherer at the Broadway Lobster Pond.[35]

---

[32] See Kleine Verbündete. Vertriebene österreichische Kinder- und Jugendliteratur. Hg. von Ursula Seeber, Alisa Douer, Edith Blaschitz und Karin Hanta. Wien: Picus 1998; Kinder- und Jugendliteratur im Exil 1933–1950. Mit einem Anhang Jüdische Kinder-und Jugendliteratur in Deutschland 1933–1938: Eine Ausstellung der Sammlung Exil-Literatur der Deutschen Bücherei Leipzig. Hg. von Andrea Thomalla und Jörg Räuber. Leipzig: Die Deutsche Bibliothek 1999. Also see: Paul Michael Lützeler: Aktualität und Inaktualität Hermann Brochs. In: Literatur und Kritik 209/210 (November – Dezember 1986), p. 406–411.

[33] J. M. Ritchie: Kurt Hiller. A ›Stänkerer‹ in Exile 1934–1955. In: The Legacy of Exile (note 3), p. 116–136.

[34] Kausi Krishnamorti: India and the Exile Experience as Mirrored in the Writings of Refugees from Nazi Germany and Indian Writers. Dissertation to be completed 2002, Wayne State University.

[35] Guy Stern: Epilog. In: G. Stern: Literarische Kultur im Exil. Gesammelte Beiträge zur Exilforschung (1989–1997). Dresden, München: Dresden University Press 1998 (Philologica: Reihe A; 1), p. 397–402.

From Exile Experience to Exile Studies 31

In short, we stand at the threshold of the next phase of exile studies. One of the great pioneers of exile studies in Germany, Werner Berthold, the founder of the exile wing of the Deutsche Bibliothek in Frankfurt, made the rash prediction in the seventies of the last century, that exile studies had just about run their course. Some have joined him in that dire prediction.[36] But to me it is clear that we stand today at the starting gate of at least ten new investigative marathons for our discipline. As prone to error or more so than my colleagues, I nonetheless would like to outline my prognosis:

1. Consonant with the overall development in the field of Germanistics exile studies will veer, as they have already done, from purely literary investigations to all aspects of culture, from biochemistry to jurisprudence. Ernst C. Stiefel and Frank Mecklenburg have written, for example, a history of refugee lawyers, Ulrike Wendland, in 1998, published a two-volume biographical guide to exiled art historians entitled *Biographisches Handbuch deutschsprachiger Kunsthistoriker im Exil*, also a lively study of exile musicians and composers exists since 1999.[37]
2. As exile studies expand in scope, they will also expand in geography. As is well known excellent monographs already exist on exile in France, Holland, Israel, Italy, the USA, the Soviet Union and most recently of Shanghai. But what of other countries of asylum? South America, as a valuable congress organized by Renata von Hanffstengel illustrated,[38] begs for further exploration. What about Africa, especially Egypt, as refuge? Or what of New Zealand? It is time that scholars in our discipline apply for some travel grants. I, personally, while on a pleasure trip to Argentina, found in Jacques Arndt the only German-speaking actor, who – once a neophyte at Vienna's Burgtheater – had made the jump to an accent-free star in the Hispanic film and theater world.[39]
3. There will ensue further comparative studies between on the one hand exiles of all ages and nations – up to the present – with the mass exodus during the Hitler years on the other. What are common elements between say Thomas Mann, Bertolt Brecht and Franz Werfel and refugee writers from Pino-

---

[36] Werner Berthold: Ausblick. Nach dem Paradigmenwechsel. Perspektiven der Exilforschung und des Deutschen Exilarchivs. Brita Eckert und Harro Kieser sprechen mit Werner Berthold. In: Berthold, Exilliteratur und Exilforschung (note 27), p. 189. A soon-to-be published article by Claudia Albert, »Ende der Exilforschung?« takes a similar position, also as a riposte to mine.
[37] See for example: Driven into Paradise. The Musical Migration from Nazi Germany to the United States. Ed. by Reinhold Brinkmann and Christoph Wolff. Berkeley, CA: University of California Press 1999.
[38] Mexiko, das wohltemperierte Exil. Hg. von Renata von Hanffstengel, Cecilia Tercero Vasconcelos und Silke Werner Franco. Mexico: Instituto de Investigaciones Interculturales Germano – Mexicanas 1995.
[39] Guy Stern: Die Odyssee Jacques Arndts. Vom Theater der Jugend in Wien zum argentinischen Musicalstar. In: Aufbau, November 22, 1985, col. 1–3.

chet's Chile, e. g. Isabel Allende, or from former apartheid-ridden South Africa, e. g. Breyten Breytenbach, or from Communist-controlled Czechoslovakia, witness Milan Kundera? A significant start for such a departure is represented by Martin Tucker, *Literary Exiles in the Twentieth Century*.[40] I personally experimented with such an approach via an undergraduate honors seminar »Exile Across Borders and Centuries« which started with the Babylonian Captivity and ended with Salman Ruschdie.[41] It brought home once again the fact that exile was and continues to be an existential human experience from Biblical times to the present.

4. Scholars have just begun to assess the impact of the exiles on their country of asylum, be it on the changed architectural skyline of New Christchurch in New Zealand or on buildings in Israel[42] or the philosophy of Theodor W. Adorno and the Frankfurt School on the philosophy of the Western World.[43] For this they garnered praise from, say, the art historians Alfred Barr, Robert Hughes and Cynthia Jaffee McCabe and, conversely, tortuously argued condemnations from Allan Bloom.[44] The exiles left no less a trace on the literature of their countries of their asylum. The German Americanist Martin Schulze and I have traced this impact on the literature of America; we found exile figures, real or imagined, in every genre of literature and from award-winning novels to subliterature.[45] It would be logical to inquire whether the motivations that impelled American writers to include exiles in

---

[40] Literary Exile in the Twentieth Century. An Analysis and Biographical Dictionary. Ed. by Martin Tucker. New York: Greenwood Press 1991.

[41] The Honors Seminar, entitled »Exile Literature: Throughout the Ages and Across Nations« at Wayne State University took place in the Winter semester of 1991. Its goal was to explore the universality of the exile experience, the various literary responses to it by thinking human beings across countries and centuries, its reflection in literature and – finally – its pertinence for our times. The complete course content was placed on the internet by the American Institute for Contemporary German Studies at Johns Hopkins University (http://www.aicgs.org/resources/daad/1992078.shtml).

[42] See Aryeh Sharon: Kibbutz + Bauhaus. An Architect's Way in a New Land. Stuttgart: Kramer Verlag 1976. Also see Myra Wahrhaftig: Sie legten den Grundstein. Leben und Wirken deutschsprachiger jüdischer Architekten in Palästina, 1918–1948. Tübingen: Wasmuth 1996.

[43] See for example Peter Uwe Hohendahl: Prismatic Thought. Theodor W. Adorno. Lincoln, London: University of Nebraska Press 1995.

[44] Alfred Hamilton Barr and Lincoln Kirstein: Art in the Third Reich. Washington/DC: American Federation of Arts 1945. See Robert Hughes commentary in the film *Degenerate Art* edited by David Grubin, Stephanie Barron and David McCullough. Los Angeles: KCET 1991. See also Cynthia Jaffee McCabe: The Golden Door. Artists – Immigrants of America 1876–1976. Washington: Hirschhorn Museum and Smithonian Institution Press 1976 and Allan Bloom: The Closing of the American Mind. New York: Simon and Schuster 1987.

[45] Martin Schulze: Geschichte der amerikanischen Literatur. Von den Anfängen bis heute. Berlin: Propyläen 1999 and Guy Stern: Zum Echo des Exils in der amerikanischen Literatur. In: Stern, Literarische Kultur im Exil (note 35), p. 360–367.

their poems, dramas and fiction also informed the writers of other nations. In America seven reasons for their inclusion obtain in American literature: Such protagonists fit into the tradition of immigrant literature. Also the exiles were used as authoritative warners against oppression and intolerance. Exile characters became catalysts within the literary setting of a static society or group. They often became the alter ego of an author who feels estranged. They served America as a belated vehicle for expiating the callous immigration policies of the United States during the Holocaust years. Finally they became paradigmatic for the existential condition of atomized modern society. But in all fairness I should add the explanation to me of one of the American authors, Leslie Epstein, who is obviously enthralled with exile figures in his novels: »Why do I fictionalize exiles? That's easy: They are so damned interesting.«[46]

Given the pervasiveness of exile figures in American literature, ranging from an apotheosized Albert Einstein to a nondescript and still persecuted survivor in an entertainment by Stephen King,[47] I venture to predict that future exile scholars will try to trace similar building blocks in the national literature of other countries of asylum and investigate the motivations, ideological and/or structural, that impelled their inclusion. Clearly such a body of literature exists in Holland. In South America the novel *Las Aguas de Mare* by the Argentinian fiction writer Marcos Soboleosky should encourage further research. In India Anita Desai has made an exile the hero of her novel, *Baumgartner's Bombay*.[48] In England Anita Brookner devoted her novel *Latecomer* to two middle-class exiles[49]. And I suspect that exile-related texts in Israel are not exhausted by Motti Lerner's dramas *Kassner* and *Exile in Jerusalem*,[50] Aharon Appelfeld's novels, for example, or, for that matter Batya Goor's detective story *The Saturday Morning Murder. A Psychoanalytic Case*, may not be isolated examples and should encourage further research.[51]

---

[46] Several of Epstein's works of fiction center around a refugee musician/composer by the name of Leib Goldstein. The latest is *Ice Fire Water. A Leib Goldstein Cocktail*, New York, Norton 1999.
[47] See Alan P. Lightman: Einstein's Dreams. London, New York: Bloomsbury, Pantheon 1993 and Stephen King: Different Seasons. New York: Viking Press 1982.
[48] For example Carl Friedman: De grauwe minaar. Verhalen. Amsterdam: G. A. von Oorschot 1996; Marcos Soboleosky: Las Aguas de Mare. Buenos Aires: Goyanarte 1960; Anita Desai: Baumgartner's Bombay. London, New York: Penguin 1988.
[49] Anita Brookner: Latecomers. New York: Pantheon 1988.
[50] Motti Lerner: Exile in Jerusalem. A play in three acts (MS), English translation: Hillel Halkin, first produced under the title Else by the Habima National Theater in Tel Aviv. Also his *Kassner*. In: Special Issue of Israeli Drama. An Anthology in Modern International Drama 27 (Fall 1993), No. 1, p. 37–98.
[51] For example Aharon Appelfeld: The Age of Wonders. Boston: David R. Godine 1981 and Batya Goor: The Saturday Morning Murder. A Psychoanalytic Case. New York: Harper Perennial 1992.

And finally in this search for exiles in literature two phenomena need singling out. The successor generation of the exiles, most of them Jewish, have almost inevitably become engrossed with the fate of their exiled parents or grandparents. No comprehensive study exists as yet – and several could certainly be undertaken – how exile characters are developed in the short stories and novels by Robert Schindel, Barbara Honigmann, Rafael Seligmann, Arno Reinfrank, Sylvia Tennenbaum, Lore Segal, Irene Dische, and poems by Israeli writer Elazar Benyoëtz, by the English poet Michael Hamburger and the Chilean writer Ricardo Loebell, he too the son of a refugee. The list could be extended at will.

And what of German-language literature itself? When looking back exiles made an early if sporadic appearance in post-World War II literature. Their presence and function has indeed commanded scholarly attention, for example by Ruth Klüger.[52] But it is time now to reach beyond Heinrich Böll's *Billard um halb zehn*, Günter Grass' *Hundejahre* and some of his poems and Alfred Andersch' *Efraim*. I detect in the new, post Group 47 generation of writers a veritable »à la recherche des exiles perdus.« Exile characters all of a sudden appear in Joseph Haslinger's *Opernball*, in Bernhard Schlink's *Der Vorleser* and W. G. Sebald's *Die Ausgewanderten* – all of them, by the way, best-sellers in Germany and Austria.[53]

All of these observations argue that we still very much need the approaches of all past stages of exile studies and that, for a long time to come, we shall complement and embellish earlier findings. But it is equally clear that new departures and challenges lie ahead. The stories of exiles have intrigued historians and creative writers since time immemorial. Shakespeare in *The Tempest* lent the wisdom and resignation of an aging poet to the exiled ruler Prospero. The Swiss author, Conrad Ferdinand Mayer introduced, in his *Hochzeit des Mönchs*, an exiled Dante as the storyteller of a novella, the genre most apposite to Mayer. The exile Peter Weiss wrote a drama *Trotzki im Exil*. Tom Stoppard, in his drama *Travesties*, uses glimpses of the exiled Lenin, as a counterpoint to farce.[54] And the Austrian writer Christoph Ransmayr links the banishment of Ovid by Emperor Augustus to a gripping fictional account of a search for Ovid's legacy by his Roman friend Cotta.[55] From this pattern we may readily assume that creative writers, fascinated by the theme of exile, will recurrently rely on one of the most extensive intellectual exoduses of human history, that of the Nazi period. And, sad to say, as our world is now constituted, exile, »the outcast state«, will remain one of the tragic results of prevailing autocracies.

---

[52] See Ruth Klüger: Katastrophen. Über deutsche Literatur. Göttingen: Wallstein 1994.
[53] Josef Haslinger: Opernball. Roman. Frankfurt a. M.: S. Fischer 1995; Bernhard Schlink: Der Vorleser. Zürich: Diogenes 1997; Winfried Georg Sebald: Die Ausgewanderten. Vier lange Erzählungen. Frankfurt a. M.: S. Fischer 2001.
[54] Peter Weiss: Trotzki im Exil. Stück in 2 Akten. Frankfurt a. M.: Suhrkamp 1969 and Tom Stoppard: Travesties. New York: Grove 1975.
[55] Christoph Ransmayr: Die letzte Welt. Roman. Mit einem ovidischen Repertoire. Frankfurt a. M.: Fischer 1991.

Taken in tandem these developments will, for a long time, claim our skills as explorers of the yet not completely charted country of exile. The past, which we have briefly scanned here, is prologue ... Or as the exiled psychiatrist Dr. Spielvogel in Philip Roth's novel, *Portnoy's Complaint* put it in the garbled English of an exile: »So. Now vee may perhaps to begin. Yes?«[56]

Perhaps new skills will be demanded of us, for example the ability to analyze fused forms of artistic expressions at a time when technology fuses music to colored laser beams or sculptures to electrically controlled movements, as witness the structures of Mark Rothko. But a desideratum of all German studies becomes all the more mandatory in exile scholarship, where a common adverse fate drew creators of various art forms closer to one another, even if not always in harmony. Cultural exile studies will probably soon heed a call for a holistic approach to the various fields of artistic expressions in exile, a call that the Leipzig Germanist Heide Eilert has compressed in the title of an article as literature's dialogue with the other arts. She writes: »Such an opening of borders [beyond literature], the glance at the various other artistic media, the other disciplines will be cemented even in syllabi and examinations.«[57] It will of necessity also inform exile studies, in order to do justice not only to exile artists working in two media, as for example Ludwig Meidner (painting and fiction writing) and Arnold Schönberg, writing some of his own texts, but also to evaluate the collaborative achievement between Kurt Weill, Franz Werfel and Max Reinhardt or to fathom the parallelism, recently pointed out by Rachael Schmidt in her Wayne State Master's Thesis, *Beyond Composition. Analogous Concepts in the Religious and Aesthetic Writings of Arnold Schönberg*, between Schönberg's atonal music of his exile years and Chagall's paintings.[58]

My quick-step march from the past to the future of exile studies must admit of a significant omission. Our colleagues in the basic sciences frequently and justly argue that the solution to a basic and theoretical problem often carries in its wake completely unexpected practical applications. But is it otherwise in the liberal arts? Novels may beget social action; Wölfflin's theories on the art of the Baroque unintendedly changed our approach to Baroque literature. The study of exile literature is a further, highly illustrative example. So far I perceive six of these ancillary effects:

1. The scholars' interest in exile literature spawned a cornucopia of rediscoveries of neglected works. Ventures by the Büchergilde Gutenberg in Germany produced an entire library of exiled authors. Suddenly the collected works

---

[56] Philip Roth: Portnoy's Complaint. New York: Random House 2002 [¹1967], p. 274.
[57] Heide Eilert: Der Dialog mit den anderen Künsten. In: Konzepte und Perspektiven Germanistischer Literaturwissenschaft. Hg. von Christa Grimm, Ilse Nagelschmidt und Ludwig Stockinger. Leipzig: Leipziger Universitätsverlag 1999 (Literatur und Kultur, Leipziger Texte. Reihe A. Konferenzen I), p. 158.
[58] Successfully defended on Nov, 16, 1998.

not only of luminaries such as Thomas Mann and Alfred Döblin, but of lesser known writers such as Friedrich Torberg and Anna Seghers emerged.
2. Libraries such as the Deutsche Bibliothek in Frankfurt and Leipzig, the Literaturarchiv in Marbach, the Akademie der Künste in Berlin added exile literature to their set of specialty collections. The Leo Baeck Institute, originally devoted to pre-war German-Jewish artifacts, extended its holdings to the exile period.
3. Because of exile studies bibliographies on German literary and cultural studies routinely include the exile period as one of its subdivisions.
4. Still more important to the public, be it in German-speaking countries or across the globe, have been made aware of the »misery and grandeur« of the exile authors by scholars of exile literature through their utilization of the public media. Reviews by colleagues in the *New York Times Book Review* or think-pieces by Peter Gay and Peter Demetz in the American media and by J. M. Ritchie in England have led to greater renown of exile authors. Also Alexander Stephan's exposé of the exiles' surveillance by the FBI made headlines.
5. A new generation of creative writers made use of our findings in their texts. Elaine Feinstein, author of a novel about Brecht, acknowledged her debt to John Fuegi, Jay Parini, fictionalizing the last years of Walter Benjamin, gives credit to Robert Alter and Bernd Witte, among others.
6. Finally exile scholars, by the weight and quantity of their expositions and the wide distributions their articles frequently received via pocket books, feuilletons in national magazines and newspapers as well as by television and radio exposure, made it impossible to ignore the achievements of exile literature. Shortly after the war a widely distributed history of German literature by Heinz-Otto Burger, in a chapter penned by the notorious, camouflaged Nazi Hans Schwerte could still devote sixty pages to arch-conservative modern writers and a bare twenty to the writers of exile.[59] A history of exile scholarship should record that after more than sixty years of pursuing our task such a flawed book would be read, at best, by the near-illiterates perusing the *Soldatenzeitung*.

Perhaps that should be today the single most important keynote or leitmotiv, as we recall the history of exile studies. The scholars of exile often wrested its achievements from oblivion. Many scholars were imbued with a near missionary zeal. Richard Exner, a poet, but also an explicator of the exile writings of Thomas Mann and Rudolf Alexander Schroeder captures that zeal in one of his poems:

---

[59] Hans Schwerte: Der Weg ins zwanzigste Jahrhundert. In: Analen der deutschen Literatur. Geschichte der deutschen Literatur von den Anfängen bis zur Gegenwart. Hg. von H. O. Burger. Stuttgart: Metzler 1951, p. 719–840.

Dichter kann man erschlagen. Namen
Werden gelöscht.
Einem, die Hoffnung
Vielleicht, brennt sich
Die Lettern ins Hirn.

They can cudgel poets to death. Names
Can be expunged.
But someone, hope incarnate
Perhaps, singes
The letters into
His brain.[60]

And by doing so, they too, will not be forgotten.

---

[60] Richard Exner: Dennoch Gedichte. In: Mit rauchloser Flamme. Gedichte. München: Schneekluth Verlag 1982, p. 13.

Sidra DeKoven Ezrahi

When Exiles Return: Jerusalem as Topos of the Mind and Soil

Something we might call ›the Jewish imagination‹ begins in an act of destruction – the destruction of ancient Jerusalem – and, in a way, ›ends‹ with the destruction of *that* culture and the restoration of Jerusalem two thousand years later. I am making a link between exile and poetics that presupposes both a destruction so vast that it marks the end of one form of civilization and the beginning of another – and survival that is not only the physical afterlife of a group of refugees but a major mutation of the culture. What happens to that culture if – and when – the exiles return?

In *Booking Passage: Exile and Homecoming in the Modern Jewish Imagination*,[1] I argue that the license for a certain kind of artistic imagination is embedded in the very concept of galut or collective exile – that Jewish culture in Diaspora was invited to remember by *imitating* the sacred. These are acts of imitation predicated on the disappearance of the original; as in the reproduction of art objects where the original model has been destroyed, imitation becomes the only means of preserving the primordial act of creation. Like the Roman copies of Greek statues, the copies may be invested over time with value in their own right, but such imitation is in the first instance an act of homage.

So when Jews imitate, they are acknowledging absence. The ruins of one form of culture become the cornerstones of its successor. In a sense, Jews today are in a position analogous to that of Jews of the first centuries of the Common Era who lived proximate to the Temple and its destruction. A civilization that was conceived out of one apocalypse was destroyed in another.

Let me add that I do not mean to draw facile analogies between the trauma of defeat in the wars against Rome in the first centuries of our common era and the trauma of genocide in the twentieth. ›Armageddon‹ has become a household word at the turn of our millennium, but not all armaggedons are equal. It is the redefinition of Jewish civilization and not the magnitude of the loss that I

---

[1] Many of the subjects and writers alluded to here are explored more fully in my *Booking Passage: Exile and Homecoming in the Modern Jewish Imagination* (Berkeley: Berkeley University Press 2000, Contraversions; 12). An earlier version of the present essay was delivered as the Brownstone Lecture at Dartmouth College in April, 1999; an expanded version will appear in *Icon, Image and Text in Modern Jewish Culture*, ed. by Barbara Mann and Leora Batnitzky, forthcoming.

am comparing here.[2] As survivors of the twentieth century, we have the dubious privilege of having been witnesses to, if not direct participants in, the radical reconfiguration of the Jewish world. The destruction, first by attrition and then by cataclysm, of European Jewish life and of the cultural forms that had sustained the peculiar condition of galut; the establishment of Jewish political and territorial sovereignty in Palestine; and the reemergence in recent decades of a new affirmative diasporic sensibility provide a unique vantage point on a civilization that lasted for two thousand years.

But the destruction of European Jewish life that resonates with the destruction of ancient Jerusalem and illuminates a culture of exile becomes all too relevant to the threat of destruction that hangs over Jerusalem today. The ›Al Aqsa Intifada‹ has generated a new, urgent sense that the fate of *two* peoples hangs in the balance. While my work focuses on the aesthetic implications for the Jewish literary imagination, on what I call in my book the *poetics of exile and homecoming*, the possibility that Jerusalem, eternal topos of mind and soil, might become another Armaggedon in our lifetime is, frankly, what animates my passion for this subject. Where I speak in the first person plural, it is sometimes as a Jew, sometimes as an Israeli – in both cases, a plurality that is meant to be fluid and inclusive.

I have asked myself over these last eighteen months of heartbreaking conflict whether there is in the cultural legacy of exile a controlling impulse for the mutually exclusive claims that threaten to bring down both houses. Whether some hard-won internal knowledge can take us beyond the dialectics of home and exile; whether it can help to defuse the peremptory ways of thinking that characterize both the Zionist-Diasporist conflict and the Israeli-Palestinian conflict.

Let me begin by mapping out the territory as an exercise in stark contrasts. The Zionist enterprise as both an act of ›return‹ and as a utopian projection is in some fundamental sense antithetical to the aesthetic norms and practices that Jews had perfected in the years of their exile. The *logic* of return to the ›original site‹ of the Jewish imaginaton threatens to revoke the very licence that we associate with a certain kind of artistic freedom.

The ›original site‹ of the Jewish imagination is the site of sacred transactions. The closer you are to the center of holiness, the more literal – and consequential – are your deeds. The tree of knowledge grows real apples only in the Garden of Eden. The literal name of God is pronounced only in the Holy of Holies and only by the High Priest once a year. Whenever holiness is site-specific, there is danger. The ›strange fire‹ that the sons of Aaron bring to the tabernacle consumes them. Eventually we learn the consolation of exile: that strange fires create less combustion in estranged places. The work of art, the very practice of the artistic representation of reality, of a peculiarly Jewish form of *mimesis*, the freedom to imagine and to create alternative worlds without fatal consequence, begins

---

[2] As Alan L. Mintz showed in his study of Jewish literary responses to disaster (Hurban. Responses to Catastrophe in Hebrew Literature. New York: Columbia University Press 1984.), paradigm shifts are not necessarily commensurate with the magnitude or the horror of the events they register.

mythically with banishment from the Garden and historically with the destruction of the sacred center and the expulsion from Jerusalem.

Still, the first impulse of the exile is a mournful renunciation of any acts of creativity on foreign soil:

> By the waters of Babylon, there we sat down, and we wept, when we remembered Zion. / There on the willows we hung our harps. / Our captors asked us there for songs, our tormentors for amusement: »sing us one of the songs of Zion.« / How can we sing a song of the Lord on alien soil? *Psalm 137:1–4*

The Lord's song, the psalm of celebration, belongs in Solomon's Temple. To be in exile is to be out of song, and yet it is the very beginning of the creative process; in no more time than it takes to draw a breath, another kind of song is born: a pledge to memory, to the word as marker for the lost world:

> If I forget thee O Jerusalem, let my right hand forget her cunning. If I do not remember thee, / let my tongue cleave to the roof of my mouth if I prefer not Jerusalem above my chiefest joy. *Psalm 137:5–6*

The tongue and the hand, metonyms of the oral and written word, are both the instruments of execution and the bodily locus of the failure of execution. This is a pledge that the exiles will carry, and that will carry the exiles, throughout years in the deserts or the fleshpots of Babylonia and all the other lands of their dispersion – but it is memory that fires, and frees, the imagination. It is a pledge to collective memory – the memory of Jerusalem – but it is spoken in the first person *singular* – if *I* forget thee – which is also the beginning of the lyric voice and the personal journey.

If the psalm of exile was articulated after the *first* destruction and expulsion at the hands of the Babylonians, it was after the *second* destruction at the hands of the Romans that a poetics of exile was fully constructed.[3] The Temple had spatialized holiness. Surely the Torah would remain, whereever it roamed, the site of primary transactions between the human and the Divine. Surely God's glory filled the earth. But the challenge was to maintain some connection to the Holy Land, to the center of cultic and national prowess, predicated on distance from it and a belated recall of the drama enacted there. Through a series of conversations conducted by conclaves of rabbis in the first centuries of the Common Era, life in the text was conceived and operationalized. The text was the Talmud, the discourse rational-dialectic, but its self-conscious

---

[3] The historical differences in patterns of grieving, of pilgrimage and of substitution between the first destruction and exile and the second are too significant to overlook, but I am here invoking the exile attendant upon the destruction of the sacred center more as *topos* and less as an historically specific event. For a lively evocation of the text culture and the playful, ironic even parodic reworking of scriptures that evolved in Hellenistic, Diasporic Judaism between the two destructions see Erich S. Gruen: Heritage and Hellenism: The Reinvention of Jewish Tradition. Berkeley: University of California Press 1998 (Hellenistic Culture and Society; 30) and id., Diaspora: Jews amidst Greeks and Romans. Cambridge/Mass.: Harvard University Press 2002.

production and its struggle with the status of symbolic languages created the rationale for the most imaginative of textual acts. The Rabbis were attempting to reinvent a religious culture that could ›go on the road‹ without relinquishing its invisible God to the rich iconic manifestations of the pagan cultures that surrounded it. The sanction of textual activity made room for what we now recognize as radical theories of artistic representation. In the debates compiled in the tractate *Avoda Zara*, the space vacated for art is that of the disabled cultic icon; while any object perceived as a function of pagan worship was emphatically excluded, the peculiar culture invented for the ›deterritorialized‹ Jews designated an arena for the aesthetic – though it was not explicitly referred to as such – that was, essentially, defined as that of the profane or the non-sacred.

Moshe Halbertal has described the rabbinic procedures by which what was considered the sacred space of the pagan world was contracted or scaled down – creating, in effect, a vacuum or no-man's-land of ›secularity‹ in which cultural and social exchanges between Jews and pagans could take place. He compares the idea of religiously neutral space in the mishnaic literature to the modern creation of neutral civic space. In the passage that has become one of the primary prooftexts for the modern discussion of Jewish aesthetics and aniconicism, Rabban Gamliel is found in a Roman bathhouse by a Greek philosopher who queries him on the propriety of his bathing in Aphrodite's space. Rabban Gamliel's answer, that he did not intrude upon Aphrodite's domain, but she upon *his*, is the rationale for much of the accommodation that the Rabbis made with the idolatrous environment in which they lived.[4] If in the *biblical* world, ancient *and* modern, the mandate in its most radical form is to rid the Holy Land of all its impurities, and of all impure others, in the *talmudic* world the exigencies of coexistence and of relinquished sovereignty produce an ingenious form of dialectical logic that allows for both the contraction of the iconic, cultic, and the expansion of religiously neutral or profane, space. This provides an arena for the emergence of the aesthetic and of cultural negotiation between theologically embattled cultures.

While none of the cultures in dialogue, neither the early Jewish nor the Graeco-Roman, nor those that succeeded them, were monolithic (and, for that matter, not all images in the so-called Pagan world were cultic), the debate over boundaries not only allows for the (albeit anxious) proximity of competing religious images; it provides legitimacy for the production of Jewish art. Kalman Bland adds to the discussion of visual representations in antiquity that it was the three-dimensional statue and not the relief or the flat painting that made the Rabbis anxious.[5] By

---

[4] *Avoda Zara*, III, 4. See Moshe Halbertal's development of this idea of the distinction between a religious and an »aesthetic« realm between Jews and pagans in »Coexisting with the enemy: Jews and pagans in the Mishnah«, in: Tolerance and Intolerance in Early Judaism and Christianity. Ed. by Graham N. Stanton and Guy G. Stroumsa. Cambridge: Cambridge University Press 1998, p. 159–172.

[5] For a more thorough exploration of the evolution of Jewish aesthetics in medieval Jewish philosophy and of modern discussions of aniconism grounded in German Jew-

this logic, one can argue that the text, being both flat and typographically non-representational, is even further removed from the lifelike sculpture that could become an object of worship. In breaking the tablets at the sight of the golden calf, Moses demonstrates that the written word both contains prohibitions against graven images and is *categorically* removed from them. (Smashing the idols, as Jewish legend represents Abraham doing in his father's shop, or as the bible reports Moses and Aaron doing to the golden calf at the foot of Mount Sinai, is a way of getting rid of them; smashing the *tablets* only invites another, even more elaborate set.)

The Talmud evolved as both a series of elaborations and commentaries on Scriptures, and as the model of a culture that could exist in exile. In the first place, again, *memory*: the Talmud is a repository for the most precise descriptions of holy space. But the memory stored in the talmudic descriptions of the Temple and of the cultic practices within it, the most exacting mnemonic blueprints of sacred architecture and vessels, also remained as constant reminders of their own surrogate status and imaginative freedom. All texts come to be defined by their distance from that space. »By the waters of Babylon, *there* we sat down and we wept ...« To be in exile is, by definition, to be *elsewhere*. The pledge to remember Jerusalem in the song of exile safeguards both the promise of eventual return and the burdens and privileges of the journey itself. From the axiom of mobility with a fixed point of origin and return comes the mandate not only to remember, but also to imagine alternative places – Babylon, its willows and its waters; Roman bathhouses and Polish bathhouses, *their* willows and waters.

The peculiar terms by which Jews in exile defined their condition as both infinitely mobile and as suspended between the memory and the vision of perfect stasis – of a territorial home that is also the *axis mundi* – gave rise, then, to a textual culture conceived as substitute for the ›real‹ one. Since by definition we are, in exile, always removed from the ›place‹ itself, the ›thing‹ itself, exile becomes culturally premised on and licensed by the principle of simulation. The synagogue is, historically and conceptually, a diasporic dwelling; it is the *not*-temple. It is referred to as a *mikdash m'at*, a sort of dollhouse of the Temple of Solomon. The destruction of the Temple invites us to build facsimiles in any and every other space as place-holders for the ›real‹, the sacred. Prayer is the not-sacrifice, marker for the ritual sacrifices that will be reinstated in messianic time (and let me add a prayer that *I* may never live to see that day!). The Sabbath is the temporal marker for Jerusalem and the world to come; *hol* is the created world in its profane manifestations, the quotidian, the time and place of our creative acts, our ›chiefest joys‹.

Some of the most magnificent Hebrew lyrics are written by poets liberated from fear of the consequences of desecration, from fear of bringing ›strange

---

ish philosophy, see Kalman Bland's *The Artless Jew. Medieval and Modern Affirmations and Denials of the Visual*, Princeton: Princeton University Press 2000; paperback edition, 2002.

fire‹. Yannai, considered to be the first *paytan* of the Classical period – but also one of the most recent of the voices to be heard, having been hidden for centuries in the treasure-trove of the Cairo Geniza – shows how far the liberated imagination can reach. Probably a Cantor in sixth century Palestine, Yannai composed verses whose metaphors are verbalizations of what would appear to be the most interdicted of visual images:

> From Heaven to the Heaven of
> Heavens; from the Heaven of Heavens
> to the Dark Clouds; from the Dark
> Clouds to the Abode; from the Abode
> to the Dwelling-place; from the
> Dwelling-place to the Skies; from the
> Skies to the Plains; from the Plains to
> the height of the Throne; and from the
> height of the Throne to the Chariot –
>
> who can be compared to You, who is
> Your equal? Who has seen You, who
> has reached You? Who can hold his
> head high, who can lift up his eyes?
> who can question, who can defy? Who
> can fathom, who can calculate? Who
> can be proud, who can be haughty?
> who is like You?
>
> For You ride on a cherub and fly on a
> wind; Your road is in whirlwind, Your
> way is in storm; Your path is through
> waters. Fires are Your emisssaries –
> thousands of thousands and myriads of
> myriads, who are changed into men,
> changed into women, changed into
> winds, changed into demons; who
> assume all shapes and fulfil every
> mission, with fear, dread, awe,
> trembling, terror, trepidation, they
> Open ... [6]

This hymn, of which the conclusion is missing, would have been inserted into the service introducing the ›kedusha‹ prayer attributed to the heavenly hosts: »Holy, Holy, Holy ...«

The license for such daring acts of metaphoric/metamorphic flight – »who can be compared to You?« (mi yidme lakh, mi yishveh lakh) – is from the book of Lamentations. But *there* the speaker, traditionally identified as Jeremiah, is

---

[6] Hymn from the Heavens. In: The Penguin Book of Hebrew Verse. Ed. by T. Carmi. Harmondsworth: Penguin 1981, p. 218–219.

addressing not God but Jerusalem after the Babylonian conquest. The image of the prophet facing the ruins of Jerusalem provides the pre-text for all subsequent acts of poetic consolation: »To what shall I compare thee that I may comfort thee? « (ma adameh lakh ... ma ashveh lakh va-anahamekh *Lam. 2:13*). But the address there is as much to the coming generations as it is to ›Jerusalem‹ and its inhabitants; it defines the poetic gaze as, potentially, the view from a distance. In lamentations for the destruction of the center of holiness, the production of metaphor is granted a role equal to that of memory in the psalm of exile. Memory and metaphor launch the poetic journey into diaspora.

It is, then, the poets' very distance from the destroyed center that frees them to construct a poetry founded on the longing to return ›home‹. The medieval *piyyut* (liturgical poem) is technically defined in architectonic terms – the two parts of a metrical line are called the *delet* (door) and the *soger* (lock); even in modern Hebrew poetry a single verse is called a *bayit* (house). My argument for the language that provides ›housing‹ as self-conscious surrogate for restless spirits is not meant to deny the metaphysical power that some traditions invest in the manipulation of language. The belief that words or letters spoken by human beings in proper combination can create or destroy worlds is deeply embedded in the Kabbalistic and other mystical traditions and comes closer to a sacramental than a symbolic, mimetic, relation to the material world. But the cultural impulse that *I* am tracing is premised on the notion of distance and alienation from the sources of the sacred as both the condition and the challenge of Jewish collective life for an unspecified – but theologically limited – time. Underlying the aesthetics of exile is the axiom of provisionality, of a state ideologically constructed between the ancient memory of domicile and the messianic promise of an (endlessly-deferred) return. Because it is theologically delimited by the vision of return, exile is non-normative and ontologically unaccountable. But because this return is endlessly deferred, the Diaspora provides a prolonged occasion for symbol-making, for substitution and replication, for maintaining the sacred center in metaphoric suspense.

In its most radical form, the imaginative license I am describing seems to have no geographic coordinates; it is an affirmation and reconfiguration of the Jewish word as nomadic exercise and Jewish exile as a kind of literary privilege. But each of the writers who ›wrote the exile‹ and their vast and scattered community of readers are bound by a commitment to the provisional status of imagined or remembered worlds, to desire as the principle of fiction and lack of closure as the structural guarantee of narrative continuity.

At this point it may be necessary to try to distinguish between mimesis as a *form of representation* and as an *act of substitution*. The distinction is as crucial for the definition of a diasporic aesthetic as for the delineation of a non-idolatrous artistic imagination. A text-based culture such as that constructed around the Talmud and sanctioned by exegetical principles and poetic practice is a culture of substitution self-consciously mimetic of and at the same time remote from the edifices and rituals that are so faithfully recorded in its precincts. It is precisely the kind of simulacrum that avoids pagan temptation because built into its language is the knowledge of its surrogacy.

I am using the term ›mimetic‹, then, less in the sense of a lifelike imitation of reality than in regard to its remove from the primordial arena of creation. We might recognize in the rabbinic move resonances of Platonic and Aristotelian ambivalences about the shadowy status of acts of representation and their moral and epistemological value. Instances of linguistic representation, such as the most explicit of the *piyyutim* of Yannai and others, that, if realized in three-dimensional marble and possibly even in two-dimensional paint would have been taboo, are the subject of debate in current reconsiderations of Jewish art and iconography.[7] In this debate, the consciousness of distance can act as a shield against the theological ›error of substitution‹ of the icon for the Deity.

The aesthetic principle I am exploring[8] also finds its expression in the many forms of a non-idealistic savoring of the material world. In the twelfth century Hebrew poetry of Yehuda Halevi, the life of a courtly poet in Andalusia and its sensual delights are delimited by their provisional status and, seemingly, overwritten by the poet's erotic desire for Zion. Exotic imagery marks his approach to the Holy Land and mingles with visions of love consummated (and consumed) in the sacred center. But Yehuda Halevi succeeded in constructing a language that held in unresolved tension a yearning for the ruined shrine with both the material pleasures of the world he was leaving behind and the practical obstacles he encountered on the actual journey to Palestine. Poems written on the first leg of the journey are saturated with erotic projection: »It / would delight my heart to walk naked / and barefoot among the desolate ruins / where your shrines once stood ...« »I'd soar on eagle-wings / if only to

---

[7] See Moshe Halbertal / Avishai Margalit: Idolatry. Translated by Naomi Goldblum. Cambridge: Harvard University Press 1992, especially the chapter on »Idolatry and Representation«, p. 37–66. Maimonides is one of the most systematic of those who argue that the ›error of substitution‹ is the cause of idolatry. See his *Laws of Idolatry* and *Guide to the Perplexed* and the discussion of this and other aspects of representation based on the presumption or rejection of resemblance to the thing represented, verbal as well as visual, in: ibid, p. 42–45 and 54. Applying C. S. Peirce's distinctions between categories of representation based on similarity, and those that derive from a causal-metonymic relation to the object of representation, or those seen as a function of cultural-epistemological conventions, Halbertal and Margalit allow for the argument that even the golden calf might have functioned as a substitute – not for the Deity but for the cherubim and the Ark of the Covenant, themselves acceptable as metonymic of rather than similar to God. Here again it is not only the issue of anthropomorphism but the question of distance from the *axis mundi* that is crucial.

[8] A discussion of the relative status of representational and non-representational art, which is beyond the bounds of this essay, cannot be divorced from the social and cultural influences in the societies in which Jews lived and created. On the rich interplay between Jewish culture and the surrounding European cultures in the modern period around the practice of visual representation, see Richard I. Cohen: Jewish Icons. Art and Society in Modern Europe. Berkeley: University of California Press 1998.

mix my tears with your dust ... I shall kiss / and cherish your stones. Your earth / will be sweeter than honey to my lips.« But such verses are interspersed with the pathos of leaving the landscapes and heartscapes of his native Spain, »denying myself a parting kiss for my child, family, companions; not even shedding / a tear over my orchard planted, watered / and pruned to blossom in abundance«[9] – and with graphic descriptions of seasickness and the omnipresent threat of pirates.

Since his traces were lost after embarking in Alexandria for Palestine, Yehuda Halevi's unknown end links death with eros as the ultimate form of arrival. The journey's anticipated consummation endangers the mimetic project of exile; the corpus of poetry loosely referred to as ›shirei yam‹ and ›shirei tzion‹ (Songs of the Sea and Songs of/to Zion) points to the ways in which both desire itself and the status of the symbolic would be fulfilled and thus superseded in the sacramental reunion with the beloved object. But close critical readings show that even in the enactment of the psalmist's pledge to ›put Jerusalem above my chiefest joy‹, the ongoing tension between the fullness of life lived in Spain and the anticipated resolution of the quotidian in the ecstatic moment of encounter with the ruined shrine, the ongoing anxiety of erotic longing for the distant beloved and expected resolution to all forms of yearning and of imagination in the Holy Land, never dissipate even in the last poems.

Yehuda Halevi's is one of many pilgrimages that fill the annals of the Middle Ages; but, since he did not survive to tell its end, his life and his writing furnish the model for the Jewish journey as an open-ended narrative; homecoming remains a deferred resolution to the condition of exile and symbolic language remains safe from realized or literalized dreams.

Although my point of departure is Andalusia and the poetry of Yehuda Halevi, the Jews who lived in the Mediterranean basin tended to regard Zion in general and Jerusalem in particular less in messianic terms and more as a central point on their local map. Europe's Jews, on the other hand, were marked more by their relation to the deferred messianism that defined the sojourn in *golus* (exile). With all the surrogate temples, surrogate houses (*batim*) and surrogate stories, what is perhaps most extraordinary is that in the many lands of their dispersion, the Jews succeeded in developing a mimetic culture that was compatible with a longing for Jerusalem. The pledge to memory held, and for most of two millennia, the Holy Land remained a ruined landscape in the minds of its rememberers, *Judea capta,* a dusty relic. The yearning for homecoming is, it turns out, consistent with the most radical form of homelessness and the most protean notion of home; the preservation of the vision of the

---

[9] Ode to Zion [Tzion ha-lo tishali]. In: The Penguin Book of Hebrew Verse (note 6), p. 348; Lovely Slopes, Earth's Delights [Yefe nof m'sos tevel]. Translated by Gabriel Levin, unpublished manuscript, p. 47; Hard Pressed for the Living God [Hatzikatni teshukati] from *On the Sea* [Shirei yam], part 5. Translated by Gabriel Levin. Jerusalem: Ibis Editions 1997, p. 26–27.

vision of the homeland in a state of desolation becomes the appropriate reference and correlative of the ongoing, indefinite exile of its people.

What I am defining as the Jewish poetics of exile was a struggle to preserve a past that had been lost in the name of a future that was its projected image. Within this seemingly rigid teleological structure, an open-ended adventure could unfold based on forms of textual repatriation, alternative stories that were conceptually one remove from the Real. As Franz Rosenzweig was to define it in his polemic with Zionism, the land that is deemed holy is also unpossessable, that is, generates its own diasporic force-field of desire.[10]

The mandate to preserve by miniaturizing what is already lost, to protect it from the ravages of history by maintaining it as a narrative memory-palace, a *mikdash m'at*, persists into the postholocaust era. As I've argued in *Booking Passage,* whether the Real is the ruined shrine waiting to be redeemed, or the ruined culture that replaced it, the shrine-replicas, the storytelling that evolves within a disaporic force-field of desire is a mode of coping with intolerable reality through fictive reinvention, through the construction of alternative history – and through imaginative representations of the world that was destroyed.

Let me not sidestep this issue. Equating Jewish Europe after its devastation with Jerusalem as sacred center may seem a bit far-fetched unless we recall that the mimetic imagination is predicated not only on distance from but also on *destruction of* the sacred center. The cultural patterns I have been tracing were defined by distance from and memory of Jerusalem. I acknowledged earlier that our generation has witnessed the greatest upheaval in 2000 years of Jewish civilization. Perhaps its most dramatic sign is that, in some fundamental sense, Europe has come to *replace* Jerusalem as the ruined shrine in the Jewish imagination – and that this move is replete with ritual and literary acts of pilgrimage and mimesis. One direction this has taken is the sacralizing of the sites of incarceration and death. The other is the creation of textual surrogates or replicas of the destroyed culture.

The attempts to keep the story alive in the wake of total destruction appear even more defiant when we consider the ways in which the triumph of the Zionist enterprise in the aftermath of the Holocaust implied certain strictures on this form of imagination. The force of a collective homecoming and of a utopian vision put the entire mimetic project of exile into question. Yehuda Halevi did not live to tell his journey's end in the Holy Land. But many of the characters who live in twentieth century narratives do, auguring the end of narrative itself. The *logic* of any messianic or utopian project, Zionism included, is that the very realization of the dream abolishes dreaming. By its very nature, that is, utopia realized makes the imagination of alternative worlds not only unnecessary but even illegitimate.

---

[10] Franz Rosenzweig: The Star of Redemption. Notre Dame: University of Notre Dame Press 1985, Part 3, Book I, p. 300.

In our liturgical and poetic representations of the long sojourn in exile, God's glory fills the earth and cannot be confined to any material dwelling-place. But the temptation to return to the place where God dwelt between the wings of the cherubim never left us. The desire to return to the space of the sacred not only as pilgrims but as settlers, the longing to dwell in its emanation, to find consummation in reunion with the beloved, has in fact fuelled all our mimetic practices in galut. We know that reconnection with the sacred raises the spectre of fatal mistakes. Unpracticed and uncouth from our wanderings, we're liable to throw our jewelry into the fire and produce a golden calf. Even in our most earnest attempts to get it right, we're in danger of bringing strange fire to the tabernacle. The results are always fatal: one false step and you're toast.

Still, when the opportunity finally presented itself, we grabbed it – as the moment we had been waiting for for 2000 years – and the history of the reconfiguration of Jewish sovereignty is, at the most fundamental level, the story of intoxication with a return to the sources of the sacred. We are only now beginning to understand the full implications of that return. They are manifested in the wars being fought between those Jews who would reconstruct the cultic world from memory's blueprints and those who would infuse the reclaimed soil with exilic habits and a post-enlightenment faith in competing narratives and never-ending journeys. Between, if you will, the ›Messiah Camp‹ and the ›Peace Camp‹.

In principle, at least, the return of the exiles seems to involve a repudiation of the aesthetic principle that allowed us to create images in all the lands of our dispersal. There never really was a danger that we'd mistake our poor imitations, our mikdashei m'at, our miserable shtiblakh (those ramshackle houses of worship), – or even our Dura Europas – for the *real thing*. A return to the sacred is a return to the place where the loose ends of the story are meant to be tied up – inviting a reification of what had been held for two millennia in a state of metaphoric suspense.

Although the idea of the sacred had been challenged long before secular pioneers with pickaxes pierced the arid soil of the Holy Land, reconnecting to the physical source of the sacred paved the way for the religious messianism that flourishes in contemporary Israel. The very appeal of a wholistic aesthetic, of a return to the site of original acts of creation, competes with the synthetic, the mimetic, the surrogate, the simulacrum that is diaspora.

I am, of course, not trying to argue, against overwhelming evidence to the contrary, that the literary imagination has not flourished in Israel – but rather that the *logic* of return to the site of negotiations with the sacred and the ›Real‹ is the resolution of mimetic desire predicated on distance and simulation. Theoretically and ideologically, that is, to reinhabit the original space of the Jewish imagination is to relinquish the license for mimicking the sacred, the license that I am identifying with the exercise of poetic freedom in exile.

On the other hand, my critique of the absolutizing, totalizing and literalizing logic of return, the defense of a diaspora aesthetic, should not be equated with the more radically ›essentialist‹ diasporist position that has evolved in recent years. Where ›Diasporism‹ congeals as an ideological platform that does not define the journey in teleological terms or acknowledge distance as a function of mimetic desire, it denies the two premises of the culture I have been tracing: the referentiality of the sacred center and provisionality as its liberating force. Diaspora becomes, then, a discursive rather than a mimetic enterprise.[11] Without the ongoing tension between the *telos* and the way, between a place designated as the Real and its replicas, between the shrine and the text, the very delicate negotiation that licensed the Jewish imagination in the first place is undermined.

Nearly all compelling instances of literary creativity in modern Israel have been a struggle *against* the utopian-messianic aesthetic, with its resolution of all the ancient grievances. Whereever the utopian-messianic mode persists, in its epic or romantic forms, the incompatibility between poetic and political measurements of time and place is denied. This is the true meaning of the rhetoric of the whole associated with the Temple Mount and Jerusalem. The elements that comprised the psalm of exile can yield all too easily to the aesthetics of homecoming. *Jerusalem*, ringed by mountains, is the most claustrophobic but in principle the most expandable space; as ultimate object of desire it admits of no negotiable borders: »May the day come when Jerusalem extends as far as Damascus, and in every direction«, says Tehila in S. Y. Agnon's story by that name (1925).[12] Confusion or fuzziness about the boundaries of the sacred was hardly consequential in the years of geographical remove from it and the construction of various topographies of the religious imagination.[13] A return to the land of the Bible is, potentially, a reversal of the process that Halbertal describes as contraction of sacred space to create a domain of ›secular‹, aesthetic exchange.

Jerusalem in its redemptive mode extends into the Hills of Judea and beyond to Damascus (!) in the north and the desert in the south – the site of revelation and the primordial landscape of the mythic soul of Israel. The desert is not only perceived as empty; it too is *original* space, Zion in mourning waiting to be redeemed through the ingathering of her exiles. The return to Zion-as-desert is configured in some of the earliest artistic and literary renderings in the

---

[11] From George Steiner's earlier polemic with Zionism, in which he designated the ›text as homeland‹ (»Our Homeland, the Text«, in: Salmagundi, No. 66, Winter – Spring 1985, p. 24–25, here p. 19), through Edmond Jabes' romantic evocation of the nomadic textuality of the Jew to the most recent work of Jonathan and Daniel Boyarin (Jews and other Differences. The New Jewish Cultural Studies. Minneapolis: University of Minnesota Press 1997), the discussion overlaps with the postcolonialist critique of Zionism.

[12] S. Y. Agnon: »Tehila«. Translated by Walter Lever. In: Firstfruits. A Harvest of Twenty-Five Years of Israeli Writing. Ed. by James A. Michener. Greenwich: A Fawcett Premier Book, 1973, p. 70. For a very different view of Jerusalem, see his »Tmol Shilshom« [Just Yesterday].

[13] On this see Maurice Halbwachs' essay on the protean geography of the Holy Land in: On Collective Memory. Ed. and translated by Lewis A. Coser, Chicago: University of Chicago Press 1992.

Yishuv (the Jewish community in pre-State Palestine) not only as a romantic encounter with desolate, untamed nature, but also as a reconnection with the ancestral self – the autochthonous Semitic self. The Bedouins – and by extension the Arabs in general – are effaced not by being overlooked but by being so fully *incorporated*: they are so fundamentally ourselves in our most authentic, ab-original state, that they cannot be Other. Return to the primordial is, then, in its aesthetic and ethical dimensions a return to the *same* as a negation of otherness, to the original as a negation of mimesis.

And that is why Tel Aviv was invented. Tel Aviv is, by definition and in its very construction, the *not-sacred*. Not the desert – and most certainly not Jerusalem. When it was no more than a dirt road, a eucalyptus tree and a few huts, it was already not-Jerusalem. Tel Aviv is the city with a horizon. It's a place that allows for comings – and goings. Every time you leave Jerusalem you have to account for it. Within the broad contours of a literature predicated on the gravitational dynamic of ingathering, the *helekh* or restless wanderer continued to act as control and reproach. The land envisioned as a haven by prophets, poets, philosophers and politicians had to make room, if only at the margins, for the yearnings and the murmurings of dislocated souls, for the reflexes of exile. Tel Aviv became their city, the place that could hold their nostalgia and their memories. Beginning in the 1920s, Tel Aviv is the evolving site of a diasporic, postmodernist, postzionist, aesthetic. It nourishes more than nostalgia. A place that has infinite horizons also has negotiable borders. It is the ultimate expression of Jewish self-representation in its non-colonialist, non-utopian dimensions.

Tel Aviv is the site of *memories*, Jerusalem the locus of *Memory*. In its collective form, as we have seen, Memory was the very elixir (and toxin) of exile – and the poetics of homecoming was meant to repatriate and redeem its vagrancy. If memory is the burden and privilege of Exile, its release in the Holy Land is a response to the temptations, and the dangers, of total recall. Memory that had been freighted for two thousand years with the fear of amnesia can be detoxified only by gently reinterring it in the place from which it was wrested:

> Let the memorial hill
> Remember instead of me,
> That's what it's here for. Let the park in-memory-of remember,
> Let the street that's-named-for remember,
> Let the well-known building remember,
> Let the synagogue that's named after God remember
> Let the rolling Torah scroll remember, let the prayer
> For the memory of the dead remember. Let the flags remember,
> Those multicolored shrouds of history: the bodies they wrapped
> Have long since turned to dust. Let the dust remember.
> Let the dung remember at the gate. Let the afterbirth remember.
> Let the beasts of the field and the birds of the heavens
> Eat and remember.
> Let all of them remember so that I can rest.
>
> *Yehuda Amichai*

Yehuda Amichai's poetic desideratum is an ironic representation not only of the burden of total recall, but of the *implications* of total recall when it is reunited with the sources of power, sovereignty and the sacred. Remember, only in the place designated as the Real are the consequences dire – even fatal. The end of Psalm 137, the part that is almost never quoted when the poetry of exile is recited, the verse that comes after the pledge to memory, is a promise to wreak vengeance on Babylon when Israel is restored to its original place – a pledge so brutal that it envisions dashing Babylon's babies against the rocks. Like the poetic dream of a borderless Jerusalem, such oaths are psychic compensation for a disempowered people. But the empowerment of ancient memories, of unredressed grievances, leads either to the deaths of children – or to self-induced acts of forgetting that make room for forgiveness, and coexistence.

»Sag, daß Jerusalem *i s t*.« Say, that Jerusalem *is*, writes Paul Celan; in the small space between his visit to Israel and his death in the waters of the Seine, he managed to dispatch eros, prayer and reading to converge once again on the Holy City: »I leaf you open, for ever, / you pray, you lay / us free.« (ich blättre dich auf, für immer, / du betest, du bettest / uns frei).[14]

---

[14] Paul Celan: »Poles«. The rather free translation is John Felstiner's: Paul Celan. Poet, Survivor, Jew. New Haven: Yale University Press 1995, p. 275–276.

Jakob Hessing

Heinrich Heine's *Reisebilder* as Images of Exile

I wish to dedicate this lecture to the memory of Jürgen Nieraad, and in doing so I shall take up certain ideas that he once expressed. Jürgen laid them down in a note to a former conference held in Jerusalem, and this note was mentioned already by Bernhard Greiner in his opening remarks.

In 1989, that conference was about Jewish aspects of the so-called ›Exilliteratur‹. I use the German term because it was coined mainly for the literature written by authors expelled by the Nazi regime, and as such it has become a matter of contention between Germans and Germans. Jürgen, himself a German who had chosen to live in Israel, was very much aware of this, and his remarks in the wake of the conference reflect upon the two languages dealing with the matter of ›Exilliteratur‹ – the one spoken by those who have experienced exile as their personal fate, the other couched in the terms of an allegedly scientific detachment, which, in fact, disregards this fate and wishes to silence the voice of the victim.

»Wie«, Jürgen asks in his note, »verfährt die Literaturwissenschaft mit einer Literatur, der in auszeichnendem Sinne Gewaltverhältnisse als Thema und biografische Erfahrung zugrunde liegen?«[1] How do scholars deal with a literature in which violence is a predominant theme and a biographical experience? Do they develop an academic discourse about it which leaves no trace of that violence and the pain it has caused? The question is of great concern to him, and he views it as a central issue underlying much of modern literature. It becomes difficult, he says, to narrate violence experienced either by oneself or by others, when no ideological framework is strong enough to contain it any longer; early instances of such a situation, he writes, should be detected at the end of the 18th century when the project of modernity begins to disintegrate, and at the latest after World War One, when no narrative can make sense of mass destruction any more.[2]

The lectures of the conference, and Jürgen Nieraad's note about it, were printed in 1993, and one year later he published a book that he had been work-

---

[1] Jürgen Nieraad: Deutsch-jüdische Exil- und Emigrationsliteratur im 20. Jahrhundert. Nach-Gedanken zu einer Konferenz. In: Deutsch-jüdische Exil- und Emigrationsliteratur im 20. Jahrhundert. Hg. von Itta Shedletzky und Hans Otto Horch. Tübingen: Niemeyer 1993 (Conditio Judaica. Studien und Quellen zur deutsch-jüdischen Literatur- und Kulturgeschichte; 3), p. 271–280, here: p. 279
[2] Ibid., p. 278.

ing on during the early 1990s. It is called *Die Spur der Gewalt*,[3] (The Footsteps of Violence), and in it, on a much broader scale, Jürgen develops the thesis hinted at in the note. There he had merely marked two points in time – the end of the 18th century, and World War One –, but in the book he fills in the gaps and presents the case of violence well into the 20th century and the literature written after the Holocaust.

Karl Philipp Moritz, he writes, had already experienced the violence of modernity in his personal life, and yet, for one more time, he tried to cling to an aesthetic theory of the sublime that remained in line with the classicism of Weimar.[4] It was only in the 19th century that violence received a totally different expression and that a poet like Baudelaire invented a new language for it.[5]

Moritz created his aesthetic philosophy at the time of the French Revolution, and *Les fleurs du mal* appeared in 1857. There is a gap of two generations between the two authors, and it is here that I aim to take up Jürgen's argument by introducing Heinrich Heine. I do not wish to read him as a missing link between Moritz and Baudelaire, but rather as a figure who, on the borderline between two historical periods, marks his own transition from a poetics of the sublime to an uncensored admittance of violence; or, to use Heine's own term, to the end of the ›Kunstperiode‹ that he associated with the name of Goethe.

»I have never attached much value to a poetic reputation«, he writes in his *Journey from Munich to Genoa,* »and I care little whether my songs are praised or found fault with. But ye may lay a sword on my coffin; for I was a brave soldier in the War of Freedom for Mankind.«[6]

Here then, there still is, or rather there still seems to be, what Jürgen Nieraad might call an ideological framework justifying the violence depicted in his poetry. Heine grew up during the Napoleonic wars, and he sees himself as a soldier in the army of the revolution; but at the same time, his self-description is already precarious. He begins his writing career *after* the defeat of the revolution, in a period when the ›War of Freedom for Mankind‹ is lost already, and the ambivalence of his situation casts a dark shadow. In the lines quoted above Heine imagines himself dead already: The image of the coffin is turned against the poet himself, for in the end he will fall prey to the violence that modernity has set free – he will not be the victor, but the loser in that War of Freedom.

Everywhere in the writings of Heine, this knowledge of a final defeat is to be found. It appears in many forms, and here I wish to take as an example some images of exile that permeate Heine's poetry. They appear from the very beginning, long before he leaves Germany and goes into exile in Paris. I shall

---

[3] Jürgen Nieraad: Die Spur der Gewalt. Zur Geschichte des Schrecklichen in der Literatur und ihrer Theorie. Lüneburg: zu Klampen 1994.
[4] Ibid., p. 98–103.
[5] Ibid., p. 117ff.
[6] Heinrich Heine: Pictures of Travel. Translated by Charles Godfrey Leland. With a Critical and Biographical Introduction by Charles Harvey Genung. New York: Appleton 1901, p. 259f.

deliberately trace them in his *Reisebilder*. They were written while he was still living in Germany, and they must be read as intimations of mortality – as the forebodings of devastation.

Heine was little older than twenty when he wrote the poem »Schöne Wiege meiner Leiden«. It is often associated with the grief over his unrequited love for his cousin Amalie, but this does not really help us to understand the poem. Instead, I wish to look at it as an early prefiguration of the homeless life ahead of him.

> Lovely cradle of my sorrow,
> Lovely tombstone of my rest,
> Lovely town, we part tomorrow –
> Fare you well! be ever blest.
>
> Farewell, holy threshold, where we
> Roamed so long, my love and I;
> Farewell, holy place! it's there we
> Met when first my love flamed high.
>
> Had I never seen or met you,
> Lovely queen of all my heart,
> Fate would never then have let you
> Rend my wretched soul apart.
>
> Never did I beg you love me,
> Never asked your love, I swear –
> Only wished a sky above me
> Where your fragrance scents the air.
>
> Now you drive me from all gladness,
> From all joy, with words of scorn;
> In my soul a raging madness
> Surges in a heart that's torn.
>
> And I'll plod on, dull and dreary,
> Leaning on my pilgrim's stave,
> Till I'm lying spent and weary
> In a cool and far-off grave.[7]

The poet, driven away by the woman he loves, is leaving behind a »lovely town«. It is a »holy place« for him, and from now on, with all gladness gone from the heart, he must drag himself from place to place until he reaches his »far-off grave«. Whatever we make of this holy town and the distance traversed by the poet, it is hard to escape an implication of Jerusalem and the Wandering Jew here: Even as a young man, long before he leaves Germany forever, Heine describes the life ahead of him in the shadow of long exile and of final death without a consolation.

Here it is a loveless woman who makes him go away. Let us now look at an episode in *The Harz Journey*, the first book of his *Reisebilder* which appeared in

---

[7] The Complete Poems of Heinrich Heine. A Modern English Version by Hal Draper. Boston: Suhrkamp/Insel 1982, p.25f.

1824. There he imagines a similar scene – the poet dreams of a woman he loves, but again he is forced to leave her. On his journey he visits Clausthal and descends into one of its mines. »And down you go, from one ladder to the next«, he writes,

> [...] with the deputy ahead of you, constantly assuring you that it is not at all dangerous, so long as you keep a good grip of the rungs, and don't look down, and don't become dizzy, and on no account step on the platform to one side where the pulley whirs up and down, and where, a fortnight earlier, some careless person fell and broke his neck. [...] From time to time you arrive in tunnels cut out of the rock [...] where the ore can be seen growing, and where the solitary miner sits all day, laboriously hacking lumps of ore out of the wall with his hammer. I did not penetrate to the lowest depths, where some say you can hear people in America shouting »Hurrah for Lafayette!« But, between you and me, the place I got to seemed quite deep enough [...].[8]

The descent into the mine, the ›Bergwerk‹, is a well known motif of romanticism. Heine turns it into a frightening and yet ironic experience: If you want to survive, the deputy seems to tell him, you will have to be careful, and here, again, all hope is lost. After a quick glance at the working conditions the poet feels that he has seen enough, and that neither the name of Lafayette nor the echoes of the revolution will make much of a difference to these wretched miners.

The mining town of Clausthal, however, has a venerable tradition, and he falls under its spell. »Although the life these people lead may appear calm and immobile«, he writes

> [...] it is none the less a genuine, living life. The ancient, tremulous woman who was sitting behind the stove opposite the big cupboard may have sat there for a quarter of a century, and her thoughts and feelings are closely interwoven with every corner of the stove and every carving on the cupboard. And the stove and the cupboard are alive, for part of a human soul has entered them.[9]

The scene, and the feelings it inspires in Heine, lead up to the following commentary:

> Only such a deep contemplative life, such a direct empathy, could have given rise to the German fairy-tale, which is characterized not only by the presence of animals and plants, but even of supposedly inanimate objects as speakers and actors. It was to meditative, inoffensive people, in the quiet seclusion of their lowly cottages amid the mountains and forests, that the inner life of such objects was revealed.[10]

Heine feels a profound sympathy with the truth of the fairy tale. He speaks of it in almost religious terms and calls it a revelation, and soon we learn how deeply this »inner life« concerns him personally. As he continues his journey through the forest of the Harz he remembers a dream that he has had during his last night at Clausthal: »But I«, we read,

---

[8] Heinrich Heine: Selected Prose. Translated and ed. with an Introduction and Notes by Ritchie Robertson. London, New York: Penguin Books 1993 (Penguin Classics), p. 44.
[9] Ibid., p. 46
[10] Ibid.

> [...] was still wrapped up in the dream I had had that night, which I could not banish from my soul. It was the old fairy-tale in which a knight descends into a deep well where the most beautiful of princesses is lying in an enchanted sleep.[11]

And then Heine draws a connection between this dream and the realities of his journey:

> I was myself the knight, and the well was the dark pit of Klausthal, and suddenly there appeared a great many lights; the watchful dwarfs rushed from holes on every side, grimaced with anger, slashed at me with their short swords [...].[12]

The fear that Heine has felt as he was descending into the mine at Clausthal, reappears in the images of the frightening dwarfs. At first, however, the knight succeeds in driving them away. For a short, illusive moment Heine imagines himself at the happy ending of his dream:

> I came to a magnificent and brightly lit hall; in its midst, wearing a white veil and as motionless as a statue, stood the beloved of my heart, and I kissed her lips, and, by the living God! I felt with rapture the breath of her soul and the sweet trembling of her lovely lips. It was as though I heard God calling: »Let there be light!« A dazzling ray of the everlasting light darted down; but at the same moment night again fell, and everything dissolved into the chaos of a vast, turbulent sea.[13]

For one happy second Heinrich Heine seems to have reached his goal. The woman that has haunted his poetry from the very beginning, the one that he has always loved and that he could never attain, is now standing in front of him – a veiled and captive princess illuminated by a celestial light. He is about to free her, but almost immediately the moment of bliss turns into a nightmare:

> A vast, turbulent sea! The ghost of the departed flew in terror over the foaming waters, their white shrouds fluttering in the wind; in pursuit, cracking his whip, came a harlequin in a motley costume, and that was me – and suddenly the monsters of the deep thrust forth their misshapen heads from the dark waves, and stretched out their claws to seize me, and my terror woke me.[14]

All of a sudden, the personality of the dreamer is splitting up: As a knight he seems to have found his princess, but at the same time, in an act of self-punishment, he turns into a harlequin and expels himself from the paradise of his wishful thoughts. In Clausthal Heine has seen the old, traditional world once again, and it has conjured up the world of fairy tales for him. But Heine knows that times have changed and that no fairy tale can ever reach its happy ending for him any more. In the closing commentary, he takes an ironic look at himself:

---

[11] Ibid., p. 48.
[12] Ibid.
[13] Ibid.
[14] Ibid.

> How the most delightful fairy-tales can sometimes be spoilt! The knight who finds the sleeping princess is supposed to cut out a piece of her precious veil; and when his bold deeds have roused her from her magic sleep, and she is once more seated on the golden throne in her palace, the knight is supposed to walk up to her and say: »Fairest of princesses, do you recognize me?« And she replies: »Bravest of knights, I do not recognize you.« And then he shows her the piece cut out of her veil, which fits exactly, and the two of them embrace tenderly, and the trumpets blow, and they celebrate their wedding.
>
> It is really a peculiar misfortune that my dreams of love seldom come to such a beautiful end.[15]

The veil that has been cut in two and is finally made whole again is an eschatological symbol: Heine dreams of his redemption, but the dream cannot reach its happy ending any more, and therefore the poet must remain in exile. In his book *Die Spur der Gewalt*, Jürgen Nieraad describes Karl Philipp Moritz' attempt to cling to an aesthetic theory of the sublime while the French Revolution has already started, and then he goes on to contrast it with Baudelaire's poetics of violence, as it is coming to the fore in the second half of the 19th century. Between the two of them, Heinrich Heine goes half the way: He transforms the sublime into irony and thus liberates the violence of modernity from the rules of the ›Kunstperiode‹. But this liberating irony is always turned against the poet himself – and so, in the end, is the violence. In his early poem »Schöne Wiege meiner Leiden«, exile still appears to be a divine judgment passed on him by the merciless priestess of a holy threshold. But now the truth has become apparent: the punishment of exile, which Heine inflicts upon himself, is the inevitable result of his modern poetics.

As long as there is no Messiah and the dead do not rise from their graves, Heinrich Heine must live in exile. Throughout the *Reisebilder*, the poet remembers the dead who have been meaningful to him in the past. Among them, there are a number of beloved women whom, like the princess in the fairy tale, he wishes to bring back to life again. In conclusion, let me look at one final example from his *Journey from Munich to Genoa*.

We have already quoted a famous sentence from that book. »But ye may lay a sword on my coffin«, he says on the battlefield of Marengo, »for I was a brave soldier in the War of Freedom for Mankind«. Heine remembers the dead, and he imagines his own death as well; as he reaches the town of Trent, even the young girls remind him of the deceased:

> Even the brisk young girls had something of that which had been dead a thousand years in their faces, and yet of revived bloom, so that almost a terror stole over me, a sweet, gentle terror such as I once felt when in the lonely midnight my lips pressed those of Maria, a wondrous lovely lady, whose only fault was that she was dead.[16]

---

[15] Ibid.
[16] Heine, Pictures of Travel (note 6), p. 223.

The dead Maria is one of many women that the poet once loved and who have long since passed away. As he remembers her he feels a deep sadness, and later, in the art gallery of Genoa, his sorrow breaks out in a lamentation:

> I cannot leave unmentioned the collection of portraits of beautiful Genoese women, exhibited in the Palace Durazzo. Nothing in the world inspires the soul with such melancholy as the sight of portraits of fair ladies who have been dead for centuries. Sadness steals over the soul when we reflect that, of all the originals of these pictures, of all the beauties who were so lovely, so coquettish, so witty, so roguish, and so dreamy – of all those May heads with April moods – of that springtide of ladies – nothing now remains but these many-coloured shadows, which some artist, who like them has long been dead, has painted on a perishable canvas, which, like the originals, must pass away, in time, to decay and dust. And so all life passes away – the beautiful as well as the hideous – without leaving a trace. Death, the dry pedant, spares the rose as little as the thistle [...].[17]

Heine visits Genoa in 1828. The revolution, a happy memory of his childhood, has failed, Italy is ruled by reactionary Austria, and the poet's heart is torn by the pains of a brave soldier defeated in the War of Freedom for Mankind. But then, in a blissful moment of artistic joy, he detects the pictures of Maria and of himself in the gallery. It is explained to him that they were painted by Giorgione many centuries ago, but Heine knows the truth. This is how he addresses the reader at the end of *Journey from Munich to Genoa*:

> And it must also be evident to you that Giorgione painted that other portrait for me, and not for some old Genoese. And it is very like – death-silent like; it even has the sorrow in the glance – a sorrow which belongs rather to an imagined pain than to one which has been experienced – and one which is very hard to paint. The whole picture seems to have been sighed upon canvas. Even the man in the black mantle is well painted, and the maliciously sentimental lips are like life – speakingly so, as though they were just about to tell a story – the story of the knight who fain would kiss his lady love to life, and as the light was blown out – – –[18]

The light is extinguished, but neither Maria nor the captive princess in the earth of Clausthal will ever come back to life. The Messiah has not come, and Heinrich Heine cannot take his place, not even in his dreams.

---

[17] Ibid., p. 264.
[18] Ibid., p. 266.

Philipp Theisohn

Erde / Papier

Kafka, Literatur und Landnahme

> Da standen die Kinder des alten Volkes in Scharen beisammen, auf den Treppen, im Korridor, im Hof, in der Kantine, in der »Schul«, galizische Köpfe mit Käppchen oder künstlichem Haar, in bürgerlicher Kleidung, mit Kaftans, die Kinder flink und lausig, die Weiber schlaff und breit, die Männer pathetisch und mit langen Weichselrohrpfeifen, die jungen Damen in hohen Stöckelschuhen und durchbrochenen Strümpfen, modisch und mit erstaunlichen Mengen von falschem Schmuck behängt. [...] Ich nehme mir's vor, in Amerika zuzusehen, wie dieses Volk sein Leben fristet. Es kolonisiert nicht. Es geht nicht nach dem Westen.
>
> Arthur Holitscher: Amerika heute und morgen (1912)[1]

> Der Boden war durchgeackert
>
> Franz Kafka: Konvolut 1920[2]

L'herbe de l'exil

In Edmond Jabès' *Le retour au livre* (1965) findet sich ein Dialog, der den Reb Acham mit dem Gleichnis anheben läßt: »La solitude est l'herbe de l'exil [...]. Si tu crois aux fleurs, tu crois à la terre.«[3] Die exilische Grunderfahrung der ›Einsamkeit‹ wird in der rabbinischen Metapher einem Bildbereich überantwortet, der im Grunde gerade nicht dem Exil zugedacht ist: dem Boden, der Wurzel und der Blüte. Nun handelt es sich, streng genommen, bei der ›solitude‹ um keines der drei, sie ist ›l'herbe‹, das ›Gras des Exils‹, sie bekundet die

---

[1] Arthur Holitscher: Amerika heute und morgen. Reiseerlebnisse. 8.–11.Aufl., Berlin: S. Fischer 1919, S. 19.
[2] Franz Kafka: Gesammelte Werke in zwölf Bänden. Nach der Kritischen Ausgabe hg. von Hans-Gerd Koch. Frankfurt a. M.: Fischer Taschenbuch-Verlag 1994 (Fischer-Taschenbücher; 12441–12452), Bd VII: Zur Frage der Gesetze und andere Schriften aus dem Nachlaß, S. 170. Alle Kafka-Zitate im weiteren mit Band- und Seitenangabe in Klammern im fortlaufenden Text.
[3] Edmond Jabès: Le retour au livre. Le livre des questions III. Paris: Gallimard 1965, S. 32f.

Fruchtbarkeit der Erde, auf der sie sich ereignet, ohne selbst den letzten Nachweis führen und deren Frucht tragen zu können. Noch mehr: sie selbst verdeckt die Erde und macht diese damit überhaupt erst zu einem Gegenstand des Glaubens, für dessen Existenz ein anderes einstehen soll – die ›fleurs‹, in deren Erblühen der Zusammenschluß mit dem Grund, die Etablierung eines verstetigten, das eigene Wesen entbergenden Kulturprozesses manifest wird. Das Gedeihen der Einsamkeit versichert dem Exilanten dagegen etwas anderes, die dialektische Grundspannung seines Aufenthaltes: daß dort, wo er wandelt, eine Erde ist, daß aber außer dem Glauben nichts dafür spricht, daß sie ihm jemals werden wird. Wo sich die Wurzeln des Vereinzelten in den Boden senken, bleibt ungewiß; er vermag seine Erde nicht zu sehen. In der Einsamkeit erhebt sich das Exil über die bloße Vergegenwärtigung des Abwesenden, über die dichotomische Fixierung auf das ›Dort‹ und das ›Hier‹, die der Exilant gegen einen Grund eintauscht, den er zwar durchqueren, auf dem er sich aber nicht ›verorten‹ kann, da dieser Grund, ›l'herbe‹, keine Verfügung kennt.

Der sich an das Gleichnis anschließende Wortwechsel bleibt nicht bei diesen Einsichten stehen, kreist er doch um die Frage, wie im Angesicht dessen, der vorgibt, ›keine Erde zu haben‹, verfahren werden kann. Wie gelangt der Exilant zu seinen Werken, auf welche Weise vermag er seine Einsamkeit zu kultivieren, kann er zum ›Leben der Wurzeln‹ (zum »vie des racines«) vordringen? Woher kommt der Reichtum des Reb Acham, aus dem dieser dem seine Besitzlosigkeit anklagenden Reb Tessié »un coin de terre«, »un coin de désert« zu versprechen vermag? Hinter der Auflösung des Problems im Hinweis, sich selbst die ›Quelle‹ – »la source« – zu sein, die unter dem Gras, den Steinen, unter dem Wüstensand (die beiden letzteren, die »existence des pierres« wie die »existence du grain de sable« als jene Erfahrungsformen verstanden, in denen sich das Höchstmaß an Statik, an Bestimmung, der Erde anheimzufallen, mit dem völligen Versagen der creatio vereint und die sich darin als ein Fehlgehen erweisen, dessen Logik wir noch kennenlernen werden) verborgen liegt, können wir ein Denken ausmachen, das die Vorstellung einer sich im Raum verstattenden Selbstverwirklichung dem Konzept eines sich von der Erde abkehrenden, sie – wie Gras – überziehenden Umgangs mit den Zeichen opfert, überhaupt dem Raum keinerlei Vertrauen entgegenbringt, ihn als eine Bedrohung, eine Gewalt der Entäußerung wahrnimmt. ›Einsamkeit‹ könnte dann als jenes Moment des Umbruchs gefaßt werden, in dem das Zerwürfnis zwischen Mensch und Erde offenbar geworden ist und andere Oberflächen ins Spiel kommen. Das Gras als der Untergrund, auf dem es kein Innehalten gibt, über den man hinschreitet, ohne bei der Blüte zu verweilen oder zu verdorren. Das Papier als der Untergrund, der selbst nicht innehält, mit dem man unentwegt fortfährt. Israel als die Seinsform, in die sich beides fügt, »le livre que, sans voir, nous écrivons de pays en pays. Nos poitrines protègent ses pages et la plume y naturalise nos larmes noires«.[4] Das Buch, das ›von

---

[4] Ebd., S. 88.

Erde / Papier. Kafka, Literatur und Landnahme 63

Land zu Land‹ geschrieben wird, die Erde bedeckend, beschreibend, das aber gleichzeitig unter der Brust, im Herzen über die Erde hinweg getragen wird.

Kaum ein Autor hat die extensive wie intensive Verdichtung von Diaspora und Literarizität wohl so konzise in seinem Werk entfaltet wie Jabès; unablässig richtet sich sein Blick auf die scheinbar tautologische Gleichung ›Exil – Literatur‹ und jede seiner Stimmen kehrt aus ihren Formeln immer wieder zu ihr zurück. Es findet sich in dieser Gleichung allerdings mehr als das selbst schon wieder Topos gewordene portable Vaterland Heines, als die wieder und wieder kehrende Reflexion der ›marges‹, als die bloße Nomadisierung der Schrift und die Einsicht, daß man dort, wo geschrieben und gelesen wird, nicht zuhause sein wird; die Gleichung verfügt über eine Tiefendimension, einen geologischen Parameter. Es verhält sich ja nicht so, daß mit dem Auftreten des Papiers die Stätten einfach verschwinden; man braucht sie noch, wenn auch als Ruinen, denn nur aus ihrem Scheitern und ihrer Zerstörung erwächst dem Literaturexil seine Legitimität. Folgerichtig liegt jenes Feld, auf dem die Schöpfung anhebt und von dem aus sie sich des Raumes bemächtigt und die Ordnung seiner Zeichen zu kontrollieren sucht – das Zentrum – in Trümmern; seine Insignien erheben sich nicht länger über die Erde, sondern der Ort, den sie zuvor bezeichneten, liegt unter ihren Überresten verschüttet. »Où est le centre? – Sous la cendre.«[5]

Kehren wir aber von hier, vom centre, zum Ausgangspunkt unserer Überlegungen, zur solitude und zum Exil zurück. Die Hypothese unserer Überlegungen war ein Zusammenhang zwischen der exilierten Schrift als Geographem (d. h. dem, das die Erde bedeckt, ohne sich mit ihr zu verbinden) und der radikalen Negation des Sich-auf/aus-der-Erde-Erhebenden. Letztere gilt dabei zum einen dem Mißtrauen gegenüber der Erde, der Drohung des Stillstandes, der sich mit dem Versuch verbindet, zur Erde zurückzukehren, dem Ende der Schrift, ihrer Verwitterung (der »existence des pierres«) und ihrem Verdorren (der »existence de grain du sable«), zum anderen auch der Höhe, dem archimedischen Punkt selbst, von dem aus ein endgültig ordnender Zugriff auf die Schrift erfolgen könnte. Das Geschriebene – um Jabès noch einmal aufzugreifen – darf vom Schreiber nicht gelesen, nicht einmal gesehen werden können, es gibt keinen Panoramablick auf Exil-Literatur. Wir werden in diesem Zusammenhang natürlich zunächst an Babel denken, plastischer wird uns diese Ansicht vielleicht eher in der talmudischen Auffassung Rabbi Šimons:

> Wer auf dem Weg geht und das Gesetz studiert und sein Studium unterbricht und spricht: Wie schön ist dieser Baum, wie schön ist dieses Ackerfeld, dem rechnet es die Schrift an, als hätte er sein Leben verwirkt.[6]

Die Gefahr des Herausfallens aus dem lebenslangen Lernen verbindet sich hier in eigentümlicher Weise mit dem Glauben an die Erde, an die Wurzeln und an

---
[5] Ebd., S. 59.
[6] Vgl. Aboth III,9.

die Blüte, an dasjenige, was sich über das Gras des Exils erhebt. Kafka hat sich diesen Satz in abgewandelter Form in sein Tagebuch notiert[7] (bezeichnenderweise hat er ihn wohl selbst nicht ›studiert‹, sondern vermutlich aus dem in Meyer Isses Pinès *Histoire de la Littérature Judéo-Allemande* [1911] abgedruckten *Lied der arbeit* entlehnt); und in der Tat, vielleicht ist das, was dann später als ›kleine Literatur‹ gehandelt wird, nur die konsequente Umsetzung eines Schriftverständnisses, welches die territoriale Gebundenheit des Schaffens der bloßen Ermöglichung des Fortgangs einer Tradierungsbewegung aufgeopfert hat. Wir haben gelernt, Kafkas Texte als Verhandlungen zwischen einem unentwegten Prozeß der Deterritorialisation und den todbringenden Momenten der Reterritorialisation zu lesen;[8] als ›Landvermessungen‹, die dort enden, wo sich das Land dem Geometer zum ersten Male zu erkennen gibt; als »eine Begründung, die aber gerade nicht Grund (im Sinne von Fundierung) sein darf, weil ja sonst das, was fundiert wird, aufhört zu sein, was es ist«.[9] Schon Benjamin hat in diesem Zusammenhang das »eigentlich Geniale« an Kafkas Werk darin gesehen, daß es »die Wahrheit preis« gibt, »um an der Tradierbarkeit, an dem hagadischen Element festzuhalten«[10] und darüber zu einem Erzählen kommt, das die Lehre bestätigen und erklären soll, sich aber immer und immer wieder verzögert, »in der Hoffnung und Angst zugleich, die halachische Order und Formel [...] könnte ihr unterwegs zustoßen«.[11] Kafka fungiert als der Kronzeuge einer Traditionslinie entwurzelten Schreibens, die von den Tradierungsmechanismen des Judentums in die Literatur der Moderne ausgreift und von dort in ihre theoretische Erfassung von Seiten der Dekonstruktion mündet. Die Veranschlagung dieser Traditionslinie hat ihre Berechtigung; vieles, was hinsichtlich des Ortes der Schrift dunkel geblieben war, ließ sich unter Berufung auf sie erhellen und verständlich machen. Es fragt sich nur, ob über Kafka nicht vielleicht auch ein anderer Weg wieder zurückführt.

---

[7] Der Eintrag wurde wohl zwischen dem 26. und dem 31. Januar 1912 gemacht (Bd X, S. 25).

[8] Den Grundstein zu dieser Art der Lektüre haben Gilles Deleuze und Félix Guattari (Kafka. Pour une littérature mineure. Paris: Les éditions de Minuit 1975) gelegt; eine Gegenlektüre wird deswegen zunächst auch das Territorialkonzept, das dort zum Tragen kommt, welches aber seine Grundlegung bei Deleuze/Guattari wiederum im Zusammenhang mit anderen Überlegungen findet, an Ort und Stelle aufsuchen und hinterfragen müssen.

[9] Bernhard Siegert: Kartographien der Zerstreuung. *Jargon* und die Schrift der jüdischen Tradierungsbewegung bei Kafka. In: Franz Kafka: Schriftverkehr. Hg. von Wolf Kittler und Gerhard Neumann. Freiburg i. Br.: Rombach 1990 (Rombach Wissenschaft: Reihe litterae), S. 222–247, hier S. 239.

[10] Benjamin an Scholem, Paris, 12. Juni 1938. In: Walter Benjamin: Briefe. Hg. und mit Anmerkungen versehen von Gershom Scholem und Theodor W. Adorno. Frankfurt a. M.: Suhrkamp 1978, Bd II, S. 763.

[11] Walter Benjamin: Franz Kafka. Beim Bau der Chinesischen Mauer. In: W. Benjamin: Gesammelte Schriften. Hg. von Rolf Tiedemann und Hermann Schweppenhäuser. Frankfurt a. M.: Suhrkamp 1991, Bd II/2, S. 676–683, hier S. 679.

Das Marginale und sein Territorium

Es mangelt fraglos nicht an Informationen, die eine kulturwissenschaftliche Vernetzung von Kafkas Schreiben mit den zionistischen Umtrieben seiner Zeit erlauben würden. So dokumentieren die Tagebücher etwa eine intensive Beschäftigung mit der Wiederbelebung einer jüdischen Nationalkultur, auch mit Kolonisierungsplänen, den Besuch von einschlägigen Veranstaltungen etc.[12] Man mag vielleicht auch an jenes sonderbare Versprechen denken, das Kafka bei seinem ersten Zusammentreffen mit Felice Bauer dieser sogleich abgerungen hat, »im nächsten Jahr eine Palästinareise mit ihm machen zu wollen«.[13] Ausgiebig beleuchtet wurde Kafkas Besuch des Propagandafilms *Schiwath Zion* 1921,[14] in seiner Bibliothek finden wir ausreichend Informations- und Agitationsmaterial der Bewegung[15]. Das alles sagt freilich nichts aus über Möglichkeiten und Wirksamkeit einer zionistischen Poiesis, an deren Stelle vermeintlich die radikale Materialisierung der Sprache, das – wie es Adorno formuliert – ›nackte Wort‹ als Künder einer »ungemilderten Negativität«,[16] als ein Erscheinen des Erzählens vor dem Gesetz tritt. Der Rekurs auf das Materielle, rein Stoffliche, das Tierische steht immer im Dienste einer Bewegung in das Unbestimmte und Unbestimmbare, das nicht zu Ortende, d. h. im Dienste einer Deterritorialisierung. Der Ort des Gesetzes dagegen ist der Ort schlechthin: wer ortbar ist, der hat sich bereits in jenes Netzwerk aus Beamten, Vätern, Richtern, ›Dritten‹ eingepaßt, das seinerseits – wie Deleuze und Guattari zu zeigen bestrebt sind[17] – selbst wieder deterritorialisiert werden kann, indem man das ödipale System universalisiert, und dann ist der bestimmende, ›lokalisierende‹ Mechanismus selbst wieder ein ganz unbestimmter, ubiquitärer. Die Wahrheit des Territoriums ist seine Negatio, das Bekenntnis zu dieser Wahrheit wiederum das Abschwören des ›croyance au terre‹, das Eintauschen der

---

[12] Vgl. beispielsweise den Tagebucheintrag vom 24. (vielleicht 23.) Mai 1912: »In den letzten Tagen ausgezeichneter Vortrag von David Trietsch über Kolonisation in Palästina.« (Bd X, S. 72)

[13] Vgl. Brief vom 20. September 1912 an Felice Bauer. In: F. Kafka: Briefe 1900–1912. Hg. von Hans-Gerd Koch. Frankfurt a. M.: S. Fischer 1999, S. 170f. Bemerkenswert auch, daß Kafka seine Kommunikation mit Felice unversehens auf diesen Grund zu stellen versucht, indem er bereits im Folgeabsatz (man merke, daß es sich um eine Art Vorstellungsbrief handelt, mit dem sich Kafka bei Felice überhaupt erst in Erinnerung bringen will) von der ›Notwendigkeit‹ spricht, »dass wir schon von jetzt ab über diese Reise uns zu verständigen suchen«.

[14] Vgl. etwa Hanns Zischler: Kafka geht ins Kino. Reinbek: Rowohlt 1996, S. 145–153.

[15] Vgl. die Zusammenstellung bei: Jürgen Born: Kafkas Bibliothek. Ein beschreibendes Verzeichnis. Mit einem Index aller in Kafkas Schriften erwähnten Bücher, Zeitschriften und Zeitschriftenbeiträge. Frankfurt a. M.: S. Fischer 1990, insbs. S. 109–132.

[16] Theodor W. Adorno: Ästhetische Theorie. Hg. von Gretel Adorno. Frankfurt a. M.: Suhrkamp 1970 (Gesammelte Schriften; 7), S. 296.

[17] Deleuze/Guattari, Kafka (Anm. 8), S. 17–28.

›fleurs‹ für ›l'herbe‹, der Erde für das Papier, der großen Werke für eine ›kleine Literatur‹. (Das geht dann soweit, daß wir – um etwa auch der hebräischen und jiddischen Literatur, dem weniger *dezentrischen* als vielmehr *azentrischen* Schreiben eine Partizipation an poetischen Innovationsprozessen zugestehen zu können – die Dichotomie von Deterritorialisierung/Reterritorialisierung letztendlich ganz auflösen und Modernismen in allen Literaturen zu »deterritorialized expressive systems« erklären.[18]) So besitzt auf einer anderen Ebene die Debatte um Kafkas Verhältnis zum Zionismus – die in der Regel auf ein Reflektionsverhältnis hinausläuft, innerhalb dessen die Literatur das Problem einer modernen, genauer: einer modernen jüdischen Identitätsstiftung aufgreift, durchexerziert und die politische Offerte des Zionismus schließlich als ein ihr Wesensfremdes wieder entläßt – vor allem eine Funktion: die Initiation des Schriftstellers Kafka, der dem Akt der Landnahme die fortwährende Durchstreichung des Ortes, das Schreiben, gegenüberstellt.[19]

So gilt es zunächst darauf hinzuweisen, daß der Zionismus sich für Kafka keineswegs jenseits der Literatur ereignet, sondern er kommt dieser »dazwischen«, bevor sie sich zu »einer Kabbala entwickeln« kann.[20] Dort, wo aus dem Schreiben eine Lehre hätte werden können, in der sich der »Ansturm von unten« und der »Ansturm von oben« durchdringen, an diese Stelle tritt Zion als ein Ort, dem man sich eben nur dadurch nähert, daß man von ihm herkommt, und der sich nur in den Monumenten eines Schreibens zu erkennen gibt, welches »die entgegenstehenden Welten auseinanderhält, statt sie zu verknüpfen«[21] und dabei eine Bresche für ihn zu schlagen vermag. Es handelt sich um ein Ereignis, von dem viel, wenn nicht alles zu erwarten ist: einen Ort, an dem sich die Menschheit

---

[18] Diese Überbietungsstrategie bei Chana Kronfeld: On the Margins of Modernism. Decentering Literary Dynamics. Berkeley, Los Angeles, London: University of California Press 1996 (Contraversions; 2), S. 13.

[19] Dies exemplarisch etwa bei Baioni, für den an die Stelle der »Geburt des Zionisten Kafka [...] die des Schriftstellers Kafka« tritt. Giuliano Baioni: Kafka. Literatur und Judentum. Aus dem Ital. von Gertrud und Josef Billen. Stuttgart: Metzler 1994, S. 33. Ähnlich auch bei Ritchie Robertson: ›Antizionismus, Zionismus‹. Kafka's Responses to Jewish Nationalism. In: Paths and Labyrinths. Nine Papers Read at the Franz Kafka Symposium, Held at the Institute of Germanic Studies on 20 and 21 October 1983. Ed. by J. P. Stern and J. J. White. London: Institute of Germanic Studies 1985 (Publications of the Institute of Germanic Studies; 35), S. 25–41.

[20] Eintrag vom 16. Januar 1922 (Bd XI, S. 198f.). Bloom hat zurecht darauf hingewiesen, daß die durch Scholem auf uns gekommene Lektüre Kafkas im Lichte »einer Verbindung zwischen der Kabbala des Isaak Luria, dem Messianismus der Sabbatianer und Frankisten und dem politischen Zionismus« hier Risse bekommt (Harold Bloom: Kafka. Unbestimmter Wohnsitz. In: H. Bloom: Kafka – Freud – Scholem. Aus dem Engl. von Angelika Schweikhart. Basel, Frankfurt a. M.: Stroemfeld/Roter Stern 1990, S. 7–29, hier S. 12).

[21] Bernhard Greiner: Mauer als Lücke. Die Figur des Paradoxons in Kafkas Diskurs der Kultur. In: Arche Noah. Die Idee der ›Kultur‹ im deutsch-jüdischen Diskurs. Hg. von Bernhard Greiner und Christoph Schmidt. Freiburg i. Br.: Rombach 2002, S. 173–195, hier S. 187.

von Neuem gründet, ein ›Gegen-Babel‹, das in der Tiefe, im »Schacht« zu suchen ist, der nicht zuletzt auch durch die Ahnengräber, in die Katakomben führt (VII, 170f.). Es wird dieser Literatur schließlich zur »ursprünglichste[n] Aufgabe« werden, den sie vereitelnden »Mangel des Bodens, der Luft, des Gebotes« zu beheben. (Und das ist gerade im Einklang mit der im gleichen Zusammenhang geäußerten Bekundung zu betonen, nicht »wie die Zionisten« »den letzten Zipfel des davonfliegenden jüdischen Gebetmantels [...] gefangen« zu haben, sondern »Ende oder Anfang« sein zu wollen [VI, 215]). In der sich in Kafkas Werk (zumal in den späten Fragmenten) drängenden Motivik der Grabung spricht sich das Verlangen der Schrift nach ihrem Eingehen in die Erde aus, nach einer Materialisierung, die eben nicht in eine universale Deterritorialisierung ausläuft, sondern gerade dadurch besticht, daß sie das Papier durchschlägt, hinabsteigt, ›Gravur‹ wird. Das Moment der ›Kerbung‹ ist nicht mehr von einem ›Mapping‹ her oder auf dieses hin zu denken (und ist damit auch der bloßen Entgegensetzung ›glatt‹-›gekerbt‹ überhoben), mit ihm etabliert sich vielmehr ein ganz neues – geo-logisches – Verhältnis zum Nomos.[22] Am Ende, nach eingehender Lektüre, werden sich Kafkas Phantasmata der Vertiefung als Vorzeichen einer Territorialpoetik erweisen, in deren Zentrum wiederum – wie könnte es anders sein – eine territoriale Reflexion auf das Gesetz hin steht. Wenn wir nach den Zusammenhängen zwischen Literatur und Landnahme fragen, so werden wir auf all dies zu sprechen kommen müssen; zuvor gilt es allerdings, jene Grenzverläufe zwischen Land und Literatur, Geschichte und Gesetz in Augenschein zu nehmen, die Kafkas Texte unablässig skizzieren. Diese Grenze stellt weitaus mehr dar als lediglich ein »étroit défilé« zwischen der »sémiotique contre-signifiante des nomades« und der »sémiotique signifiante elle-même, dont la nostalgie ne cesse de les [les Hébreux] traverser, eux-mêmes et leur Dieu«.[23] Sie wird nicht nur permanent in polaren Abweichungen in immer wieder neuen Kartographien ausgeschrieben und definiert, sondern verläuft vielmehr selbst zwischen kartographischer Logik und territorialer Logik und ist nicht ohne weiteres zu durchbrechen.

An besagter Margo entlang bewegt sich etwa das Textkonvolut um den *Bau der chinesischen Mauer*, in dem der Zwiespalt zweier Zeichenordnungen und ihrer Lektüren – die Kluft zwischen den »Pläne zeichnenden Händen der Führerschaft«, auf denen der »Abglanz der göttlichen Welten« (VI, 70) ruht, und der Mauer als der Schrift des »Tatsächliche[n]«, »der Mühe und des Lebens von Hunderttausenden« (VI, 69) – ausgiebig verhandelt wird. Die Karten, die in den

---

[22] Für Deleuze/Guattari verbinden sich mit Logos und Nomos zwei sich durchdringende räumliche Organisationsprinzipien, das der ›Aufteilung‹ (partage) eines geschlossenen Raumes und das der ›Verteilung‹ (distribution) innerhalb eines offenen Raumes. Insofern die Rede von der ›déterritorialisation‹ essentiell von genannter Konzeption des Verhältnisses von Logos und Nomos abhängt, Kafkas Literaturentwurf aber sich aus ganz anderen – eben nicht *nomadischen* – Überlegungen zum ›Gesetz‹ speist, begegnen wir hier bereits einer höchst problematischen Prämisse der ›littérature mineure‹. Vgl. Gilles Deleuze / Félix Guattari: Mille Plateaux – Capitalisme et Schizophrénie II. Paris: Les Éditions de Minuit 1980, S. 600f.
[23] Ebd., S. 154.

Planungsbüros entstehen, ergeben, bezogen auf das Territorium, seine Abgrenzung und Sicherung keinen ›zweckmäßigen‹ Sinn, sie sind auch nicht zu lesen, sondern lassen sich allenfalls ›nachbuchstabieren‹. Ebensowenig ergibt sich aus den umherstehenden Teilbauten, der Schrift der Steine, irgend etwas, das als »ein sicheres Fundament für einen neuen Babelturm« zu dienen vermag, wie jener Gelehrte aus »den Anfangszeiten des Baues« behauptet (ebd.). Der Abstieg vom Papier zur Erde, der Impetus, mit dem sich die Zeichen »in den Boden einsenken«, entmächtigt zugleich die Interpreten, insofern von der Erde kein Weg mehr zurück- und hinaufführt, das Moment der Deszendenz einhergeht mit einem Kontrollverlust über die Relation von Karte und Territorium, der allerdings gerade nicht ihr Zusammenfallen bedeutet, sondern sich in einem unentwegten Auseinanderdriften von Kartographie und Geologie Ausdruck verleiht.

Kafkas Erde sperrt sich in jeder Hinsicht gegen das Eingehen in einen perpetuierenden Prozeß von Deterritorialisierung und Reterritorialisierung; die Territorien öffnen sich ihr nicht als einem ›ailleurs‹, wie sie auch keine Territorien vergibt oder gar zurückgibt.[24] Was bei Horkheimer und Adorno für den Raum überhaupt gilt, so finden wir auch bei Kafka die Erde als »absolute Entfremdung«[25]. Von ihr führen keine Fluchtlinien und ihre Weiten sind auch nicht die des Gesetzes, zumindest nicht eines Gesetzes, welches vorrangig als ›Verlangen‹ bestimmt werden könnte und das sich mit Vorliebe in Nebenzimmern aufhält. Dementsprechend verläuft Landnahme hier auch nicht in den Bahnen von Polis und Nomadismus, sondern beschreibt eine Macht der Selbstgründung, die sich den Entzugstendenzen der sich einer dauerhaften Einschreibung widersetzenden Erde dadurch überhebt, daß sie dem Anderen Raum gibt, daß in der »gewaltsame[n] Struktur der stiftenden Tat« kein »Schweigen [...] eingeschlossen oder vermauert« wird.[26] Man wird der nomadischen Bedrohung nicht dadurch Herr, daß man sich ihr verschließt, sondern indem man die Spannung zwischen geschlossenem und geöffnetem Raum in der Bewegung eines Zusammenschlusses im Offenstehen still stellt.[27] Wenn die Nomaden »geängstigt durch den Mauer-

---

[24] Vgl. Gilles Deleuze / Félix Guattari: Qu'est-ce que la philosophie? Paris: Les Éditions de Minuit 1991, S. 82.

[25] Max Horkheimer / Theodor W. Adorno: Dialektik der Aufklärung. In: Th. W. Adorno: Gesammelte Schriften. Hg. von Rolf Tiedemann. Frankfurt a. M.: Suhrkamp 1997, Bd III, S. 205. Das Tier in *Bau* wird folgerichtig von der Erde und den in ihr lebenden Wesen behaupten, daß »hier [...] auch nicht [gilt], daß man in seinem Haus ist, vielmehr ist man in ihrem Haus« (Bd VIII, S. 167).

[26] Jacques Derrida: Gesetzeskraft. Der »mystische Grund der Autorität«. Aus dem Frz. von Alexander García Düttmann. Frankfurt a.M.: Suhrkamp 1991 (Edition Suhrkamp, N. F.; 645), S. 28.

[27] Es handelt sich bei dieser Spannung um eine Anziehungskraft, die umso stärker wird, je größer die Bemühungen sind, sich ihren Verdrängungsmechanismen zu entziehen. Dementsprechend werden die Nomaden auch durch den Palast des Kaisers, das Insignium des statischen Raumes, »angelockt« und indem man das Tor vor ihnen verschließt und die Wache »früher immer festlich ein- oder ausmarschierend, [...] sich hinter vergitterten Fenstern« hält, »versteht [der Palast] es aber nicht sie wieder zu vertreiben.« (Bd VI, S. 82)

bau mit unbegreiflicher Schnelligkeit wie Heuschrecken ihre Wohnsitze wechselten«, so galt ihre Furcht nicht dem Auftauchen des ihnen antithetisch zugeordneten Raumprinzips, sondern der Auslöschung der Antithetik als solcher, welcher der panische Versuch, den Raum des Nomos wiederzugewinnen, gegenübergestellt wird. Freilich wäre es ein leichtes, die »in öder Gegend verlassen stehenden Mauerteile« zu zerstören, doch dort, wo sich das Schließen aus der Öffnung, die Mauer aus der Lücke fügt, laufen derlei ›Grenzaufhebungen‹ ins Leere, vielmehr drohen sie, den Angreifer selbst zu verschlingen. So bleibt nurmehr ein letztes verzweifeltes Aufbäumen der Deterritorialisierung, die Verwandlung des Menschen in den Heuschreckenschwarm, der von Wohnsitz zu Wohnsitz flieht.[28] Die Fragilität seiner Margo bewahrt das »unendliche China« vor potentiellen Invasoren und schlägt diese in die Flucht; jener Raum, der dem einfallenden Grenzvolk nichts entgegenzusetzen hat, läßt sich weder aufheben noch besetzen, *man wird mit ihm nicht fertig*. Abseits des Wechselspieles von Yischuv und Expulsatio ereignet sich Territorialität letztendlich nur dort, wo Marginalisation immer bereits in die eigene Territorialisierung mit hineingenommen wird und die ›Marken‹ selbst nicht endgültig bestimmt, verunklärt werden, keinem (machtpolitischen) Ordnungssystem völlig gehören und dienen können.[29] Das ist – fernab jeglicher Stilisierung des Judentums zum postmodernen Paradigma – natürlich auch eine jüdische Perspektive par excellence. Wenn etwa Graetz in seiner *Volkstümlichen Geschichte der Juden* (1888) sich der Besiedlung Palästinas widmet, so gilt sein Augenmerk ganz diesem Moment.

> Indessen war das diesseitige Land keineswegs durchweg eingenommen und den Stämmen zugeteilt, ganze Strecken waren noch in der Gewalt der Urbewohner verblieben. Es läßt sich nicht mehr ermitteln, wie viel Josua selbst Schuld daran trug, daß die Eroberung unvollendet geblieben ist. [...] Jeder Stamm und jede Stammesgruppe war auf sich selbst angewiesen. Den vereinzelten Stämmen ward es daher schwer, gegenüber den Urbewohnern sich abzurunden. So blieb der ganze Küstenstrich, die zum Teil fruchtbare, zum Teil sandige Niederung von Gaza [...] bis Akko unterworfen. [...] Der nördliche Teil gehörte den Phönikiern und der südliche den Philistern. So wohnten viele Stämme entweder in der Nachbarschaft oder inmitten von heidnischer Bevölkerung. Die von den übrigen völlig getrennten Stämme Jehuda und Simeon wohnten noch mehr untermischt unter fremden Völkerschaften und zwar unter solchen, welche das Hirtenleben mit dem der Wegelagerer vertauschten. [...] Wie öfter im Leben des Einzelnen und der Völker

---

[28] Die Triebkraft dieser Bewegung ist, wie der Text richtig erkennt, der Wahnsinn: denn nur wer »das menschliche Wesen«, das »von der Natur des aufliegenden Staubes« ist, verleugnet und sich selbst fesselt, wird am Ende »bald wahnsinnig an den Fesseln zu rütteln anfangen und Mauer Kette und sich selbst in alle Himmelsrichtungen zerreißen.« (Ebd., 70)

[29] So ist dann etwa auch »der eigentliche Zugang zum Bau [...] so gesichert, wie eben überhaupt etwas auf der Welt gesichert werden kann, gewiß, es kann jemand auf das Moos treten oder hineinstoßen, [...] kann eindringen und für immer alles zerstören.« (Bd VIII, S. 166)

verwirklichte sich auch diesmal die Hoffnung ganz anders, als sie geträumt war. Das Land gehörte allerdings den Söhnen Israels; aber es gehörte ihnen kaum halb, und der errungene Besitz konnte bei kraftvoller Verbindung der zurückgebliebenen Urbewohner ihnen wieder entrissen und sie wieder in die Heimatlosigkeit zurückgetrieben werden.[30]

Es geht von dieser Schilderung doch eine ganz eigentümliche Faszination aus; eine Faszination, die – wie wir den Tagebuchaufzeichnungen entnehmen können[31] – auch Kafka bei der Lektüre ergriffen hat. Wir sind geneigt, die von Graetz beschriebenen Verfehlungen der Kolonisation dem Auge weniger als ein folgenschweres Scheitern, sondern eher als einen Akt der Selbstbestimmung, als Weigerung, sich eines Territoriums anzunehmen, »der Scholle anheimzufallen« (wie in Genesis 34,10 aufgetragen), aufzufassen. Im Mißlingen der Margo, im Mangel an »Abrundung«, an stabiler Unterscheidung zwischen dem Eigenen und dem Anderen, mithin der Vorwegnahme der eigenen Marginalisierung durch andere, scheint sich die Ahnung zu verbergen, daß eine der Erde vermachte Identität ein Irrtum sei und das »menschliche Wesen, leichtfertig in seinem Grunde, von der Natur des aufliegenden Staubes, [...] keine Fesselung« (VI, 70) vertrage. Womöglich hätte man es hier dann mit einer Vorgeschichte der Literatur zu tun, dem Opfern der Erde für das Papier, des Reiches für das Bekenntnis zu einer Geschichte und Welt umspannenden Literarizität.

Freilich sagt uns Kafka in seinem Text doch etwas ganz anderes. Sein Augenmerk gilt ganz der Eröffnung der Erde für das Schreiben, dem Verharren der Zeichen in der Tiefe, das aber nur solange möglich ist, wie für eine gewisse Unmittelbarkeit der Setzung gesorgt ist. Diese Unmittelbarkeit verhindert zwar das Werk, die Geschlossenheit, das Planvolle, allein dadurch vermag dieses Schreiben aber das Papier zu durchschlagen und »Einheit« zu stiften. Garantiert wird die Schrift dabei durch ein Nicht-Verstehen, durch Bestimmungen hinsichtlich der Grenzen von Lektüre (und es verwundert nicht, daß deren Erläuterung ebenfalls wieder des Rekurses auf ein Territorialgeschehen bedarf[32]). Der Weg von den Karten, auf denen der »Abglanz der

---

[30] Heinrich Graetz: Volkstümliche Geschichte der Juden in drei Bänden. Erster Band: Von der Entstehung des jüdischen Volkes bis zur zweitmaligen Zerstörung Jerusalems unter Kaiser Vespasian. Leipzig: Leiner 1888, S. 13.
[31] Eintrag vom 1. November 1911: »Heute Geschichte des Judentums von Grätz gierig und glücklich zu lesen angefangen. Weil mein Verlangen das Lesen weit überholt hatte, war es mir zuerst fremder als ich dachte und ich mußte hie und da einhalten, um durch Ruhe mein Judentum sich sammeln zu lassen. Gegen Schluß ergriff mich aber schon die Unvollkommenheit der ersten Ansiedlungen im neu eroberten Kanaan und die treue Überlieferung der Unvollkommenheit der Volksmänner (Josua, der Richter, Elis).« (Bd IX, S. 168)
[32] Wer den Plänen der Führerschaft zu lange nachsinnt, ohne zum Stein zu greifen, bei den Karten und Anordnungen verweilt, statt zur Erde zu gelangen und mit dem Bau zu »verwachsen«, dem ergeht es »wie dem Fluß im Frühjahr«: er »übersteigt [...] seine Ufer, verliert Umrisse und Gestalt, verlangsamt seinen Abwärtslauf, versucht

göttlichen Welten« ruht, zur monolithischen Écriture führt nicht über das Verstandesvermögen, sondern über eine Dynamik des Zirkels (und bleibt darin gleichwohl nicht unkantisch). Durch das Wegfallen der ›Zweckmäßigkeit‹ des Baues wird nämlich sogleich die Frage aufgeworfen, welche der beiden Schriften denn die ursprünglichere sei. Immerhin ist das, worin die unterschiedlichen Erklärungen des Bauvorganges konkreszieren, eben nur der Kommentar, der Mittlungsversuch zwischen Papier und Erde. Die große Idee des Mauerwerkes, des Babelschen Fundamentes, welches die »Einheit« des Volkes erstehen läßt, indem es die Arbeiter, das »Blut, nicht mehr eingesperrt im kärglichen Kreislauf des Körpers, sondern süß rollend und doch wiederkehrend durch das unendliche China« (VI, 68) treibt, diese Idee scheint nur hinter der endlichen Konkretion des Teilstücks auf und der Verzicht auf Überschaubarkeit führt zum sofortigen Versiegen der geistigen Kräfte. Auf der anderen Seite haben wir dann aber eben diese durchbrochenen Anordnungen von Zeichen territorialer Herrschaft, die nach ›oben offen‹ stehen und denen man Erzählungen des Unendlichen unterlegen muß, in denen die Materialisierung aber nicht aufgeht. (Und auch hier gilt, daß derjenige, der die Lücke zu schließen versucht und den einen Text aus dem anderen lesen will, im Geiste verdorren muß.) Die Zirkulation der beiden Schriften mündet dann schließlich im Hinblick auf die Negation, auf das Nicht-Verstehen, die Nicht-Vollendung, das Nicht-Gemäß-Werden, darin, daß sich Karte und Territorium durchdringen, in ihrem Kräfteverhältnis ununterscheidbar werden; so daß Kafkas Textkonvolut als solches sowohl den Teilbau selbst als auch den Versuch seiner Kartographie darstellt. Mit den Lücken in der Mauer wird nicht nur die horizontale Grenze zwischen Polis und Nomadentum, sondern ebenso die vertikale Grenze zwischen Papier und Erde fraglich, denn im Grunde ist es zuallererst die Mauer des Erzählens, die durchbrochen wird, Krisen der Tradierbarkeit zeitigt, das Zeitgefüge zersetzt und letzten Endes nurmehr aus erratischen Blöcken besteht, welche sich dem Gesetz des ›Fortschreibens‹ entziehen. Die Aufkündigung der räumlichen Dichotomie zwischen Eigenem und Anderem, geschlossenem und offenem Raum, Papier und Erde ist gleichzusetzen mit der Aufkündigung pharisäischer Lektüre. Die Verhandlungen zwischen Nomadismus und Polis verlaufen bei Kafka somit durchaus um ein Vielfaches komplexer, als Deleuze und Guattari glauben machen wollen, denn sie bleiben stets gekoppelt an das Ziel eines Erschreibens des Bodens, auf dem die Schrift gedeihen kann, der Erde, die sich nur zeigt, wenn der Prozeß deterritorialisierenden und reterritorialisierenden Schreibens stillgestellt werden kann.

---

gegen seine Bestimmung kleine Meere im Binnenland zu bilden, schädigt die Fluren, und kann sich doch für die Dauer in dieser Ausbreitung nicht halten, sondern rinnt wieder in seine Ufer zusammen, ja trocknet sogar in der folgenden Jahreszeit kläglich ein.« (Ebd., 71)

HaMakom

In der Tat ist es nicht ganz unmöglich, die im *Bau der chinesischen Mauer* zutage tretenden Konstellationen zwischen dem Universalen und dem Partikularen, dem Eigenen und dem Anderen im Hinblick auf Kafkas eigene Rezeption auch durch innerjüdische religionsgeschichtliche Debatten zu kontextualisieren.[33] So finden wir in seiner Bibliothek etwa Moritz Friedländers Abhandlung über *Die religiösen Bewegungen innerhalb des Judentums im Zeitalter Jesu* (1905), in der Friedländer erstmals seine – ihm doch bis zu seiner Wiederentdeckung durch die politische Theologie eigen bleibende – Umwertung des jüdischen Hellenismus und dem sich dort ausbildenden Antinomismus zur eigentlichen Fortführung des Mosaismus vollzieht. Mit der nach den Makkabäersiegen einsetzenden Herrschaft pharisäischer Gesetzesauslegung sieht er

> [...] die natürliche Entwicklung des Judentums gewaltsam unterbrochen, seinen Lebensnerv unterbunden, es seiner ureigenen Mission entfremdet und seinen Geist in andere, von den Propheten nie geahnte Bahnen gelenkt, auf denen es die schiefe Ebene des Partikularismus hinuntergleitt, so daß es in der Folge zur Mitwirkung an dem Aufbau der Weltreligion untauglich wurde.[34]

Demgegenüber steht das hellenistische Diasporajudentum als legitimer Nachkomme des mosaischen Universalitätsanspruchs; es vermag die jüdische Identität gerade dadurch zu bewahren, daß es den Fremdkulturen offensteht, das Gesetz verinnerlicht und die Ethik über das Wort stellt.

Diesen sicherlich sehr weitreichenden Betrachtungen (denen Kafka offensichtlich nicht allzuviel Aufmerksamkeit geschenkt hat – er hat Friedländers Buch überhaupt nur bis Seite 42 aufgeschnitten) steht die wohl rege Lektüre eines Beitrages »zur Erneuerung des Judentums« des Karlsbader Rabbiners Ignaz Ziegler über *Die Geistesreligion und das jüdische Religionsgesetz* (1912) gegenüber. Für Ziegler ist »gerade das Geistig-Sittliche das eigentlich Mosai-

---

[33] Die Frage, ob eine solche Kontextualisierung des Fragments vonnöten ist, muß an dieser Stelle nicht beantwortet werden; allein soll deutlich werden, daß diese Debatten dann doch etwas zu weit reichen würden, um bei den Feststellungen stehen bleiben zu können, die Mauer repräsentiere »the partial protection of the tradition«, der Erzähler habe seinen Glauben an die Weisheit dieser Mauer aber schon verloren. Hieraus gar zu folgern, »Kafka could help rebuild neither the wall of faith nor the alternative wall of political homecoming« und den Text als Präludium der Confessio einer von Religiosität wie von politischer Verwirklichung exilierten jüdischen Existenz zu lesen, läuft auf eine völlige Verkennung der sich hinter dem Konvolut verbergenden poetischen wie religionsgeschichtlichen Diskurse hinaus. (Dies bei Arnold M. Eisen: Galut. Modern Jewish Reflection on Homelessness and Homecoming. Bloomington: Indiana University Press 1986 [The Modern Jewish Experience], 189f.)

[34] Moriz Friedländer: Die religiösen Bewegungen innerhalb des Judentums im Zeitalter Jesu. Berlin: Georg Reimer 1905, S. VI.

stische oder Sinaitische am Mosaismus«[35] und nur in einer Rückführung der Ausprägungen der historischen jüdischen Religion, der »Vereinfachung der Objektivierung bei Heilighaltung des Prinzips«[36] ist das Judentum des 20. Jahrhunderts inmitten der es umgebenden Kulturen aufrechtzuerhalten. Wiewohl Ziegler in seiner Hinwendung zur Ethik, durch welche allein die »Beschäftigung mit der Gotteswelt« erfolgt und die »Religionsidee [...] ein wesentlicher Teil unseres Seelenlebens wird«[37], Friedländer durchaus sehr nahekommt, so sieht er sich genötigt, gerade die Pharisäer als Bewahrer der Tradition einer »gelebten Lehre« zu verteidigen,[38] insofern der Pharisäismus die Verteidigung der Gotteswelt gegenüber der »kleinmenschliche[n] Umwelt« dadurch gestärkt hat, indem er immer neue »Wälle und Mauern um die Seele aufzurichten versteht.«[39] Ziegler bewegt sich in seinen Ausführungen permanent an der Problemstellung des chinesischen Mauerbaues entlang, indem sein Plädoyer für die ›gelebte Lehre‹ natürlich stets um die Frage kreist, in welcher Weise die »Religionsideen [...] als etwas Reales, Faßbares, anschaulich Erreichbares, Stoffliches in die Menschenseele hineingearbeitet, hineingeknetet werden« können.[40] Das ›seelische Erbteil‹ ist der Grund, auf dem sich der jüdische Reformer zu bewegen und seine Neuordnungen vorzunehmen hat. In Zieglers Fall geht es dabei in gezielter Weise um eine Refragmentierung der pharisäischen Mauern, wobei in Kauf genommen wird, daß nach dem Abbau der »zahllosen Normen« möglicherweise »die Idee auch nicht klar vor den Geist« kommt und dieser sich mit einem »Ahnen« begnügen muß, das bereits als eine »reinigende Tat« gewertet werden kann.[41]

Nun ist eine solche Revision des Verhältnisses von Lehre und Leben nur scheinbar ein lediglich korrektiver Vorgang und kann auch nur als ein solcher verstanden werden, solange man der Weisung und dem gewiesenen Tun einen gemeinsamen, gleichzeitigen, unverschütteten Ort zukommen läßt. Die Lehre erfüllt den Zweck, diesen Ort als den ›meinen‹ zu markieren, mich an ihn zu binden und mich zu seiner Gegenwart anzuhalten; in meinen Handlungen vergegenwärtige ich Sinai und selbst dort, wo mir Sinai aus meinem Handeln nicht in Sicht kommt, läßt es sich ›erahnen‹. Probleme ergeben sich erst dann, wenn die Vorschriften diesen Ort zu begraben drohen und ihn zur Fremde werden lassen, in der das handelnde Subjekt sich nicht wiederfindet. Die ›Vereinfachung der Objektivierung‹ meint im Grunde auch eine ›Vereinfachung

---

[35] Ignaz Ziegler: Die Geistesreligion und das jüdische Religionsgesetz. Ein Beitrag zur Erneuerung des Judentums. Berlin: Georg Reimer 1912, S. 14.
[36] Ebd., S. 150.
[37] Ebd., S. 126.
[38] Dies geschieht nicht zuletzt wohl in Reaktion auf Rudolf Leszynskys Aufwertung des Sadduzäismus. Leszynsky selbst gibt in seiner Schrift *Pharisäer und Sadduzäer* (Frankfurt a. M.: J. Kauffmann 1912) den Hinweis auf Debatten mit Ziegler.
[39] Ziegler, Die Geistesreligion (Anm. 35), S. 126.
[40] Ebd., S. 127.
[41] Ebd., S. 146.

der Subjektivierung‹ und das teilweise Abtragen pharisäischer Erbschaften steht gleichzeitig für die Stabilisierung jüdischer Identität. Diese In-Eins-Setzung Zieglers, die Korrespondenz zwischen Subjekt und Objekt, Leben und Lehre, auf deren Grundlage ein neues Judentum erstehen soll, schuldet sich natürlich ganz der Annahme einer Unverstelltheit des Gesetzes und seines Ortes. Demzufolge muß sie übersehen, daß die Verschiebung des Primats von ontologisierender Schrift zur Ethik eine Umkehrung an jenem Punkt erzeugt, an dem das ans Gesetz gebundene und in seiner kulturellen Konstitution von ihm abhängende Subjekt in den Blick kommt.

In der Perspektivierung von Kafkas Text erscheinen die in der Kontextualisierung aufgeworfenen Fragestellungen sodann in einem gänzlich neuen Licht. Der Grund, auf dem sich die Identitätssuche des chinesischen Volkes abspielt, läßt sich nicht mehr beschreiben, die »Mitte der Welt« erweist sich »hochgeschüttet voll ihres Bodensatzes« (VI, 76) – als ein »centre sous la cendre« – und die Hierarchie zwischen ›Idee‹, ›Lehre‹ und ›Leben‹ scheint aus den Fugen geraten. Die Aufgabe, an der sich Kafkas Text abarbeitet, lautet dementsprechend nicht mehr: dieses Terrain zu sichern, sondern vielmehr: allererst zur Erde zu gelangen und ›Einheit‹ dort erstehen zu lassen, wo jedes Aufsteigen von der Materialisation zur ›Idee‹ versagt bleibt. Dies wiederum kann nur bewerkstelligt werden, wenn realisiert ist, daß die Idee des ›Unendlichen‹ – und nur um sie geht es hier – gegenwartslos bleibt, in dem Sinne, daß sie »mit einer Bedeutsamkeit bedeutet, welche der Gegenwart, jeder Gegenwart, jedem Ursprung im Bewußtsein vorausgeht und somit an-archisch zugänglich ist in ihrer Spur« und »welche immer schon älter als ihre Zurschaustellung ist [...], ihren Sinn nicht aus ihrer Manifestation zieht«.[42] Wir wissen, daß Kafka ein außerordentliches Gespür für die Tücken vorbewußter Bedeutsamkeit entwickelt hat, denen er seine Protagonisten unentwegt aussetzt, indem ihnen Eingänge ›bestimmt‹ sind, die aber niemals passiert werden können. Das Gesetz war immer schon vor ihnen da und hat sie immer schon dazu verurteilt, ›außen vor‹ zu bleiben. Kafkas Helden können sich am Ort des Gesetzes nicht einfinden, geschweige denn diesen als den ›ihren‹ kennzeichnen – und ihr Verhängnis liegt schlichtweg darin begründet, daß sie an der Vorstellung einer Gleichzeitigkeit dieses Ortes haften bleiben und in der Annahme gehen, eine neue Signifikanz produzieren, noch ›etwas ausrichten‹ zu können, wiewohl die Zeichen ihnen schon längst nicht mehr gehören und sie selbst bereits angefangen haben zu bedeuten, ohne gesprochen zu haben.

Diese Fixierung auf eine Rückkehr des marginalisierten Subjekts an den Ort, von dem aus das Gesetz seinen Anfang nahm, hat Kafka in ihrem Scheitern experimentell vorgeführt. Nehmen wir an, wir hätten es bei Graetz' »zurückgebliebenen Urbewohnern« vielleicht auch mit jenen »barbarischen Gebirgsbe-

---

[42] Emmanuel Levinas: Gott und die Philosophie. In: Gott nennen. Phänomenologische Zugänge. Hg. von Bernhard Casper. Freiburg i. Br., München: Alber 1981 (Alber-Broschur Philosophie), S. 81–123, hier S. 99.

wohner[n]« zu tun, von denen das »unbeholfene[s] Gekritzel« auf den Steinen stammt, die in einem der späten Fragmente Kafkas (im Oktavheft H) zum Tempelbau dienen sollen. Betrachten wir diese kleine Passage etwas genauer:

> Alles fügte sich ihm zum Bau. Fremde Arbeiter brachten die Marmorsteine, zubehauen und zueinandergehörig.
> Nach den abmessenden Bewegungen seiner Finger hoben sich die Steine und verschoben sich. Kein Bau entstand jemals so leicht wie dieser Tempel oder vielmehr dieser Tempel entstand nach wahrer Tempelart. Nur daß auf jedem Stein – aus welchen Brüchen stammten sie? – unbeholfenes Gekritzel sinnloser Kinderhände oder vielmehr Eintragungen barbarischer Gebirgsbewohner zum Ärger oder zur Schändung oder zur völligen Zerstörung mit offenbar großartig scharfen Instrumenten für eine den Tempel überdauernde Ewigkeit eingeritzt waren. (VI, 223)

Wie bereits beim *Bau der Chinesischen Mauer*, so entsteht Marginalisierung auch hier als eine bereits im Akt der nationalkulturellen Manifestation angelegte Tendenz; allerdings erscheint diese beim Tempelbau nicht als Zielvorstellung ›unzweckmäßiger‹ architektonischer Planung, sondern als Resultat des Auftauchens eines zweiten, ›barbarischen‹ Systems von Kulturzeichen, das in Konkurrenz zum Bauprinzip des Tempels selbst tritt, dieses subvertiert und schließlich überwinden wird. Vielleicht könnten wir statt ›Überwindung‹ auch von einem ›Widerruf‹ sprechen, dann wären wir wieder in einem uns eher vertrauten Schema angelangt: das Fremde ist immer schon dem Eigenen eingeschrieben und verlangt seine ständige Neupositionierung und Abgrenzung; das Material der Zeichen zersetzt das Werk, welches sich daraus konstituiert; der aus den Brüchen gehauene, in Kultur überführte und systematisierte Stein führt die Zerstörung der Kultur bereits mit sich; das »Gekritzel«, die »Eintragungen« beseitigen und substituieren den ›croyance au terre‹, der wohl kein größeres Bekenntnis fordern kann als den Bau. Aber was wird dann genau widerrufen? Worin besteht die ›wahre Tempelart‹, so sie dasjenige darstellt, was wir hier als Angriffspunkt der barbarischen Negationsleistung veranschlagen sollten?

Natürlich geht es hier nicht und gerade nicht um Architektur, sondern um das Gesetz und seinen Wohnsitz, um *Positio*. Positio ist nie Konstrukt, planvoll, symbolisch, vielmehr hat das, was wir als die Tätigkeit des Architekten bzw. des ›Bauleiters‹ begreifen, das Abmessen, jeglichen symbolischen Charakter verloren, es ist weder Order noch Nachvollzug, sondern schon der Bau selbst. Der Tempel ›fügt sich‹, *ohne daß* dazu eine Menschenhand gefordert würde, *ohne daß* eine Hierarchie der Schöpfung einsetzen muß. Zwischen das Gesetz und den Ort, den es sich erwählt hat, tritt keine vermittelnde Instanz, keine Kraft, nichts, das der Errichtung des Baues hemmend sich entgegenstellen könnte. Das Subjekt ist mit dem Tempel ganz alleine gelassen, alleine in der »Selbstgegenwart, die das Bewußtsein ist«.[43] Tatsächlich ist aber auch bereits dieser Vorgang Text, הםקום ersteht aus den Bruchstücken einer undekodierbaren Schrift, die dem Gesetz und seinem Ort vorgängig ist und im

---

[43] Ebd.

Durchschneiden der Schreiboberfläche irreversibel wird. Die Zerstörung des Raumes, den das Höchstmaß an Grenze umgibt, nämlich die Grenze zwischen profanem und sakralem Raum, kann nur dadurch erreicht werden, indem der Nomade selbst wieder zu den Kerbungen greift und dem Zeichen der absoluten Dislozierbarkeit ein absolut lokalisiertes Schreiben entgegengesetzt. Der Tempel entsteht als die Negation seines eigenen Bauprinzips, denn freilich sind die einzelnen Bausteine ›zueinandergehörig‹, aber ihre Markierungen deuten darauf hin, daß diese Zusammengehörigkeit ihren Ursprung an einem anderen Ort hat und Transpositionen ausgesetzt war. Nun ist aber der Tempel gerade der Raum, welcher jegliche Transposition untersagt, aus dem die Schrift nicht austreten darf und der keine fremden Zeichen kennt. Die Nomadisierung des Logos, die wir mit der Zerstörung des Tempels verbinden, hat nicht allein dadurch statt, daß sich die »barbarischen Gebirgsbewohner« der nomadischen Zeichenordnung entschlagen und selbst das Material zur absoluten räumlichen Verstetigung liefern (und es müssen natürlich »fremde Arbeiter« sein, die den Marmor herbeischaffen), sondern daß sie darüber hinaus die Tiefendimension der Schrift, das territoriale Schreiben anerkennen, Gravuren erzeugen, ihrer Écriture einen unauslöschlichen Ort geben. So, wie die einzige Botschaft der chinesischen Mauer an die Nomaden diejenige ist, daß es immer nur den einen Ort geben wird, das unendliche China, so entziffern sich dem Tempelbauer die Eintragungen auf den Steinen nur dergestalt: daß es schon immer ein Zweites gibt. Der Bau öffnet nicht mehr allein den Grund, auf dem er steht, sondern ihm werden Korrespondenzen unterlegt, über die er nicht mehr selbst verfügt; er wird Bestandteil einer kartographischen Logik, die als das Produkt »sinnloser Kinderhände« erscheinen muß und sich nicht in das Tempelgefüge übersetzen läßt.

Seinen Rang in Kafkas loser Folge einer alternativen jüdischen Historiographie erhält dieses Fragment zudem dadurch, daß sich unter den zahlreichen Bänden der »Religionsgeschichtlichen Volksbücher für die deutsche christliche Gegenwart« in Kafkas Bibliothek auch Immanuel Benzingers Traktat *Wie wurden die Juden das Volk des Gesetzes?* (1908) findet. Benzinger vertritt dort gleich zu Eingang die These, daß das »israelitische Gesetz [...] aus dem geschriebenen Recht, das zur Zeit in Kanaan in Geltung war« – dem Hammurabirecht –, hervorgegangen ist; er selber kommt zu diesem Gesetz durch den im Dezember 1901 von französischen Archäologen in Susa gefundenen Dioritblock, dessen »Inschrift [...] in 44 Zeilen die Gesetzessammlung des Königs, die älteste der Welt« enthält.[44] Verfolgen wir die Weggeschichte dieses Blockes, so ist die Vermutung, daß es sich bei den »barbarischen Eintragungen« um ein »lange vor der mosaischen Zeit [...] geschriebenes Gesetz« handelt, durchaus nicht abwegig. So war der »Stein ursprünglich im Sonnentempel Ebabbara zu Sippar gestanden; von da hatte ihn ein elamitischer Eroberer nach

---

[44] Immanuel Benzinger: Wie wurden die Juden das Volk des Gesetzes? Tübingen: Mohr 1908 (Religionsgeschichtliche Volksbücher für die deutsche christliche Gegenwart, Reihe 2: Religion des Alten Testaments; 15), S. 6.

Susa verschleppt. Auch im Tempel Esagila in Babel war nach der Inschrift ein solcher Stein mit einer Abschrift der Gesetze aufgestellt.«[45]

Widerrufen wird im Tempelfragment dabei nicht nur die Möglichkeit einer Subjektivierung des Gesetzes (und dementsprechend auch die Möglichkeit einer Anpassung der Lehre an das Leben, der Objektivierungen an das Subjekt), sondern darüber hinaus die Vorstellung der Gleichursprünglichkeit von Subjektivität und Transzendenz. Die zerstörerische Wirkung nomadischer Inscriptio erweist das wahre Verhältnis im Negativen, der chinesische Mauerbau dagegen im Positiven: ein Land erschließt sich nicht auf dem Weg vom Zentrum zu seinen Grenzen, die Einheit eines Volkes ersteht nicht aus der Abgrenzung nach außen, das Subjekt konstituiert nicht seine Lebenswelt per Gesetz. Vielmehr – und allein dies spricht sich in der Errichtung jener offenstehenden Grenze aus – bin ich zuerst und schon immer außer mir gewesen und gelange nur von der Margo zu mir zurück. Keine Weisung ist mein Eigen, sondern ich eigne der Weisung als »der Tempel oder das Theater der Transzendenz«.[46] Die Pläne der Führerschaft lassen sich nicht einsehen, die Idee Chinas, die Idee des ›Unendlichen‹ läßt sich nicht anordnen, sondern ihr gehört ein Volk, das sich, von ihr getrieben, eines Landes bemächtigt, indem es sich von seinen Rändern herschreibt.

Das Exil als Zeichenmaschine

Nun ist der Einwand, daß wir es hier mit Nachlaßfragmenten zu tun haben und eine Projektion der dort vorgefundenen Strukturen auf eine breitere, ›repräsentative‹ Ebene sicherlich nicht unproblematisch sein dürfte, durchaus berechtigt und somit gilt es, dem Verlangen der Schrift nach der Erde, den Experimenten eines ›Re-Centerings‹ auch im ›gewichtigeren‹ Œuvre Kafkas nachzugehen. Wenn dabei die Wahl auf den 1912 begonnenen und 1914 endgültig unvollendeten *Verschollenen* – einen »ins Endlose« angelegten Roman[47] – fällt, so weist bereits der von Kafka gewählte Projekttitel auf eine sich auf Dislozierung gründende Identität. ›Verschollen‹, fernab der ›Scholle‹ zu sein, das meint auch hier nicht nur eine geographische, sondern darüber hinaus eine geologische Entsetzung, die das seinem kulturellen Zusammenhang entrissene Subjekt den einander ablösenden Instanzen des Dritten überantwortet und es einem anonymen, in seinem Ursprung nicht ortbaren Strom der Zeichen, entsprechend etwa den elektromagnetischen Wellen Marconis, die in Holitschers Amerika-

---

[45] Ebd.
[46] Levinas, Gott und die Philosophie (Anm. 42), S. 119.
[47] Brief an Felice Bauer vom 11. November 1912 (Kafka, Briefe 1900–1912 [Anm. 13], S. 225).

Reisebericht die Verbindung »zwischen uns Verschollenen und der sicheren Welt« herstellen,[48] aussetzt. Das Schicksal des Verschollenen wird bestimmt durch Signifikanten, die in ihrem Verschwinden und (Wieder-)Auftauchen ein paranoisches Zeichenregime etablieren, welches das exilierte Subjekt unablässig dazu nötigt, die es anfallenden Geschehnisse in einen Bedeutungszusammenhang zu fügen, ohne es in die Lage zu versetzen, das Bedeutete zu ermitteln.[49]

Der Preis, den Karl Roßmann zahlen muß, um dieses Regime, um Amerika zu betreten, ist der Verlust seines Koffers – das ist der Signifikant, an dem die Atmosphärisierung der Zeichen aus der Heimat anheben muß, birgt er in sich doch Reste eines fremden Regimes, »Dinge [...], die man vor allen Leuten geheim halten mußte« (II, 195). Die im Koffer enthaltenen Gegenstände – Bibel, Anzug, Elternphotographien, Salami – bilden kein Sammelsurium, sie gehorchen nicht den Gesetzen des Exils, des geheimnisvollen Wechselverweises, sondern sie verschmelzen zu einer »alten Umgebung«, in der sich Gewißheit über das ›Eigene‹ und sein Herkommen verschaffen läßt (II, 103).[50] Als Karl auf mysteriösen Umwegen den Koffer wiedererhält und sich dieser »alten Umgebung« gewahr wird, ist diese – obgleich »[n]icht das geringste fehlte« – bereits in den Amorphisierungsprozeß des Romans eingetreten und selbst zum Bedeutungsträger in einer endlosen, in sich kreisenden Zeichenkette avanciert. Allmählich verschwinden die Insignien der verlassenen Ordnung, nicht zuletzt unter Beteiligung der rigorosen Agenten Delamarche und Robinson, zunächst die Veroneser Salami, dann, nachdem der Koffer einmal gewaltsam aufgebrochen wurde, fehlt das Herrschersiegel der verlassenen Ordnung: die Photographie der Eltern, die wichtiger wäre als alles andere, gegen die der verbliebene Rest sogar einzutauschen wäre. ›Richtig hergestellt‹ ist der Koffer dann erstmals und ein einziges Mal wieder im ›Repräsentationszimmer‹ der Oberköchin, inmitten einer Vielzahl alter Photographien, die »wohl noch aus Europa«

---

[48] Holitscher, Amerika (Anm. 1), S. 25.
[49] Vgl. dazu: Deleuze/Guattari: Mille plateaux (Anm. 22), S. 141f.
[50] Man wird zurecht darauf hinweisen, daß die Repräsentation Europas keinesfalls für sich in Anspruch nehmen kann, frei von jenem Verhängnis zu sein, welches das amerikanische Exil überschattet; vielmehr spricht viel, wenn nicht alles dafür, daß das Exil keinen eigenen Kontinent, kein ›ailleurs‹ braucht, sondern schon existierte, bevor es ein ›ailleurs‹ gab. Freilich ist die Initiation in den Prozeß fortwährender Repression, der Verstoß gegen das Gesetz des Vaters, eine europäische Initiation. Dennoch und gerade deshalb scheint es mir geboten, die Bedeutung, welche die Zeichenmaschine für die exilische Grunderfahrung bei Kafka besitzt (und zu deren europäischer Ausprägung allenfalls ein »undeutlicher Zusammenhang« besteht), zu pointieren. Erst die Maschine produziert aus jenem Verstoß einen »Œdipe trop gros«, erst sie kann auch jene sich einzig und allein auf topologische Identität Selbsterschreibung des amerikanischen Bürgers, der sich von seinen »europäischen Verwandten vollständig abgetrennt« haben will (32) und dennoch auf ihre Erfindungen und Zeichen angewiesen bleibt, leisten, insofern sie diese Zeichen technisch neu zu organisieren und ins Monströse anzuhäufen vermag.

stammen, bevor er schließlich durch Therese in die Pension Brenner geschickt wird – Karl wird ihn dort vermutlich nicht mehr abgeholt haben, er bleibt im Roman verschollen.

Die Botschaft des amerikanischen Exils ist deutlich: es gibt keine patria portabile mehr, das Land im Koffer löst sich unter der Sogwirkung des signifikanten Zeichenregimes auf. Man mag die Bibel zur Hand nehmen, in ihr blättern, man liest sie aber nicht mehr, auch sie ist nurmehr ein Signifikant in einem amorphen, maschinell angetriebenen Kontinuum. Zeichen zu lesen und Zeichen zu setzen, das ist jenseits des Atlantiks zu einem vollkommen entpersönlichten, ritualisierten, von Maschinen übernommenen Akt geworden. Man deponiert das Geschriebene in überdimensionierten Schreibtischaufsätzen, in denen es »langsam oder unsinnig rasch« zirkuliert, verschwindet, wiederkehrt. Die Evokation und der Wirkungsgrad von Zeichen obliegt in dieser Welt nicht mehr dem Subjekt, das sich mit all seinen Habseligkeiten ganz dem Kosmos der Verbannung übergeben hat. Es beherrscht auch seine Worte nicht mehr, zurück bleiben leere Zimmer mit verlassenen Schreibtischen und eine Ohnmacht der Rede, wie wir sie in der Hauptkassa des Schiffes beobachten können – auch dies ein Raum, in dem die Dokumente, angetrieben von einem unsichtbaren Regulator, zirkulieren und in dem ›man weiß, wo man ist‹. Gegenüber diesen Apparaturen muß jede Rhetorik wirkungslos bleiben; Kleists Bären gleichend lesen sie keine Finten. Das gilt für die Schiffsoffiziere wie für die Bediensteten im Telegraphenamt des Onkels oder auch die Angestellten in der Portiersloge des Hotel Occidental. Amerika reißt den Zeichenhaushalt des es heimsuchenden Exilanten an sich und treibt ihn durch seine Kommunikationsmaschinerie, zu der Karl Roßmann keinen Zugang erhält: so mahnt ihn der Onkel unter falschem Vorwand, »den Regulator möglichst gar nicht zu verwenden« (II, 48), auch der Oberportier bringt erst bei seinem letzten, sich nach der offiziellen Entlassung ereignenden Zusammentreffen mit Karl (dessen einziger Zweck ja in der Einsichtnahme in jene Maschinerie des Hotels bzw. in der Vermittlung der Ausgeschlossenseins von dieser besteht) eine mögliche Anstellung in der Portiersloge zur Sprache. (II, 201) Die Machtlosigkeit vor den Schreib- und Sprachmächtigen, die über die Kommunikationsautomatik verfügen, das Verlangen, sich dieser zu bemächtigen, treibt Roßmann durch den Roman und setzt ihn erst dann frei, als ihm nichts mehr geblieben ist, er weder Schirm, noch Koffer, noch Rock, noch Papiere, noch eigene Sprache, nicht einmal mehr seinen Namen besitzt. Wenn Exil etwas bedeutet, dann doch dies: die Kontrolle über seine Zeichen vollkommen verloren zu haben, das Arsenal an ›persönlichen‹ Signifikanten einer Welt zu vermachen, die schon immer bedeutend war, »bevor man wußte, *was* [sie] bezeichnet«. Es charakterisiert demnach weniger die Befindlichkeiten dieser Welt, daß ein verlorener Raum in der Fremde imaginiert wird, als daß dieser Raum erst und eigentlich verloren wird und zur eigenen Zeichensetzung nicht mehr zur Verfügung steht. In diesem Sinne steht das Erzählte auch für ein Erzählen ein, welches wir als den radikalen Drang zur Marginalisierung begriffen haben, als ein Erzählen jenseits der Öffentlichkeit, jenseits der Maschine[51], jenseits der Nation: eben als »littérature mineure«.

Hatten wir eingangs mit Jabès von der Einsamkeit als dem ›l'herbe de l'exile‹ gesprochen, welches dem Exilanten bedeutet, daß er auf einer Erde wandelt, die ihm niemals werden wird, so beweist sich Kafkas Amerika als der Kontinent, auf dem dieses Gras besonders gut gedeiht. Amerika ist keine Wüstenei, kein zeichenloser, sondern im Gegenteil ein unendlich kultivierter Raum – allerdings organisiert dieser seine Kulturzeichen in einer Art und Weise, die ihn unlesbar werden läßt. Im Floating der Signifikanten, in Unkenntnis der Gesetze ihres Erscheinens, Verharrens und Abtauchens läßt sich selbst von prädestinierten Aussichtspunkten die Poetik der Fremde nicht entziffern. Wie gesagt: es gibt keinen Panoramablick auf Exil-Literatur, und so bietet sich auch Karl Roßmann »nicht viel mehr als de[r] Überblick über eine Straße«, eine – wie sich herausstellen wird – kaleidoskopische Perspektive,

> [...] eine aus immer neuen Anfängen ineinandergestreute Mischung von verzerrten menschlichen Figuren und von Dächern der Fuhrwerke aller Art [...], von der aus sich noch eine neue vervielfältigte wildere Mischung von Lärm, Staub und Gerüchen erhob, und alles dieses wurde erfaßt und durchdrungen von einem mächtigen Licht, das immer wieder von der Menge der Gegenstände zerstreut, fortgetragen und wieder eifrig herbeigebracht wurde und das dem betörten Auge so körperlich erschien, als werde über dieser Straße eine alles bedeckende Glasscheibe jeden Augenblick immer wieder mit aller Kraft zerschlagen. (II, 46)

Das Kontinuum der Signifikanten entlarvt sich hier als ein Kontinuum der Zertrümmerung, hinter dem das maschinelle Herz des Exils schlägt und zerschlägt. Denn auch die amerikanische Poetik des Raumes unterliegt den gleichen a-rhetorischen Mechanismen wie der Schreibtischaufsatz oder die Portiersloge: man verfährt »nach schlauen Plänen der besten Raumausnützung« (II, 155), d. h. man vereinigt nicht nur das Heterogene an ein und demselben Ort, sondern man ›reguliert‹ auch dessen Raumverteilung permanent, das Auftauchen und Verschwinden der Zeichen aus dem Blickfeld des Betrachters mittels eines undurchschaubaren und zweifelsohne gewaltsamen Mechanismus von Öffnungen und Schließungen. Auch die amerikanischen Häuser, Städte und Zimmer sind Monumente des signifikanten Zeichenregimes, im besten Sinne ›heterotop‹, sie verfügen über eine Vielzahl unterschiedlichster Kodierungen/Aktenfächer auf engstem Raum (etwa im Schlafsaal der Liftjungen, in den New Yorker Quartieren, »wo angeblich in einem kleinen Zimmer mehrere Familien wohnten und das Heim einer Familie in einem Zimmerwinkel bestand«), so daß sich für diejenigen, die keinen Zugang zur Maschine besitzen, nicht entscheiden läßt, »ob sie [...] in zwanzig Häusern oder in zwei oder gar nur in einem Haus gewesen waren« (ebd.). Unabhängig davon, ob es sich dabei um Photographien, um Apparaturen oder um Menschen handelt: Ameri-

---

[51] Vgl. Friedrich A. Kittler: Aufschreibesysteme 1800 · 1900. 3., vollst. überarb. Neuaufl., München: Fink 1995, S. 457ff.

ka gleicht einem gigantischen Repräsentationszimmer, in dem die gewaltsam geeinten und ausgestoßenen Signifikanten der alten Welt sich drängen und changieren, über die Maschinerie in Beziehung zueinander treten, sich in der Maschinerie verlieren, anstatt diese in ein Bedeutungsverhältnis, die Aktenablage wieder in ein messianisches Geschehen überführen zu können.

Das ›Offenstehen‹ von Bauten wird dabei durchweg als Bedrohung erfahren. Wer – wie Thereses Mutter – als Kalklöscherin auf einer Baustelle arbeitet, die »kaum bis zum Erdgeschoß gediehen, wenn auch schon die hohen Gerüststangen für den weitern Bau, allerdings noch ohne Verbindungshölzer, zum blauen Himmel ragten« (II, 156), der, so die unmißverständliche Botschaft, zahlt mit dem Leben. Das Unheil weht Amerika von den unbeschriebenen Flächen an, von der »dunkle[n] Leere«, die Karl entdeckt, als er sich ein einziges Mal in einem Haus verirrt, in dem die Architektur angefangen hat, rhetorisch zu werden, Umwege zu produzieren und »eine Raumverschwendung sondergleichen« zu betreiben, nämlich im Landhaus des Herrn Pollunder. Der »große tiefe Raum« der Kapelle, die durch nichts als durch die Leere identifiziert werden kann – in ihm scheint die einzige Möglichkeit zu liegen, zu etwas anderem zu gelangen, mit seinen Symbolen auf eine andere Weise umzugehen als sie der Gesetzesmaschinerie anzuvertrauen (und schon allein deswegen ist es dem Diener eine Pflicht, anzumerken, daß die Kapelle »später unbedingt von dem übrigen Haus abgesperrt werden muß«). Den Agenten der Zeichenmaschine, die Karls Weg säumen, treten nun die unscheinbaren, aber erfahrungsgemäß wirkungsmächtigen Agenten des Vorgesetzlichen und Unzweckmäßigen gegenüber: die Bauarbeiter, von denen Karl erstmals während der Fahrt zum Landhaus Notiz nimmt. Wo immer sie zugange sind, lassen sie Räume offen stehen; daß man »viel Ärger mit so einem Bau« hat, scheint weniger ein Allgemeinplatz, sondern ein machtpolitisches Problem zu sein. So sind dann auch im Landhaus ein »paar große Durchbrüche gemacht worden, die niemand vermauert« (II, 80) – zweifelsohne ein ›chinesisches‹ Prinzip, von dem her der amerikanischen Heterotopie ihre Auflösung droht.

Während Karl es nicht verstattet ist, sich ins Nichts zu setzen und die Kapelle bei Tag wieder aufzusuchen, bezeichnet diese allerdings exakt den Ort, aus dem der Roman entsteht. Jost Schillemeits Kommentar verdanken wir die Information, daß der *Verschollene* sich nicht nur einem »neuen Modus des ›zusammenhängenden Schreibens‹« verdankt, in dem kompositorische Planung und literarische Ausführung zusammenfallen, sondern daß dieser Modus sich in erster Linie auch durch autokommunikative Verfahren auszeichnet.[52] In

---

[52] Vgl. auch Jost Schillemeit: Das unterbrochene Schreiben. Zur Entstehung von Kafkas Roman ›Der Verschollene‹. In: Kafka-Studien. Hg. von Barbara Elling, New York et al.: Peter Lang 1985 (New Yorker Studien zur neueren deutschen Literaturgeschichte; 5), S. 137–152. Schillemeit macht darauf aufmerksam, daß sich das Innehalten des Schreibaktes in der Regel mit einer Hemmung des Sprech-/Bewegungsablaufs der Figuren verbindet, während die Wiederaufnahme des Schreibens u. a. durch die sich im Roman textualisierende Aufforderung, ›wieder an die Arbeit zu gehen‹ eingeleitet

eigentümlicher Verschränkung affizieren sich Text und Autor gegenseitig; in die dunkle Leere hinein ruft der Schreibende sich ins Schreiben zurück bzw. evoziert die Schrift den Schreiber. Mit der Kerze leuchtet Kafka in die Tiefe hinab, aus der ihm sein Roman entgegenkommt. Nichts ist hier vermittelt, es gibt kein papiernes Schaffen, man hinterläßt keine Akten, die zu ordnen, zu bearbeiten oder zu ›regulieren‹ wären. Im Gegensatz zur Kolonisation des erzählten Raumes nehmen die Zeichen vom erzählenden Raum in einer ganz anderen, radikal selbstbezüglichen Weise Besitz: sie konstituieren zuallererst die Fläche, auf die sie sich verteilen. Wie der Reb Acham ›sich selbst Quelle zu sein‹, das ist das eine; aus dieser Quelle aber sich selbst zu schöpfen, das ist ein anderes. Einem Regime, das aus Zeichen besteht, die schon immer bedeuteten, tritt ein Regime gegenüber, das aus Zeichen besteht, die daselbst schon immer waren, ohne auf ein Anderes zu verweisen. Die erzählte Welt fürchtet das Einbrechen dieser Macht und ist bemüht, ihre Lücken zu vermauern, um sich gegen ihr Vordringen, das Einströmen der Zugluft als Pneuma der Erzählinstanz zu verwahren. Der Durchbruch zur Kapelle wird somit zum ersten ›systemimmanenten‹ Streitfall des Romans, insofern mit erzähltem und erzählendem Kulturprinzip auch die beiden Facetten zionistischer Poiesis aufeinandertreffen: Eine Literatur, der Zion »dazwischen« kommt, mag »klein« sein, sie mag ihr marginales Wesen im Bezug auf alles forcieren, was man ihr zur Seite stellt, sei es Nation, Tradition oder Gesetz. Sie ist es jedoch nie im Rückbezug auf sich selbst, denn gerade dadurch, daß sie sich innerhalb jener »Vätersysteme« nicht verorten läßt und aus ihnen heraus immer wieder in die eigene Materialität entkommt, zeugt sie selbst die Stätte, an der sie zu lesen wäre. Letztendlich fällt die Entscheidung über den Ausgang dieser Konfrontation aber nicht auf dem Grund des Gesetzes, sondern abseits der Mauern: im Westen.

Staats-Theater

Die Bewegung der Romanhandlung und ihres Protagonisten westwärts, ins Landesinnere, konterkariert von Beginn an Karls Gang durch die sich allmählich verlierenden Institutionen der ›Dritten‹, an dessen Ende er seinen gesamten Zeichenvorrat eingebüßt hat. Das Recht an dieser Bewegung liegt eindeutig nicht auf der Seite der erzählten, sondern der erzählenden Instanz. Erzähllogisch ist sie überhaupt nicht zu motivieren – dies verrät sich nicht zuletzt im Beschluß des Herrn Green, Karl »eine Karte Dritter nach San Francisko« zu kaufen, da »die Erwerbsmöglichkeiten im Osten [...] viel bessere sind« (II, 98).

---

wird. Im konkreten Fall endet die Niederschrift just in jenem Moment, in dem der dunkle Gang in das »eiskalte[s] marmorne[s] Geländer« übergeht, welches in die »Dunkle Leere« hinausführt. (S. 78)

Es findet sich in der Tat keine Begründung, den Osten zu verlassen – außer der Aussicht auf die Möglichkeit einer neuerlichen inneren wie äußeren Kolonisation, auf unbeschriebene Flächen, die noch nicht durch das signifikante Regime besetzt und verwaltet werden.

Das finale Aufbrechen des Textes, das Hervortreten der Tiefe unter dem Papier ergibt sich nicht von selbst, sondern wird bedingt durch einen veränderten Umgang mit den Zeichen, einen Bruch mit der Maschinerie des amerikanischen Exils und den durch sie geschaffenen Räumen. Im Anfangsstadium des Romans, an der Ostküste fanden wir diesen Transfer verbürgt durch das Tun der Bauarbeiter, den Fragmenten wird dagegen eine Institution geschenkt, welche das signifikante Regime nicht nur unterminiert, sondern auslöst: das »Teater von Oklahoma«.

Das Versprechen der Werbetruppe ist gewaltig: es richtet sich an all jene, die ohne Ort geblieben sind, die ›Stellungslosen‹, die in den Schreibtischaufsätzen des Romans nicht untergekommen sind. Der Margo ein Theater zu vermachen (und sie in einer »Bude am äußersten Rand« zu rekrutieren) heißt, ihr einen Weg zum Zentrum zu eröffnen, den Kategorisierungsmechanismen der sie beherrschenden und dezentrierenden Ordnung zu entkommen. Gerhard Neumann hat darauf aufmerksam gemacht, daß, so im Muster der theatralen Inszenierung dem Akt der Signifikation Spontaneität unterlegt und dem theatralischen Subjekt somit »in einem respektierten Rahmen« Transgression und Selbstsetzung ermöglicht wird, im Aufrufen der ›Theater‹-Vorstellung den ritualisierten Bedeutungsprozessen der amerikanischen Gesellschaft scheinbar eine Komplementärmacht gegenübersteht, die selbst aber wieder als ein durch und durch ritualisiertes und gänzlich a-theatralisches Geschehen bewahrheitet und desavouiert wird.[53] In der Tat hat man auf dem Rennplatz von Clayton alle Elemente theatralischer Befreiung beseitigt und ersetzt durch ebenjene amerikanischen Mechanismen, von denen sie befreien sollen. So findet der seiner Zeichen entledigte Protagonist keine Bühne, auf der er sich neu erschaffen, beschreiben könnte oder die sich in Beschlag nehmen ließe (denn das, was ihm auf der Photographie als Bühne erscheint, entpuppt sich bei näherer Betrachtung als ein dem Präsidenten der Union vorbehaltenes Terrain). Statt dessen, so scheint es, opfert Karl im Angesicht dieser letzten, überdimensionalen und weltumspannenden Registratur auch noch das letzte, was ihm geblieben ist, seinen Namen, und löscht sich damit ganz aus. Von den beim Theater ›Stellung‹ Suchenden wird keiner als Schauspieler aufgenommen, die Identität, die man den Bewerbern zukommen läßt, ist ebenjene, mit der sie gekommen sind.

---

[53] Gerhard Neumann: Ritual und Theater. Franz Kafkas Bildungsroman »Der Verschollene«. In: Franz Kafka. Der Verschollene. Le Disparu/L'Amérique – Écritures d'un nouveau monde? Textes réunis par Philippe Wellnitz. Strasbourg: Presses Universitaires 1997, S. 51–78. Vgl. auch ders., Der Wanderer und der Verschollene. Zum Problem der Identität in Goethes *Wilhelm Meister* und in Kafkas *Amerika*-Roman. In: Stern/White, Paths and labyrinths (Anm. 19), S. 43–65.

Und doch: »Es ist ja ein Teater.« (II, 303) Wenn wir vergeblich nach den Momenten theatralischen Umschlagens Ausschau halten und in der Mobilisierung des Marginalisierten durch den Ruf des Theaters nicht mehr erkennen als eine letzte perfide Strategie des herrschenden Regimes, sich Karl vollständig gefügig zu machen und in seine Schubfächer zu plazieren, so unterschätzen wir die Kraft der Affirmation. Die Personalabteilung des Theaters unterscheidet sich von ihren Doppelgängern im Roman durch ein kleines, allerdings entscheidendes Detail: sie liest Finten. Sie benötigt keine Papiere, nichts Amtliches, sie verläßt sich auf das gesprochene Wort und da sie ohnehin jeden aufnimmt, benötigt sie nicht einmal das. Die Radikalität dieser Institution liegt nicht darin, daß sie ein neues, anderes Prinzip verkörpert, Freiräume schafft, sondern darin, daß sie selbst ›Maschine spielt‹, ›Staats-Theater‹ betreibt. Kafka ist in Oklahoma im Zentrum einer zionistischen Exilpoetik angelangt, und das hat zunächst nichts mit den naheliegenden Assoziationen zu tun, welche in der Praxis der ›Werbetruppe‹ leicht ein Instrument zionistischer Galuthpolitik, ein Aliyah-Unternehmen erkennen lassen. Was hier tatsächlich vonstatten geht, ist die Reproduktion der amerikanischen Repressionsverhältnisse, ihr Bestimmungs- und Kategorisierungsverfahren, das über keinerlei Referenz(en) verfügt. Für die tatsächliche Existenz des Theaters gibt es keinen Bürgen, auch und gerade unter den Agenten der Persuasion bleibt Oklahoma ein Gerücht, ein Territorium, das man »selbst noch nicht gesehn« hat (II, 300) – und aus verstohlen herumgereichten Bildern (von denen man zudem nur ein einziges zu sehen bekommt) hat die Wahrheit noch selten gesprochen, sie maskieren lediglich die Leerstelle des Transfers, die der Betrachter passieren soll. Natürlich ist das Theater von Oklahoma ohne Theater, wie auch der zionistische Staat der Kongresse und Tagebucheinträge ohne Staat ist, sondern das Theater existiert nur, insofern es Staat, der Staat, insofern er Theater ist. Tatsächlich verfährt die Werbetruppe nach einer Strategie, die es demjenigen, welcher durch die Mühlen des signifikanten Regimes gegangen ist und über kein Zeichenmaterial mehr verfügt, welches er in eine neue Identität einbringen könnte, gestattet, den Zustand signifizierter Ohnmacht unbemerkt zu überwinden. Indem man die Mechanismen der herrschenden, ausgrenzenden Instanzen nachbildet, diesen aber ein unendliches, völlig nachgiebiges Prinzip, das schlichtweg jeden berücksichtigt, unterlegt, konstruiert man die Maschine als eine sich im Verschließen öffnende Instanz. Auf der einen Seite verfügen die Kanzleien durchaus über die sich in ›Aufschriften‹ manifestierende Autorität des Gesetzes und können mit dieser denjenigen, der sich nicht zu den Aufschriften bekennen kann, mit der Bemerkung zurückweisen, nicht dazu zu gehören. Auf der anderen Seite sind die Schreiber völlig machtlos, wenn der Befragte die Gesetzeskonformität soweit ausschreitet, daß er sich vollkommen ausstreicht und eine Identität auf ›Zuruf‹ annimmt.[54] Während die Registratur

---

[54] Überhaupt scheint das Wesen des Theaters doch recht treffend als eine affirmative Übernahme von Anrufen charakterisiert zu sein, so etwa, wenn die »Leute auf dem Bahnhof [...] einander die Truppe« zeigen und dabei »Ausrufe wie ›Alle diese gehören zum Teater von Oklahoma‹« zu hören sind (Bd II, S. 317).

ihre ganze Ohnmacht dadurch unter Beweis stellt, daß sie der Lüge zwar gewahr ist (»Er heißt nicht Negro«), aber sie dennoch hinnehmen muß, hat der Exilant im Moment seiner Selbstdurchstreichung die Kontrolle über die Zeichen und ihre Wirksamkeit wiedergewonnen.[55]

So, wie die Bauarbeiter die Grenzen der Romanwelt errichten, um sie letztendlich unvermauert stehen zu lassen, so hat die Überprüfung der Identität in der Personalabteilung des Theaters die (theatralische) Funktion, ihren an zahlreichen Verhörinstanzen geschulten und konditionierten Klienten den Weg zur Neubeschreibung zu öffnen, indem sie »gewaltsam die Kontrollabsperrungen [öffnet] und [...] die Verpflichtung [vereitelt], alles, was von draußen hereintritt, genehmigen oder adoptieren zu müssen«.[56] Auf der anderen Seite ist es der zeichenlose Karl, der auf diese ›unzweckmäßige‹ Organisation mit einer ebenso ›unzweckmäßigen‹ Strategie antwortet und in der Selbstnichtung vor einer sich selbst nichtenden Repression[57] die Autorität der amerikanischen Verhältnisse affirmiert und sie gleichzeitig dabei durchbricht. Das Theater wird somit gerade dadurch zu einem ›Umschlag-Platz‹ des Exils, insofern es auf nichts verweist, was über die Strukturen des signifikanten Zeichenregimes hinausreichen würde, sondern statt dessen durch Übersignifikation das Gesetz ins Leere laufen und anfällig werden läßt für eine Infiltration durch diejenigen, welche es auslöschen, indem sie es erfüllen. Zum Vorschein kommt dabei eine Nation der Margo, deren Angehörige sich in nichts von den durch Amerika Marginalisierten unterscheiden – außer durch die Tatsache, daß sie die Maschinerie gänzlich durchlaufen haben und in eine Welt eingetreten sind, die *erst mit diesem Eintritt* beginnt zu bedeuten, über deren Zeichen und Einschreibungen sie gebieten können.

Maschine zu ›spielen‹, das heißt nämlich auch, eine bestimmte Zeichenpraxis, die das Kontinuum der Signifikanten autonomisiert, kaleidoskopisch immer neue Kartographien erzeugt und das um topologische Gewißheit nachsu-

---

[55] Dies ist ein Vorgang, der verständlicherweise vor allem in den Gender Studies verstärkt ins Licht gerückt wird. »Hier erzeugt die performative Äußerung, der Ruf des Gesetzes, der ein gesetzmäßiges Subjekt zu erzeugen trachtet, eine Reihe von Folgen, die über das hinausschießen und das durcheinanderbringen, was dem Anschein nach die disziplinierende Absicht ist, das Gesetz herbeizuführen. Die Anrufung verliert somit ihren Status als eine einfache performative Äußerung, als eines Aktes des Diskurses, ausgestattet mit der Macht, das zu erschaffen, von dem die Rede ist. Sie erschafft mehr, als sie jemals zu schaffen vermeinte, da sie über jeden beabsichtigten Referenten hinausgehend signifiziert.« Judith Butler: Körper von Gewicht. Die diskursiven Grenzen des Geschlechts. Aus dem Amerikanischen von Karin Wördemann. Frankfurt a. M.: Suhrkamp 1997 (Edition Suhrkamp, N. F.; 1737: Gender Studies), S. 174.

[56] Levinas, Gott und die Philosophie (Anm. 42), 99.

[57] Die Bedeutung dieser Figur (wie wir sie ja auch etwa im »Schweigen der Sirenen« vorfinden) für die Bewertung des ›Teaters von Oklahoma‹ erstmals bei: Horst Seferens: Das »Wunder der Integration«. Zur Funktion des »großen Teaters von Oklahama« in Kafkas Romanfragment »Der Verschollene«. In: Zeitschrift für deutsche Philologie 111 (1992), S. 577–593.

chende Subjekt diesen Kartographien unterwirft, zu fiktionalisieren. In der Befragung Karls demonstriert die Personalabteilung des Theaters eine semiologische Verfügungsgewalt, die sie gar nicht besitzt: sie ist nicht mehr Staatsinstanz und ihre Kommunikation mit den marginalisierten Subjekten ist nicht mehr Ausdruck eines vorgezeichneten Machtverhältnisses, das im wesentlichen eben die conditio exul, die Aussperrung von der Erde unter Maßgabe des Papiers, beinhaltet. Wenn nun aber diese Autorität hier gar nicht vorliegt, sie gleichwohl ›gespielt‹ wird, dann ist die spielende Institution – das Theater – unversehens in eine Funktion gerückt, in der sie die ganze Relation von Erde und Papier alleine zu verantworten hat.[58] Ihr subordinierender, in seinen Ursprüngen auf eine territoriale Ordnungsmacht sich gründender Gestus ist zweifellos vorhanden; er verweist aber auf keinen Raum mehr. Gleichwohl evoziert die bloße Strukturwiederholung der maschinellen Registratur ein Territorium, das sich nicht von diesem Experiment eines Bezeichnen-Bezeichnens abtrennen läßt, das aber keinesfalls identisch mit ihm ist. Natürlich ist eine Präsidentenloge keine Bühne, aber: wo (und wenn) eine Loge ist, so muß es dort doch auch eine Bühne geben. Natürlich ersetzt eine auf einem Rennplatz zusammengekarrte überdimensionale Rezeption keinen Staatsbetrieb, aber: wo (und wenn) man mir einen Ort zuweist, so muß es dort doch auch ein Land geben.

Mit dieser über das Spiel des ›Staats-Theaters‹ herbeigeführten Umkehrung, welche das Territorium aus der Karte erst hervorgehen läßt, öffnet sich aber auch das Geschriebene wieder dem Schreiben, öffnet sich eine Literatur, die an den Rändern der Nationen sich auf ihre Marginalität besinnt, einer Literatur, die sich selbst den Grund gibt, öffnet sich das Papier der Erde noch ein letztes Mal. So zeigt sich im Schlußfragment den Reisenden die territoriale Schrift des neuen Kontinents, spüren sie dessen wahre »Größe«:

> Bläulichschwarze Steinmassen giengen in spitzen Keilen bis an den Zug heran, man beugte sich aus dem Fenster und suchte vergebens ihre Gipfel, dunkle schmale zerrissene Täler öffneten sich, man beschrieb mit dem Finger die Richtung, in der sie sich verloren, breite Bergströme kamen eilend als große Wellen auf dem hügeligen Untergrund und in sich tausend kleine Schaumwellen treibend, sie stürzten sich unter die Brücken über die der Zug fuhr und sie waren so nah daß der Hauch ihrer Kühle das Gesicht erschauern machte. (II, 318)

Die Besonderheit dieser Passage liegt gewiß nicht darin, daß sich aus einer paradigmatischen Darstellung von Erhabenheit ein Rückverweis auf die Unabhängigkeit des Subjekts und seines Geistesvermögens von der physischen Gewalt der Natur einstellen könnte. Diese Landschaft dient niemandem, sie wird ihren Betrachter nicht seiner Integrität versichern, sondern ihn vielmehr mit der Tatsache konfrontieren, daß zwischen der Dynamis der Erde und ihrer ›Beschreibung‹ eine unüberwindbare Kluft liegt und kein Weg hinüberführt,

---

[58] Zu den Veränderungen der Karte-Territorium-Relation unter Spielbedingungen vgl. Wolfgang Iser: Das Fiktive und das Imaginäre. Perspektiven literarischer Anthropologie. Frankfurt a.M.: Suhrkamp 1991, S. 426–430.

Erde / Papier. Kafka, Literatur und Landnahme 87

sondern sich die territoriale Schrift im Moment ihres kartographischen Nachvollzugs sofort ›verlieren‹ muß. In den Tiefen des Westens wartet auf den Roman der Gewahrsam des defizitären Abstands zwischen Erde und Papier und erneut wird dieser Mangel erfahren in einer ›Kühle‹, die von außen her in den Zug hineindringt – so, wie im Landhaus die von der unvermauerten Wand hereinströmende Zugluft es den Diener nicht mehr ›aushalten‹ ließ. Für die erzählte Welt der Exilanten birgt diese Erfahrung mehr als ein weiteres Abgestoßen-Werden; die Schrift erliegt für einen Moment dem Atem der Macht, der sie sich verdankt; das Land sucht die Literatur schließlich doch noch heim und gibt ihr eine letzte Rechtfertigung.

Erde und Papier sind die beherrschenden Kräfte des Exils Literatur. Sie korrespondieren nicht, sondern schließen einander aus; sie bedingen sich gegenseitig und geben sich doch den Anschein, die Gegenkraft nichten zu können. Das Exil findet nicht dort sein Ende, wo das Gesetz, die Schrift gänzlich erfüllt und ausgelöst wird, eine Umkehr erfolgt ist. Im Gegenzug ist es auch nicht dort erst vollkommen und aufrichtig, wo diese Umkehr von vornherein ausgeschlossen wird und die Welt ein Bündel von Karten bleibt. Wir haben uns vielleicht allzusehr mit dem Gedanken angefreundet, daß Marginalität eine ganz und gar papierne Erscheinung ist, der nichts Irdenes mehr entspricht, und daß in der Konsequenz das Exil auch keinen Ort hat, da es ein universales Exil geworden ist. Mit Kafka aber kehrt das Land wieder zur Margo zurück: nicht, um ihr Exil zu beschließen, sondern um ihr zu bedeuten, *daß eine Erde ist*, der sie entstammt, die sie sich selbst eröffnen kann und an der sie sich messen lassen muß. Ein Land, das einzunehmen die Literatur ausgezogen war, ohne welches sie nicht ist, das sie jedoch – und so bleibt sie mosaisch – nur von seinen Rändern her erschauen wird.

Pierre Bouretz

Yichouv as *Teshuvah*: Gershom Scholem's Settling in Jerusalem as a Return from Assimilation

At the end of August 1923, Gershom Scholem was leaving Berlin. One month later, September 30th, he arrived in Jerusalem. Emphatically said, this move from Berlin to Jerusalem could be seen for this generation as an exit out of exile, a second departure from Egypt, a kind of a new liberation from the house of bondage, which was Assimilation and its falseness: freedom without; enslavement within. From this point of view, coming to Zion was the radical expression of the rediscovery of the self-awareness denied by the generation before, and settling meant a return in the strict sense of the word.

Concerning this personal adventure which was also a collective one, we have four main sources. The first is Scholem's autobiographical writings. These consist of his autobiography properly speaking, in two versions: *From Berlin to Jerusalem*, written in German in 1977; the enlarged text of 1982, written in Hebrew before to be translated in German, *Mi-Berlin l-Irushalayim*.[1] Devoted to Walter Benjamin, the *History of a Friendship* can also be considered as an autobiographical book.[2] Secondly, and perhaps most important, are the two volumes of Scholem's *Tagebücher*, the second one being only published recently. With them, we can see day by day from 1913 to 1923 the rise of Scholem's hostility to the world of Assimilation, his discovery of Jewish Tradition and Hebrew language, his commitment within Zionism.[3] Thirdly, there are some interviews and analytical papers from the end of Scholem's life, mainly an article entitled »About the Social Psychology of the German Jews between 1900 and 1930«.[4] Finally, there is a strange, profound and almost

---

[1] Gershom Scholem: Von Berlin nach Jerusalem. Jugenderinnerungen. Frankfurt a. M.: Suhrkamp Verlag 1977 (Bibliothek Suhrkamp; 555); From Berlin to Jerusalem. Memories of My Youth. New York: Schocken, 1980; Mi-Berlin l-Irushalayim. Sichronoth ne'urim. Tel Aviv: Am Oved 1982; Von Berlin nach Jerusalem. Jugenderinnerungen. Erweiterte Fassung, Frankfurt a. M.: Jüdischer Verlag, 1994. References will be given to this definitive edition.

[2] Gershom Scholem: Walter Benjamin. The Story of a Friendship. Translated from the German by Harry Zohn. Philadelphia: Jewish Publication Society of America 1981.

[3] Gershom Scholem: Tagebücher. Nebst Aufsätzen und Entwürfen bis 1923. Vol. 1: 1913–1917; Vol. 2: 1917–1923. Frankfurt a. M.: Jüdischer Verlag 1995/2000.

[4] Gershom Scholem: A propos de la psychologie sociale des Juifs d'Allemagne entre 1900 et 1930. In: id., De la création du monde jusqu'à Varsovie. Trad. de l'allemand par Maurice-Ruben Hayoun. Paris: Ed. du Cerf 1990 (Patrimoines: Judaisme). See also an interview with Scholem by Muki Tsur: Devarim bego. Tel Aviv: Am Oved 1992.

pathetic text, written during the summer of 1944 for the anniversary of the Institute for Jewish Studies at the Hebrew University of Jerusalem.[5] Never mentioned, this lecture written with a kind of rage in an allegorical style has two contradictory facets. On one side, it gives a picture of Scholem's feelings during his youth that was ending when he went out of Germany: a revolt against the fathers, the spirit of Zionism, and his project of a new Science of Judaism. On the other side, it shows the despair of this generation of builders twenty years later, at the time when the destiny of the Jews in Europe was discovered.

The *Tagebücher* help us to delimitate a chronology of these years of formation. In the first pages of his diary for February 1913, Scholem notes: »I am also a Zionist.«[6] But two years later he is still asking: »Did I have a true desire to go to Palestine?«[7] He had to wait until 1918/19 to find the conceptual framework that gives a sense and an orientation to these feelings, around three Hebrew terms: *Galuth*; *Teshuvah*; *Yichouv*. Finally, Scholem shapes a formula with two Hebrew radicals making an assonance which is difficult to translate: »*teschuva* (return; Rückkehr) to Judaism comes from *jischuv* (settling; Besiedlung) in *erez Israel*.« (*teschuva la-jahadut lifne jischuv erez jisrael*)[8] This expression brings us to my subject: a whole host of impressions, that progressively become a description and an analysis of assimilated Judaism in Germany as a paradigm of Jewish exile; the social, political and intellectual project of a generation that wanted to rebuild both science and the nation in the land; the enthusiasm for settling in Palestine, but also the disenchantment that follows a paradoxical victory of Zionism.

Golusjudentum: the World of Assimilation

To describe assimilation in Germany, Scholem created November 1916 a terrible term in his diary: *Golusjudentum*.[9] The day after, he found the word that could designate in Hebrew its opposite: *Tikkun*. *Golusjudentum* is the world of the fathers, that is an illusion about political freedom, an alienation without consciousness, a refusal of Jewish life. This attitude is perfectly summarized with a classical expression by Achad Ha'am (Ascher Ginzberg): *Avdut be-Tokh Herut*; Slavery in Freedom. In Germany at the beginning of the century, there were a lot of symbols for this phenomenon. The main one was a social and political one:

---

[5] Gershom Scholem: Überlegungen zur Wissenschaft vom Judentum. In: id., Judaica 6. Die Wissenschaft vom Judentum. Hg., aus dem Hebräischen übersetzt und mit einem Nachwort versehen von Peter Schäfer in Zusammenarbeit mit Gerold Necker und Ulrike Hirschfelder. Frankfurt a. M.: Suhrkamp Verlag 1997 (Bibliobetk Suhrkamp; 1269), p. 7–52.
[6] Scholem, Tagebücher 1913–1917 (note 3), p. 10.
[7] Ibid., p. 195.
[8] Tagebücher 1917–1923, p. 365.
[9] Scholem, Tagebücher 1913–1917 (note 3), p. 437.

the *Central-Verein deutscher Staatsbürger jüdischen Glaubens*, that is a confessional organization without any other reference to Jewish identity. Another one would be the perfect loyalty of German Jews to the nation during the war, despite the suspicion in which they would be held. But these symbols also existed in everyday life. For example, the attitude towards traditional great feast days: people would respect Jewish holidays without participating in the ritual, in the name of an emancipated Judaism; but they would also celebrate Christmas, because they considered themselves as Germans. In the same way, they would refuse traditional rules, and behave sometimes in a provocative way: smoking during the Shabbat, eating the Day of Atonement and so on. Scholem adds that even the Jewish *Witz* was corrupted in that view, citing a joke of his father's he considered very shocking: to light a cigar with the Shabbat candle with a parody of benediction in favor of the *bore peri tobaqo* (creator of the fruit of tobacco).[10]

At this time, the topography of Berlin gives an image of Jewish social life.[11] The main part of the Jewish people which had arrived in the city from other places in Germany or Eastern Europe one or two generations before was living in the Old Eastern neighborhood, contrasting with a more integrated bourgeoisie which had moved to the new town in the West, like Walter Benjamin's family. Scholem's milieu was perfectly representative for this world where »few visible traces of Judaism remained«. His family had been settling in Berlin for three generations, belonging to a middle class which had adopted the German lifestyle. To show how German he was, his father refused to speak Hebrew in the family and was openly opposed to Zionism. Nobody had a particular commitment to religion or manifested any fidelity to Jewish tradition.

Later in his life, Scholem will use very sharp expressions to summarize the characteristics of this *Golusjudentum*. From a strict social point of view, it represented a conscious desire to disappear within the German society, proceeding from a renouncement to any kind of self-identity. Denying their own identity to adopt the culture and values of a foreign country, German assimilated Jewish people manifested a »voluntary self-delusion«.[12] Not only they did refuse any obligation towards the Jewish heritage, but they also wanted to repudiate it, by a kind of abdication in view of the perspective of being distinct from German people. In its ultimate manifestation, this feeling was similar to *Selbsthaß* (self-hatred).

This illusion was also present within intellectual life, by means of the idea of a »German-Jewish symbiosis«.[13] Since the time of the *Haskalah* symbolized by Mendelssohn, Jewish philosophers in Germany believed in the existence of a kind of elective affinity between the legacy of Jewish thought and German

---

[10] See »A propos de la psychologie sociale des Juifs d'Allemagne entre 1900 et 1930« (note 4), passim and *Von Berlin nach Jerusalem* (mote 1), Chap. 2.

[11] See ibid., Chap. 1.

[12] Ibid., p. 238.

[13] In order to find a synthesis on that point, see for example George L. Mosse: German Jews Beyond Judaism. Bloomington: Indiana University Press 1985 (The Modern Jewish Experience).

idealism. Hermann Cohen was the main spokesman of this harmony that could be manifested by a proximity between Maimonides and Kant, and would promote something like a secular messianism connected to the idea of an universal humanity. Furthermore, even the Science of Judaism was contaminated by an ideology that required Judaism to be diluted within occidental culture. To underline this point concerning the *Wissenschaft des Judentum*, Scholem frequently quotes a saying attributed to Moritz Steinschneider: »we must provide Judaism with a decent funeral.« In that view, the founding fathers have made a substantial effort to exhume the documents that should permit a revival of the interest for Jewish history. But their state of mind was that the authenticity of Judaism was definitely relegated to the past, becoming an object of science, nevermore a living reality. The most distressing expression of this illusion in Scholem's eyes will appear during the war, when a part of the Zionist movement will rally to the German cause. Adopting German nationalism, these people would accept to go to the front and even die for Germany. They brought to light how deep and pernicious the false historical consciousness of Jewish mankind in exile had been. Such a dramatic experience would radicalize Scholem's hostility toward assimilation and his desire to leave Europe for Palestine.

In such a light, exile was not only the historical situation of the Jews scattered all over the world, but also an unconstrained disappearance within social life, language and culture of foreign nations, meaning that prior to a return to the land, the question was one of a *Teshuvah* within Judaism. Scholem's attitude toward history cannot be understood without this idea. Conversely, this perspective will explain the commitment to Zionism and the conception of a new science of Judaism: the background to his settling in Jerusalem.

Scholem's Education Between Tradition and Zionism

Describing for Max Brod the attitude of people who were writing in German in order to leave Judaism with their fathers' approval, Kafka said: »[...] they wanted that, but their hind legs were still stuck to their fathers' Judaism and their forelegs were unable to find new ground.«[14] In order to find that ground, Scholem decided very early to learn Hebrew, to devote himself to an investigation of the old secret territories of Jewish life and finally to leave for Palestine. The reproach to Walter Benjamin for his inability to do the same would be the main shadow darkening their friendship until Benjamin's tragic death. We know how attached Scholem was to Kafka.[15] His *Letter to the Father (Brief an den*

---

[14] Franz Kafka: Letter to Max Brod, June 1921. In: id., Briefe 1902–1924. Frankfurt a. M.: S. Fischer 1958, p. 337.

[15] See, for example, »On Kafka's *The Trial*« and »With a Copy of Kafka's *The Trial*- A Poem« in: Gershom Scholem: On the Possibility of Jewish Mysticism in our Times & Other Essays. Ed. and Selected with an Introduction by Avraham Shapira. Translated by Jonathan Chipman. Philadelphia: Jewish Publication Society 1997.

Vater) was probably a kind of mirror through which Scholem looks backwards to his own youth. Kafka was a permanent object of discussion with Benjamin. His writings would become a key for Scholem's comprehension of the Kabbalah. With Kafka, Scholem also discovered one of the main questions of his life: the question of language.

The first manner to escape from the environment of assimilation was to learn Hebrew. Scholem began to do that early on, alone and with the disapproval of his family, but with the help of masters who refused any remuneration. From the age of thirteen and for many years he worked on his Hebrew one or two hours a day, noting in his diary both his progress and his difficulties, frequently adding the texts he tried to translate and explain. Rapidly, his interest would shift from the linguistic dimension to a reflection on the deepest signification of language, writing, in June 1918, a note about time in Judaism which was considered as a »metaphysics of Hebrew«.[16] Some years later, he will have his first intuition concerning the mystical dimension of language, which would serve as the starting point of an investigation that, after half a century, would become one of his main articles: »The Name of God and The Theory of Language in Kabbalah.«[17] The engagement with Hebrew, the struggle in favor of its renewal, and the translation of some pieces of traditional literature, modern literature (Agnon), or scientific papers (Bialik) into German, would remain for Scholem connected to his commitment to Zionism.[18] Moreover, the question of language was one of the factors that helped him to find his bearings among the different strains of Zionism. As an example, for Scholem, the refusal to learn Hebrew was one of the symptoms of what he called a *Salonzionimus*, that is, a kind of an unauthentic commitment, similar to an avoidance of religious questions, or a lack of consideration for a genuine educational project.[19]

These considerations, coming from Scholem's diaries and first writings, shed new light on his conception of Zionism at the time of his youth and probably forever. First of all, if Zionism can appear as a revolt against the father, it must be taken seriously, being neither the adventure offered to young people bored with their families, nor simply the dream leaving the atmosphere of an old country for a new world. Such a view discriminates between the different organizations. Scholem had no regard for the youth movements which only proposed a regeneration of bodies through a sort of romanticism. Similarly, he is

---

[16] »Bemerkungen über die Zeit im Judentum«, in: Scholem, Tagebücher 1917–1923 (note 3), p. 235–240.

[17] Gershom Scholem: Der Name Gottes und die Sprachtheorie der Kabbala. In: Eranos-Jahrbuch 39 (1970), p. 243-299, reprinted in: id., Judaica 3. Studien zur jüdischen Mystik. Frankfurt a. M.: Suhrkamp 1973 (Bibliothek Suhrkamp; 333), p. 7–70.

[18] Examples of Scholem's translations between 1918 and 1922, in: id., Tagebücher 1917–1923 (note 3): Die Klagelieder (Lamentations), p. 112–127; Ein mittelalterliches Klagelied, p. 607–611; S. J. Agnon: Die Geschichte von Rabbi Gadiel dem Kinde, p. 627–631; Chaim Nachman Bialik: Halacha und Aggada, p- 559–580.

[19] Scholem, Tagebücher 1913-1917 (note 3), p. 309.

frequently ironical about the attitude of Martin Buber and his followers, particularly when they seemed mainly preoccupied by the personal dimension of actual experience and self-realization (*Erlebnis*).[20] On the other hand, he remained suspicious of the socialist currents that called for a pure atheism and preferred social analysis to a more speculative reflection concerning the historical situation of the Jews. From this point of view, having belonged during all his time in Berlin to the *Jung Juda* movement, he would never be attracted by organizations like Ha-Po'el ha-Za'ir, in the same way that, although he would considered himself a *haluz* (pioneer) in Palestine, it would be in the precise perspective of someone who makes no separation between the political level and the intellectual or spiritual one.

Reading Scholem's intimate papers, we must be impressed by the number of pages devoted to the religious dimension of Zionism, which would almost disappear in his narrative books. Scholem frequently uses biblical quotations to express the intimate being of his ideal. For example, in December 1917: »I may walk before the Lord in the land of the livings.« (Psalm 116,9) Or, in a note significantly devoted to Hermann Cohen's remembrance at the day of his death in April 1918: »[...] would we be like Cohen, that Zionism will be fulfilled, and we could become properly speaking a *kingdom of priests.*«[21] Just as he quotes biblical expressions, Scholem commonly writes with allusions to the Bible, or concepts coming from Jewish theology, particularly in some aphorisms collected for Walter Benjamin: *Historie ist der Terminus für das innere Gesetz der Lehre*; *Hermann Cohens Dasein ist Torah*; *Die Lehre ist der Strom, der zwischen den Polen der Offenbarung und des messianischen Reiches strömt.*[22] Once again, for him, Zionism could not only be a return from exile to the land, but also the rediscovery of the Jewish heritage which had been buried beneath a foreign culture and by a sort of self-denial of the Jews during the time of *Galuth*.

In the end, Scholem's attempt to save Judaism from its downfall maintained an intellectual dimension that made him one of the greatest scholars of his generation. But it must be said that before it turned out to be a scientific approach, this project was similar to traditional study: prior to *Wissenschaft* was *Lernen* in the classical sense of the term within East-European Judaism.[23] A consideration of Scholem's training in *Lernen* gives us an occasion to underline some particularities of Jewish life in Germany at this time. First of all, it was very difficult to find places and masters to study in Berlin. Some Zionist

---

[20] See, for example, ibid., p. 396–399. Reading many years later Kafka's correspondence, Scholem will discover that Kafka's fiancée was present at this meeting (see Kafka's letter to her, September 22, 1916. In: id., Briefe an Felice und andere Korrespondenz aus der Verlobungszeit. Hg. von Erich Heller und Jürgen Born. Frankfurt a. M. S. Fischer 1967, p. 703f.).

[21] Scholem, Tagebücher 1917–1923 (note 3), p. 190.

[22] Scholem, 95 Thesen über Judentum und Zionismus. In: ibid., p. 300–306.

[23] On this sense explained by Scholem himself, see: Three Types of Jewish Piety. In: id., On the Possibility of Jewish Mysticism in our Times & Other Essays (note 15), p. 180.

groups were able to propose classes in Jewish history, but courses in the true religious tradition were rare. On the other hand, such an education had lapsed within the familial environment, where it provoked hostility, if not contempt. Young people like Scholem were obliged to find someone to study with by themselves, which meant an exploration of the Berlin synagogues in search of the appropriate person. Scholem would meet such a man in Isaak Bleichrode, who was the rabbi of the orthodox synagogue in Dresdner Straße, not so far from his house.[24] With him, he would work several hours every Sunday and during the week for many years, considering him as a real master and a model. The best illustration of these years of education within traditional Judaism would be a day of Gerhard Scholem's life at the age of fifteen. On Sunday the fourth of April 1913: from seven to nine, two hours of *Gemara* with Bleichrode; after that, a religious training by Rabbi Eschelbacher, concerning *Ketuvim*; then lessons with the liberal rabbi Martin Joseph in study of the *Michnah*, before yet another meeting with Bleichrode in the evening, devoted to Rachi's commentaries[25].

Scholem will continue this sort of training in Hebrew language, traditional literature and religion almost during his entire stay in Germany. But he would progressively discover some more arcane aspects of Jewish life and thinking. First he read something about the Kabbalah in Heinrich Graetz' *Geschichte der Juden*, which he received from his parents for his *Bar Mizva*.[26] But generally speaking, the *Wissenschaft des Judentums* was obliterating the role and importance of mysticism within Jewish history. On the other side, Isaak Bleichrode was forced to recognize that he was unable to help him with the *Zohar*. So it was necessary to study by oneself, beginning with new forms of language, unknown concepts and a strange vision of the world. Scholem would rapidly be convinced that the Kabbalah was »the place in which the hidden life of Judaism had once dwelled«.[27] But what he would pick up from it would be more than an ancient forgotten literature or a sort of magical system, irrelevant for modern Judaism. In the Kabbalah, its language and concepts, he would find a spiritual world that was like a mirror in which Jewish life within exile takes sense despite of the suffering, hopelessness and even despair generated by the dispersion, the persecutions and the slowness of time.

---

[24] Scholem, Von Berlin nach Jerusalem (note 1), Chap. 3.
[25] Scholem, Tagebücher 1913–1917 (note 3), p. 21–22.
[26] Around October 1916, Scholem also discovered Franz Joseph Molitor's Philosophie der Geschichte oder über die Tradition. Münster: Verlag der Theissing'schen Buchhandlung 1857.
[27] Gershom Scholem: A Candid Letter About My True Intention in Studying Kabbalah [1937]. In: id., On the Possibility of Jewish Mysticism in our Times & Other Essays (note 15), p. 4. On the same topic, in the same book, see: My Way to Kabbalah [1974], p. 20–24.

Scholem's Art of Writing Jewish History

This discovery is the core of Scholem's conception of Jewish history and the key to his personal art of writing. For him, science will never be a peaceful work concerning cold objects, but an investigation within the dialectical aspects of historical phenomena, in order to promote an understanding of the more mysterious facets of Jewish life. From this point of view, he would be fascinated by the comprehensive attitude of the kabbalists toward the *Galuth*. As an example, Isaac Luria built a real system giving an explanation of exile: in order to realize the Creation, God was obliged to resort to a self-contraction, necessary to produce the world *ex nihilo*; but just after, his light had been disseminated all over the world, as a symbol of Jewish dispersion amongst the nations; at the end, the sparks of this light would be gathered again, within a process of reparation of the world (*Tikkun*) that means the Redemption for the Jews.[28] On an other side, Abraham Abulafia or Isaac the Blind had been able to promote a linguistic theory that explains the form of God's Name and its presence, but also described within the language a circular process which could be an image of the world and mankind from their appearance to the time of Redemption.[29]

Scholem's purpose when considering such doctrines was to show how they produced a system of symbols by which Jewish sufferings could be explained, distress relieved and hope revived. At the same time, his interest was focused on the practical efficiency of this symbolism of Exile and Redemption. The main field for such an inquiry was the role played by messianism in Jewish history. In Scholem's eyes, messianic movements were a response to the people's dereliction at the times of hopelessness, when it seemed that there was no other alternative than to withdraw from a depressing unredeemed world. From this point of view, messianic experiences which had been considered as a dangerous phenomenon and the negative face of Jewish history must be understood as a vital process and the main factor explaining the survival during the exile. By a fascinating paradox, it was only the disruptive force of messianism that could break the sclerosis that was threatening Judaism, despite the dialectical aspect of a process that could also provoke the destruction of Jewish life.[30]

---

[28] On Luria's Kabbalah, see: Gershom Scholem: Major Trends in Jewish Mysticism. New York: Schocken Books 1954, Chap. VII.

[29] See Scholem, Der Name Gottes und die Sprachtheorie der Kabbala (note 17).

[30] On Scholem's conception of messianism in Judaism: Gershom Scholem: Zum Verständnis der messianischen Idee im Judentum. In: Eranos Jahrbuch 28 (1959), translated in: id., The Messianic Idea in Judaism, and other Essays on Jewish Spirituality. New York: Schocken Books 1971; Zionism – Dialectic of Continuity and Rebellion. Interview with Gershom G. Scholem. In: Unease in Zion. Ed. by Ehud Ben Ezer. With a Foreword by Robert Alter. New York, Jerusalem: Quadrangle Books, Jerusalem Academic Press 1974, p. 263–296.

This explains why Scholem would devote such a long time of his life and his major book to Sabbatai Sevi.[31] Through the »mystical messiah«, and its fantastic adventure, many things could be shown. First of all, it made clear why it was necessary to break with scientific rationalism to understand one of the strongest historical experiences of Jewish people, which extended to all the classes of society, all over the Diaspora, and for a long time after its catastrophic end. Because this rationalism was »shrinking the historical perspective«, it had been unable to see »the sparks of Jewish life« that were lying under the appearance of a so-called fatal experience. By breaking with it, it would be possible to promote a new understanding of the secret dimensions of Jewish history. Secondly, a study of this kind of messianic movement would permit us to underline the long-lasting influence of doctrines which had been censored by rabbinical Judaism and official historiography. In that case, the question is to understand why and how the Lurianic Kabbalah had, one century after the events, been a response to the trauma provoked by the expulsion of the Jews from Spain. And the answer is that it gave, through mystical concepts, an explanation of this dramatic moment, an interpretation of the process of Redemption, restoring hope and confidence. Finally, Scholem's intention was to put the Sabbatian messianism in its true light: the first movement that had been capable of »sweeping all the house of Israel«, by way of the forces generated through the symbol of a »gathering of the exiled«.

At the time of this discovery, Scholem's question would become: »what price for messianism?«[32] On the one hand, this price seems to be the highest. Radical messianism was tempted by a kind of antinomism, that is the possibility to realize the Law by the negation of the Law. From this point of view, Scholem will study what he calls »the redemption by the sin«, or how transgression appeared to be the only way to accelerate a destruction of the world that must precede the coming of the Messiah.[33] This explains the mysterious idea of eschatological messianism: »Far from being the result of a historical process, redemption arises from the ruins of history, which collapses amid the ›birth pangs‹ of the messianic age.«[34] But at the same time, we must explain why the utopian aspect of apocalyptic messianism could appear as a factor of renewal within the history of Judaism. Scholem's answer is that »in the closed world of narrowly circumscribed Jewish existence messianic utopia represented the possibility of something radically and wonderfully different.«[35] This means that the success of Kabbalah within the Jewish experience was connected to the fact that it was able to provide »a valid answer to the great prob-

---

[31] Gershom Scholem: Sabbatai Sevi. The Mystical Messiah, 1626–1676. Translated by R. J. Z. Werblowsky. Princeton: Princeton University Press 1973 (Bollingen Series; 93).
[32] See ibid., preface and Scholem, Zum Verständnis der messianischen Idee im Judentum (note 30), passim.
[33] Gershom Scholem: Mitzva ha-baah ba-averah. In: Keneset 2 (1937), p. 347–392.
[34] Scholem, Sabbatai Sevi (note 31), p. 9.
[35] Ibid., p. 10.

lems of the time«, and thus this answer »illuminated the signification of exile and redemption and accounted for the unique historical situation of Israel within the wider, in fact cosmic, context of creation itself«.[36]

When asking what is the price for messianism within Jewish history, Scholem answers that it is a powerful dynamic, which is »both constructive and destructive«. On the side of construction, its main contribution is to promote an idea which is susceptible to illuminate the Jewish life in exile: the idea of *Tikkun*, that is, a process which associates the gathering of the Jews dispersed all over the world with the reparation of this world, in the perspective of the »world to come«, connected to the messianic age. On the other side, by its practical effects, radical messianism will be a disruptive force within Jewish life, provoking a revolt against authority, a destructive attitude vis-à-vis the Law and an impatience concerning the time to be redeemed. But between the enchantment it could promote and the catastrophic consequences it may have, it remains one of the main forces able to produce a religious enthusiasm and above all the only way to elevate the depressing experience of exile and the dereliction of the world to the level of the process of the redemption, giving them a significance on historical scale. For Scholem, this *Weltanschauung* and the historical movements associated with it would not only be an object of scientific inquiries, but also a kind of a mirror in which the contemporary experience of Judaism could be reflected.

To conclude, it must be underlined that for Scholem at the time of his departure to Jerusalem, it was impossible to dissociate the three levels of a radical critique of assimilation, the project of Zionism and the program for a new science of Judaism. The best account of this point remains his 1944 lecture, written for the anniversary of the creation of the Jerusalem Institute. At this time, Scholem is at the middle of his life, being settled in the land since around twenty years, taken this moment as a occasion to make a sort of a personal and collective examination. But the epoch is a tragic one. That moves him to be intransigent on both sides of the reconstitution of the dreams of his youth and an evaluation of the achievement that had been obtained.

There is no doubt that in Scholem's mind when he was coming to Palestine, his thoughts would be better expressed in Hebrew than in German: the rejection of *Galuth* must conduct to an *Aliya*, *Yichouv* being in the true sense a *Teshuvah*. The connection between an historical analysis of exile, the meaning of Zionism and a conception of scientific work does appear in this text through an allegorical language which is adapted to an age of anxiety. Mainly devoted to science, this never noticed lecture does not speak of *Wissenschaft des Judentums*, but *Chochmat Israel*, evoking an affinity between »Jewish studies« and »Israel's wisdom«. Remembering Bialik's appeal for a renewal of the science of Judaism twenty years before, Scholem writes that such a project was to make this science »settle again in its only language, after its exile within

---

[36] Ibid., p. 20.

Occident's jargon«.[37] We must understand that for Scholem and his friends, the founding fathers of the *Wissenschaft des Judentums* have effectively been like gravediggers celebrating Judaism's funeral, within a movement of »liquidation and decomposition« as old as the Haskalah itself. Confronted with their radical failure, which looks like a betrayal of the Jewish heritage, this generation wanted to be one of builders. From this point of view, to build a new society in the land was synonymous with rebuilding the »house of Israel«. But at the same time, the reconstruction of Jewish identity from the ruins that had been abandoned within the nations of exile required the construction of an authentic knowledge of Judaism. On one hand, a new science of Judaism was impossible out of the land, without the Hebrew language. On the other, a renewed understanding of Jewish history would take its place on the »dream's wings« of Zionism. In that view, because exile within foreign countries had also been a self-forgetfulness within foreign languages and cultures, return would be in both social and spiritual reigns a *Teshuvah*.

Jerusalem: Paradise Regained?

This is not the place to explore all the aspects and meanings of Scholem's settling in Palestine, which he frequently calls *Altneuland*.[38] At the end of his autobiography, he meticulously writes down what was important concerning aspects of land, people and events.[39] On the first level, Scholem draws a precise topography of Jerusalem at this time, around his own house in *Me'ah Sche'arim*: the orthodox neighborhood, where he can meet the last Kabbalists and find obscure precious old books; the »profane street«, which is the limit of the new town; the areas that symbolized the »new *Yichouv*«. Adding to this description that of some *Kibbutzim* located at the frontiers in the desert, he shows people belonging to both second and third *Aliya*. On doing so, he liked to record not only geographical origins of the people he meets, but also their genealogies, religious, social or political milieu, and frequently the way they spoke Hebrew. Thus appears the formation of the group that will be the base of the imagined new science of Judaism in the land, the founders of the »historical School of Jerusalem«, around the library managed by Shmuel Hugo Bergmann: David Beneth, Benzion Dinur, Yitzhak Baer and Gershom Scholem.[40]

---

[37] Scholem, Überlegungen zur Wissenschaft vom Judentum (note 5), p. 9.
[38] Scholem, Tagebücher 1913-1917 (note 3), p. 195. This was the title of a book published by Theodor Herzl in 1902.
[39] Scholem, Von Berlin nach Jerusalem (note 1), Chap. 10.
[40] On this subject, see David Myers: Re-inventing the Jewish Past. European Jewish Intellectuals and the Zionist Return to History. New York: Oxford University Press 1995 (Studies in Jewish history).

The main event in this time will be the inauguration of the Hebrew University, in April 1925. Here, where we are today, on the mount Scopus, the scene is a majestic one. First the landscape, in front of the biblical land: Judean Desert; Jordan valley; the Dead Sea; Moab's hills. The ceremony was presided over by the most representative personalities of Zionism: Chaim Weizmann; the Rabbi Kook; Nachman Bialik; Achad Ha'am. But, in Scholem's eyes, most important of all was Judah Leon Magnes, who had been battling in favor of the creation of an university for many years. Lord Balfour's address was the climax of this day: » a magnificent old man standing in front of the setting sun, he praises Jewish people for what they have accomplished in the past and promise for the future.«[41]

Once again, Scholem uses metaphorical images to summarize his feelings during his first period in Jerusalem, saying that they were »wonderful years«: he was really living »within an allegory«; *Me'ah Sche'arim*, where he had settled, looks like »a rather dialectical paradise, which is probably inherent to the true nature of paradises«.[42] But this last expression dissimulates what would rapidly emerge: the other side of such a dialectic which would affect the three levels of the old dream, that is, the Zionism's project, the revival of language and the building of a new science of Judaism.

First of all, he will write to Walter Benjamin in 1931 that maybe Zionism is self-defeating, dying from its own victory:

> [...] our existence, our sad immortality that Zionism wanted to definitively stabilize is now secured within time, that is, for the two next generations; but, for that, we have paid the most hideous price.[43]

Similarly, as soon as 1926, he had sent to Franz Rosenzweig a distressed confession »about our language«.[44] In this letter, he wrote that he was scared by the secularization of the Hebrew language as it became an every day one, that is, when it was losing its »apocalyptic point« to become a profane instrument of communication. Because he henceforth heard in the streets a sort of an inexpressive »volapück«, he asked himself if the Sacred language would not some day revolt against such a phenomenon, as a symbol of the price of secularization within Judaism.

Let us turn again some moments to the 1944 lecture. Here, Scholem expresses a sort of despair. His generation wanted to rebuild the house of the Jewish

---

[41] Scholem, Von Berlin nach Jerusalem (note 1), p. 234.
[42] Ibid., p. 216.
[43] Scholem's letter to Walter Benjamin, August 1, 1931. In: id., Walter Benjamin – Die Geschichte einer Freundschaft. Frankfurt a, M.: Suhrkamp 1975 (Bibliothek Suhrkamp; 467), S. 211–217.
[44] Thoughts About Our Language. Letter to Franz Rosenzweig, December 26, 1926. In: Scholem, On the Possibility of Jewish Mysticism in our Times & Other Essays (note 15), p. 27–29.

studies, in order to give to *Chochmat Israel* its true meaning. In such a view, the purpose was to propose a new examination of Jewish tradition, to assure a »liquidation of the liquidation« that had been provoked by the generation before. But at this tragic time, it was perhaps an illusion. A terrible suspicion had arisen: »Is it possible that some souls had woken up from the world of the *tohu* in order to put the confusion within the world of the *tikkun* we were working for?«[45]. As a last light of hope, maybe Jewish studies must pursue once more their *Tikkun*, with the energy of the »little rest« which escaped from the destruction of Jewish people in Europe. But this perspective remains an uncertain one, surely unable to dispel the present anxiety.

In less emphatic terms, the source of this kind of disenchantment could be identified within something Leo Strauss accurately formulates:

> The establishment of the state of Israel is the most profound modification of the *Galouth* which has occurred, but it is not the end of the *Galouth*: in the religious sense, and perhaps not only in the religious sense, the state of Israel is a part of the *Galouth*.[46]

Scholem was all the more convinced of this idea since he had virtually formulated a similar one as soon as 1929: »the Jewish people's salvation, I hope for as a Zionist, is on no account similar to the religious redemption I hope for concerning the world to come.«[47] It is probably not possible to imagine that Gershom Scholem definitely had no confidence in the possibility for the dream of his youth to be one day realized in Israel. *Mi-Berlin l-Irushalayim*, his settling had effectively been a return from assimilation, *Yichouv* being from this point of view a *Teshuvah* in its first meaning, that is, a return to something like an origin. But even if it gives an image of a »dialectical paradise«, the settling in the land cannot be seen as the rediscovery of the *Pardes*. In other words, you can make a return from exile, but it will never be the same thing as a true *Teshuvah*.

---

[45] Scholem, Überlegungen zur Wissenschaft vom Judentum (note 5), p. 50.
[46] Leo Strauss: Preface to Spinoza's ›Critique of Religion‹. In: id., Jewish Philosophy and the Crisis of Modernity. Essays and Lectures in Modern Jewish Thought. Ed. with an Introduction by Kenneth Hart Green. Albany: State University of New York Press 1997 (SUNY Series in the Jewish Writings of Leo Strauss), p. 143.
[47] Gershom Scholem: Al sheloshah peshaei berith shalom. In: Davar, December 12, 1929.

Mark H. Gelber

Stefan Zweig's Conceptions of Exile

The very perception of Jewish perspectives of exile in Stefan Zweig's works has changed in important ways over the last quarter century, that is roughly since the Zweig centenniel in 1981. This external context, as well as its connection to Zionism must be appreciated from the start. First, it was just twenty years ago that the fact of a secret relationship between him and the Jewish National Library in Jerusalem became widely known, although the news had been revealed for the first time ten years after his death, in 1952, or thus almost thirty years previous to the centenniel. It is a complicated story in its own right, which has in the interim been interpreted differently, but it has certain implications for the following consideration.[1] Here, at the outset, it is important merely to emphasize that Zweig chose Jerusalem as the repository for some of his most precious correspondence and manuscripts, when he decided to dissolve his household in Salzburg and voluntarily head off into exile in late 1933/early 1934. In December, 1933, he referred to the Jewish National Library, in a letter to its director, Hugo Bergmann, as *our* library (»unsere Bibliothek«).[2] This is certainly an unambiguous expression of Jewish-national solidarity at a precarious moment in his life, which is directly linked to the issue of exile.

Secondly, it is only in the last 15 years or so that the predominance of Zionism in Jewish life throughout the world has come to be fully appreciated, after the State of Israel has absorbed more or less successfully the massive waves of former Soviet and Ethiopian immigration, helping to make the Jewish community in Israel probably the largest Jewish community in the world today. For a long time it has been and continues to be the only one in which the Jewish population increases annually owing to natural reproduction. Quantity or demographic concentration is not the main issue in this discussion; rather what is important is the very existence of a viable and vibrant

---

[1] See Mordekhai Nadav: Stefan Zweigs Übersendung seiner Privatkorrespondenz an die Jewish National and University Library. In: Bulletin des Leo Baeck Instituts 63 (1982), p. 67–73; Margarita Pazi: Stefan Zweig, Europäer und Jude. In: Modern Austrian Literature 14 (1981), No. 3/4 p. 291–311; Mark H. Gelber: Stefan Zweig und die Judenfrage von heute. In: Stefan Zweig Heute. Hg. von Mark H. Gelber. New York et al.: Peter Lang 1987 (New Yorker Studien zur neueren deutschen Literaturgeschichte; 7), p. 160–180.

[2] Cited in Gelber, Stefan Zweig und die Judenfrage von Heute (note 1), p. 163.

Jewish State, which as one of its *raisons d'être* serves as a place of potential or permanent refuge for persecuted Jews. While the State of Israel did not yet exist during Zweig's lifetime, the option of Zionist affiliation or activity was presented to him. But, he never really considered Zionism as a serious option, which might provide a solution to the dilemma of his exile. Had I written this paper before the latest wave of violence began to rock Israel in the fall of 2000, it would have been much more sanguine in its overall assessment of Zionism. And, it would have taken, probably, a more stringent line regarding aspects of Zweig's own Jewish perspectives, to the extent that he doubted the cogency of practical Zionism or distanced himself from the ideology and activities of the movement.

Variegated conceptions of exile appear in Stefan Zweig's writings, and in order to understand their difference and development, it makes some sense to divide his career roughly into three periods from the point of view of exile. The first period encompasses the bulk of his career and his pre-exilic writings, which were written before he took the decision, in late 1933 in wake of rising Nazi sympathy in Austria and given the harsh tenor of anti-Semitic events just across the border, to abandon Salzburg. The second period, which he himself designated as his half exile (»Halb-Exil«), includes the years in the thirties up through the Anschluß and the beginning of the War. During this time he resided mostly in England, while he still visited Austria and other addresses on the continent. He was in constant touch with his family in Salzburg and with his secretary there. At a certain point, he sought to obtain British citizenship, in order to facilitate travel and avoid bureaucratic troubles, without, of course, coming to identify culturally in the least as British. The last period covers his last few years and several stations of exile, as he moved from Bath in England to New York, New Haven, and Ossining in the United States, and then on to his final destination, Petropolis in Brazil, where he committed suicide in 1942.

Although this division is fairly artificial, for the purposes of this paper, it will be useful to focus on one textual example for each period under discussion: first, the Biblical drama, *Jeremias* (»Jeremiah«), written during World War One and first staged in Zurich in 1917. This example is, of course, a pre-exilic one. The second example, his Jewish legend, *Der begrabene Leuchter* (»The Buried Candelabrum«), is taken from the period of his ›half-exile‹. It was first published in 1936 by Herbert Reichner in Vienna, that is before the Anschluß. At this time, Zweig's works could no longer be published or distributed in Nazi Germany. The final example, written shortly before his suicide, is his posthumously published memoirs, *Die Welt von Gestern* (»The World of Yesterday«). This work is an example of exile literature par excellence.[3]

---

[3] Mark H. Gelber: ›Die Welt von Gestern‹ als Exil-Literatur. In: Stefan Zweig – Exil und Suche nach dem Weltfrieden. Hg. von Mark H. Gelber and Klaus Zelewitz. Riverside: Ariadne Press 1995 (Studies in Austrian Literature, Culture, and Thought), p. 148–163.

The different conceptions of exile manifested in these works may be considered within the context of the Zionist discussion concerning exile, in Hebrew ›Galuth‹ (in Yiddish, ›Golus‹), as it evolved in the first half of the century. One particular, extended discussion of exile within Zionism deserves special attention, because Zweig had direct access to it, namely the discussion initiated by Jakob Klatzkin (1882–1948) in Martin Buber's *Der Jude,* beginning in 1916 and continuing through 1917. Klatzkin's sharp arguments against diaspora Jewry and against its continued existence elicited some negative or corrective responses, which were also subsequently published in *Der Jude.* Thus, a lively debate ensued. This is the exact same time of the genesis, gestation, and completion of Zweig's *Jeremiah* play, as well as the period of the intensive correspondence between Buber and Zweig, concerning the possible publication of part of *Jeremiah* in *Der Jude* and failing that, what the nature of the potential contribution of Zweig to the journal in another or related area might be. Incidentally, although he expressed keen interest in *Der Jude,* as well as a desire to publish work in it, he never did publish anything in *Der Jude.* It is this correspondence and the final disagreement between Buber and Zweig that ensued, which served to mark the ultimate break in their relationship.

The Zionist discussion focuses on the concept of the negation of the Exile, »Shlilat HaGaluth«, which is relatively complex and which has numerous aspects. It is fair to label it as one of the central concepts that were elaborated and discussed in early Zionist theory. The concept itself was formulated in several different versions and these were certainly not accepted uniformly, or even accepted at all, within the movement. The concept had a checkered reception and it was debated vigorously. One might even say that it is still being debated throughout world Jewry today, although the parameters of the discussion have changed considerably in the interim. Klatzkin, a Hebraist who was born in Poland, completed his university education in Germany, and is perhaps best known today as the editor-in-chief of the major *Encyclopedia Judaica* project in German which was terminated at volume ten (the letter K) with the rise of Nazism. He wrote a short study entitled »Grundlagen des Nationaljudentums,« which was published in three chapter-installments in *Der Jude* in 1916.[4]

In this study, Klatzkin refuted an important tenet of the spiritual or cultural Zionism proferred by Ahad Ha-am, namely, Ahad Ha-am's view that the reconstitution of a vibrant, Jewish national culture in Hebrew in the land of Israel by an intellectual elite would radiate to the diaspora and serve to invigorate Jewish life there. Ahad Ha-am's cultural or spiritual Zionism was designed in this way as a solution to what he perceived as the general, widespread vitiation and degeneration of the Jewish spirit in the diaspora. In his essay, Klatzkin rejected the Galuth in uncompromising terms. He predicted that the regeneration of Jewish life in the land of Israel would in fact weaken,

---

[4] Jakob Klatzkin: Grundlagen des Nationaljudentums. In: Der Jude 1 (1916/17), p. 534–544, 677–648, 825 833.

rather than fortify, Jewish existence in the diaspora. In fact, the new Hebrew human type, a complete human being, that would come into existence in Zion would represent such a radical break with the Jewish being in the diaspora that two separate peoples, with totally different cultural agendas, would eventually distinguish themselves from each other and go their separate paths. The cleavage of the nation that he foresaw would result ultimately in the disappearance of diaspora Jewry, which was in any case moribund. Klatzkin argued that Zionist efforts were in practice only hampered by »Galuth-Romantik«, the romanticization of, and preoccupation with, diaspora Jewry. According to Klatzkin, Zionism was weakened by Jewish interest in the diaspora to any extent and by a preoccupation with the implications of Zionism for the diaspora. Rather, Zionism needed to marshall all of its various strengths for the daunting tasks of nation building and invest all of its energy in the land of Israel and leave the diaspora decisively behind in every possible way.

A number of separate reactions to Klatzkin appeared in *Der Jude*, each taking exception to various aspects of his exposition, including his harsh rejection of the idea of a continued Jewish existence in the diaspora. For example, Hermann Glenn, in a contribution entitled simply »Galuth«, countered that while the diaspora existence of Jewry was indeed responsible for much of the worst suffering of the nation, at the same time it was the source of tangible enrichment for, and a deepening of, Jewish spirituality.[5] Furthermore, Jewry was indebted to the exile in world-historical terms for fructifying the Jewish spirit in tremendous, world-historical proportions through the encounter with the shining cultural phenomenon of Europe. Rafael Seligmann, in his essay »Bejahung und Verneinung des Galuth«, (»Affirmation and Negation of Exile«) rejected the idea that the physical dispersement of the Jews of antiquity by the Romans was the cause of the Jewish condition of exile.[6] Rather, as Seligmann viewed it, exile was integral to the Jewish essence; it was an original, inner Jewish spiritual orientation, which was always striving forward, and it served to give a specifically Jewish signature to all that Jewry absorbed from the world.

And, in perhaps the most elaborate response to Klatzkin published in *Der Jude*, Heinrich Margulies, writing from Poland, argued that by no means was the diaspora fated to disappear. In a response entitled »Das Galuthproblem im Zionismus«, he argued that Zionism would not only have to reckon with the diaspora's continued existence; it would have to accomodate its future blossomings.[7] The realization of the Zionist goal would by no means signalize the end of the diaspora, according to Margulies. Instead, the Jewish enterprise would eventually reach higher stages of existence partially through mutually

---

[5] Hermann Glenn: Galuth. In: Der Jude 2 (1917/1918), p. 517–523.
[6] Rafael Seligmann: Bejahung und Verneinung des Galuth. In: Der Jude 2 (1917/1918), p. 595–601.
[7] Heinrich Margulies: Das Galuthproblem im Zionismus. In: Der Jude 2 (1917/1918), p. 601–607.

beneficial relations and interactions between the actualized Jewish homeland and a sporadically blooming diaspora Jewry. The diaspora's continued existence and its repeated blossomings appeared to Margulies to be conditions for the success of the Zionist enterprise in the land of Israel.

This particular discussion in *Der Jude* was in fact part of an ongoing, multifaceted debate about the role of the diaspora in Zionist theory. Since Zweig read *Der Jude*, and commented about it to Buber in their correspondence, there is little doubt that he was aware of this specific exchange. The discussion may be contextualized further by way of citing an essay, which Zweig also would have known, written by another contributor to *Der Jude*, Max Brod, whom Zweig knew quite well. Brod's essay is entitled »Die dritte Phase des Zionismus«, and it was published in *Die Zukunft* in Berlin in 1917, that is, at this exact same time.[8] It is important to emphasize that the variety of Zionism trumpeted in this essay is ultimately diaspora-oriented. Brod expressed here his basic vision and the historical sense of a diaspora-oriented Zionism. He expressed satisfaction regarding the rapid pace and particular nature of the inner development of the Zionist idea over the last twenty years, that is, since the time Herzl took up the cause. His argument attempted to delimit three phases of Zionism. The first phase was constituted by the political, diplomatic, and organizational activity initiated by Herzl and his wing of the movement. The second phase consisted in the series of small-scale, practical colonization attempts in the land of Israel itself. And, the third phase, the crowning achievement as Brod saw it, appeared to have just begun in the present, that is, around 1916/17. He identified it with decidely Jewish-national social and cultural projects and activities initiated in the diaspora. One major example of a locus for this Zionism in the third phase, according to Brod, was Martin Buber's *Der Jude*. Brod argued that the Jews as a nation were essentially cosmopolitans with strong inclinations toward totalizing Weltanschauungen. Jewish national activity was designed to benefit humankind at large. Thus, *Der Jude* itself, by discussing the issue of ›Galuth‹ within Zionism, was in this sense actually doing so in order to reach beyond Jewry to impact on more global issues, for example, issues of national identity in what we would now call a global, multi-cultural, international world, or issues of national displacement, or of national demographic concentrations and their importance in terms of international relations.

Keeping this particular discussion about ›Galuth‹ in mind, because it may be seen to have provided a frame of reference to which Zweig had unmediated access, his *Jeremiah* may be interpreted as an unreserved affirmation of the spiritual beneficiality of ›Galuth‹ existence. The play ultimately projects an image of spiritually fortified Jews in face of their physical destruction. It is a dramatic demonstration of what became Zweig's pet notion: the spiritual superiority of the vanquished. At the end of the drama, the prophet Jeremiah leads

---

[8] Max Brod: Die dritte Phase des Zionismus. Offprint from: Die Zukunft, No. 16, January 20, 1917, p. 1–13.

the defeated Jews into exile, who nevertheless march off triumphantly, owing to the cognizance of their spiritual victory despite the physical destruction of Jerusalem. ›Galuth‹, thus, has an avowedly positive essence. Concomitantly, in letters to Buber written in 1917, Zweig wrote about how much he loved the diaspora existence of Jewry, which was the expression of its cosmopolitan pan-humanist calling. Jewish unification and strengthening were purely spiritual issues, unrelated to practical Zionist efforts. The realization of a spiritual homeland, an eternal Jerusalem of the spirit, was independent of practical Zionist activity. For Zweig, the diaspora was an exalted state of existence and the source of the substantial Jewish contribution to civilization.[9]

This positive evaluation and idealization of exile subsequently found its way into a number of Zweig's writings which were unrelated to Jewish issues. The most elaborate rhetorical formulation of this conception, which focuses on the various strengths to be derived from exile, may be found in his 1929 biography of Joseph Fouché. There he described exile in general as »eine schicksalschöpferische Macht, die im Sturz den Menschen erhöht«,[10] a »fatefully creative power, which by way of human downfall elevates the human being«. Zweig indicated that some of the most significant contributions to civilization were generated by exile experiences. He cited the founders of the world religions in this context: Moses, Christ, Mohammed and Budda, but also many of the lonely geniuses of world culture. He wrote:

> Nur das Unglück des Exils gibt Tiefblick und Weitblick in die Wirklichkeit der Welt. Harte Lehre, aber Lehre und Lernen ist jedes Exil. [...] Immer ist dem wahrhaft Starken das Exil keine Minderung, sondern nur Kräftigung seiner Kraft.[11]
>
> (Only the unhappiness of exile provides insight into, and an overview of, the reality of the world. Hard teaching, but every exile is this teaching and learning. For the truly strong, exile is always no dimunition, but rather a fortification of his strength.)

From the evidence at hand, it seems that his own experience of exile was the catalyst for a revision in his thinking.

By the time Zweig saw the refugees from Nazism cross the border into Salzburg in 1933, the issue had become a personal one which affected him directly. In the same year with the deterioration of the political situation in Austria, he discussed the possibility of his leaving Salzburg and going into exile, for example in letters to his friends Romain Rolland and Scholem Ash. For the most part, he was by no means pessimistic about the prospect. He compared it theoretically, and a bit naively no doubt, to the time of his world travels before the first World War. Zweig may have been encouraged in this attitude by Rolland's rather cavalier attitude towards exile altogether, as he was

---

[9] Martin Buber: Briefwechsel aus sieben Jahrzehnten. Hg. und eingeleitet von Grete Schaeder. 3 Vols, Heidelberg: Lambert Schneider 1972–1975, Vol. 1, p. 430ff.

[10] Stefan Zweig: Joseph Fouché. Bildnis eines politischen Menschen. Leipzig: Insel 1929, p. 148.

[11] Ibid.

convinced of its many intangible benefits. For example, in July, 1933, as Zweig was trying to make a decision about leaving Salzburg, Rolland wrote to him about exile as follows, referring specifically to the former's Jeremiah:

> Es ist hart, nach der Lebensmitte den Weg ins Exil zu gehen, wie Ihr Jeremias. Ich habe trotz allem die Hoffnung, daß dieses Exil nicht lang sein wird; und ich bin sicher, daß Sie durch diese Schicksalsprüfung wachsen werden.[12]
>
> (It is hard to go into exile in the middle of one's life, like your Jeremiah. Still, I am hopeful, that this exile will not last long. And, I am certain, that you will grow as a result of this fateful test.)

It was shortly thereafter that Zweig initiated contact with the Jewish National library in order to arrange secretly for the establishment of an archive, where he could send some of his most precious correspondence, like the letters from Rolland, and items from his autograph collection. His mind was made up, and he planned to abandon Austria and head into exile. Little did he anticipate that this exile experience would lead to his demise and suicide. In this context, it is the measurable change in his longstanding belief in the benefits of exile which requires analysis.

But, the Zionist idea, which had led to the realization of a Jewish National Library in Jerusalem, might have appeared at this specific juncture more compelling than ever in face of his personal dilemma. Still, he kept this development, that is, his relationship with the Jewish National Library, entirely confidential. In his personal correspondence, up through 1935 and even into 1936, he sometimes presented a rather optimistic sense of the meaning of exile for him to some of his addressees, but this appears to be posturing of a sort. For example, in a letter to Hermann Hesse written in January, 1935, he described his uncertain situation in relatively positive terms:

> Ich hänge ziemlich unsicher an einem schwachen Ast [...] so lebe ich jetzt beinahe studentisch, bald da, bald dort und spüre es beinahe als Glück, aus diesem sicheren Behagen herausgestoßen zu sein. Ich habe viel gelernt in dem Londoner Jahr und nun in Amerika.[13]
>
> (I am hanging somewhat precariously on a weak limb [...] so I am now living almost like a student, now here, now there. And, I perceive it almost as good fortune to have been thrown out of my previous secure contentment. I have learned a lot during the year in London and now in America.)

In another letter to Hesse, written in May, 1935 he wrote metaphorically about how much he was enjoying his »nomadic existence«.[14] Around the same time,

---

[12] Romain Rolland / Stefan Zweig: Briefwechsel 1910–1940. Hg. von Waltraud Schwarze. 2 Vols, Berlin: Rütten & Loening 1987, Vol. 2, p. 187.

[13] Stefan Zweig: Briefe an Freunde. Hrsg. von Richard Friedenthal. Frankfurt a. M.: S. Fischer 1978, p. 264.

[14] See Donald Prater: Stefan Zweig and Hermann Hesse. In: Modern Austrian Literature 3/4 (1981), p. 1–70, here p. 66.

in a letter to Scholem Ash, he wrote more seriously about how innerly disturbed he was, even to a great extent, severely troubled (»verstört«), by the situation of exile with which he was presented.[15]

In terms of the exile discussion in Zionism, *Der begrabene Leuchter*, written in 1936 in England, represents an attempt to retreat somewhat from his earlier idealization of the diaspora, without however embracing Zionism unambiguously in fiction. There is no celebration of the condition of exile, of Jewish suffering, or of weakness in the legend, as one finds in the earlier *Jeremiah*. Rather, the work seems to formulate an expression of general doubt about the possible meaningfulness of the condition of exile, while the prospect of a return to the ancient homeland is mentioned more than once as a possible solution to the Jewish condition. The long-suffering protagonist concedes at one point: »Kein Volk kann so leben ohne Heimstatt und Ziel, wandernd und ewig umgrenzt von Gefahr.«[16] (»No people can live like this, without a home and goal, wandering and eternally bound by danger.«) Or, as he proclaims in another passage: »Doch vielleicht – und mein Herz ist voll dieser Zuversicht – vielleicht wird sein Wille es wollen, daß unser Volk heimkehre zur Heimat.«[17] (»But perhaps – and my heart is full of this confidence – perhaps it will be his will that our people return to the homeland.«) I have previously argued that *Der begrabene Leuchter*, given its medieval setting and accompanying fictionally verisimilitudinous, religious literary idiom could not convincingly convey any pertinent Zionist message, except perhaps by way of a cogent illustration of the necessity for radical change in Jewish life.[18] But, it is precisely here that the legend, from the point of view of the Zionist discussion of the diaspora, falls short, because it does not stake out an unambiguous position, while it does inch closer to the view of those, like Klatzkin, who rejected exile and the diasporic existence of Jewry.

In *Die Welt von Gestern,* his autobiographical statement written shortly before his suicide in exile and published posthumously, Zweig confessed clearly the detrimental effects of exile in general and upon the self in particular: »Jede Form von Emigration verursacht an sich schon unvermeidlicherweise eine Art von Gleichgewichtsstörung [...] man wird unsicherer; gegen sich selbst mißtrauischer.«[19] (»Each form of immigration inevitably causes a kind of disturbance of equilibrium [...] one becomes more uncertain, more mistrusting of the self. «) Or: »Etwas von der natürlichen Identität von meinem ursprünglichen und eigentli-

---

[15] Stefan Zweig to Scholem Ash. In: Ash Collection, Beinecke Library, Yale University.

[16] Stefan Zweig: Der begrabene Leuchter. In: id., Legenden. Frankfurt a. M.: S. Fischer 1959, p. 189.

[17] Ibid., p. 208.

[18] Mark H. Gelber: Sholem Ash, Josef Leftwich, and Stefan Zweig's *Der begrabene Leuchter*. In: Identity and Ethos: A Festschrift for Sol Liptzin on the Occasion of his 85th Birthday. Ed. by Mark H. Gelber. New York et al.: Peter Lang 1986, p. 101–120.

[19] Stefan Zweig: Die Welt von Gestern. Erinnerungen eines Europäers. Frankfurt a. M.: S. Fischer 1978), p. 373f.

chen Ich blieb für immer zerstört.«[20] (»Something from the natural identity of my original and true ›I‹ remained destroyed for ever.«) Yet, the work is inconsistent in that it contrasts his own precarious and deteriorating predicament with the more positively constructed paradigmatic exile figure, which appears in a few places. There are several examples one might cite, but here, it will suffice to discuss perhaps the most important example in the text, Sigmund Freud.

Towards the very end of the memoirs, which chronologically finish with the outbreak of the Second World War, Zweig sketches an image of Sigmund Freud as the outstanding figure of the present exile, but also as that of the paradigmatic Jew. It is the conflation of these two images which is of utmost importance in the context of this discussion. It appears at first, perhaps tentatively, that Zweig wished to revert to the positive, idealistic sense of exile, which he had proferred earlier in his career. According to Zweig's presentation, it was the entire world which really rejected Freud, although it appeared merely that he had been ostracized by the university. The only exception proved to be a small, closed circle of devoted followers. In actuality, according to Zweig's account, an entire epoch feared him and there was a general boycott of the medical profession against him, just as later the Nazis feared and boycotted the Jews.

Still, in Zweig's embroidered narration, as an exile Freud, although elderly and ill, was neither weary nor distressed. Zweig described their encounter in London, as the octogenarian Freud found refuge there from the Nazis after the Anschluß. Zweig found him in exile to be full of energy and happier than ever. At 83 his mind was clear and he remained productive, writing daily, as in his most prolific periods of creativity. Zweig wrote: »[...] sein starker Wille hatte alles überwunden, die Krankheit, das Alter, das Exil ...«[21] (»[...] his strong will had risen superior to everything, illness, age, exile [...]«) Exile might be seen to be responsible for further beneficial consequences, since for Zweig, Freud had even mellowed to a degree, owing to the displacement and the trials he had endured. Zweig reported how he and Freud discussed the tragedy of Jewry in wake of Nazism, but psychoanalysis provided neither a formula nor a solution to this seemingly eternal problem. Freud, so reported Zweig, was non-plussed by the Jewish predicament and even he could not explain it. Taken together, the passages on Freud appear to function as a model of encouragement to the exiled writer, since Freud managed to carry on and remain productive despite all of the difficulties. Even though he could not provide the answer to the problem of Jewry in the Nazi period, he persevered and remained creatively alive. In one sense, Zweig probably hoped to derive badly needed personal support from his constructed example of Freud, as if to try to convince himself, despite the harsh reality of exile, that he, Zweig himself, could also persevere, be creative and continue to write, and survive.

---

[20] Ibid., p. 374.
[21] Ibid., p. 382.

This section of the *Die Welt von Gestern* comes to a climax in a veritable lament for the difficult predicament of modern Jewry. There is an interesting rhetorical turn which pertains to the Zionism debate. In the passage which comes after a rhetorical question about the possible reason for the sense of the persecutions of Jewry by the Nazis, in effect admitting that there appeared to be no sense or meaning in the present Jewish suffering and exile, Zweig writes about the Jews: »man trieb sie aus den Ländern und gab ihnen kein Land. Man sagte: lebt nicht mit uns, aber man sagte ihnen nicht, wo sie leben sollten.«[22] (»They were told that they were not wanted, but they were not told where they might live.«) In other words, despite Zweig's reticence in this passage and his failure to address the Zionist debate, there was certainly one compelling ideological movement within Jewry at that time, which tried to make the case for the land of Israel as the »land to go to«, in this sense. Despite all of the practical problems for exiles from Nazism in terms of actually seeking refuge there in the 1930s and during the War, the Zionist option existed. It was a factor.

One possible explanation for this omission within the context of *Die Welt von Gestern* is that the answer to the Zionist discussion was already provided much earlier in the text, specifically in the section where Zweig depicted his youthful encounter with Theodor Herzl. Although the meeting, as it is remembered in Zweig's literary depiction, was patently about the beginnings of his career as a writer, – indeed Zweig sought out Herzl in the latter's capacity as feuelliton editor of the *Neue Freie Presse* – one may read this section as a comment about the Zionism discussion emanating from the period of exile and War, despite the fact that it is based on one of Zweig's earlier accounts of his meeting with Herzl.[23] His enthusiastic description renders Herzl one of the true heroes of the book, the first man of world importance whom he had encountered in his life. However Zweig admitted that he did not then know »[...] how great a change his person was destined to bring about in the fate of the Jewish people and in the history of our time« (»[...] welche ungeheure Wendung seine Person im Schicksal des jüdischen Volkes und in der Geschichte unserer Zeit zu erschaffen berufen war.«).[24] This hyperbole seems to make more sense now, in 2001, than it would have made at any time Zweig was alive. It is certainly out of place in terms of the mentality of the fin-de-siècle and the first years of the 20th century until Herzl's death in 1904. In real terms, Herzl had accomplished preciously little and the movement he had brought into existence existed on the margins of mainstream Jewish life. Furthermore, it would have been impossible for Zweig to attempt to praise Herzl and Zionism in such unmitigatingly glowing terms at all, except from an exile perspective in the midst of World War II and perhaps as a strong wish for the future at a time of his deep despair about the impossible, totally vulnerable situation of Jewry at the mercy of Nazism.

---

[22] Ibid., p. 388.
[23] See Stefan Zweig: Erinnerungen an Theodor Herzl. In: St. Zweig: Menschen und Schicksale. Frankfurt a. M.: S. Fischer 1955, p. 216–217.
[24] Zweig, Die Welt von Gestern (note 19), p. 100.

Simply, Herzl and Zionism had not changed palpably the destiny of the Jewish people during the time of Zweig's life, and it is only much later in the century, in actuality at the very end of the 20th century, that such a statement can be made cogently in retrospect. The exile discussion in Zionism is pertinent here, to the extent that for Zweig, Herzl was destined to change the fate of the Jewish people and exert a seminal impact on modern history. This kind of literary acknowledgement of Herzl and Zionism within the greater context of *Die Welt von Gestern* can also be plotted in the framework of the Zionist debate about the diaspora. If Zweig, even at this very late stage, could not join those like Klatzkin, who had preemptorily rejected the diaspora, he could at least pay homage to Herzl, who had pointed the way to a solution for the condition of Jewish exile. Yet, as Zweig distanced himself geographically from Zion and from Europe, the specific Zionist discussion of ›Galuth‹ and the practical Zionist option itself receded in importance for him. For a time, survival alone came to dominate his literary agenda, until survival also receded in importance as well.

Christoph Schmidt

Deus sive natura
The Transformation of the Jewish Apocalyptic Version of History into a Natural History in Jizchak Fritz Baer's Treatise of »Galut« (Exile)

1. Preface

Jizchak Fritz Baer's little investigation of the concept and of the history of »Galut« (Exile)[1] from 1936 is in fact a little *Tractatus Theologico-Politicus*. Written under the impression of the national-socialist seizure of power, the author explicitly refuses to give only an account of the idea (›Begriffsgeschichte‹) of Galut, but wishes to define the Jewish existential question with this investigation. It is the quest for the real causes for the continuation and the negation of Galut, which – if correctly understood – should lead to the negation of the modern historical thought of Judaism, since »this historical thought suffers« – according to Baer – »from the confusion of a misunderstood *religious-political heritage*.« (p. 99f.)

To write the history of Galut in this very moment of ultimate danger – this means, to define this heritage and to act upon it in the right way. For the historian, out of this task derives first and for all the necessity to explain history in *natural* and *causal* terms; in this case, he has to explain the historical fact and self-understanding of the *Galut*, which belongs to an »unnatural« = *theological* picture of history. The modern Jewish historian will not thus deal with God's action in history but rather with man's action who tends to derive his action from the supposed action of God. This means that the theological understanding of history becomes a factor for man's behavior, not *per se*. He himself will thus replace the moral-theological explanation for the Galut, according to which it is a function of Israel's sin, repentance and forgiveness, by a natural explanation. Against the moral causality he will insist on the fact that the little

---

[1] Jizchak Fritz Baer: Galut. Berlin: Schocken Verlag 1936 (Bücherei des Schocken Verlag; 61). (All further citations of this text are documented by page in brackets, all translations by Christoph Schmidt.) This text has been published in the Schocken publishing house together with other important investigations in the time after the nationalsocialist seizure of power in Germany, such as Leo Baeck: *Die Pharisäer. Ein Kapitel jüdischer Geschichte* (Berlin 1934), Leo Strauss: *Philosophie und Gesetz. Beiträge zum Verständnis Maimunis und seiner Vorläufer* (Berlin 1935), Gershom Scholem: *Zum Verständnis des Sabbatianismus – Zugleich ein Beitrag zur Geschichte der Aufklärung* (Berlin 1936), Elias Bickermann: *Der Gott der Makkabäer. Untersuchungen über Sinn und Ursprung der makkabäischen Erhebung* (Berlin 1937), Nachum Norbert Glatzer: *Geschichte der talmudischen Zeit* (Berlin 1937). They all reflect in a deep sense the catastrophic historical moment.

Jewish state could possibly not win a war against the imperialist super power of the Roman empire, especially in a time of civil war.

So far. So clear.

Precisely now, because the natural historian is ready to accept the theological interpretation of history as a real, causal factor for his explanation of the Jewish attitude, this attitude itself becomes in fact *unnatural*. The surviving of the small Jewish minority within European Christian culture contradicts – so to speak – the laws of natural causality – according to which weak nations are absorbed, if not extinguished by the strong nations. If Jews have survived 2000 years of Galut, the natural historian has to admit, that thereby the laws of natural political history have been actually *suspended*. To assume the political-theological heritage of modern Judaism in the right way implies the demand to bring this *unnatural* and *unnormal* existential situation to an end and to create a Jewish state for the stateless Jewish community. This means to suspend the Galut or better: *to suspend the suspension of the natural law*.

Baer is a *Zionist*. For the historian this means to naturalize history completely, i. e. to politicise the theological hope for redemption: here and now. Baer calls this political naturalization »a work of redemption« thus confusing the *theological* (p. 102) and the *political* dimension that he is supposed to separate properly. But by defining political action in theological terms he may be indicating that with political action the content of the theological belief is fully realized – so that in fact it can be described in a theological language which receives a rather metaphorical status. In this sense Baer hopes, »that for us the last consequence of the modern causal-historical thinking will coincide with the last conclusion« of the antique Jewish picture of history« (p.103).

One can say that in this hope for conversion of the *natural* and the *theological* picture of history we can find the strong ambivalences which haunt the history of the modern Jewish state from its beginnings, whether this state is the ›atchalta de geula‹ (beginning of redemption) as Rabbi Kook would say or whether it is free of all messianic implications as Gershom Scholem would hold against Rabbi Kook.[2] However interesting this issue may be, I wish to talk here rather about the condition of its possibility. And here is my claim: If we read Baer's historical account carefully we have to conclude that the condition of the possibility of the conversion of theology and politics is a function of the peculiar change of perspective of the historical events, which happens at the beginning of the 16th century – after the expulsion from Spain. This change could be best described as a change from the *apocalyptical vision* of history to its *natural description*. It is precisely the radicalised theological and mystical account of the Galut history *as apocalypse* which describes *Jewish existence* under the rule of the emperors and popes as a *being among the apocalyptical beasts* – think of book Daniel – and

---

[2] Compare in: Gershom Scholem: Od Davar. Pirqe morasa u-tehiyya. Kînnes we-ara'k Avraham Sapira. Tel Aviv: Am Oved, 1989 [Hebrew], Introduction of A. Shapira: Tradition as the origin of resurrection – on Gerschom Scholem's intellectual identity, p. 13–26, here p. 15.

which thus contains the possibility of analysing the *natural* behaviour of these beasts – the *Zoon Politikon* – in order to predict historical action and to protect oneself against it. When later on – in the 17th century – Jewish intellectuals like Simone Luzzato and Menasse Ben Israel (p. 69) will adopt this naturalistic point of view they will recommend Jewish presence before the kings not only in terms of economic and cultural benefits, but because they can assure the king that they – the weak Jewish Nation without a state – are no danger for the king, since – as Luzzato contends – the Jews have lost their *natural wildness* since their last rebellion against the Roman emperors (p. 83). No vanity and pride characterizes this community of loyal citizens.

When Baer analyses the situation of modern Jewry and modern Judaism and blames them for heavy confusions in their historical picture of the world he will point to the extreme distortions that the Jewish *natural* body politic has suffered – since this transformation from the mystical body. According to Baer *naturalisation* has stopped half way, since the natural rules have been accepted only as rules of description and not as rules which serve as a guide for proper political action. The apocalyptical turn into natural history after the Spanish expulsion has now, in the apocalyptical situation in Germany 1936, to be completed in its practical meaning; i. e. as the full restitution of the Jewish natural body through sovereign political action.

To know how to take over the politic-theological heritage means then to turn back to its *apocalyptical origins* in order to transform *natural description* into *natural-Zionist-practice*.

2. The definition of Galut

> Political servitude, dispersion, longing for liberation and reunification – sin, repentance and reconciliation – these are the lines which define the essence of Galut. (p. 6)

Baer introduces in this short drawing two systems of explanation of the Galut: The natural-political logic and the theological grammar.

– System 1: Political servitude, dispersion, reunification.
– System 2: Sin, repentance and reconciliation.

The theological self-understanding depends on a reduction of the real-political events to the religious grammar. The fact, that the Jewish people has been expelled from its homeland, is an act of God's punishment who has instrumentalized the Roman empire to perform his will. This divine judgement creates the very hope for a reconciliation with God through repentance and the redemption of the Jewish nation through God's action.

Baer obviously prefers the political description to the theological one. He describes the concept of the Galut for the second temple period as a unified trinity of *nation, land* and *Tora* (the latter he defines with Philo as *Politeia*, the constitution of law and study; p. 6). In this first period Galut is still perceived in its relation to a really existing political center of Jewish life in Palestine. If Baer defines the *trinity* of *Tora, land, people* as a *holy structure* in which the *Politeia* constitutes itself and does not forget to add to the concepts ›servitude‹, ›actual situation‹ and ›reunification‹ the attribute ›political‹ then he himself, the natural historian, already reduces the two systems in the opposite way. The concepts ›sin‹, ›repentance‹ etc. do not appear in Baer's own accord.

After the fall of Judea in the year 70 A. D. the *holy* structure of the trinity is transformed into a basically binary structure, based on *nation* and *Tora* alone. With this transformation the essential characteristics of Galut are defined. The synchronic unity of *Politeia, land, nation* is reduced to a binary structure of *nation* and *Politeia*, a constitution without a state. This transformation is parallel to the diachronic succession of Exile, political servitude and return, which is the restitution of the holy trinity.

3. The history of Galut

The history of Galut is described by Baer in a sequence of epochs which shows certain modifications and exchanges of dominant features in this structure; certain elements disappear, others step into the foreground. It is metaphorically visualized as the history of a body, corpus or statue which in the course of time splits into a mystical body on the one hand, and a natural/historical body on the other hand which, in consequence of the sufferings becomes more and more distorted, until the body is found dead with its bones lying scattered on the earth.

Baer distinguishes between seven main periods of this history – from the Roman times to the Christian domination of Europe, the time of the crusaders, the expulsion from Spain, the time of the early still religious enlightenment and finally the radical crisis of modern Judaism as a result of the abolition of the concept of the Galut. (I skip the details.) If we overlook the development according to Baer's reconstruction we can distinguish three main tendencies:

1) Because of the expulsion from the land »the system of ever growing interpretation of the Tora« becomes the decisive factor of the life of the people. This tendency even intensifies in the mystical interpretation of the Halacha and history which seems to be a compensation for the delay of redemption:

> Through the systematic kabbala which increases into enormous dimensions the problem of Galut is now integrated into a cosmic metaphysical framework in such a manner that the return into a reality is not possible any more. (p. 59)

Baer defines mystical Judaism as a kind of overcompensation, according to which the mystical consolation leads to the dissolution of the reality it came to console for.

2) Vis à vis this mystical reduction of history we find – from the time of the Spanish expulsion – an opposite tendency towards naturalization and political realism which defines the historical situation from the perspective of its politi-

cal, social and economical conditions. Baer traces this tendency down to Don Izchak Abravanel and recognizes it in its full articulation in Shlomo Ibn Virga (1520; p. 40) who becomes the founding father of modern Jewish *natural* historiography (p. 64). It is Virga who in fact enforces already a full reduction of the theological grammar of being to a natural and physical one.

3) It is this dialectics of the extremes, of a radical mystification on the one hand and the natural perspective of the events on the other hand which leads to the consciousness of a constantly widening gap. As already mentioned Judaism is now described metaphorically as a body which dissociates into two bodies: the holy and eternal body and the natural body. While the one holy body becomes so spiritual, the natural body suffers from the real political events and becomes more and more distorted. It is the ultimate dissociation of *Judaism's two bodies* which leads to the final sabbatian collapse of Judaism – which is the early signal for the total crisis of modern Judaism as a whole.

To know how to assume the political-theological heritage of this history means not only to recognize the fundamental dynamics which are at work here but it means to be able to recognize the mystical apocalyptical origins of modern naturalistic historiography *and* to bring this turn from the apocalypse to natural history to its full completion.

4. Apocalypse and nature

Now I want to go a bit into the details of this history of the Galut, but only in order to show why and how the transformation from apocalypse to natural history is actually working. We already mentioned the reduction of the Galut conception from the trinity of Politeia, land and nation to the binary structure after 70 A. D. According to Baer the history of the Galut from now on is interpreted in an analogy to the 7-days creation.

> After the first days of the holy history, when the temple still stood, the fifth and sixth day bring the domination of the wild beasts, i. e. of the great empires, until the world Sabbath will lead to the restitution of the harmony in heaven and on earth. (p. 8)

The galut consists basically of an especially cruel situation, which is a consequence of the opposition between the natural logic of the history of these empires and the holy logic of the history of Israel. When the natural agents of history act according to the principle of political power, the Jews, following their moral understanding of history are unarmed and defenseless and handed over to the martyrdom.

The condition of the Exile became aggravated with the Christian domination of the antique world, since Christianity claims to be the true community of God while the Galut existence of the Jews is perceived as the punishment for the *deicide* and as a symbol for the glorious victory of the Church. With the Christian age »the Jews were now degraded in the whole world to *a politically and religiously persecuted class«*. (p. 12) In the context of the destruction of the very last Jewish community in Palestine by the crusaders Baer speaks of a total retreat of the Jewish people from all active-political history: »The Jewish people« – he says – »withdraws from the line of the fighting nations and puts its history entirely into God's hand. This is a peculiar historical fact, which no historian has ever appreciated in the right way.« (p. 14) This retreat from history which results from the degradation of Galut into a more and more purely theological understanding which is reinforced by mystical-apocalyptical speculation.

In the treatise *Megilat Hamegale* by Abraham bar Chija (1129) the analogy (p. 21) between creation and history is apocalyptically intensified since the author of this book is convinced that with the destruction of the last Jewish community in Palestine the apocalyptical prophecy of Daniel is fulfilled: »The holy sanctuary is profaned and the Jews are expelled from Jerusalem.« (p. 21) In this context – 1) the growing gap between religious hope and historical reality, 2) the medieval rationalism on the one hand and the Christian apologetics on the other hand which both shake the foundations of traditions – mysticism takes over a decisive role in creating a new spiritual and halachic pillar for this tradition.

> The whole miraculous world of the tradition was now illuminated in a magic brilliance which spreaded even over the horrors of Galut. But the *renewed body* of the *nation* appeared much more like the *heavenly body* with which the dead are clothed after the last judgement. (p. 42)

In Samuel Usque's mystical treatise on redemption this process of spiritualization as a process in face of the catastrophic reality is reflected as the mystical transfiguration of Israel into a pure heavenly kingdom.

> While the Jewish people carries the yoke of the great empires of the world it in fact ascends in heaven step by step up to the very highest sphere where Israel is offered the *crown of the highest martyrdom*. (p. 82f.)

Usque's text is a fascinating document for the process where the aggravation of political servitude is compensated with the idea of the heavenly kingdom.

With the end of the Middle ages we can witness a growing elucidation of the natural-political conditions of the Galut as this very existence under the domination of the world empires. Such an approach Baer detects in the writings of the great Spanish statesman, humanist and mystic Don Izchak Abravanel. In fact Abravanel still believes that the Jewish people obey another – theological – causality than the other peoples who act according to the laws of nature (p. 53). But at the same time Abravanel analyses the constitutions and the political literature of Greece and Rome as well as the constitutions of his time with natural, causal and even aesthetical categories, very much in the humanist manner, and he concludes that the very natural *greatness* and *beauty* that characterizes these constitutions can be seen even in Jewish history which he implicitly includes in the realm of nature. He confines this natural Jewish history to the time of the Jewish kings though, i. e. before Galut (p. 53). These remarks are actually written when – as Baer contends – Abravanel writes his most important exegetic works, in a time of the greatest revolutions in Jewish history. It is also the time of intense messianic and apocalyptic speculation.

From these remarks one can conclude, what Baer does not do explicitly, that the modern Jewish historian is born in the apocalyptical scene, since the political realm – the realm of the beasts – is now interpreted according to its inner natural logic, the logic of the political animal: the *zoon politikon*. It is the very vision of history as the realm of the beasts and animals which allows at least implicitly a transformation of the perspective on historical events. This transformation from the pure theological/apocalyptical perspective to the historical-natural point of view is obviously mediated through the aesthetic dimension which reveals the connection between natural *greatness* and natural *beauty*. The state which develops from the play of natural forces can come to an ideal organization when these forces can be balanced out, so that they create a beautiful harmony.

This tendency towards the naturalisation of history becomes quite dominant in Shlomo Ibn Virgas *Schewet Jehuda* from 1520, another Jew who had to flee from Spain. His treatise is in fact an »investigation of the real and psychological causes of the expulsion of the Jews from Spain« (p. 64). This already hints – as Baer's own declaration – to a certain historical interest. Ibn Virga universalizes the natural perspective by expanding it from the history of the Jewish state to the period of Galut itself. »The oppression of the Jewish state happened according to a natural law. After the height of historical fortune it had inevitably to fall down« (p. 65). This means for Virga that »the Jews have accelerated their subjugation by inner conflicts which led strange powers to intervene in the affairs of the Jewish state« (p. 65).

In fact the destruction of the Jewish state was a consequence of the theological understanding of history which proved illusionary, because the Jews »began to neglect their military training in favour of their trust in God's help. When God deprived the Jews of his grace because of their sins they were left without any help«. (p. 65) In other words: the theological point of view remains pro forma valuable, since Ibn Virga calls Galut the time of God's examination of man, but the analysis just quoted offers the possible interpretation that the *sin* consisted in the fact, that Israel neglected its political, military and economical skills. *Sin* would be nothing else than *natural weakness*. Possibly *sin* consists in the fact that Israel relied on the theological interpretation of the events which culminates in messianic hope. So one can find here the beginning of the process of the reduction of the theological meaning to a purely political meaning. *Thus God appears as the principle of nature itself which is nothing else but the principle of self-conservation.*

Ibn Virga even analyses anti-Semitism in naturalistic terms as a function of social tensions. He drops the idea that it is a sign of God's punishment. As a political realist he offers a series of real-political solutions to this tension, among them practical laws which should regulate the relations between the Christian majority and the Jewish minority. He is ready to consider the possibility of a return of the Jewish people to their homeland and of the construction of a Jewish state, but he is convinced that inner conflicts will lead again to the destruction of this state. Baer summarizes: Ibn Virga does not give up »the hope for a full political redemption, but he criticizes the belief that Galut is a divine punishment« (p. 66f.).

Now Baer is constantly constructing an analogy between the situation of the Spanish Jews after 1492 and the German Jews after 1933. This analogy can be applied as well to the Marranian character of both already before the actual catastrophe. Although German Jews in modern Protestant Germany were not compelled to convert to Christianity like the Spanish Jews, their assimilation and conversion to Protestantism is, according to Baer, a consequence of enormous social pressure. But with all the differences between the two, both forms of Marranism are part of the apocalyptic picture that characterizes the two historical situations. Baer's analogy serves as a key for his implicit construction of the transformation from apocalypse to political naturalism. To my opinion and interpretation of what I would call Baer's historiographic subtext, the second apocalyptic situation serves as the background for a completion of the naturalistic turn that began around 1500. When Ibn Virga initiates the first transformation from apocalyptic vision to natural description, then Baer – the German ›reincarnation‹ of Ibn Virga – will complete this apocalyptical transformation and expand it from description to political action: where Ibn Virga refrains from the consequence to negate Galut by sovereign action, Baer will plead for this naturalistic consequence in favour of a Jewish state.

5. The Jewish nation's two bodies

Between these two historical moments of danger, between the Spanish expulsion and the rise of national socialism in Germany modern Jewish historiography unfolds. This historical understanding develops from the radical opposition between the mystical and the political point of view of history, the first indulging in mystical fantasies of messianic redemption, the other becoming more and more interested in a legal-political reform of the situation of the Jews. The latter's approach is technical in the sense that it is looking for practical solutions of a problem, which is considered to be basically a political one.

This dissociation of the theological and the political point of view is – as already indicated – reflected in Baer's rhetoric of the national body. On the one hand this body is transfigured into a *mystical body* and on the other hand this body becomes *natural*. The mystical body is similar to the heavenly body, while the earthly body is deformed and distorted by the historical sufferings. The natural body can only be cured by a natural therapy, while the heavenly one is secured by God. Natural therapy is basically a political therapy which tries to adjust to the political affairs of the moment. One could argue that only now the Jewish *civitas dei* has actually received its real political counterpart: the *Jewish civitas terrena*.

Deus sive natura

The natural perspective of the Galut leads to an effort to convince the former apocalyptic beast, the Christian Sovereign, of the natural advantage he can gain from the presence of the Jews in his state. This usefulness is not so much a result of the economic and diplomatic skills of the Jews, but – as Simone Luzzato claims in his defense of the rights of the Venetian Jews from 1638 – the fact that Jews are no threat to the state. Although the Jews practice solidarity they are a weak nation, so that there is no reason to be afraid of any Jewish rebellion or revolution against the existing power. The last Jewish rebellion – Luzzato writes – was the upheaval against the Roman emperor Trajan (p. 72). Since then Jews have lost their »original wildness«. In other words: Among the animals one can only exist politically if one renounces one's own animality, that is: one renounces the political claim for sovereignty. Jews, Luzzato adds, are without »pride and vanity«. Considering the fact that the modern sovereign state is – as Thomas Hobbes will say in his famous *Leviathan* from 1649 – constructed against human *pride and vanity*,[3] both being the source of rebellion and disobedience, Luzzato's description of the Jews becomes clear in its political intention. Baer cites an illuminating allegory Luzzato uses here in order to recommend the Jews in the eyes of the sovereign ruler. It is formulated in aesthetic terms referring to concepts of Renaissance humanism, which seems to be the medium sphere which enables the transformation of the theological into a natural point of view:

> When the weather beaten fragment of an old statue from Phidias or Lysipp is worth its price, then the relic of the old Hebrew people should not be despised, although it is distorted by the sufferings and by the long servitude. According to a general agreement this people has been once created by the greatest artist who has saved it in its form of administration and institution of life. (p. 75f.)

The mystically revived body is equaled by a real torso now, who is distorted by the sufferings as well as by the self-conception of the Jewish political body as a non-rebellious ›being in the world‹.

6. The final forgetfullness of Galut

From here Baer draws a direct line to the modern enlightenment, which leads to the final collapse of a genuine Jewish culture in Western Europe. Baer deduces this breakdown from the breakdown of the dialectics of the nation's two bodies.

I shall leap here over the details of this reconstruction, however interesting and sum up the main issues of Baer's reconstruction which is influenced by

---

[3] Thomas Hobbes: Leviathan. In: The English Works of Thomas Hobbes of Malmesbury. Ed. by William Molesworth. 2. Reprint, Aalen: Scientia-Verlag 1966, Vol. III, p. 307: »Hitherto I have set forth the nature of man, whose pride and other passions have compelled him to submit himself to government.«

Scholem's thesis[4] about the origins of the enlightenment in Sabbatean theology. Baer in fact believes that the Sabbatean messianic movement collapsed due to the unbearable dissociation of the two realities: the existence as a Civitas Dei and its real political misery. He mentions basically three important issues in this context of the aftermath of the Sabbatean movement.

1) The impact of the collapse of this movement for the understanding of history;
2) The antinomian aspect of Sabbatean theology;
3) The idea that Galut has a hidden mystical meaning as the period of the liberation of the sparks being scattered in the world of evil.

These three lead to what might be called the final forgetfulness of Galut in the enlightenment. It is the process of emancipation and assimilation which Baer describes as a will to political self-negation and self-liquidation which creates the modern Jewish marrano, who, different from his Spanish forefather, is actually willing to lose his hidden identity. All this, Baer says, can be seen from Mosche Chagis' analysis of the modern Jewish mind in *Sefat Emet* (1707; p. 96f.).

7. Deus sive natura – between Spinoza and Kabbala

In this context of the total collapse of the integrating concept of a unique Jewish history reflected in the idea of Galut and at the beginning of the total destruction of Jewish culture in national-socialist Germany, Baer, the historian, says: »Galut has indeed returned to its point of departure. It is and remains what it always has been: political servitude.« (p. 101) And it is this political servitude which – from the naturalized perspective of the modern historian, has to be suspended. This suspension as the suspension of the suspension of the natural causality is called by Baer a »Zionist work of redemption«. So what Baer does here, is: he calls for a redefinition of the political reality in Europe as Galut, in order to negate this Galut in national-political terms.

Indeed, if theology can be naturalized and politicized, if *God is nature*, then the natural political action, which draws all the consequences of the naturalistic turn from 1520, can indeed be called a *work* of redemption as the naturalistic view of history can adopt the theological term and define the historical situation as Galut. With this rhetoric Baer proves to be a Zionist Spinocist. *Deus sive natura* is the well-known metaphysical axiom of this Marrano's Tractatus Theologico-Politicus. Baer does not miss the apocalyptic dimension here when he, the follower of Ibn Virga, employs a retranslation of the natural picture into an apocalyptic vision. It is the *torso*, the distorted natural body,

---

[4] Scholem: Zum Verständnis des Sabbatianismus (note 1); id., Die Theologie des Sabbatianismus im Lichte Abraham Cardosos [1928]. In: id., Judaica. Frankfurt a. M.: Suhrkamp 1963 (Bibliothek Suhrkamp; 106); id., Die Metamorphose des häretischen Messianismus der Sabbatianer in religiösen Nihilismus im 18. Jahrhundert. In: Judaica. Studien zur jüdischen Mystik. Frankfurt a. M.: Suhrkamp 1970 (Bibliothek Suhrkamp; 333).

Deus sive natura

which has died in the course of the history of Galut and which Baer integrates into a biblical, apocalyptical vision, namely the prophet Hesekiel's vision of the dry bones scattered, on the earth. In Baer's own words:

> From the living national body there were left only scattered dry bones, of which nobody could foresee that they would – according to the words of the prophet – be unified to one vital whole. (p. 99)

But this unification of the scattered bones to one vital whole is – against the apocalyptical dimension – translated into simple natural action, into a *work of political redemption*.

Baer prefers kabbalistic pantheism on Spinoza's pantheism for obvious reasons. The Kabbala contains a national myth while Spinoza has transgressed the borders of national loyalty. Baer's conversion of the theological and the political seems best defined by the great kabbalist Maharal, whom Baer quotes at the very end of his *Zionist Tractatus*:

> God has assigned every nation its place and to the Jewish nation he has assigned the Land of Israel as its place. Galut is the abandonment of the natural place. But all things which abandon their natural place loose their natural hold until they return to their natural place. The dispersion of Israel among the people is something unnatural. [...] According to the order of nature it is unbearable that one nation dominates another nation, because God has created every nation for itself. Galut cannot persist according to the law of nature. (p. 102)

This quotation is introduced without any clear context, but Baer adds to this kabbalistic vision of the unity of *God and nature*:

> We may refer to such conceptions of Galut with the consciousness that the *old belief* has received *a new meaning*. (p. 102)

Doerte Bischoff

Exile, Trauma and the Modern Jewish Experience: The Example of Else Lasker-Schüler

For literary critics, to deal with the concept of exile in the 20th century always means to enter extremely complex and precarious territory. On the one hand, in this period of mass expatriations exile becomes a widespread experience, while on the other hand exile becomes a prime metaphor for a modern condition, in particular the condition of the modern writer who cannot rely on metaphysical truths any more.[1] The emergence of psychoanalysis may be regarded as only one symptom, though a highly telling and influential one of a new awareness of a foreignness that is not caused by any act external to the individual but that reveals itself to be bound into the very structure of subjectivity and identity itself. It has been argued that it is no coincidence that it was a Jew from an assimilated German-Austrian background who founded this new science, a science which fundamentally calls into question all scientific striving for objective knowledge. The fascination and scandal which marked the reception of psychoanalysis both reacted to an ambivalence inherent in the Freud's attempt to explore and explain what had been regarded as essentially unexplainable. While the interpretation of dreams, myths and mysteries which Freud proclaimed as the *via regia* to the subconscious presented itself as a consistent implementation of the Enlightenment paradigm, it also demonstrated the impossibility of ever getting hold of identity or truth as such by exposing their dependence on language and rhetoric.[2] Transforming the world into a readable text, psychoanalysis also suggests that there is no privileged vantage point which ensures a definite, final reading.[3] Thus

---

[1] The question of what modern literature is and when it begins has, of course, been subject to debate and different categorizations. Since in this paper texts belonging to literary modernism in the narrow sense of the word, e. g. implying the historical and aesthetic condition of the *fin de siècle* and the first half of the 20th century, are discussed in relation to what has been called ›the project of modernity‹ which is usually identified with the Cartesian turn and the dialectics of Enlightenment, the two most common usages of the word and their connections and continuities are evoked here. For a discussion of exile and modernity see Terry Eagleton: Exiles and Émigrés. Studies in Modern Literature. London: Chatto & Windus 1970; Andrew Gurr: Writers in Exile. The Identity of Home in Modern Literature. Brighton, Sussex et. al.: Harvester Press 1981 (Harvester Studies in Contemporary Literature and Culture; 4).

[2] See Stephen Frosch: Psychoanalysis, Science and ›Truth‹. In: Freud 2000. Ed. by Anthony Elliott. Cambridge: Polity Press 1998, p. 13–37.

[3] See Zygmunt Bauman: Moderne und Ambivalenz. Das Ende der Eindeutigkeit. Aus dem Engl. von Martin Suhr. Hamburg: Junius 1992 (Modernity and Ambivalence,

the position that is invested with an unprecedented power and knowledge, the position of the analyst himself, appears at the same time to be bound to the contingencies and ambiguities that determine all human attempts to construct worlds and bestow them with meaning. The Freudian hermeneutics is not guided by the struggle to find a meaning behind the words, to discover an original state where language and the real coincide, but instead is characterized by an ongoing process of reading and interpretation that does not come to a standstill.

Susan Handelman and others have described this mode, that constantly refers epistemology to an irreducable mediality, knowledge to the ways in which it is achieved and presented, as a resurgence of a rabbinic reading practice in modern literature and theory.[4] Even though the assumption of such a proximity might not be unproblematic, since it recalls the antisemitic verdict of psychoanalysis as a ›Jewish science‹,[5] it leads to the question as to whether exile as a central category of the Jewish tradition still manifests itself in the Europe of the 20th century, where Talmud readings and a firm belief in the biblical account of exile as constitutive for Jewish identity for most Jews did not belong to a common experience and practice any more. Rather, the gradual assimilation process in the 18th and 19th centuries had thoroughly alienated Western Jews from these continuities and traditions. If, in this process the Jews had become the touchstone for the possibility of emancipation that had been at the core of modern concepts of individual and collective identity, by the turn of the century they were the ones to experience the limits of these universalist promises most directly. The moment they set out to achieve complete assimilation it turned out that they were rejected again: while the rejection in the past had always referred to their (self-proclaimed) otherness, however, modern antisemitism constructed it anew as a difference going beyond self-definition and relying solely on the ›scientific‹ judgment of the hegemonic culture.

The Jews, finally classified as vermin and parasites, were assumed to embody not another culture but the other of all culture. Thus the totalitarian effort of Nazi-ideology to define once and for all cultural value and meaning can be regarded as a phantasmatic attempt to eliminate all difference by establishing an absolute community beyond the contingencies of human action and imagination. Its own signifying practices appear as unmediated acts of self-creation which deny any difference between the sign and the real. Its specificity – and at the same time its

---

Cambridge: Polity Press 1991), p. 216f. [References refer to the translated edition in cases where I did not have access to the original edition.]

[4] Susan A. Handelman: The Slayers of Moses. The Emergence of Rabbinic Interpretation in Modern Literary Theory. Albany: State University of New York Press 1982 (SUNY Series on Modern Jewish Literature); Renate Schlesier: Hermeneutik auf dem Königsweg zum Unbewußten. Freuds *Traumdeutung* (1900). In: Jahrhundertbücher. Große Theorien von Freud bis Luhmann. Hg. von Walter Erhart et al. München: Beck 2000 (Beck'sche Reihe; 1398), p. 14–37.

[5] See Georges-Arthur Goldschmidt: Als Freud das Meer sah. Freud und die deutsche Sprache. Aus dem Frz. von Brigitte Große. Zürich: Ammann 1999 (Quand Freud voit la mer, Paris: Buchet/Castel 1999), p. 173.

modernity in a certain sense[6] – lies in the megalomaniac attempt to posit an omnipotent subject that does not *project* itself towards a utopian, spiritual or metaphysical horizon, but *identifies* itself with this ultimate borderline where human symbolizing processes merge with visions and myths of the absolute.[7] Other interpretations of this phantasmatic confusion of word and reality also suggest a certain connection to a Christian idea of redemption according to which the word becomes flesh, while in the Jewish tradition the coming of the Messiah and therefore a divine materialization on earth is deferred to an incalculable future.[8]

As Zygmunt Bauman has argued, it was precisely this totalising belief in the word and the attempt to assert identity beyond difference which prompted Jewish intellectuals and artists to explore the ambiguities and contradictions inherent in the project of modernity.[9] Many of those who were exposed to the radically excluding violence of signification transformed this experience into cultural documents giving testimony to the internal coincidence of representation and exclusion, self-assertion and rejection.[10] If Jews were called the »pioneers of modernism«,[11] this did not only refer to Jewish engagement for various emancipation processes but also to a specific sensitivity for their blind spots and hidden violence. In this context exile no longer means separation from a Jewish homeland and the memory of the destruction of the Temple as a specific Jewish

---

[6] For an interpretation of the Holocaust as an ultimate consequence of modern instrumental and totalising thinking, which is of course a central point in Horkheimer and Adorno's *Dialectics of Enlightenment*, see also Zygmunt Bauman: Modernity and the Holocaust. Ithaca: Cornell University Press 1989 and id., Moderne und Ambivalenz (note 3), p. 69.

[7] See Philippe Lacoue-Labarthe: Die Fiktion des Politischen. Heidegger, die Kunst und die Politik. Aus dem Frz. von Thomas Schestag. Stuttgart: Edition Schwarz 1990 (La fiction du politique. Heidegger, l'art et la politique. Paris: Bourgois 1988), p. 110: »Die im Grund der neuzeitlichen Metaphysik angelegte Verunendlichung oder Absolutsetzung des Subjekts stößt hier auf das Resultat ihrer *Operation*: die Gemeinschaft am Werk und an der Arbeit (National*sozialismus* als National*ästhetizismus*) bearbeitet und bewerkt, wenn man so sagen kann, sich selbst, und vollendet so den subjektiven Prozeß par excellence, den Prozeß der Selbsterschaffung und Selbstbildung.« See also Jean-Luc Nancy: La communauté désœuvrée. Paris: Bourgois 1986 (Collection »Détroits«), p. 13.

[8] Margarete Susman: Der jüdische Geist. In: id., Das Nah- und Fernsein des Fremden. Essays und Briefe. Hg. von Ingeborg Nordmann. Frankfurt a. M.: Jüdischer Verlag 1992, p. 209–226, here p. 212f.: »Dem Christen wurde das Wort Fleisch, dem Juden blieb das Wort Geist.«

[9] Bauman, Moderne und Ambivalenz (note 3), p. 234.

[10] This is not to suggest that Auschwitz, which clearly stands for the extreme elimination of space for expression and resistance generated creativity. However, literary and philosophical writings after the Holocaust have often taken up modernist modes, and in particular postmodern criticism of representation and identity often explicitly refers to a specific Jewish experience in the 20th century.

[11] Michael A. Meyer: Jüdische Identität in der Moderne. Aus dem Amerikanischen von Anne Ruth Frank-Strauss. Frankfurt a. M.: Jüdischer Verlag 1992 (Jewish Identity in the Modern World. Seattle et. al.: University of Washington Press 1990), p. 116.

symbol for the oneness of place and (absolut) meaning. The split between self and origin, actual dwelling place and home, which had been a mark of a Jewish difference (and had also been connected with their being the Chosen People), now concerns the intimate connection between universal concepts of humanity and their radical other.

This new quality which exile has taken on in modernity was already noted by contemporaries. In 1933, for example, Margarete Susman published an essay on ›the Jewish spirit‹ in which she emphasizes changes in the Jewish experience in the modern world. Only with the assimilation into the Western world did the »desertedness and homelessness of the Jew complete itself«.[12] »We understand nothing of the life in which we stand [...]. [...] We are absolutely and totally in exile.«[13] Jean Améry describes his exile experience as an expulsion from familiar contexts and beliefs provided by the language of his childhood. After he was forced to leave Nazi-Germany in 1939, the perception of his senses suddenly no longer naturally coincided with meaning and orientation.[14] Even if in exile he gradually learned to ›see through‹ the signs which at first impose themselves on him like a mysterious ›Etruscan Script‹, he never again feels totally at one with a symbolic world he has acquired intellectually and not – like the mother-tongue and the semiotic code of his native land – intuitively.[15] Remarkably, Améry also observes the difference between a Yiddish-speaking Polish Jew he meets in Belgium and himself: while the former embodies for him the ›wandering Jew‹ for whom homelessness and the change of places belongs to an old tradition and routine, thus to a certain extent providing identity, the assimilated ›modern‹ Jew loses all his normal ties and support, finding himself in a radical exile which deprives the self of all possibilities to ground his identity in a collective symbolic.[16] Home, the mother-tongue, childhood, all this is not only irretrievably lost, but fundamentally called into question, as it is claimed by an enemy who does not leave any space for difference. In retrospect it appears as a construct that relies on the illusion of self-evidence which – after the violent expulsion – is shattered and can never be regained. The condition of exile thus appears, as Joseph Brodsky has put it, »first of all, [as] a linguistic event«.[17] This accounts for the

---

[12] Susman, Der jüdische Geist (note 8), p. 219f. [Translation mine, if not indicated otherwise].

[13] Ibid., p. 221.

[14] Jean Améry: Jenseits von Schuld und Sühne. Bewältigungsversuche eines Überwältigten. Stuttgart: Klett-Cotta 1977, p. 82: »Gesichter, Gesten, Kleider, Häuser, Worte (auch wenn ich sie halbwegs verstand) waren Sinneswirklichkeit, aber keine deutbaren Zeichen. In dieser Welt war für mich keine Ordnung.«

[15] Ibid., p. 82f.

[16] Ibid., p. 78: »Der Wanderjude hatte mehr Heimat als ich.« Und: »Ich war ein Mensch, der nicht mehr nicht mehr ›wir‹ sagen konnte und darum nur noch gewohnheitsmäßig, aber nicht im Gefühl vollen Selbstbesitzes ›ich‹ sagte.«

[17] Joseph Brodsky: This Condition We Call Exile. In: The New York Review of Books, January 21 1988, p. 16, 18. Cit. after Elisabeth Bronfen: Exil in der Literatur. Zwischen Metapher und Realität. In: Arcadia 28 (1993), p. 167–183, here p. 172.

experience that the signs lose the neutrality and self-evidence they usually have for someone growing up in a certain speech community which, in its ritualised signifying practices, closely links language and meaning. The moment the referential function of language is no longer sure the signs become opaque and draw attention to the production of meaning and the limits of understanding and representation. This struggle with language, which asserts itself as the only accessible home left while at the same time bearing the mark of absence and loss,[18] is shared by the person forced out of his/her native places and contexts and the intellectual or artist whose creativity springs from the absence of a truth beyond or before the words. Although there may be many good reasons for differentiating between political exile and the use of the word in aesthetic and philosophical discourse, literary criticism is very often confronted with the indissolubility of the two. In focussing on the ways in which signifying processes and the limits of re-presentation surface in narratives of exile, however, exile as metaphor and as (biographical, historical) reality can be discussed in correlation.[19] Exile studies then direct their interest to the structure on the narrative, to the ways it constructs referential ground and reflects an ›in-between‹ that marks the language that problematizes home in the sense of given meaning and identity instead of presupposing it. This perspective might prevent the critic from basing the argument primarily on the knowledge of the writer's life and from projecting assumptions about the existential meaning or subversive power of exile onto the text instead of analysing its ›exilic modes‹ which might reveal much less unambiguous ›messages‹. But it also makes it possible to account for specific historical and political conditions of exile and the questions of how they affect modes and limits of representation.

If, in her inspiring essay on *Exile in Literature: Between Metaphor and Reality*, Elisabeth Bronfen cites and operates with plenty of Jewish examples, this is certainly no coincidence.[20] Although functioning as a prime metaphor in Jewish narratives, exile has also always had a historical and political meaning in the Jewish experience. However, what seems characteristic is that the actual condition of being marginalized, oppressed or persecuted by the host countries, a condition which to a large extent has dominated Jewish life in history, is never completely identified with the meaning of Jewishness, even though it essentially marks its material being. To be a Jew is not just to be the flip side

---

[18] See Shmuel Trigano: Le Temps de l'Exil. Paris: Éditions Payot & Rivages 2001, p. 33: »Une des première découvertes que fait l'exilé est ainsi celle de la puissance et de l'épaisseur du langage, capable de porter le monde [...]. Avant le départ, les mots désignaient ce qui existait en dehors d'eux. Dans l'exil ce sont les mots qui portent l'extériorité, l'abstrait porte le concret. L'identité devient un récit, la réalité, une mémoire. Il n'y a plus de paysage sans la narration qui le dépeint, ou plutôt le reconstruit dans le prisme de la mémoire. L'habitation devient effet de langage, sans perdre de sa consistance ni de son épaisseur.«

[19] See esp. Bronfen, Exil in der Literatur (note 17), p. 172f.

[20] Bronfen does not explicitly comment on it, nor does she develop a thesis concerning the relation of a Jewish notion of exile and the connection of exile as metaphor and reality.

of antisemitic projection and provocation. Rather, the tradition and experience of the Jews, as Maurice Blanchot notes, gives them the possibility to be more than what has been assigned to them, to go beyond signification and names given by others, by the hosts, by antisemites.[21] Its positive meaning is that it brings something to the fore that can be described as a relationship to oneself and to the other human being which preserves singularity against unifying and universal definitions.[22] If modern Jews can be regarded as symptoms that seismographically recorded the described shift towards a radical exile which cannot be attributed to a specific symbolic tradition, exile at the same time takes on a universal meaning.[23] It appears not as a relative term signifying the loss of a certain home, truth or substance, nor the fate of only a certain group of people, but characterizes the human condition as marked by a coincidence of self-assertion and separation.[24] In describing the Jewish existence as a paradoxical living in exile and in the kingdom at the same time,[25] André Neher articulates a notion of exile that has been elaborated by modern as well as postmodern literature and theory. It signifies a resistance against unity insofar as it exposes the impossibility of signs or symbolic systems to signify completely, to exhaust and to appropriate reality. Since this mode of exilic existence does not aim at transcending the material world, but rather takes it as momentary dwelling places which always reveal their contingent character, it differs from a concept of spiritual exile that has dominated Western philosophical discourse. In his recent book on the *Time of Exile* which owes much to other French thinkers like Blanchot, Edmond Jabès, Emmanuel Lévinas, Jean-Luc Nancy or Jacques Derrida, Shmuel Trigano differentiates between the Socratic tradition of Western thought and the Jewish tradition.[26] While the former conceptualises the material world as something that has to be overcome in order to reach the ›real‹ world of ideas and thus establishes a hierarchy be-

---

[21] Maurice Blanchot: Jude sein. In: M. Blanchot: Das Unzerstörbare. Ein unendliches Gespräch über Sprache, Literatur und Existenz. Aus dem Frz. von Hans-Joachim Metzger und Bernd Wilczek. München et al.: Hanser 1991 (Edition Akzente) (L'indestructible. In: M. Blanchot: L'entretien infini, Paris: Gallimard 1969, p. 180–200), p. 181–193, here p. 183.

[22] Ibid.

[23] Bauman, Moderne und Ambivalenz (note 3), p. 196f.

[24] Ibid., p. 234: »Die Universalität der Abwesenheit und das Leere sind die einzige Universalität, die es gibt; die jüdische Einzigartigkeit ist die einzige Universalität, die es gibt; alle Universalität ist jüdisch.«

[25] André Neher: Jüdische Identität. Einführung in den Judaismus. Aus dem Frz. von Holger Fock. Mit einem Nachwort von Rudolf Pfisterer. Hamburg: Europäische Verlagsanstalt 1995 (L'identité juive. Paris: Editions Seghers 1989), p. 24. As Sidra DeKoven Ezrahi points out, for Jewish memory and imagination »the yearning for ultimate homecoming is compatible with the most radical form of homelessness« (S. DeKoven Ezrahi: Booking Passage. Exile and Homecoming in the Modern Jewish Imagination. Berkeley: University of California Press 2000 [Contraversions; 12], p. 7).

[26] This and the following: Trigano, Le Temps de l'Exil (note 18), p. 24f.

tween the sensual and the spiritual, Judaism does not categorically separate senses and spirit. Rather, it regards both as constitutive of reality, the form and meaning of which, however, is constantly transgressed and reshaped. Both concepts connect exile and existence: while the Socratic vision identifies it with an inferior, unredeemed state, in the Jewish perspective it holds the promise for another world which appears not beyond the material, beyond flesh, blood and stone, but in and through their ever new manifestations.[27] This does not necessarily contradict the above-mentioned tendency of Western (Christian) thought to orient itself towards an incarnation of the spiritual and metaphysical, since in its eschatological, teleological or dialectical striving it typically depends on the projection of a sublation of the oppositions into an ideal all-encompassing unity.[28] Contrary to this view which usually implies the notion of an original wholeness, of an origin ›in God‹ which in some sense has to be regained, the primal scene of the Jewish imagination as depicted by Trigano as well as Blanchot is departure and separation.[29] Abraham, called by God to leave everything behind and go towards an unknown future, abandons all possessions and securities to deliver himself up to an exile that links identity to an ongoing movement of separation and the crossing of boundaries.[30]

Clearly, this notion of exile that subverts all efforts to assert and legitimize identity by suggesting an original or final truth transcending the materiality of

---

[27] Ibid., p. 25: »L'exil abrahamique délivre, contrairement à la voie socratique, la possibilité d'une existence dans le monde, d'un autre rapport à l'être. Il porte le germe d'une connaissance de la vérité qui ne renonce pas au sensible ni à la réalité. [...] Ce n'est pas à ses sens qu'il l'appelle à renoncer (pour acquérir la capacité purement intellectuelle de contempler les idées), c'est à une plus grande conscience qu'il le convoque, sur tout son être. Non pas renier sa chair dans le monde mais à continuer la marche, à faire du déracinement, un exil.« For the connection of the sensual and the spiritual in Judaism, see also Neher, Jüdische Identität (note 25), p. 128.

[28] In his essay on Jewishness, Blanchot also emphasizes the difference between Greek and Christian thinking on the one hand and the Jewish condition on the other. While the first essentially reduces all difference to a universal same (die Herrschaft des Selben) this is avoided by the Jewish mode which is directed against totalising assimilation projects. See Blanchot, Jude sein (note 21), p. 187f.

[29] Ibid., p. 187: »Der Jude ist der Mensch des Ursprungs, der sich auf den Ursprung bezieht, nicht indem er bleibt, sondern indem er sich entfernt und so zum Ausdruck bringt, daß die Wahrheit des Anfangs in der Trennung liegt.« See also Neher, Jüdische Identität (note 25), p. 19–21: »Der Hebräer ist der abrahamitische Mensch. Wenn der Jude sich als Hebräer fühlt, ist er bereit, Abrahams Entscheidung noch einmal zu treffen und sie zu wiederholen; bereit, sich vom Bestehenden loszureißen [...] Es ist die Bereitschaft, die Seinsbedingung des Hebräischen in seiner etymologischen Bedeutung anzunehmen. Hebräisch: *ivri*, das setzt die Erfahrung des *Übergangs*, des *Übersetzens* voraus. [...] Das Exil ist eine Mission, die den Juden überall hinführt, wo ein Übersetzen stattfinden soll, und so versetzt das Hebräischsein den Juden in eine Art weltweiten Taumel, macht es zu seiner Bestimmung, im Handeln Bruder aller Menschen zu sein.«

[30] Blanchot, Jude sein (note 21), p. 185; Trigano, Le Temps de l'Exil (note 18), p. 14f., 25, 30, 44.

the world as well as of the symbols and signs signifying it, enjoys much attention among postmodern thinkers. In literary criticism it has been received in connection with various readings of texts from all centuries, whereby the specific reference to a Jewish tradition (biblical accounts and aspects of the Jewish diaspora) from which Blanchot, Trigano and others draw their arguments usually do not play a significant role any more. Rather, deconstructive readings tend to generalize textual strategies and lose sight of historical and political contexts and their possible impact on narratives. This, of course, can be very unsatisfactory when it comes to the discussion of texts the production of which is closely linked to an actual exile experience which threatens to lose all specificity when conflated with a universalising concept of exile as the condition of art or humanity as such. However, as my introductory remarks suggest, it is not only possible, but also very promising and revealing, to take into account a certain historical dimension when discussing or implying a Jewish notion of exile. Reflections on the mutual influence of modernism and the Jewish condition in the late 19th and early 20th century can open up the field towards a broader semiotic approach that includes not only literary documents but also analyses signifying practices which manifest themselves in ideologies and narratives of political action and reaction.

Here also lies the chance to explore relations between two academic traditions which have both dealt with exile as their central concern but until now have hardly taken notice of each other. While French thinkers especially like the ones discussed above, privilege a Jewish tradition of exile and emphasize its linguistic aspects and implications, »Exilforschung« as a field of study in German literatury studies that developed in the 1970s has focussed almost exclusively on the period between 1933 and 1945, and thus on texts written by those who had to leave Nazi-Germany. In recent years there has been much self-reflection and self-criticism within this field, claiming that the presupposition that everything written in exile at this time was somehow part of a larger project to liberate and unite all forces against a barbarian claim for power produced its own myths and blind spots.[31] While few earlier contributions had pleaded for an appropriate consideration of the aesthetic dimension of exile literature and warned against it being reduced to merely a function of historical, political or moralistic presumptions,[32]

---

[31] Lutz Winckler: Mythen der Exilforschung? In: Exilforschung 13 (1995), p. 68–81; Bernhard Spies: Exilliteratur – ein abgeschlossenes Kapitel? Überlegungen zu Stand und Perspektiven der literaturwissenschaftlichen Exilforschung. In: Exilforschung 14 (1996), p. 11–30; Claudia Albert: Ende der Exilforschung? Eine Überlegung anläßlich neuerer Veröffentlichungen zum Thema Exilliteratur. In: Internationales Archiv für Sozialgeschichte der Literatur 24 (1999), No. 2, p. 180–187.

[32] See Renate Werner: Transparente Kommentare. Überlegungen zu historischen Romanen deutscher Exilautoren. In: Poetica 9 (1977), p. 324–351; Guy Stern: Prolegomena zu einer Typologie der Exilliteratur. In: G. Stern: Literatur im Exil. Gesammelte Aufsätze 1959–1989. Ismaning: Max Hueber 1998, p. 37–52, here p. 38 (the paper was originally presented at a conference on »Schreiben im Exil. Zur Ästhetik der deutschen Exilliteratur 1933–1945« in 1982); Wulf Koepke: Die Wirkung des Exils auf Sprache und Stil. Ein Vorschlag zur Forschung. In: Exilforschung 3 (1985), p. 225–237.

the latest criticism is even more comprehensive when it attacks the »circle of legitimation« in which these studies of exile have been trapped: by assuming unifying characteristics or messages in the texts examined they really only produced a seemingly coherent ›other‹ to national socialist ideology which then could serve as a matrix for various projections of alternative visions of cultural and/or political identity.[33] This should not be a general verdict against a field of study – since to a certain extent it holds true for any research project – but it is clear that by now a general paradigm shift in literary and cultural studies has occasioned new methodological approaches and differentiations. Already at the beginning of the 1990s Ernst Loewy, a prominent figure of German »Exilforschung«, remarked (self-)critically that the predominant orientation towards antifascism which had characterized the study of exile literature in the 1970s and 1980s might have served the function of a »kind of historical screen memory« which prevented the thematisation of the mass expatriation and extermination of the European Jews for a certain period of time in which it seemed impossible to find concepts or proper words to account for it.[34] In fact, it is striking that the question of a Jewish perspective on this radical exile which clearly presented a limit to all possible transformations of an exterior threat into an active and creative self-definition, is addressed only rarely in this field of research.[35]

Of course, Zionism is the most obvious answer to this threat, however, since it relies on a specific reading of the Jewish notion of exile – namely interpreting it as something that can, and has to be, ended by a return and recovery of a Jewish homeland – it marks a break with a tradition in which identity and exile had been linked in a paradoxical way. So structurally there were indeed similarities between Zionist and assimilationist rhetoric since the former advocated, as Hannah Arendt argued, that the Jewish people become like other peoples in terms of home, possessions and identity.[36] In her recent work on *Exile and*

---

[33] See Spies, Exilliteratur (note 31), p. 12–18.

[34] Ernst Loewy: Zum Paradigmenwechsel in der Exilliteraturforschung. In: Exilforschung 9 (1991), S. 208–217, here p. 212. See also his contribution to the volume Deutsch-jüdische Exil- und Emigrationsliteratur im 20. Jahrhundert. Symposion der Hebräischen Universität Jerusalem Mai 1989. Hg. von Itta Shedletzky und Hans Otto Horch. Tübingen: Max Niemeyer 1993 (Conditio Judaica. Studien und Quellen zur deutsch-jüdischen Literatur- und Kulturgeschichte; 3), p. 15–28.

[35] In addition to the volume cited above, see Manfred Schlösser: Deutsch-Jüdische Dichtung des Exils. In: Emuna 4 (1968), No. 2, p. 250–265. This paper was reprinted in: Exilliteratur 1933–1945. Hg. von Wulf Koepke und Michael Winkler. Darmstadt: Wissenschaftliche Buchgesellschaft 1989 (Wege der Forschung; 647), p. 279–299. Schlösser asks if Jewish literature in exile was not a tautology, since Jewish literature is always one of exile. This approach, however, conflates totalitarian signification with a Jewish concept of self in a problematic way which calls for further analysis.

[36] Hannah Arendt: The Jew as a Pariah. Jewish Identity and Politics in the Modern Age. Ed. with an Introduction by Ran H. Feldman. New York: Grove Press 1978, p. 145f. For a further discussion of this correspondence which cannot be developed here, see Carl E. Schorske: Fin-de-Siècle Vienna. Politics and Culture. London: Weidenfeld and Nicolson 1979; Bauman, Moderne und Ambivalenz (note 3), p. 114f., 184f.

Homecoming in the Modern Jewish Imagination, Sidra DeKoven Ezrahi has pointed out that political Zionism, by taking the »inherited model of Homecoming that was essentially ahistorical« literally has dangerously moved away from the traditional idea of Jewish exile.³⁷ The traditional notion of the Jews as ›people of the book‹ for whom texts constitute a homeland which always bears the mark of being ›not the real thing‹,³⁸ is bound to the idea of Jewish culture as maintaining a provisionality by conceiving itself a substitute for an endlessly deferred sacred space. This is fundamentally challenged by the Zionist attempt to reunite and identify text and territory, imagination and reality. This, however, does not only question the existence of the space of literary imagination with its characteristic mode of suspended implementation; it also threatens to cut off what had seemed to be a Jewish privilege, i. e. the flexibility of a symbolic which is not tied to a specific manifestation or original state, but exposes an irreducible incongruity of language and the real, of signifier and signified. In its call for a realization and materialization of symbolic and imaginative archives, the Zionist enterprise aims at the conflation of a symbolic and the real ›home‹ that Trigano and other postmodern Jewish thinkers describe as essentially non-Jewish. According to this concept the Jewish tradition resists binary oppositions as guiding principles of a theology or philosophy that eventually aspires to reconcile the differences and dissolve them into an encompassing whole. Between the extreme possibilities of on the one hand a transcendence of the material towards a pure world of ideas or a divine realm and on the other hand the materialization and incarnation of ideal spiritual visions, it steers a middle way, encouraging an endless process of creation of material worlds and ›homes‹ which are, however, never hypostasised as being the only possible, real manifestation of truth and identity.

If it would be presumptuous and unproductive in this context to play off one notion of Jewish identity against another (of course, the Zionist notion is also a Jewish notion of exile), it nevertheless seems rewarding to explore their respective potentials for new paths and paradigms in exile studies. One starting point might be the observation that in current debates about Zionism arguments and critical objections are raised that structurally resemble those put forward in the (self-)critical revision of German Exilforschung. According to their critics, both adhere to an understanding of exile as a negative foil which generates visions of a ›better world‹ and the appeal to realize them.³⁹ Both tend to subordinate the word to the idea, denying symbolization processes their specific dynamics and contingency. In this they obviously can be said to reflect

---

³⁷ Ezrahi, Booking Passages (note 25), p. 3, 18.
³⁸ See e. g. George Steiner: Our Homeland, the Text. In: Salmagundi 66 (1985), p. 24–25, cit. after Ezrahi, Booking Passages (note 25), p. 11. Here Ezrahi also quotes Edmond Jabès: »Gradually I realize that the Jew's real place is the book.«
³⁹ Ezrahi analyzes Zionist visions of a »utopia ›realized‹«. For the assumption that the exiles represented the ›other, better Germany‹ see Winckler, Mythen der Exilforschung (note 31), p. 72f.; Spies, Exilliteratur (note 31), p. 18.

to a certain extent a tendency of European modernism to complete representation or assimilation by eliminating the difference between the symbolic and the real. It seems, however, that the dissatisfaction surfacing in current debates, also implies the chance to develop a new look at exile in the 20th century. By explicitly turning back to the other aspect of modernism, namely the intellectual and artistic attention to the ambiguities of symbolizations and to the impossibility of exhausting creative (re-)conceptualisations of the world, another notion of exile can be retrieved. For reasons outlined above this is closely linked not only to resistance to the totalitarian trends in modern Europe but also to a specific Jewish role in modern critical thought. Thus drawing attention to this tradition which has been neglected both in Zionist thinking and in the treatment of exile in German Exilforschung, can seek to bring together two notions of exile which have both marked dominant discourses in the 20th century but have seldom been reflected in terms of their correlations and mutual exclusions. As these brief reflections on Zionism have shown, it is not possible to speak about *a* Jewish perspective on exile as opposed to a non-Jewish tradition that manifests itself, for example, in the reception of Platonic and Christian ideas. However, the various Jewish and non-Jewish concepts of exile all seem to be part of a complex symbolic network of modernism which can be described satisfactorily only in an analysis that does not implicitly favour one of the positions described but that reflects their historical and structural relations.

In the two literary texts of the 20th century I now propose to analyse exile plays a significant role. The first was written and published in Swiss exile after its Jewish author had fled Nazi-Germany, and the second is a short text by the same author and was written in Berlin in 1921. The first text has been classified as exile literature in the sense in which German Exilforschung has used the term; however, it has not received much attention in this field of study, the reason evidently being its silence about Nazi Germany and the absence of any explicit antifascist or humanistic message. The second text, which also hasn't attracted much critical attention on the whole, has been read as a statement on assimilation and Zionism. So far they have not been discussed in relation to each other, so the question as to whether they approach the theme of exile in a similar or an altogether different way has not yet been asked.

Else Lasker-Schüler was, beyond doubt, a modern writer, a German Jew living through the most changing years in German-Jewish relations. Born in 1869, she grew up in an assimilated family, was confronted with antisemitism at an early age, lived in Berlin amongst Jewish and non-Jewish avantgarde writers and artists, came into contact with Zionist ideas and representatives of the Jewish Renaissance, and, from 1933 until her death in Jerusalem in 1945, she was an exile in the political sense of the word: she left Germany for Switzerland in 1933, and after a journey she finally stayed in Palestine from where she could not return because of the outbreak of the war in 1939. All this suggests a complex interrelation of the different concepts and traditions of exile outlined in the first part of this paper. Consequently, in order not to subordinate the texts to one of the concepts of exile that modern and postmodern thought, Zionism or Exilforschung have developed, the following reading focuses on the question as to how the texts reflect signifying practices while at the same time taking historical and biographical factors into account. Thus the possibility to read them in the context of a modern (Jewish) experience will be explored as well as the potential of postmodern French thought in order to highlight the texts' approaches to exile.

Das Hebräerland, which several recipients already shortly after its publication in Zurich in 1937 criticized for its disregard of all reality and violence and and thus as escapist and naive,[40] presents itself as a montage of very heterogeneous fragments: impressions from Lasker-Schüler's second journey to Palestine that preceded the writing of the book border on phantastical, dreamlike elements. Characters from all her earlier books and from other texts, especially the Bible appear next to historical personalities like Theodor Herzl, Leo Baeck, Hugo Bergmann, Gershom Scholem and S. Y. Agnon. Descriptions of the Zionist cultivation-project are contrasted with fairytale-like accounts on the divine act of creation and on the narrator's own process of creativity while writing the book *Das Hebräerland*. Thus the text manifests its own textuality by exposing the autonomy and heterogeneity of the different elements out of which it is constituted. By mingling ›reality bites‹ with quotations from poetic and mythical texts it focuses attention on their fabric, on the modes and processes of their making rather than on a firm state one could call home, identity or God. If it is true that the prime gesture of the text is not referential, this is because it is characterized by a performative language that keeps positing

---

[40] In the reception of her work, the term exile has played a central role, without – in most cases – having been defined or differentiated sufficiently. Thus the assertion that Lasker-Schüler was an outsider as a woman writer and a Jew is recurrently conflated with the fact that she modelled herself Tino von Bagdad or Jussuf von Theben, and therefore – it is assumed – invented alternative worlds. This argument, which is already a conglomerate of different aspects, most of them external to the texts themselves, is sometimes additionally combined with her Jewishness. Thus for Alfred Bodenheimer (and others), for whom it is evident that Lasker-Schüler was an exile in German culture while Palestine was naturally her home, arrives at the remarkable conclusion that the reason why Lasker-Schüler was not very productive in Palestine was because there she had finally arrived in the land (Orient and Bible) that had been the object of her imagination before, but now revealed itself as higher reality. Alfred Bodenheimer: Die auferlegte Heimat. Else Lasker-Schülers Emigration in Palästina. Tübingen: Max Niemeyer 1995 (Conditio Judaica. Studien und Quellen zur deutsch-jüdischen Literatur- und Kulturgeschichte; 9), esp. p. 48. Sonja Hedgepeth: »Everywhere I search for a homeland.« Exile in the work of Else Lasker-Schüler. Ann Arbor: UMI 1991. For a more comprehensive discussion of the reception of *Das Hebräerland* see my paper: Avantgarde und Exil. Else Lasker-Schülers *Hebräerland*. In: Exilforschung 16 (1998), p. 105–126, esp. p. 109–111 and chapter V.5.1 of my book: Ausgesetzte Schöpfung. Figuren der Souveränität und Ethik der Differenz in der Prosa Else Lasker-Schülers. Tübingen: Max Niemeyer 2002 (Hermaea, N. F.; 95).

universal meaning while at the same time marking it as an ongoing process that cannot be concluded. Throughout the text fictional images and reality fragments become confused, their categorical difference obviously being denied, and already at the beginning the described space is emphatically associated with revelation,[41] recalling associations of a coincidence of signs and truth as final meaning. However, in the *Hebräerland* the assertion of identity and presence cannot be separated from the playing with texts, names, images or narratives that are continuously rearranged and refigured.

I would like to look at some examples that seem to classify the text as an account of an experience of a holy, Jewish homeland. In one episode, for example, Jerusalem's district of Rehavia is described as a miraculous place which, with its winged houses, is just about to take off into heaven (p. 812). A closer look reveals, however, that it is constituted of very divergent elements: the arrangement of the flowers in the gardens reminds the narrator of toys she played with in childhood on the floor of her parental home. This is followed by the remark that in the ›other continent‹ where she has lost this home the soil is black and brown. The next sentence informs the reader that in Europe she had already admired the delicate »blooming toys«, cared for by a gardener. The few references to Nazi-Germany do not suffice to create a whole picture of it; the colours black and brown (»like hazelnuts«, p. 812[42]) are surely unambiguous allusions, but at the same time they are ›broken‹ from this ideological context and placed into a semantic field of gardening, cultivating and love, all of which indicating an attitude towards nature or ›the other‹ in general that does not impose a fixed order on them but arranges their elements playfully.[43] Since they are not really related to one another – which is also emphasized by the unmediated succession of the sentences – a hermeneutic approach seems futile. It is not so much the meaning of the single things – flowers and toys seem insignificant enough – nor of the their composition as a whole, but rather playing as a poetological principle that raises the question of meaning as well as of authorship. Apparently no categorical difference is made between natural and artificial elements, between reality and fiction. If this is, as has often been observed, characteristic of most of Lasker-Schüler's literary texts and of her general self-fashioning, it does not mean that her work is simply ›fantastic‹. Nor does it imply though, that the text constitutes

---

[41] »*Ganz Palästina ist eine Offenbarung!*« (p. 788) All page numbers in brackets refer to Else Lasker-Schüler: Gesammelte Werke in drei Bänden. Bd 2: Prosa und Schauspiele. Hg. von Friedhelm Kemp. Frankfurt a. M.: Suhrkamp 1996.

[42] Translations are mine.

[43] This operation of ›breaking‹ elements from their contexts in order to ›liberate‹ them for resignifications and thus restore their polyvalence can be compared to a practice of signification that Walter Benjamin described as allegorical (in his book on the origin of the German tragedy) or messianic (in his theses on the philosophy of history). See Walter Benjamin: Ursprung des deutschen Trauerspiels. In: W. Benjamin: Gesammelte Schriften. Hg. von Rolf Tiedemann und Hermann Schweppenhäuser. Frankfurt a. M.: Suhrkamp 1991, Vol. I.1, p. 203–430, here p. 355, 364, 373, 382; Walter Benjamin: Über den Begriff der Geschichte. In: ibid, Vol I.2, p. 691–704, hier p. 701, 703.

an alternative reality, referring to an existing land or sketching an ideal home. The example, picked out at random, shows that playing is more than just an innocent, childlike activity and that it provides a way to account for heterogeneous worlds and experiences without eliminating breaks and fissures. While exile as loss of the country of birth is reflected as a radical state which threatens even childhood memories which are the precondition of any later self-reference and identity,[44] the exterior violence – the National Socialist appropriation of everything German – is not addressed explicitly. Rather, the breaks and separations it produces are repeated in the text and this transforms them into an exilic mode of writing denying closure and finality.

Interestingly, playing as prime mode of expression in the *Hebräerland* is also attributed to God. He not only loves the playing child but even appears as his playmate who can be touched and teased without taking on a clear shape or individuality.[45] In fact, God Himself is even called a child who playfully arranges the various elements of the Creation. Palestine is said to have been ›built‹ after a drawing made by the divine child, so that now it can be referred to as a child's masterpiece.[46] God and child are joined by a certain totalising attitude towards the world. Like a little God, the child refers to the worlds it creates in its playing as to whole universes (Freud speaks about the omnipotence of thought which characterizes an early narcissistic period in the development of the psyche, or in analogy a ›primitive‹ state in the development of human religion and society[47]). Especially in Jerusalem, one reads, the little boys like to play with their spinning tops, which for them are small wooden universes.[48] Similarly, the divine process of creation, which naturally concerns the world in its totality, appears as an act or process in which the creating authority does not precede the Creation as its origin or author. Rather, it is constituted through play in this very process – just as children gain an idea about themselves as subjects through playing with things, images and persons. In contrast to a form of playing in which an already constituted authority subjects and abuses objects and other people, the playing mode outlined in the *Hebräerland* is not instrumental but creative in a comprehensive way. If it implies moments of reduction and destruction (when elements are ›broken‹ from their former contexts) these are never final; single elements or meanings are not negated and foreclosed once and for all but only temporarily, and will always

---

[44] See the account Jean Améry gives of his exile experience (notes 14ff.)

[45] »Gott liebt das spielende Kind, Er läßt spielen mit Sich, ja zerren an Sich und seinen Himmeln.« (p. 928)

[46] »Palästina, nach Gottes Kinderzeichnung Meisterbild erbaut, Palästinas Flur ist das Meisterkinderwerk Gottes.« (p. 907)

[47] See e. g. Sigmund Freud: Totem und Tabu. Einige Übereinstimmung im Seelenleben der Wilden und der Neurotiker. In: S. Freud: Studienausgabe. Frankfurt a. M.: S. Fischer 1989, Vol. IX, p. 287–444, here p. 374–379.

[48] »Es spielen so gerne, besonders hier in Jerusalem, die kleinsten Knaben mit ihren Kreiseln und lassen die kleinen hölzernen Weltalle sich drehen, als wäre jedes von ihnen Kindern – ein kleiner lieber Gott.« (p. 929)

be rescued in subsequent play. This, however, preserves the memory of a traumatic loss or wound that is connected with the experience, that identity cannot be gained without symbolizing which, at the same time, implicates the loss of any immediate self-reference.[49]

What is also and consistently preserved in this kind of playing is the notion of a vulnerable God who in a way is dependent on human action and care. This is also suggested by the recurrent image of the Torah as a delicate child that needs to be carried and supported by the Hebrews.[50] The mode of exile is thus also reflected in an ethical dimension of the text: since there is no divine or metaphysical truth to rely on, support and orientation depend solely on symbolizing activities. In order to do justice to the contingencies of different conceptions of the world, they have to reflect their own constitutive processes, be open to change, and thus leave room for the incalculable other.

Since playing, creation and the literary process are inextricably interwoven, the ethical aspect is implicit in the text's poetics. One image that combines the realm of childhood and that of writing is that of a *Poesiealbum*[51] that the narrator one day finds on the road (in the sand, p. 809). It belongs to somebody, evidently a little girl named Ruth, who is not the author, but a collector of pictures, poems and letters which were ‚given' to her by friends. The narrator picks it up and starts to reconstruct who the owner is and how she can give it back to her. For a while the book directs her ways in Palestine, and in her attempt to restore the precious possession to the owner she finds people whose names are in it such as that of Meskin, a famous actor at the Habimah theatre company, who appears to be the girl's uncle. Thus the journey not only connects textual traces and real encounters but also leads to a site where playing takes place. *Poesiealbum* and theatre both comment on each other as places that provide a framework or platform where alien texts can playfully be performed. The text also closely relates the owner and the finder of the book. The little girl who, the reader is informed,

---

[49] The prototypical game that preserves the notion of this trauma bound into the structure of subjectivity is the *fort-da* game described by Freud in: Jenseits des Lustprinzips. In: Freud, Studienausgabe (note 47), Vol. III, p. 213–272, here p. 224–227.

[50] »Voller Ehrfurcht [...] betrachtete ich in den kleinen Quergassen in den seraphidischen und aschkenasischen Synagogen nach dem Gottesdienste die Thoraïm, mit einem Schellenband um den Hals, trägt der Knecht Adoneus mit besonderer Obhut, das Wundertragkind, zurück in den Heiligen Schrein. Der gute Hebräer wacht über den Schatz des Herrn, über die Gebote und Gesetze, vor allem über die ewige Liebe, die *Sein Lächeln* über die Welt breitet.« (p. 814) »Der Hebräer [...], der vom Inhalt seiner göttlichen Bürde weiß, trägt die verantwortliche Last, das holde Kind der Gebote ... die Thora lächelnd in seinen Armen. Die Thora ist ein Wunderkind; die Gebote Gottes: Glieder.« (p. 883) For the specific conflation of the Law and the Body of the Divine see also Bischoff, Ausgesetzte Schöpfung (note 40), chap. V.4.3.

[51] This term which does not have an English equivalent – commonplace book would probably be the closest translation – indicates a book often owned by girls who have their friends and acquaintances contribute poems, proverbs, images, personal greetings and the like.

sometimes also plays under her uncle's direction, lags behind at school, something the narrator relates about herself as well (p. 866). When she was a child, she says, she used to dream herself into *being* the biblical Joseph, thus playing a role that becomes indissoluble from her ›real‹ personality. Also, it is certainly no coincidence that the little girl's name is Ruth, which evokes the association of the biblical figure who became one of the mothers of the Jewish people by leaving her Moabite home, crossing the boundaries of lands and religions, thus representing origin and otherness at the same time.

The close relation between the two female figures also emphasizes the similarity between the child's *Poesiealbum* and the book called *Hebräerland*. Neither constitute an entity with clear boundaries and a set order. Instead they appear to be a work in progress that relies on encounters with others and that sets up a stage on which personalities appear in changing roles and configurations to such an extent that it is no longer possible to distinguish between actor and role, real and fictional identity. This is – in parenthesis – a prominent feature of Lasker-Schüler's epistolary novel *Mein Herz* which reflects its own poetics by labelling itself a ›comedy for the masses‹ (»Massenlustspiel«) performed on a revolving stage (»Drehbühne«, p. 336) and of her drama *IchundIch* which is called »my heart's stage«[52] by ›the poet‹ (»die Dichterin«) who acts as one of its characters. If in these texts it is obvious that the author is affected by the playing mode that blurs the distinction between reality and fiction, this is also true in the *Hebräerland*. Not only is the narrator who is presented as autobiographical self subject to abrupt changes disregarding the logic of time and space,[53] the writing of the book is also explicitly analogised with the journey. Just as the stay in the Holy Land turned out to be extremely hard for the traveller, it is claimed that the act of producing the *Hebräerland* became a similar hardship, because the narrator had to pave her way »between stone and stone« (p. 959). The reference the title of the book seems to indicate is questioned at this point since the ›real‹ stones in Palestine are interchanged with the textual fragments the writer deals with. Land and text become indistinguishable, their common characteristic being a performativity that continuously produces reality without fixing it to one specific order or appearance. The creative process that on the one hand is emphatically associated with bringing into life, is on the other hand bound to difference and distance. If bodies and homelands (which both appear as ›Heimat‹) usually signify

---

[52] *Mein Herz* is included in the Volume cited above (note 41), p. 289–392. For the later drama, written in exile, see: Else Lasker-Schüler: IchundIch. Eine theatrische Tragödie in sechs Akten, einem Vor- und einem Nachspiel. In: E. Lasker-Schüler: Gesammelte Werke in acht Bänden. München: Deutscher Taschenbuchverlag 1986 (dtv; 10641–10648), Vol. 7: Die Wupper und andere Dramen, p. 227–343. In the Prologue the ›author of the play‹ presents herself as listener to the hellish play on her »Herzensbühne«. See also my paper: Herzensbühne und Schriftkörper. Transformationen des Briefromans in der Moderne am Beispiel von Else Lasker-Schülers *Mein Herz*. In: Mutual Exchanges. Sheffield-Münster Colloquium II. Hg. von Dirk Jürgens. Frankfurt a. M. et. al.: Peter Lang 1999, p. 41–58.

[53] For this, see in greater detail Bischoff, Avantgarde und Exil (note 40), p. 115–119.

the foundations of identities which are the precondition for any further development of subjectivity, in Lasker-Schüler's prose they become bound into the process of construction, thus exposing not only the ›ideal‹ convergence of sign and reality, but at the same time marking the abysses that write themselves into the fabric of a text which does not rely on a referential frame or an authority. For, if author or Creator in fact seem to manifest their presence *in* the text, they also appear subject to difference and repetition. The journey through the »bibleland« is marked by abrupt changes (the street on which the narrator travels suddenly ends, ascending to the height of Jerusalem, p. 795) as is also the text called *Hebräerland* which reveals its mode of production. If Palestine is described primarily as a construction site of enormous proportions, it is emphasized that the process of construction always implies destruction – splittings and burstings are part of the divine process of creation – God breaks the stone from the »bibleland« to build the other worlds (p. 824, 897) – as well as the construction of the *Hebräerland* as a home that is in fact a continuous building process: collection and gathering of stones, splitting and dispersing of stones over and over again. (p. 832, 894) Thus the responsibility of the Hebrews, who, as the Chosen People, appear as a vanguard or model for all mankind, does not lie in taking possession of any given land and soil, but rather in observing differences and irreducible otherness inherent in their constructions of home. Zion, the text asserts, is not the home for only one people, but characterized by multiplicity and heterogeneity: with the narrator the reader moves between peoples and even the different tribes of Judah can be discerned in this »construction kit of images« (»Bilderbaukasten«, p. 791). God does not manifest himself at the moment identity is firmly grounded, but in the spaces in-between, in the marks and scars that indicate an openness and an otherness resisting representation.

So far this analysis has demonstrated that the text cannot be reduced to a document of exile literature in a narrow sense, reflecting the split between fascist Germany and the ›other Germany‹ constituted by the voices of the exiles, although it is certainly part of them too. The question arises, however, if it, above all, should be regarded as document of a typically Jewish perspective on exile. In fact, there are many indications in the text that point to different strands and motifs of this multifaceted tradition. Clearly Zionist activity and perspective play an important role, but, as I have tried to show, they constitute only some of the elements the text assembles. There are, for instance, also cabalistic and messianic elements which are characteristic of all of Lasker-Schüler's work.

I now would like to look at the earlier text, *Der Wunderrabbiner von Barcelona*, published in 1921, and ask if the notion of exile that informs the poetics of the *Hebräerland* can already be found in a text that thematically does not so much refer to the characteristics of the Holy Land and to exile from Nazi Germany as focus on the question of the Jewish Diaspora.

As the title suggests, the story plays in Barcelona, very probably before the expulsion of the Jews from Spain, but there are also many references to the current situation of the beginning of the 20th century. The narrative, which is much shorter than *Das Hebräerland*, at first seems to be more coherent in terms of plot and characters, but at a closer look turns out to be very dense and highly ambiguous. It comprises two major strands that are closely intertwined. They reflect different attitudes towards identity and difference which are each associated with a Jewish character. On the one hand there is the Rabbi Eleasar who resides in a splendid palace on a hill outside the city, which, with its dome built of wood from Lebanon and pure gold, recalls the Temple of Jerusalem. On the other hand there is Amram, the daughter of the Jewish architect who is introduced as a poet. Eleasar is described as a very impressive figure who resembles the archangel Gabriel and is respected and feared not only by the Jews but also by the Spanish for his »magically enlarged head«[54]. For the Jews he is more than an ordinary rabbi – the palace is not identical with the synagogue which is wedged between the houses of Spanish nationalists and antisemites – Eleasar takes on an important position to preserve a delicate equilibrium between the two peoples. As long as he is at home there is no major incident, but the moment he leaves the place a pogrom starts. The story describes an escalation of this violence which is caused by the events that occur when the Wonder Rabbi does not leave in time for his annual study trip to ›Ancient Asia‹, but actually witnesses the appalling violence of the pogrom in which the bodies of the Jews are mutilated and dismembered.[55] This sight shatters his belief in God; he wrestles with him like Jacob until the pillars of his palace collapse »like arms« (p. 504) and the golden dome breaks into pieces. A huge avalanche of rocks and stones, fragments of the broken temple, pours down the hill and destroys everything and everybody – a total annihilation that strikes even the Spaniards who had remorsefully buried the Jews (p. 504). This, however, is only the end of one strand of the narrative. In the other, Amram and Pablo, the son of Barcelona's Mayor, go aboard a miraculous ship that suddenly appears in the marketplace just before the pogrom, and disappear in it.

If one wants to make sense of the story, the first impulse surely is to ask if there are reasons why Eleasar is subject to, and in a way causes, the horrifying apocalyptic scene, and if, likewise, the text justifies Amram's wondrous survival. Is Eleasar guilty of excessive violence? A closer look at Eleasar shows him to be a very differentiated and ambiguous figure. The description of the book he reads (while the pogrom is taking place) is not at all disparaging. On the contrary, the very account of how the Jewish people were chosen by God is very poetic: Eleasar reads that God took one of the stars off His robe and

---

[54] The remarkable size here is also connected with the notion of ›realization‹: »Sein ehrerbietiger Kopf rätselhaft wie durch die Lupe vergrößert und verwirklicht, neigte sich umrahmt im Bogenfenster des Palastes freundlich jedem Vorüberschreitenden zu, ob Jude oder Christ.« (p. 494)

[55] »Und die Juden, die an den Namen Jehovahs immer von neuem erwacht waren, lagen alle verstümmelt, zerbissen, Gesichte vom Körper getrennt, Kinderhände und Füßlein, zartestes Menschenlaub auf den Gassen umher, in die man die Armen wie Vieh getrieben hatte.« (p. 501)

placed it on the forehead of the Jews, the »child« among the peoples. (p. 502) While all the other peoples are given homelands, the Jews ›possess‹ just this sublime ray of light that implies a special responsibility to serve God in all countries and all peoples. This responsibility is also grounded in a certain lack in God – for the moment He gives away one of His stars signifying His glory to the Jews, it is they who have to take care of this divine light. The text speaks of a »delightening« (»Entlichtung«, p. 502) in God, which is probably an allusion to the Lurianic Cabala, i. e. the theme of the broken vessels and the fallen sparks of light that recurs several times in Lasker-Schüler's work. Eleasar evidently adheres to a messianic attitude towards Jewish exile; he does not really believe in Zionism. If he does not state this explicitly it is because he thinks that the suffering Jews who long for a home where they are not subject to pogroms could not cope with it. Thus while he himself indulges in Cabala and *Galut* studies, he puts them off again and again, leaving them in the belief that the realization of a Jewish home on earth is dependent only on their devotion. Considering his motive, though – he loves his people and does not want to hurt them – he can hardly be called guilty here; surely he cannot be blamed for the final catastrophe. If there is guilt, it is not confined to the individual, it cannot be anticipated or explained within the logic of a given system of thought.

The story gives no hint that a Zionist ›solution‹ might have prevented the catastrophe. However, the narrative strand around Amram is characterized by elements that are certainly different: the girl, dressed like a boy, joins her father, the architect, in order to visit the houses that are under construction. While Eleasar's splendid residence is described in detail, we do not learn where Amram lives – rather, her mode is to submit herself to the building process and to the incomplete. Thus she is not protected by a precious roof as he is, but moves freely without support. When she once climbs into the as yet unfinished dome (»unfixed crown«, p. 496) of the palace, she falls, and, lying in the sand, she is found by Pablo. This first encounter is not mediated by any common language or symbol – on the contrary, it is precisely the imperfectness of the dome/crown as a sign of a divine presence that brings the two together. Also in the following episodes around Amram and Pablo difference is neither eliminated nor explicitly stated: on the ship that takes them away, a big sail hides them, leaving unity and difference undecided (p. 500). The ship that Eleasar does not even notice because he refuses to receive the bewildered people, does not only contain Jew and non-Jew, but is also a metaphor for a discontinuous passage, without a firm ground, without origin (Barcelona is destroyed) or destination.

Even though the text picks up elements of contemporary discussions about Zionism, messianism and *galut*, it clearly does not take a stand. Even the contract between Eleasar, who – as Itta Shedletzky has pointed out – bears a striking resemblance to Martin Buber[56] (in fact, some passages are modelled almost

---

[56] Itta Shedletzky: Bacherach and Barcelona. On Else Lasker-Schüler's Relation to Heinrich Heine. In: The Jewish Reception of Heinrich Heine. Ed. by Mark H. Gelber.

verbatim on Buber's essay *Der Heilige Weg*[57]) and Amram serves only in some respects as a starting point for an interpretation. If Amram, the playful poet who exposes herself to the incomplete and to coincidence, anticipates the poetics of the *Hebräerland*, Eleasar's messianic attitude towards exile does too.

The remarkable comment attributed to him, that Palestine is only the »observatory of home« (»*Sternwarte* ihrer Heimat«, p. 503) is taken up in the *Hebräerland* as well (p. 789). There, the mentioning of stars falling down onto the earth (p. 905) and especially the notion of *Zimzum*, God contracting in order to make room for the construction of the world (p. 922, 928), represent cabalistic elements which in the *Wunderrabbiner* are attributed to Eleasar. It is also striking that Eleasar and Amram are interrelated by many motifs: they are both described as ›children‹ and angels, they have both seen God, and they are both modelled as figurations of Moses.[58] It seems as if this couple represent two sides of the Moses-figure: the father who, being in direct contact with God, leads his people and gets into difficult situations when the people demand immediate relief from their sufferings and anxieties – first they want to return to the fleshpots of Egypt, then they stop waiting for Moses to come down from Mount Sinai and start worshipping the Mammon (the golden dome in the *Wunderrabbiner* may be regarded as an allusion to this). Moses' problem is thus one of transmission: how to relate evidence of a God who is not visible. The other aspect which Amram and Eleasar both share with the biblical Moses is the predominance of passage and transition. The ship in the *Wunderrabbiner* is an allusion to Noah's Ark, but it also recalls the ark of bulrushes in which Moses is hidden and left floating in the water shortly after he is born. Like Amram, who, after falling from the dome, is found by Pablo, Moses is found and brought to the Pharaoh's daughter who raises him as her son although she knows about his being Jewish.[59] Later, when Moses leads his people through the desert, this for him is also a passage that does not terminate in the Holy Land, for he only sees it but dies before he can set foot on it.

As a result, one can regard Eleasar and Amram, the priest and the poet, as two sides of one of the central figures of Jewish identification that is closely connected with the idea of a passage between exile and home, a passage, which is not finally concluded. Consequently, the two endings of the narrative might also be read as two radically opposed sides of the same. Not only do they both deal with the fate of the Jews, but they focus on events involving Jews and non-Jews

---

Tübingen: Max Niemeyer 1992 (Conditio Judaica. Studien und Quellen zur deutsch-jüdischen Literatur- und Kulturgeschichte; 1), p. 113–126, here p. 122.

[57] For a detailed discussion see Bischoff, Ausgesetzte Schöpfung (note 40), chap. V.3.3.

[58] Itta Shedletzky suggests this when showing that they are both invested with characteristics of the biblical Moses; however, she does not discuss possible consequences for the structure of the story.

[59] See also Lasker-Schüler's self-fashioning as Joseph of Egypt: it is in Egyptian exile that Joseph asserts his power and identity which, however, always remains marked by separation and difference.

alike: total destruction is contrasted with miraculous salvation, both are strongly associated with biblical images and motifs. They are also both linked to a gesture of complete exposure to the ›other‹ that is not at all intelligible or translatable into human speech and symbols. The dome as visual site and symbol of God's presence is in the end completely shattered and fragmented as is the representative figure of the Wonder Rabbi who in a strange way merges with the people he represents,[60] setting free a power that goes beyond human will and action because it destroys the human order. The moment of destruction presents the Jewish people as a powerful avalanche of separate stones (the texts uses the expression »Steinbruch« which seems to contradict the idea of stones coming down from the hill, but emphasizes the violent fragmentation that separates the single elements). Here, it seems, striking similarities can be seen with the *Hebräerland*. In the *Wunderrabbiner* destruction and salvation appear as two extreme conclusions in a text that relates them closely and therefore denies an unambiguous ending. In the *Hebräerland* these two modes become part of the repetitive structure of the text which does not even try to narrate a coherent story any more, but reveals its breaks and abysses as well as the process of composing new entities from heterogeneous elements.

Concluding this comparative reading of the two texts, I would like to take up again my opening remarks about different perspectives of exile. Clearly, Lasker-Schüler's texts refer to very different notions of exile without manifesting one as a prime idea or message. Instead, they ›break‹ the elements of political, existential, Zionist and messianic concepts of exile from their original contexts, thereby depriving them of their referential functions. Particularly in the *Wunderrabbiner* interpretation and reference is always connected with antisemitism: the Spaniards interpret everything Jewish that they do not understand as dangerous and sinful,[61] every pogrom is in fact based on such an act of interpretation. Similarly, on the Jewish side the signs of identity and meaning, especially those that presume divine presence, reveal their destructive potential and they are finally destroyed themselves. Exile, in these texts, is thus closely associated with exposure to a traumatic event or experience that can neither be understood by the individuals nor represented by privileged signs. In

---

[60] »Ein ungeheurer Steinbruch aber, Er, der große Wunderrabbiner, ein Volk stürzte sich vom heiligen Hügel, den das goldene, zerbröckelte Mosaik der Kuppel verklärte, auf die Christen Barcelonas, die den letzten gequälten Juden reuevoll zur Ruhe legten, und erlosch ihre Erleuchtung, zermalmte ihre Körper.« (p. 504)

[61] This is especially clear in the interpretation the Christian Mayor of Barcelona finds for the Jewish books (written in Hebrew and therefore to be read in a strange way »von außen nach innen«, p. 499). For him, the Jewish eyes which, because of these books, do not rest but always go back to the materiality of the book and its gaps and fissures (»Augen, die sich nicht am Ziel zu bleiben getrauten, Augen, die sich versteckten in des Buches Heftung, sich flüchteten immer zurück in den Spalt«). He interprets this as a criminal act: »›Augen, die stehlen‹ – meinte der Bürgermeister betonend zu seinem erbleichenden Sohn.« (p. 499)

fact, it affects the very symbols of unity and identity by reversing the process of their construction and setting free a violence that separates and disperses their single parts. It is quite clear that this trauma is not caused by any specific enemy or political condition (exile or persecution), but that it is inherent in this concept of identity. If there is an ethical impetus to be found in these narratives which do not prescribe any specific moral or political action, it is the responsibility to make space for difference that cannot be represented. This difference exceeds the possibility to differentiate between individuals, religions or peoples because it affects each identity in itself.[62] The texts both refer to a particular reality of exile suffered by Jews at a particular historical time and place (Barcelona in the 15th century) and/or to the radical antisemitism at the time they were written, and at the same time question reference as a way to relate signs and reality systematically. While they can be read as documenting a Jewish perspective on exile, both structurally and thematically, they cannot be reduced to it. Discussing them in the context of a modern Jewish experience that reflects the phantasmatic strife for a totalitarian conflation of the symbolic and the real in the 20th century, however, makes it possible to bring out their universalist impulse without losing sight of the Jewish fate and tradition through with it is articulated.

---

[62] See Julia Kristeva: Fremde sind wir uns selbst. Aus dem Frz. von Xenia Rajewsky. Frankfurt a. M.: Suhrkamp 1990 (Edition Suhrkamp, N. F.; 604) (Etrangers a nous-même. Paris: Fayard 1988), p. 23. Here Kristeva speaks of an exile that essentially characterizes a modern art of living, the cosmopolitanism of the abused; it implies a radical estrangement towards oneself, towards the notion of unity and wholeness as points of reference for individual and collective identity.

Adi Gordon

German Exiles in the ›Orient‹

The German-language Weekly *Orient* (Haifa, 1942–1943)
between German Exile and Zionist Aliya[1]

This article will attempt to shed some new light on the self-understanding of the German-speaking emigrants to Palestine – the »Yekkes« – by means of a close examination of the *Orient*: a German-language periodical that appeared in Palestine for one year beginning in the spring of 1942 – a short but tormented period for the Yishuv and for the Jewish people as a whole.

As an historical source, the weekly *Orient* reveals some lesser known elements both regarding the character of the Jewish emigration from the Third Reich to Palestine and the manner in which it was absorbed. Some scholars have proposed a distinction between three sub-groups within the German Aliya: the Old-Zionists, the New-Zionists and the emigration out of desperation[2]. The term *Old-Zionists* relates to the relatively small segment who were Zionist activists prior to their arrival in Palestine. The term *New-Zionists* refers to those who made up their minds to immigrate to Palestine only as a result of the Nazi rise to power, after having experienced bitter disappointment with the old homeland. This was, incidentally, not only the largest sub-group within the German Aliya, but also the one whose absorption was the least problematic. Paradoxically, having arrived with no great expectations, the new-Zionists were spared the disappointments that affected many of the old-Zionists so deeply. The third sub-group emigrated out of desperation – these were people who came as refugees seeking a temporary haven from Nazi persecution. The oxymoron »Non-Zionist Olim« has occasionally been applied to them. Many of them eventually struck root and integrated into the new homeland. Others, however, continued to lead an existence of exiles for the duration of their stay in Palestine/Israel, and left the country after the end of the war and the fall of the Third Reich. It was from this sub-group of Non Zionist emigrants. In this

---

[1] The article is based on my MA thesis: In Palestine. In a foreign Land. The Weekly *Orient* between ›German Exile‹ and the ›Yekke‹ Aliya. Jerusalem 2001 [hebr.].

[2] Miriam Getter: Immigration from Germany to Israel, 1933–1939. Socio-Economic Absorption versus Socio-Cultural Absorption [hebr.]. In: Cathedra for the History of Eretz Israel and its Yishuv, No. 12, July 1979, p. 126; Gideon Stachel: The Jewish Immigration from Germany to Palestine during the Years 1933–1939 and Its Meeting with the People of the Yishuv from the Immigrants' Point of View. (Ph. D.) Jerusalem 1996 [hebr.], p. 189–191. This distinction is presented also in: Evelyn Lacina: Emigration 1933–1945. Sozialhistorische Darstellung der deutschsprachigen Emigration und einiger ihrer Asylländer aufgrund ausgewählter zeitgenössischer Selbstzeugnisse. Stuttgart: Klett-Cotta 1982 (Beiträge zur Wirtschaftsgeschichte; 14), p. 384.

sense, the weekly represented an exile's outlook rather than the perspective of the ›Olim Chadashim‹ and many notions conveyed by the *Orient* were truly unique and marginal within the human landscape of the Yekkes.

It must nevertheless be mentioned that at the same time some notions that were expressed by the *Orient* with pungency and resolution could be found in varying degrees in the consciousness of the Central European Aliya in its entirety, although most Yekkes would not have dared to articulate such ideas in those years in the nation-building Yishuv. I am alluding here to the motivation to maintain strong bonds to the old homeland, and to practice a certain cultural separatism advocated by the *Orient*. This included focusing on matters of the German intellectual world, consistently ignoring the Hebrew culture and ridiculing the ways of the ›Ostjuden‹.

It is only natural that the perception of those who experienced life in Palestine as some form of exile found an utterly different expression than that of the ›Olim Chadashim‹, the people who made a new beginning in the Zionist homeland – a process which was meant to draw a final line over their German past. In this article, I will attempt to examine some of what the *Orient*'s contributors wrote about their immigration to Palestine and the ensuing harsh confrontation with the establishment of the Yekke Aliya, which had a radically different interpretation of that emigration.

The *Orient* is the only periodical published in Palestine to be considered by scholars to be a part of the ›Exilpresse‹, the German press in exile.[3] To be sure, there were quite a few other German-language publications written for and by German-speaking immigrants. At least two of them exist to this very day. But in those years, in a nation-building Yishuv, the *Orient* stood out as the only German speaking publication that had no Zionist alibi whatsoever. Indeed, it had a very distinct character.

Although the *Orient* proclaimed, time and again, to be a part of the Yishuv and specifically a part of the German speaking Aliya, serious doubt was cast regarding its true affiliation both in those days and in retrospect. The editorial board, however, repeatedly denied being a part of a German Exile. Both contemporaries and, in later years scholars, remained justifiably very skeptical vis-à-vis such declarations.

The periodical entitled *Orient. Independent Weekly. Current Affairs – Culture – Economy* appeared in Palestine for the first time in April 1942. Politically it had a leftist, pro-Soviet orientation and from its outsider's position, combined a strictly oppositionary line with provocative rhetoric.

* * *

---

[3] See e. g. Angela Huß-Michel: Literarische und politische Zeitschriften des Exils 1933–1945. Stuttgart: Metzler 1987 (Sammlung Metzler; 238); Hans Albert Walter: Deutsche Exilliteratur. Stuttgart: Metzler 1978, Vol. 4: Exilpresse; Walter A. Berendsohn: Die Humanistische Front. Einführung in die deutsche Emigranten-Literatur. 2 Vols, Worms: Heintz 1976 (Vol. 1: first published Zürich: Europa-Verlag 1946).

Who, then, were the founders of the weekly and its contributors, and in what sense were they exiles or refugees rather than ›olim‹? Two editors are mentioned on the front page of the *Orient:* the well known author Arnold Zweig and Wolfgang Yourgrau – an almost-unknown journalist and academic. Yourgrau (born 1908) was the heart and mind behind the weekly. He was the one who initiated the idea of establishing the periodical, and who wrote all editorials and many of the other articles – often using pseudonyms. Yourgrau coordinated all of the weekly's activities, occasionally financed it, and even delivered copies to kiosks and private subscribers. He held a doctorate in physics but was also very learned and knowledgeable in the fields of Economics, Philosophy and Oriental Studies. Back in Germany, he used to contribute to left-wing publications (including the famous left-wing Berlin periodical, the *Weltbühne*) and was an active member of the SAP (Socialist Workers-Party).

Following the Nazis' rise to power, Yourgrau became a target for Nazi assaults. He was attacked by SA-men and was forced to go underground for an extended period of time. In December of 1933, he fled Germany for Poland. Shortly thereafter, he was required to leave Poland due to activity with left wing circles which was considered subversive. From there, Yourgrau left for Latvia, where the story repeated itself once again, and he was forced out. At this stage, Yourgrau himself admitted, he did not know where to go next. He had two options available to him: he was offered to continue eastwards into the USSR and at the same time, due to contacts with Robert Weltsch, one of the leaders of German Zionism, he was offered a certificate for emigration to Palestine. Yourgrau took the latter offer. A few years later, his skills enabled him to acquire a certain position both within the ranks of the Association of German Olim and in the *Histadrut* – but all this does not change the fact that he had no Zionist background prior to his arrival to Palestine. He left Palestine in the late 1940s and eventually settled in the USA.

Before finally deciding to establish the *Orient*, Yourgrau asked Arnold Zweig for a limited contribution to the periodical that would list him as co-editor. Naming the well-known writer as editor lent the new weekly a certain respectability, as most of its contributors were quite unknown in Germany and completely anonymous in Palestine. Zweig saw himself as the »patron who stood behind the periodical«[4] though in practice Yourgrau was the sole editor and Zweig's title was merely honorary. He may have contributed to most issues, but often using reprinted old texts.

Upon his arrival in Palestine, Zweig was already a very well known figure in the world of German literature. He was a proclaimed pacifist but had also been a Zionist for some twenty years prior to his 1932 visit to Palestine. It was specifically that visit, however, that had resulted in a weakening of his Zionist convictions. That year, his critical *De Vrient kehrt heim* was published in Germany. The book, inspired by the assassination of Dr. Jakob Israel de Haan by members of the Haganah, was regarded by the Yishuv as a writ of divorce

---

[4] Walter, Deutsche Exilliteratur (last note), Vol. 1, p. 680.

from Zionism. A few months later, Hitler was elected chancellor and the leftist Zweig was forced to emigrate.

In December of 1933, the no longer ardent Zionist Zweig settled in Haifa. A concise remark in his notebook tells us of his feelings: »In Palestine. In a foreign land.« (»In Palästina. In der Fremde.«)[5] On January 21, 1934 Zweig wrote to Sigmund Freud:

> I don't care anymore about »the land of our fathers«. I haven't got any more Zionistic illusions either. I view the necessity of living here among the Jews without enthusiasm, without any false hopes and even without the desire to scoff.[6]

From the outset, his choice of Palestine as a destination was made with mixed feelings and grave misgivings. From his home on Mount Carmel, Zweig never ceased to explore the possibilities for emigration to Britain or the United States. For various reasons, however, these plans did not materialize until the end of the Second World War. His years in Palestine were very trying. He had arrived at the age of forty-six, as a writer at the peak of his success, and left at the age of sixty-one, a bitter man, looking much older than his actual age. During these years, Zweig nearly lost his eye-sight and lived in social and professional seclusion. Most of his time in Palestine was spent in his home, surrounded by his many books.

The celebrated writer was all but ignored in Palestine – a phenomenon that was interpreted at least by Zweig himself as a deliberate ban against him resulting from his allegedly ›anti-Zionist‹ book *De Vrient kehrt heim*. He made ends meet by writing for the *Orient* and for the *Palestine Post*, and was also provided financial support by friends from abroad and by Soviet funds. In 1948, following the end of the Second World War and the declaration of Israeli independence, the Zweig family returned to East Berlin. As in the case of Yourgrau, the reasons for Zweig's decision to immigrate to Palestine and for staying there through the late 1940's cannot be easily established. It can be assumed, however, that some of the considerations were personal rather than ideological.

Apart from the editors, the weekly was produced by a group of some ten writers who contributed on a regular basis and two dozen or so additional writers. Among the regular contributors were Franz Goldstein, Walter Zadek, Sally Friedrich Grosshut and Louis Fürnberg. Like Yourgrau and Zweig, most of this central core of the *Orient* staff had not come to Palestine out of Zionist convictions.[7] One year after his arrival in Palestine, Louis Fürnberg, who later became one of the German Democratic Republic's national poets, wrote in his

---

[5] Quoted in: Arnold Zweig. Mit Selbstzeugnissen und Bilddokumenten dargestellt von Jost Hermand. Reinbeck: Rowohlt 1990 (Rowohlts Monographien; 381), p. 74.

[6] The Letters of Sigmund Freud and Arnold Zweig. Ed. by Ernst L. Freud. London: Hogarth Press 1970, p. 55–58.

[7] Due to limitations of space, I have not sketched the biographies of these members of the *Orient*'s central core in this article. For these biographical details, see the biographical appendix to my MA thesis *In Palestine* (note 1).

diary: »My life is too shattered into pieces. I would have wanted to be able to arrange it ... but who can do it in such a disgusting land?«[8]

The core of the *Orient* circle consisted of Jews who had emerged from within the German, Austrian or Czech left scene. In referring to precisely such people, George Mosse wrote that the »German-Jewish tradition reached its climax in a left-wing identity«.[9] The *Orient*'s contributors were persecuted after the Nazi seizure of power and were forced out of their homelands primarily for political reasons rather than because they were Jews. They should therefore be understood as belonging to the circles of political refugees from ›the German Reich‹ and not only to the Jewish emigration, notwithstanding the fact that the distinction between these two groups was not always obvious. Whatever remained of Zweig's former Zionist ideology after his arrival to Palestine was not sufficient to make him consider himself an ›Ole Chadash‹.[10] He saw himself as the exiled German writer that he was. This is apparent in light of his limited connections with the Yishuv intelligentsia on the one hand, and his extensive correspondence with German-speaking exiled intellectuals, such as Sigmund Freud[11] and Kurt Tucholsky[12] on the other hand. This pattern in the conduct of the *Orient* circle is unique, and is closely related to their former background. Generally speaking, they – as opposed to ›Brith Shalom‹ figures, for example, such as Martin Buber and Akiba Ernst Simon – had been extremely integrated into the political scene in their old homelands and became bystanders of sorts and critical spectators in the context of the country in which they had arrived. It must nevertheless be mentioned that some of the *Orient* contributors had a different background and held distinctly Zionist views. Max Jungmann and Schalom Ben-Chorin were two such figures. Although clearly a minority in what regards their ideology and personal backgrounds, these contributors nonetheless constituted a substantial part of the core of the weekly's staff.

* * *

The programmatic editorial that appeared in the first issue of the weekly provides a glimpse into the self-understanding of the *Orient* – did its contributors consider themselves a part of the Yekke immigration or of German exile? At

---

[8] Quoted in: Der Briefwechsel zwischen Louis Fürnberg und Arnold Zweig. Dokumente einer Freundschaft. Hg. im Auftrag der Akademie der Künste der DDR von Rosemarie Poschmann und Gerhard Wolf. Berlin, Weimar: Aufbau 1978, p. 12f.

[9] George L. Mosse: German Jews beyond Judaism. Bloomington: Indiana University Press 1985 (The Modern Jewish Experience – Jewish studies – A Midland Book), p. 55.

[10] This view is generally accepted by most of the scholarship on Zweig: Hermand, Arnold Zweig (note 5); Manuel Wiznitzer: Arnold Zweig. Das Leben eines Deutsch-jüdischen Schriftstellers. Königstein/Ts: Athenäum 1983; Wilhelm von Sternburg: »Um Deutschland geht es uns«. Arnold Zweig, die Biographie. Berlin: Aufbau 1998.

[11] Cf. The Letters of Sigmund Freud and Arnold Zweig (note 6).

[12] Cf. Exil. Literarische und politische Texte aus dem deutschen Exil 1933–1945. Hg. von Ernst Loewy Stuttgart: Metzler 1979, p. 265–279.

the same time, however, this article, like many others that would follow, was somewhat vague and does not provide us with a clear-cut picture:

> Our periodical appears in the German tongue [...] it is meant to reach the reader for whom it will remain impossible to acquire the Hebrew language during the war. We aim at this circle only [...] This periodical is not an organ of the emigrants'-literature. Our stage is open to the old Zionist activist just as much as it is open to the emigrant in this land who still seeks to clarify his political views. Ideas can never be vanquished merely by declaring them Taboo [...][13]

An examination of the manner in which the German-speaking immigrants were received in Palestine, which appeared in the following issue, was somewhat more revealing with regard to the self-understanding of the weekly's participants. The initial willingness to embrace ›Alija Chadasha‹, the left-liberal party of Central European Aliya, reflects the paper's commitment to the cause of these new immigrants. The Yishuv, the *Orient* claimed, greeted German immigrants not only with indifference but in fact with a certain hostility. They had been exploited and were being discriminated against for the past nine years. The *Orient*'s aggressive line on this matter was first fully expressed by Walter Zadek in an article called »Speak Hebrew or perish!«[14] In this article, Zadek claimed that the struggle for the domination of the Hebrew language was being excessively intensified, motivated not by ideological considerations, but rather by the selfish economic interests of the veteran Yishuv People (the ›Vatikim‹). The ›Grabsky-Olim‹ from Poland, he argued, had become Hebrew language fanatics only in order to get potential economic competition on the part of German immigrants out of the way. Similarly, the *Orient* accused ›Youth Aliya‹ of using immigrant youngsters for menial labor;[15] and Yourgrau wrote about the Histadrut's systematic deception of, and discrimination against, people from Germany.[16]

A heated debate on the way in which German Aliya was received by the Yishuv ensued in a series of articles written by Arnold Zweig. It followed a violent clash at Cinema Esther – perpetrated by the revisionist ›Beithar‹ during a meeting of the pro-Soviet ›League V‹ in which its president, Arnold Zweig, intended to give a speech in German. Zweig responded in the *Orient* condemning the »fascists« within the Yishuv, as he called them. Among other things, he put the following imaginary sentence in their mouth:

> Are the New Immigrants from Germany at all entitled to speak up and to have seats in the Yishuv's institutions? Is it really about absorbing and accepting them and permitting them to raise their heads in the only language which would enable them to participate in the ongoing intellectual discourse? What actually do these shreds of

---

[13] Wolfgang Yourgrau: Auftakt. In: Orient, No. 2 (April 10, 1942), p. 1–2.
[14] Walter Zadek: Sprich Hebräisch oder stirb! In: Orient, No. 7, May 10, 1942), p. 15–17.
[15] Cf. Ein Vater: Hat die Jugendalija versagt? In: Orient, No. 8, May 22, 1942, p. 15–19.
[16] Cf. Wolfgang Yourgrau: Geprellt. In: Orient, No. 4, April 24, 1942, p. 1–5.

a defeated Legion want? We don't need them, nor their experience or advice. It is their cash we want.[17]

In the following issue, Zweig launched another article titled »Rootedness« (»Verwurzelung«),[18] in which he described the process of his own absorption in a manner which raised the ire of many. Zweig spoke against those who had accused him of »not striking root in the land«. A seed, he claimed metaphorically, that was dropped by chance on an arid rock, devoid of rain and heat, will not strike root. It will remain small and dry and will be swept away by the mildest wind. Zweig claimed that in Palestine he was deprived of the possibility of exercising his calling: no Hebrew theater, periodical or publisher was interested in his services. Faced with hostile indifference towards him, he emphasized the fact that prior to his arrival in Palestine other possible destinations for emigration had been opened to him, and that honour and respect were still bestowed upon him abroad. He was told that the Yishuv should have »borne him high on their hands« (»In Palästina müsse man mich doch auf Händen tragen«). In this article, Zweig exposed a central and important vein in the *Orient*'s understanding of the absorption process. It seems that he viewed it as a trade-off of sorts, in which the Yishuv was to support the immigrant and at least provide for his material needs. Only then would the question of the immigrant's cultural-and spiritual strikingroot arise. The article revealed an interpretation of the concept of Aliya/immigration that was intolerable and subversive to the ears of the Yishuv mainstream. First, the understanding of immigration to Palestine as a random act rather than as the fulfilment of destiny, and second – and this is the key issue – the understanding of striking root as a sacrifice brought by the immigrant rather than as something that is at his own interest and his own goal.

The article infuriated Gustav Krojanker, an old Zionist and acquaintance of Zweig, who in August 1942 wrote a pungent response in the bulletin of the Central European Olim, the *Mitteilungsblatt der HOGOA*.[19] Krojanker rejected the *Orient*'s criticism of the absorption of Jews from Germany as hypocritical since, as he claimed, they would leave the land as soon as they could, and their criticism stemmed only from the mental necessity to express resentment, nostalgia and arrogance. This was just »the vicious view of the stranger, the barren criticism of the ›Welbühne‹«. His article, titled »Sentiment und Ressentiment«, opened with the following analysis:

> When one reads the weekly Orient published in the German language here, in this land, one gets a vivid picture of some segments of our German speaking Aliya: namely those who, given the opportunity, will once again leave the Land, without

---

[17] Arnold Zweig: Cinema Esther Pantomime. In: Orient, No. 13, June 26, 1942, p. 1–4. I would also argue that Zweig was paraphrasing here Tucholsky's final letter to him (cited in note 12).

[18] Arnold Zweig: Verwurzelung. In: Orient, No. 14, July 3, 1942, p. 5–7.

[19] Gustav Krojanker: Sentiment und Ressentiment. In: Mitteilungsblatt der HOGOA, No. 33, August 14, 1942, p. 3–4; id., Der Unterschied. In: ibid., No. 39, September 25, 1942, p. 4–5.

ever having really been there in the first place [Diejenigen nämlich, die das Land, wenn möglich, wieder verlassen werden, ohne vorher dagewesen zu sein]. For as far as this periodical has a face [...] it can be defined by three features: the sentiment [Sentiment] of reminiscing, the resentment [Ressentiment] towards what surrounds them, and arrogance. Basically it is one single trait: People who have not formed any attachment to this land maintain a spiritual existence in yesterday's world. Aware of the abnormality of their existence they put the blame on »the Others«, on those who impeded them – the talented and highly cultural – from developing. [...] It is the periodical of those who have no attachments and who elevated this into an ideology.[20]

* * *

The enlistment of the Yekke establishment into the campaign against the periodical was a landmark in the story of the *Orient* and marked the beginning of its end. It illustrates the extent to which the German immigrant mainstream had internalised the norms and values that prevailed in the Yishuv. The struggle was by no means confined merely to the writing of articles, but soon turned into violence and culminated within less than one year when, on February 2nd 1943, a bomb demolished the *Orient*'s printing-house. This was already the fourth printing-house in the periodical's short existence. The former three had been forced in one way or another to cease working for the *Orient*. After the bombing, Yourgrau managed somehow to publish one final issue, but this was the end of the *Orient*.[21]

In many ways this struggle shaped the character and rhetoric of the *Orient* and the manner in which it was to be remembered. It resulted in the *Orient*'s use of increasingly inflammatory language to depict the Yishuv as a totalitarian society; to describe certain circles within it as »Fascist«; to use terms such as »Yishuv-Nazis«, »our SA-men«, »Stürmer-Style« actions.

The violent struggle against the *Orient* on the one hand, and the harsh expressions used by the periodical on the other, eclipsed some very central perceptions that constituted the foundations of its raison d'être. This included scorn and arrogance vis-à-vis the Yishuv's cultural life: the new Hebrew culture and art were generally ignored, whereas contempt was expressed towards the Eastern European Jewish culture – which the *Orient*, like many other Yekkes, thought to have detected at the foundation of the dominant Yishuv culture. The *Orient* complained that local art critics in the Yishuv »had just graduated from a youth spent in a Cheder« (»die sich gerade von einer im Cheder zugebrachten Jugend emanzipiert haben«).[22]

It further lamented that the Yishuv's education system was under the influence of Melamed-Type teachers (»Wir wollen nicht den Typ des Melamed züchten, wir brauchen frohe, nicht verbitterte Pädagogen«).[23] It ridiculed the »Shtetl-practices« which it identified in the Yishuv and attributed to the Yishuv leader-

---

[20] Krojanker, Sentiment und Ressentiment (last note), p. 4–5.
[21] The struggle is described in detail in my Master's thesis *In Palestine* (note 1), p. 21–26.
[22] Walter Zadek: Das Dilemma unserer Kritik. In: Orient, No. 5, May 1, 1942, p. 7–9, here p. 8.
[23] Wolfgang Yourgrau: Lehrerstreik. In: Orient, No. 8, May 22, 1942, p. 1–2.

ship a »shtetl mentality«, or alternatively, a »ghetto mentality« (»Ghetto-Mentalität«, »die engstirnige Städtelmentalität«)[24] and yearned for a takeover of clear European minds (»klare europäische Köpfe«).[25]

* * *

One of the most manifest expression of the *Orient*'s exile perspective can be found in examining their strong and tormented relationship to their old homeland. Articles dealing with the great assets of German culture and their continuation in exile appeared with great frequency. Works by German writers, including those in Palestine, coupled by articles relating to the world of German culture, constituted approximately one-third of the weekly's material. Yourgrau and others responded to the allegations that identified the roots of Nazism as stemming from the depths of German culture. While not denying these claims, they regarded them primarily as disproportionate demagoguery, and often as shallow exaggerations.

It is probably revealing that the most extensive article to have been published in the *Orient* was Zweig's piece against anti-Germanism. It was so long that it was printed in seven sequences. Three central points which Zweig raised will command our attention in this context:

1. The allegation that Nazism represents Germaness (Deutschtum) was not only false, but originally a Nazi claim. The victims of this regime, those who had been hurt and disappointed by it, should not let their rage mislead them to adopt this allegation.[26]
2. The true enemy was to be found in those who enabled the Nazis to accede to power in the first place. For Zweig – and this is, of course, a very problematic line of reasoning – this enemy was identified as anti-bolshevist forces, rather than as the German people.[27] Notwithstanding the horrendous crimes perpetrated in the name of the German people, Zweig stated that the real enemy »was not the German soldier, nor the Nazi party apparatus«, but rather the reactionary forces.[28]
3. To understand defeat of the Germans as the war's goal would be a fatal mistake which would render this world war, like the previous one, another unnecessary war fought in vain. It was not only a battle between nations and armies, but primarily »a struggle of unprecedented dimensions between social forces«.[29]

---

[24] Wolfgang Yourgrau: Nach einer Bombe. In: Orient, No. 6–8, April 7, 1943, p. 1–15, here p. 6.
[25] Ibid.
[26] Arnold Zweig: Antigermanismus. 1933 erlebt. In: Orient, No. 32/33, November 20, 1942, p. 5–8, here p. 7.
[27] Arnold Zweig: Antigermanismus. Die Realität dieses Krieges. In: Orient, No. 38, December 25, 1942), p. 6–8, here p. 7.
[28] Ibid., p. 6.
[29] Ibid.

In this vein, it was the Zionist Ben-Chorin who expressed extensive concern with regard to Germany's future:

> This lost war will be followed in Germany by bloody retribution, in which thousands and thousands (but not millions) of murderers...and mass executioners will be mercilessly treated [...]. Those responsible should be stood against the wall! But this should be followed by planning a genuine reconstruction. There are productive elements in Germany and in exile who must be harnessed in order to found a Germany (regardless of the political system) so that a European viewpoint will prevail in Europe. A foreign rule might drive even the positive forces among the Germans – those who might still exist as a minority – back into the arms of demagogues.[30]

Accordingly, it is no wonder that Arnold Zweig, when referring to what he believed to be the readership of the *Orient*, repeatedly used the expression »We, German Republicans« (»Wir, deutsche Republikaner«).[31]

* * *

The story of the non-Zionist émigrés in the Palestinian exile has yet to be told. They have been elbowed into the position of a footnote in the Israeli-Zionist and the German anti-Fascist narratives. In the most comprehensive research so far of the ›Yekkes‹, Yoav Gelber, for example, mentions them only rarely and very briefly. He did not go much beyond representing Zweig's case, not neglecting to advise his readers that

> [...] due to Zweig's difficult personality one should not take him as an example from which one can draw general conclusions. The radical conclusions which Zweig drew from his own failure to integrate into Yishuv society, moreover, made him part of a negligible minority among the Olim.[32]

Most existing research is biographical in nature, stressing the personal circumstances rather than the milieu and emphasizing psychological motivations without attempting to represent these individuals as belonging to a group with a particular ideology.[33] The *Orient* is representative of German exiles in Palestine in the sense that they in fact constituted a group that was cohesive and self-conscious. Although they kept among themselves, these exiles had an active and organized cultural and political life. Separatist cul-

---

[30] Schalom Ben-Chorin: Deutschland – Morgen. Eine Antwort an Alfred Kerr. In: Orient, No. 23/24, September 11, 1942, p. 31–32.

[31] Arnold Zweig: Antigermanismus. Nach drei Kriegsjahren. In: Orient, No. 30, October 23, 1942, p. 10–11.

[32] Yoav Gelber: New Homeland. Immigration and Absorption of Central European Jews 1933–1948. Jerusalem 1990 [hebr.], p. 231. For further remarks by Gelber on this group, see also p. 70–77 and esp. p. 233–236 (the subchapter »Emigration from Eretz Israel of central European immigrants«).

[33] Arie Wolf: Größe und Tragik Arnold Zweigs. Ein jüdisch-deutsches Dichterschicksal in jüdischer Sicht. London et al.: World of Books 1991, p. 358. The entire 7th chapter of this book is in fact replete with psychologistic interpretation of Zweig's political opinions and activity.

tural evenings³⁴ were held regularly in the big cities of Palestine;³⁵ there was, for example, at least one active branch of the SAP³⁶ in Tel-Aviv; one might also mention ad-hoc formations aimed at facilitating the return to Germany and Austria after the war.³⁷

The Zionist narrative uses terms such as »Aliya« and »absorption« and avoids the use of expressions such as »emigration« and »exile«. Apologetically, Yekkes tended to view their story in terms of their contribution to the Yishuv and to the state of Israel, minimizing the conflict and hardships they encountered. Generally speaking, the surface aspects took precedence over internal dimensions, such as the identity problems experienced by immigrants.³⁸

The arrival of emigrants in Palestine has been described by historians as some kind of »Stunde Null«. The circumstances and background prior to emigration have not been dealt with, as if this chapter was self-explanatory or irrelevant to the story of these immigrants' Aliya and their integration in the new land. Thus any continuity that might have existed in the emigrants' self-understanding was completely ignored, and a break was established between the history of Central European Jewry and that of the Yekkes.

The *Orient* challenges us to question the existing narrative. Examining this periodical can help us not only to understand the demarcation line between Zionist Aliya and German Exile, but can also help us to bridge the gap between the history of Central European Jewry and the story of the Yekkes. Based even on the few citations presented here, it is clear that, even in Palestine, the *Orient*'s writers preserved at least something of the German-Jewish tradition and that variant of it which Mosse termed »left-wing identity«. The *Orient* clearly does not represent the majority of the Yekkes, but it does provide a striking illustration of the problematics which were – albeit in a much milder and a more repressed manner – typical to many German Jews in Palestine/Israel.

---

³⁴ For a long list of such artistic-literary circles, see: Berendsohn, Die Humanistische Front (note 3), Zweiter Teil: Vom Kriegsausbruch 1939 bis Ende 1946, p. 164f. For a list of German publications by members of these very circles, see ibid., p. 170f.

³⁵ The author's interview with Walter Grab (April 25, 1999).

³⁶ See the text on Alfred Moos (who contributed to the *Orient* under the pseudonym Peter Zink) in: Biographisches Handbuch der deutschsprachigen Emigration nach 1933 / International Biographical Dictionary of Central European Émigrés 1933–1945. Hg. vom Institut für Zeitgeschichte München. Unter der Gesamtleitung von Werner Röder und Herbert A. Strauss. 3 Vols, München et al.: Saur 1980–1983, Vol. 1, p. 507. See also: Signs of Life. Jews from Wuerttemberg. Reports for the Period after 1933 in Letters and Descriptions. Ed. by Herbert A. Strauss. New York: Ktav 1982, p. 213–215.

³⁷ Israel State Archives, Division 2, D 198/46 and I 583/46.

³⁸ For criticism of similar approaches, see Henry Wassermann's Review of Gelber's book (*New Homeland*, 1990), in: Aschkenas 2 (1992), p. 285–292. For a beginning of a different approach, see Guy Miron's doctoral dissertation, which is based on the writings of emigrants and thus focuses on the emigrants perspective: Guy Miron: From ›There‹ to ›Here‹ in First Person. German Jews in Palestine/Israel. Self Consciousness through Patterns of Autobiographical Memory. Jerusalem 1998 [hebr.].

Bernhard Greiner

Re-Präsentation: Exil als Zeichenpraxis bei Anna Seghers

Kafka, der sich in einem Brief an Milena als der »westjüdischste der Westjuden« bezeichnet,[1] wählt, um seine Existenz als eine des Exils oder der Diaspora zu fassen, nicht einen Psalmisten oder Propheten der Bibel zum Wortgeber, sondern den aus der Verbannung sprechenden Dichter Ovid. In einem seiner Briefe an Felice Bauer (22./23. Januar 1913) berichtet er von einem Traum,

> [...] wo ich [...] zu einer Brücke oder einem Quaigeländer hinlief, zwei Telephonhörmuscheln, die dort zufällig auf der Brüstung lagen, ergriff und an die Ohren hielt und nun immerfort nichts anderes verlangte, als Nachrichten vom »Pontus« zu hören[2].

Das Traum-Ich vermag keine Verbindung zu dem anderen exilierten Dichter herzustellen, aber, so der Erzähler, »ich ließ nicht nach und ging nicht weg«.[3] Die Reverenz an den Autor der »Tristia« und »Epistulae ex Ponto« mag in der paradoxen Leistung dieser Texte gründen, im Sprechen aus der Trennung von der kulturellen Gemeinschaft, der sich der Autor zurechnet, gerade eindringlich eine Verbindung zum Entzogenen herzustellen. Wenn Ovid von Rom als dem Verwehrten spricht, wird dieses in unerhörter Leuchtkraft nahe gerückt. Die Elegie lebt von dieser Dialektik, sie ist zugleich die Grundfigur der Literatur des Exils. Goethe entfaltet sie umfassend im Schlußabschnitt der *Italienischen Reise*. Der Abschied von Rom, die Trennung von der Stadt, in der das Künstler-Ich sein wahres Zuhause erfahren hat, läßt die Rückkehr in die Heimat zum Gang ins Exil werden. In der Abschiedsstunde wandert das beschriebene Ich durch das nächtliche Rom und beschwört dabei das ihm noch gegenwärtige Rom in Versen Ovids, die ihrerseits aus dem fernen Tomi den eigenen nächtlichen Abschied von Rom in Erinnerung rufen. So entwirft Goethe in der noch gegenwärtigen Erfahrung Roms das Getrennt-Sein von der Stadt, indem er einen Text aneignet, der im Beschwören von Abgetrennt-Sein das Entzogene gerade anwesend sein läßt. Solch potenzierte Verschränkung von Distanznahme und Vergegenwärtigung führt in das Zentrum der Literatur des Exils.

---

[1] Franz Kafka: Briefe an Milena. Hg. von Willy Haas. Lizenzausg., 1.–6. Tsd, New York: S. Fischer 1952, S. 247.
[2] Franz Kafka: Briefe an Felice und andere Korrespondenz aus der Verlobungszeit. Hg. von Erich Heller und Jürgen Born. Lizenzausg., 6.–9. Tsd, Frankfurt a. M.: S. Fischer 1967, S. 264.
[3] Ebd.

Denn deren spezifische Leistung erschließt sich aus der Frage, wie in der Erfahrung und Vorstellung des Abgetrennt-Seins von der jeweils zugehörigen Gemeinschaft der Bezug zum Entzogenen gerade hergestellt oder bewahrt wird. Poetologisch ist dies die Frage, wie in der Re-Präsentation, die immer Vergegenwärtigen eines Abwesenden ist, mit dem Moment der Präsenz umgegangen wird. Damit sind die Grundlagen benannt für eine poetologische Bestimmung von Exilliteratur: als Literatur, die sich durch spezifische Strategien ausweist, die paradoxe Verschränkung von Entzug und Vergegenwärtigung im Akt der Repräsentation zu leisten und zu sichern. Solch eine Definition würde beim literarischen Charakter dieser Literatur ansetzen, was angemessener erscheint als eine historisch-soziologische Bestimmung (im Rekurs auf die Exilerfahrung des Autors) oder eine thematische. Für diese gattungsbegründende Leistung von Exilliteratur aber, d. i. ihre spezifische Verschränkung von Re-Präsentation und Präsenz, hält die jüdische Erfahrung und Tradition komplexe Denkfiguren und Handlungsmuster bereit, da im jüdischen Selbstverständnis der Exilgedanke eine überaus prominente, zugleich paradoxe Stellung innehat.[4]

Schon in die Konstitution des jüdischen Volkes, nicht erst in seine Geschichte seit dem babylonischen Exil und weit mehr noch seit der Zerstörung des Tempels ist der Exilgedanke maßgeblich eingeschrieben. Den Beginn des endlichen Daseins des Menschen faßt die Bibel als Vertreibung (aus dem Paradies). Auf den Bund mit Noah nach der Sintflut folgt das Gebot Gottes an Noahs Nachkommen, sich zu zerstreuen, was das Volk in Babel mit dem bekannten Ergebnis verweigert hat. Die anschließende Geschichte Abrahams setzt damit ein, daß Gott Abraham gebietet, seine Heimat zu verlassen, also in die Fremde zu gehen, die hier allerdings ein von Gott gewiesenes Land ist. Nach solcher Vorgeschichte überrascht es nicht, daß die Geburtsstunde des jüdischen Volkes, die Offenbarung und der Bund am Sinai, in die Übergangszeit und den Durchgangsraum eines Auszugs gelegt ist: das Land der Knechtschaft ist verlassen, aber die Landnahme steht noch aus. Und noch ehe diese erfolgt ist, noch ehe mithin die Gemeinschaft einen Ort hat, wird schon das Elend eines erneuten Exils – als Strafe bei Nichteinhalten der Gebote – in fürchterlicher Weise ausgemalt (»[...] und ihr werdet herausgerissen werden aus dem Lande, in das du jetzt ziehst, es einzunehmen. Denn der Herr wird dich zerstreuen unter alle Völker von einem Ende der Erde bis ans andere. [...] Nacht und Tag wirst du dich fürchten und deines Lebens nicht sicher sein. Morgens wirst du sagen: Ach daß es Abend wäre! und abends wirst du sagen: Ach daß es morgen wäre.« [5 Mose 28,63 u. 66–67, vgl. auch 3 Moses 26]). Ist derart Exil, Vertreibung, Knechtschaft unter fremden Völkern im kollektiven Gedächtnis wie im religiösen Bewußtsein des Judentums ein integraler Bestandteil der Vorstellung von gelungener Gemeinschaftsbildung im verheißenen Land, so ermöglicht dies auch die Umkehrung, gewissermaßen die Gegen-

---

[4] Hierzu: Yosef Hayim Yerushalmi: Exil und Vertreibung in der jüdischen Geschichte. In: Y. H. Yerushalmi: Ein Feld in Anatot. Versuche über jüdische Geschichte. Berlin: Wagenbach 1993 (Kleine kulturwissenschaftliche Bibliothek; 44), S. 21–38.

Lektüre: wo der Entzug, das Abgetrennt-Sein von der zugehörigen kulturellen Gemeinschaft bzw. der Verlust ihres Zentrums benannt werden muß, ist in der jüdischen Tradition das Moment der Vergegenwärtigung im Benennen des Entzugs, des Eines-Seins im Benennen der Zerstreuung immer stark. Für die Verschränkung von Re-Präsentation und Präsenz in der Exilliteratur, insbesondere für das Befestigen des Momentes der Präsenz in der Re-Präsentation, finden sich in der jüdischen Tradition drei große Felder der Verwirklichung, denen dann auch spezifische poetische Strategien zugeordnet werden können.

1. Das Moment der Präsenz in der Repräsentation kann im Akzentuieren der »Antinomie des Allegorischen« im Sinne Benjamins befestigt werden,[5] theologisch und historisch führt dies zum Messianismus im Judentum. Wenn das geschichtliche Dasein als eines des Exils nicht mehr auf ein existierendes Zentrum bezogen werden kann, rückt es in den Status des Vorläufigen.[6] Dann wird jedes Geschehen, jeder geschichtliche Zeitpunkt, jedes Ding gleich-gültig, Vor-Geschichte. Es entwertet sich unter dem allegorischen Blick. Zugleich wird es jedoch ungeheuer aufgewertet, da nun jeder Augenblick der des Umschwungs, jedes Ding zum Gefäß der Verheißung werden kann. Auf die Exilexistenz, das Leben im Aufschub angewandt, besagt dies: dem Exil als Sühne des Volkes muß irgendwann die Rückführung folgen; denn der Bund ist ewig: »Der Israel zerstreut hat, der wird's auch wieder sammeln« (Jer. 31,10),[7] resp. das rabbinische Vertrauen: »am Tag, als der Tempel zerstört wurde, ward der Erlöser geboren.«[8] In Walter Benjamin kann ein prominenter Vertreter dieser allegorisch-messianischen Möglichkeit des Exilliteratur erkannt werden, literarisch hat wohl Kafka diese Denkfigur am eindringlichsten ausgeschrieben.

2. Das Moment der Präsenz in der Re-Präsentation erscheint in der jüdischen Tradition auch durch eine Art theatralisches Zugleich beider befestigt, als paradoxe Verschränkung von ›Assimilation‹ und ›Dissimilation‹. Exilexistenz als Zerstreuung in andere Kulturen, woraus aber auch ein Sich-Einrichten im Fremden werden kann, Exil als Domizil,[9] solche Exilexistenz wird in dieser Denkfigur mit der Erfahrung verknüpft, sich bewahrt zu haben resp. sich be-

---

[5] Walter Benjamin: Ursprung des deutschen Trauerspiels. In: W. Benjamin: Gesammelte Schriften. Hg. von Rolf Tiedemann und Hermann Schweppenhäuser. Frankfurt a. M.: Suhrkamp 1974, Bd I/1, S. 350.

[6] Gershom Scholem: Zum Verständnis der messianischen Idee im Judentum. In: G. Scholem: Über einige Grundbegriffe des Judentums. Frankfurt a. M.: Suhrkamp 1970 (Suhrkamp-Taschenbuch; 414), S. 121–167, hier S. 166.

[7] Vgl. auch 3 Mose 26, 44–45: »Auch wenn sie schon in der Feinde Land sind, habe ich sie gleichwohl nicht verworfen und ekelt mich ihrer nicht also, daß es mit ihnen aus sein sollte und mein Bund mit ihnen sollte nicht mehr gelten; denn ich bin der Herr, Ihr Gott. Und ich will über sie an meinen ersten Bund gedenken, da ich sie aus Ägyptenland führte vor den Augen der Heiden, daß ich ihr Gott wäre, ich, der Herr«.

[8] Yerushalmi, Exil und Vertreibung in der jüdischen Geschichte (Anm. 4), S. 23.

[9] Ebd.

wahren zu können in der kulturellen Besonderheit, in diesem Sinne als ›Präsenz‹ des Jüdischen. Die Bildungsidee des 18. und 19. Jahrhunderts und die Kulturidee der Kulturphilosophie des frühen 20. Jahrhunderts waren Konzepte, auf die die Erwartung solch eines Zugleichs projiziert wurden. Es ist die Denkfigur einer immanenten Transzendenz: im Hinübergehen zum anderen, in der Entgrenzung, gerade nicht ›hinüberzugehen‹, vielmehr das Prinzip der Unterscheidung stark zu machen.[10] In der jüdischen Überlieferung ist die Esther-Geschichte hierfür das Paradigma: eine Erzählung der Makkabäerzeit,[11] zurückprojiziert in die Zeit des persischen Großreiches. Die Assimilation der Juden in den Ländern des Großreiches erscheint weit fortgeschritten, das gleichzeitige Beharren auf dem eigenen, Jüdischen (der Part Mardochais) führt zuerst in größte Gefährdung des Judentums als ganzem, dann aber zu einer umfassenden Restituierung des Eigenem im Fremden: die Dissimilation. Das Purim-Fest wiederholt dieses Paradox: Entgrenzung, Ausgelassenheit, die aber nicht kompensatorisch freigegeben ist als Ausgleich für Ich-Schwäche und mithin das Ich in seinen Grenzen bedrohend, sondern als Manifestation des Ich in seiner Besonderheit, also seines Beharrens auf Grenzen. Die Esther-Erzählung als Paradigma dieser Spielart von Exildichtung macht die Figur der immanenten Transzendenz explizit, in der nicht-jüdischen europäischen Tradition, soweit sie in Ovids Elegien ihr Urbild erkennt, blieb diese Figur verborgen, obwohl Ovids ›Exil‹-Dichtung viele Signale bereithält, daß die Exilexistenz des sprechenden Ich eine fiktive ist: in Rom, d. h. ›immanent‹, in einem Dasein im Zentrum der eigenen Kultur, wird das furchtbare Geschick eines Verbannt-Seins ans Ende der Welt, die ›Transzendenz‹ in einen kulturlosen Raum entworfen.[12]
3. In der jüdischen Tradition findet sich noch eine dritte Strategie, das Moment der Präsenz in der Re-Präsentation zu befestigen. Es ist das Bilden und Tradieren von Zeichen einer humanen Welt in der Perspektive ihrer ›Materialisierung‹, d. h. der geschichtlichen Verwirklichung des im Zeichen Vorgestellten. Die ›Verwirklichungs‹-Idee des Zionismus ist hier selbstverständlich zu nennen (›hagschamah‹, mit der Wurzel ›geschem‹: Realisierung, Materialisierung).[13] Als ein geschichtsphilosophisch-materialistisches

---

[10] Im Sinne von Kafkas Parabel »Von den Gleichnissen«, in: Franz Kafka: Die Erzählungen und andere ausgewählte Prosa. Hg. von Roger Hermes. Frankfurt a. M.: Fischer Taschenbuch-Verlag 1996 (Fischer-Taschenbuch; 13270), S. 463.
[11] Hierzu Elias J. Bickerman: The God of the Macabees. Studies on the Meaning and Origin of the Macabean Revolt. Leiden: Brill 1979 (Studies in Judaism in Late Antiquity; 32), insb. Vorwort) und E. Bickerman: Four Strange Books of the Bible. Jonah, Daniel, Koheleth, Esther. New York: Schocken Books 1967.
[12] Die These, daß Ovid gar nicht im Exil gewesen sei, verdanke ich Heinz Hofmann: Ovids Verbannung in seinen Gedichten (unveröffentlichtes Vortragsmanuskript).
[13] Zu den verschiedenen Orientierungen dieses Verwirklichungsdenkens: The Zionist Idea. A Historical Analysis and Reader. Ed. and with an Introduction and Biographical Notes by Arthur Hertzberg. 2. ed., Philadelphia, Jerusalem: Jewish Publication Society 1997.

Pendant dieses Verwirklichungsdenkens kann der Marxismus erkannt werden.[14] Anna Seghers' Schreiben ist grundlegend diesem Weg der Verschränkung von Repräsentation und Präsenz verpflichtet. Es soll hier in den Blick gerückt werden, weil es diese Figur der Exilliteratur radikal befragt, in eine umfassende Krise führt, aus der ein Weg heraus entworfen wird in einer neuen literarischen Begründung von Autorschaft. Nebenbei stellt sich damit die Frage, wie weit das historisch-materialistische Geschichts- und Gesellschaftsverständnis, das Anna Seghers' Schreiben leitet, sich gerade in seinem Akzentuieren des Verwirklichungsgedankens auch aus zionistischen Quellen speist. Anna Seghers ist in einer orthodoxen jüdischen Familie aufgewachsen,[15] sowohl in diesem Umfeld als auch an ihrem Studienort Heidelberg[16] wäre eine Auseinandersetzung mit Grundgedanken des Zionismus nicht ungewöhnlich. Bisher ist unerforscht, ob es konkrete Verbindungen zu zionistischen Gruppen gegeben hat, etwa während des Studiums, das Anna Seghers (Netty Reiling) bekanntlich mit einer Dissertation über *Jude und Judentum im Werk Rembrandts* (1924) abgeschlossen hat.

Abgesehen von all ihrer stofflichen und thematischen Vielfalt, auch den großen Schwankungen ihrer literarischen Qualität, zeigen Anna Seghers' Erzählungen und Romane eine erstaunliche strukturelle Gleichförmigkeit. Ein Geschehen wird aufgebaut, das nicht nur in der vorgestellten Welt, sondern ebenso im Akt des Erzählens ausgerichtet ist auf die Bildung eines Zeichens, in dem das Versprechen einer humanen Welt, gegen die gezeigte Wirklichkeit der Klassenkämpfe, positiv oder ex negativo gesetzt ist. Das Zeichen ist auf Verwirklichung des in ihm Vorgestellten hin gespannt, so muß das Erzählen diese Spannung ausmessen. Diese ist aber immer auch ein Effekt des Erzählens selbst; denn das Erzählen bestimmt durch die gewählten literarischen Verfahren, etwa eine spezifische Allegorese, nicht nur die Chance, daß das Zeichen wirklich werde, der literarische Bestimmungsakt ist vielmehr selbst schon ein Teil des Verwirklichungsgeschehens.

Eindringlich führt der erste Abschnitt der frühen Erzählung »Aufstand der Fischer von St. Barbara« (erschienen 1928), mit der Anna Seghers in der literarischen Öffentlichkeit bekannt wurde (im gleichen Jahr wurde ihr der Kleist-Preis zuerkannt) diese Struktur vor:

---

[14] Eine Verbindung beider Konzepte zeigt z. B. das Schaffen Max Nordaus.
[15] Hierzu Christiane Zehl Romero: Anna Seghers. Eine Biographie 1900–1947. Berlin: Aufbau 2000; Friedrich Schütz: Die Familie Seghers-Reiling und das jüdische Mainz. In: Argonautenschiff. Jahrbuch der Anna-Seghers-Gesellschaft 2 (1993), S. 151–173; id., Juden in Mainz. Katalog zur Ausstellung der Stadt Mainz im Rathaus-Foyer, November 1978.
[16] Über jüdische intellektuelle Kreise in Heidelberg s. z. B. Scholems Autobiographie: Gershom Scholem: Von Berlin nach Jerusalem. Jugenderinnerungen. Erweiterte Fassung. Aus dem Hebr. von Michael Brocke und Andrea Schatz. Frankfurt a. M.: Jüdischer Verlag 1994, S. 79–83.

> Der Aufstand der Fischer von St. Barbara endete mit der verspäteten Ausfahrt zu den Bedingungen der vergangenen vier Jahre. Man kann sagen, daß der Aufstand eigentlich schon zu Ende war, bevor Hull nach Port Sebastian eingeliefert wurde und Andreas auf der Flucht durch die Klippen umkam. Der Präfekt reiste ab, nachdem er in die Hauptstadt berichtet hatte, daß die Ruhe in der Bucht wiederhergestellt sei. St. Barbara sah jetzt wirklich aus, wie es jeden Sommer aussah. Aber längst, nachdem die Soldaten zurückgezogen, die Fischer auf der See waren, saß der Aufstand noch auf dem leeren, weißen, sommerlich kahlen Marktplatz und dachte ruhig an die Seinigen, die er geboren, aufgezogen, gepflegt und behütet hatte für das, was für sie am besten war. (I, 7)[17]

Der Beginn nimmt das Ende vorweg. Ein Aufstand hat stattgefunden, aber die alten Verhältnisse bestehen fort. Den Repräsentanten der etablierten Macht stehen zwei Gruppen gegenüber. Zum einen Figuren, die mit Namen benannt werden, sie waren offenbar die ›Seele‹ des Aufstandes, als solche figurieren sie als Repräsentanten einer humaneren Welt, zum andern die Fischer, die den Aufstand gemacht haben. Das ›innerste Innere‹ der Fischer, so wird die Erzählung dann zeigen, wurde eins mit den revolutionären Repräsentanten (als Anwälten der Realisierung der Freiheitsidee), das ›innerste Innere‹ wurde in diesem Verschmelzungsakt zugleich erweckt und kenntlich, d. h. wahrnehmbar und somit körperlich:

> Über den Tisch weg sahen die Frauen in den Augen ihrer Männer ganz unten etwas Neues, Festes, Dunkles, wie den Bodensatz in ausgeleerten Gefäßen. (I, 58)

Die Vereinigung des Innersten der Fischer mit den revolutionären Repräsentanten schuf aber nicht eine neue Wirklichkeit, vielmehr – unter dem Druck der siegreich gebliebenen alten Macht – ein Zeichen: die Allegorie des Aufstands, die der Erzähler auf den leeren Marktplatz projiziert. Bemerkenswert ist die Umkehrung der Vorstellung, die der Erzähler dabei vornimmt: der Aufstand »dachte ruhig an die Seinigen, die er geboren, aufgezogen, gepflegt und behütet hatte für das, was für sie am besten war«. Der Aufstand, der stattgefunden hat, bestand im Handeln der Figuren, so ist dieses die Ursache, ist der Aufstand als Allegorie das Produzierte; demgegenüber macht der Erzähler den Aufstand zum Produzierenden, d. h. zur Instanz, die etwas in die Wirklichkeit bringt, also verkörpert. Ein literarisches, wenn man will: rhetorisches Verfahren – metonymisches Vertauschen von Subjekt und Objekt in der Allegorese –, befestigt derart den Verwirklichungsgedanken. Nach solchen Befestigungen muß aber gesucht werden, soll die Aussage nicht zynisch sein, daß die in Subjektposition gerückte Allegorie das Beste für die Seinigen besorgt habe; denn dieses ›Beste‹ ist, folgt man der berichteten Handlung, ein gänzlich erfolgloser Kampf gewesen.

Das geschaffene Zeichen muß eine Gewähr seiner Verwirklichung mit sich führen. Das ist die eingangs genannte Frage nach Strategien, das Moment der

---

[17] Zitate aus den Werken von Anna Seghers werden, wenn nicht anders vermerkt, im Text nachgewiesen, wobei folgende Ausgabe zugrundegelegt wird: Anna Seghers, Werke in zehn Bänden, Darmstadt, Neuwied: Luchterhand 1977.

Präsenz in der Re-Präsentation zu sichern. Es ist ein textfremdes Argument, in diesem Zusammenhang auf die Biographie der Autorin zu rekurrieren, die 1928 Mitglied der kommunistischen Partei geworden war, also die marxistische Geschichtstheorie zu bemühen, die einen notwendigen Gang der Geschichte hin zur sozialistischen Revolution postuliert und so einem hierauf verweisenden Zeichen die ›letztendliche‹ Verkörperung garantiert. Zu fragen ist vielmehr nach den literarischen Strategien des Textes selbst. Die erste Antwort war, daß das geschaffene Zeichen, die Allegorie »Aufstand«, in umspringenden Vorstellungen sowohl als Produziertes als auch als Produzierendes entworfen wird. Dadurch wird Verwirklichung suggeriert, allerdings zirkulär, insofern das Ergebnis des Prozesses für diesen schon immer vorausgesetzt ist. In eben solch einem Zirkel zeigt sich aber auch die Kulturidee des Zionismus verstrickt. Im Begriff der Kultur sind die Vorstellungen von Aneignung, Bebauung und Verstetigung eines Raumes zentral, für das Judentum ist jedoch, seit der Zerstörung des Tempels, Raumlosigkeit kennzeichnend bzw. Bezug zu einem entzogenen Raum, den Gottesstaat, den der Messias begründen wird. So müssen die kulturellen Akte einerseits den Kulturraum erzeugen, in dessen Bebauung und Verstetigung sie sich andererseits doch erst als Akte der Kultur begründen. Das Ergebnis des kulturellen Aktes liegt diesem immer schon als Bedingung voraus.[18]

Anna Seghers' Texte entwerfen eine bemerkenswerte literarische Strategie, aus diesem Zirkel herauszukommen: das im Zeichen zur Debatte stehende Versprechen der Verwirklichung wird befestigt durch performative Verkörperung. Denn schon das Schaffen selbst des Zeichens – die Allegorisierung des leeren Marktplatzes zum Aufstand – ist Teil seiner Verwirklichung und bürgt entsprechend für diese, allerdings nicht in der vorgestellten Welt, sondern auf der Ebene des literarischen Diskurses. Wieder erfolgt dies in umspringenden Vorstellungen. Das Zeichen wird in der Wirklichkeit der dargestellten Welt situiert, dort bleibt es aber eine Setzung, bewahrheitet nur durch das Handeln der Fischer. Zugleich wird dieses Zeichen in der Wirklichkeit des literarischen Prozesses geschaffen, es fungiert auf beiden Ebenen, der Text vollzieht, wovon er spricht. Das gibt der Allegorisierung auf der einen Ebene (der ›histoire‹) Schlüssigkeit durch ihre Verwirklichung auf der anderen Ebene (des ›discours‹) und umgekehrt. Verwirklichung des Zeichens, das Moment der Präsenz in der Re-Präsentation, wird performativ befestigt als Verkörperung im literarischen Prozeß selbst, der die Semiosis zugleich vollzieht, die er darstellt. Der literarische Diskurs ist selbst schon ein Vorgang der Verkörperung. Diese an der Erzählung »Aufstand der Fischer von St. Barbara« herausgearbeitete Struktur leistet noch in einem zweiten Zirkel eine Selbstbegründung (wenn man im beschriebenen Wechselerweis von histoire und discours im Hinblick auf den Verwirklichungsgedanken den ersten Zirkel erkennt). Es ist der Zirkel,

---

[18] Hierzu Philipp Theisohn: Aus dem Nichts. Der Raum der Nation im jüdischen Kulturdenken zwischen Idealismus und Zionismus. In: Arche Noah. Die Idee der ›Kultur‹ im deutsch-jüdischen Diskurs. Hg. von Bernhard Greiner und Christoph Schmidt. Freiburg: Rombach 2002, S. 95-123.

daß der Text mit der erläuterten Struktur wiederholt und damit literarisch vollzieht, was die Autorschaft ›Anna Seghers'‹ begründet hat.

›Anna Seghers‹ ist bekanntlich ein Pseudonym, das auf die historische Person Netty Radvany, geb. Reiling und deren umfangreiches literarisches Werk verweist. Der Name ›Anna Seghers‹ wurde aber nicht einfach als Verfassername unter einen Text gesetzt, er wird vielmehr in der ersten veröffentlichten Erzählung der Autorin begründet, d. i. die Erzählung »Die Toten auf der Insel Djal«, erschienen 1924 in der Weihnachtsausgabe der *Frankfurter Zeitung*. Die nachfolgenden Texte schreiben die in dieser Erzählung gesetzte Struktur in immer neuen Varianten aus, so ist dieser Text nicht nur Ursprungstext des Autorennamens, sondern diskursbegründend für die Autorschaft ›Anna Seghers'‹. Die Erzählerin stellt in diesem Begründungstext der Autorschaft ›Anna Seghers'‹ durch einen dem Protagonisten wie der Erzählerin gemeinsamen Familiennamen eine Verbindung zur Welt des Textes her. Der Protagonist trägt den Namen Jan Seghers, die Erzählung hat den Untertitel »Sage aus dem Holländischen, nacherzählt von Antje Seghers«. Ein Erzähler, der sich mit seinem Namen in einem Text artikuliert – z. B. in einer Autobiographie – verweist nie genau auf eine reale Person dieses Namens, sondern auf ein alter ego. Foucault spricht daher von der »Funktion Autor«, die den Bruch vollziehe zwischen fiktionalem Sprecher und wirklichem Schriftsteller.[19] Dieser ›Bruch‹ wird im Ursprungstext der Autorschaft ›Anna Seghers'‹ selbst zum Thema. Denn er entwirft eine Welt, in der die Relation zwischen Text und Leben nicht eine der Repräsentation ist, sondern der Metamorphose: von einem Text geschieht Verwandlung in Leben, Leben wird zugleich überführt in Text, soll dort stillgestellt werden. Der Protagonist Jan Seghers,[20] Pfarrer auf der Insel, ist aus einem Text – er führt seinen Besucher zu einem Grabstein, auf dem sein Name steht – ins Leben gelangt. Er habe, so berichtet er, nach seinem Tode Gott so lange bestürmt, bis dieser ihn in seiner alten Gestalt wieder ins Leben gelassen habe. Die »Wollust«[21] des Pfarrers aber besteht darin, Leben in Text/Schrift zu verwandeln. Er sorgt dafür, daß die an der Insel zerschellten und auf ihr begrabenen Seeleute, die auch im Grab keine Ruhe geben (Hände aus dem Grab strecken, als Revenants wieder auftauchen), in ihren Gräbern zur Ruhe kommen. So setzt er die Opposition von Text (Schrift auf den Grabstei-

---

[19] Michel Foucault: Was ist ein Autor? [Qu'est-ce qu'un auteur?] In: M. Foucault: Schriften zur Literatur. Aus dem Frz. übersetzt von Karin von Hofer. Ungekürzte Ausg., Frankfurt a. M., Berlin, Wien: Ullstein 1979 (Ullstein-Buch; 35011: Ullstein-Materialien), S. 7–31.

[20] Anna Seghers: Die Toten auf der Insel Djal / Sagen von Unirdischen. Berlin, Weimar: Aufbau 1985 (erster Wiederabdruck nach der Erstveröffentlichung von 1924 in: Blätter der Carl Zuckmayer-Gesellschaft 6 [1980], S. 223–226). In der Zeichnung des Pfarrers wird eine Durchlässigkeit auch zwischen transzendenter und immanenter Welt angezeigt: »Er hätte der Leibhaftige sein mögen, wenn er nicht gerade der Pfarrer von Djal gewesen wäre.« (Die Toten auf der Insel Djal, wie oben, S. 223)

[21] Ebd., S. 223.

nen) und Leben endgültig durch (als Re-Präsentation ohne Präsenz). Ist er derart Instanz der Unterscheidung, so widerruft er diese aber zugleich durch sich selbst, da er sie ja durchbrochen hat. Diesen Widerruf spiegelt der Text noch einmal darin, daß die Handlung damit vorankommt, daß der Pfarrer einer Bibelstelle nachsinnt, die wiederum von nichts anderem handelt als dem Übergang von Tod in Leben:

> »Und es ging ein Brief an die Gemeinde von Laodicea« sagte er zum dritten Mal vor sich hin und schlug auf den Tisch; denn aus irgendeinem Grund schien ihm diese Stelle besonders wohlklingend und eine Zierde des Neuen Testamentes zu sein [...].[22]

Der Satz spielt auf die Offenbarung des Johannes an (vgl. Off. 3,14), worin eine Stimme zu schreiben befiehlt, die sich mit den Worten einführt: »Ich war tot und siehe, ich bin lebendig von Ewigkeit zu Ewigkeit.« (Off. 1,18) Was der Text zu lesen gibt – u. a. soll der Gemeinde von Laodicea geschrieben werden: »Siehe, ich stehe vor der Tür und klopfe an. So jemand meine Stimme hören wird und die Tür auftun, zu dem werde ich eingehen [...]« (Off. 3,20) – das ereignet sich dann sogleich in der Wirklichkeit des Pfarrers, allerdings gekappt um die Erlösungsperspektive: in die Stube des Pfarrers tritt ein aus dem Totenreich Wiedergekehrter, der vom Pfarrer aber vergeblich eine Befestigung seiner Rückkehr aus dem Totenreich zu erzwingen sucht. Das Gelesene gewinnt so Körperlichkeit. Repräsentation wird ersetzt durch Verkörperung hier und jetzt des im Zeichen Vorgestellten wie umgekehrt die Verkörperung das vom Zeichen Repräsentierte bewahrheitet als ein Wechselerweis von vorstellendem Sagen und Performanz des Sagens. Die Autorschaft ›Anna Seghers‹ ist Effekt dieses Wechselspiels, zugleich vollzieht sie es aber schon in diesem Begründungstext und wiederholt sie dieses dann in jedem ihrer weiteren Texte. Denn alle diese Texte sind gespannt auf den Aufbau eines leitenden Zeichens hin, für das Präsenz in der Repräsentation performativ befestigt wird: Verwirklichung als Verkörperung im literarischen Akt selbst. Der Zirkel des Wechselerweises von Präsenz und Repräsentation in der Zeichenbildung – daß das Zeichen, das die Texte jeweils schaffen, Effekt der erzählten Handlung ist (am ersten Beispiel: die Allegorie »Aufstand« als ein Produziertes), daß dieses Zeichen zugleich aber die treibende Kraft der Handlung ist (die Allegorie »Aufstand« als das Produzierende) –, diesen Zirkel versuchen die Texte aufzubrechen, indem sie ihn in einem zweiten Wechselerweis spiegeln, bei dem die beiden Glieder nun aber auf systematisch verschiedenen Ebenen situiert sind (in der vorgestellten Welt und in der diskursiven Wirklichkeit des Erzählens). Im Prinzip wiederholt sich aber auch hier nur der Zirkel und dann noch ein weiteres Mal, insofern jeder Text mit diesen zirkulären Verfahren die Struktur des Ursprungstextes der Autorschaft wiederholt und fortschreibt. Die Spiegelungen verstärken die Suggestion des Wirklich-Werdens des Zeichens durch immer neue performative Verkörperungen.

---

[22] Ebd., S. 224.

Die Texte der Autorschaft ›Anna Seghers‹ folgen dieser Struktur. In ihr ist die konstitutive Aufgabe von Exilliteratur, ein paradoxes Verschränken von Entzug und Vergegenwärtigung semiologisch, als Aufgabe, das Moment der Präsenz in der Re-Präsentation zu befestigen, scharf herauspräpariert und mit der Strategie der literarischen Performanz beantwortet. Entsprechend zeigt dieses Schreiben keinen systematischen, sondern allenfalls einen graduellen Wandel seiner Grunddisposition, wenn für die Autorin und ihre literarische Öffentlichkeit das Exil real wird. Eines der erfolgreichsten literarischen Werke der deutschen Exilliteratur (›Erfolg‹ am Kriterium der Verbreitung gemessen), Anna Seghers' Roman *Das siebte Kreuz* (geschrieben 1938/39, erschienen 1942) zeigt die genannte Grundstruktur überaus sinnfällig.

Repräsentant einer humaneren Welt ist in diesem Roman ein Antifaschist, einer von sieben Flüchtlingen aus einem KZ, für die die Kreuze schon stehen, an die man sie schlagen wird, sobald sie aufgegriffen sind. Die Flucht des Protagonisten bleibt aber erfolgreich und mithin sein Kreuz leer, weil er immer wieder Menschen trifft, die ihm unter größten Gefahren helfen, wobei sich diesen Menschen durch ihre Hilfe für den Flüchtling ihr verschüttetes oder verhärtetes Inneres neu belebt:

> Wir fühlten alle, wie tief und furchtbar die äußeren Mächte in den Menschen hineingreifen können, bis in sein Innerstes, aber wir fühlten auch, daß es im Innersten etwas gab, was unangreifbar war und unverletzbar. (III, 288)

Das Zeichen, das in diesem Roman gebildet wird, das leer bleibende Kreuz, ist auch hier zirkulär begründet. Es ist Effekt des Handelns der Personen, zugleich bringt es als Bereitschaft zum Opfer für andere die Handlung voran; so ist das Bewirkte ein Bewirkendes. Und wieder wird die Verweisungskraft des Zeichens performativ befestigt; denn es wird nicht nur in der vorgestellten Welt, sondern ebenso in der Wirklichkeit des literarischen Prozesses geschaffen, auf dieser Ebene erweist es sich allerdings als widersprüchlich. In der vorgestellten Welt ergibt sich aus der Handlung zwingend, daß das Zeichen seine Verweisungskraft daraus gewinnt, daß das Kreuz leer bleibt. In der Wirklichkeit des literarischen Prozesses, d. h. für den Leser, ist die Bildung solch eines Zeichens jedoch paradox. Zum einen wird mit ihm das zentrale christliche Zeichen zitiert, so steht das Erlösungswerk, auf das dieses verweist, für die Verwirklichung des vom Roman im Zeichen Vorgestellten ein. Zum andern ist am christlichen Zeichen aber eine Negation vorgenommen; denn das Kreuz bleibt leer. Das Versprechen, daß das Zeichen wirklich werde – im ersten Schritt als Verkörperung im literarischen Prozeß –, ist derart daran geknüpft, daß am Zeichen der Körper gerade ausgespart wird. Ein analoger Wandel der erläuterten Grundstruktur der Autorschaft ›Anna Seghers‹ läßt sich an all ihren Texten des Exils erkennen: am jeweils geschaffenen Zeichen wird eine Negativierung vorgenommen, während sich an der Strategie nichts ändert, das Versprechen der Verwirklichung des Zeichens performativ zu befestigen. Im Roman *Transit* (geschrieben 1940/43, erschienen in spanischer und englischer Übersetzung

1944, deutsch 1948) ist die Negativierung am Zeichen so weit fortgeschritten, daß die Grundfigur dieses Schreibens, ihre Semiosis, in Frage steht. Im radikalen Zu-Ende-Schreiben seines eigenen Prinzips, also seiner Selbstaufhebung, ist dieser Text einmalig im Corpus der Autorschaft ›Anna Seghers‹.[23]

Der Roman entwirft zwei Repräsentanten einer humaneren Welt: einen verstorbenen Dichter und eine französische Familie. Letztere hat den einen der Protagonisten, einen deutschen Emigranten, aufgenommen und ihm damit erstmals eine Erfahrung von ›Heimat‹ vermittelt. Mit diesen Repräsentanten einer humaneren Welt verschmilzt das neu erweckte Innere der beiden Protagonisten des Romans. Das ist zum einen Marie, die Frau des Dichters, die diesen im Stich gelassen hat, ihn jetzt sucht, von seinem Tod nicht wissend. Sie verzichtet darauf, ihre Liebe zum anderen Protagonisten des Romans zu leben, um statt dessen dem toten Dichter die Treue zu halten, ihn in immer neuen Exilländern zu suchen, wissend: »Sobald ich suche, weiß ich es, es gibt den Mann. Solange ich suche, weiß ich, ich kann ihn noch finden.« (IV, 152) Der Protagonist und fiktive Erzähler verzichtet reziprok auf seine Liebe zu Marie, obwohl ihm nach vielen Wirren wunderbarerweise die Möglichkeit offenstünde, mit ihr nach Amerika zu emigrieren. Er wird statt dessen eins mit dem Volk, das ihm Zuflucht gewährt hat:

> Was sie trifft, wird auch mich treffen. Die Nazis werden mich keinesfalls mehr als ihren Landsmann erkennen. Ich will jetzt Gutes und Böses hier mit meinen Leuten teilen [...]. (IV, 186)

»Transit« ist am Ort der Handlung, dem Fluchtort Marseille, das magische Papier, dem alle die Emigranten nachjagen, weil es Flucht ermöglicht. Es beinhaltet aber nicht rettende Ankunft in einem anderen Land, sondern, einen Raum zu passieren, ohne sich mit ihm zu verbinden. So steht es für das Transitorische, d. i. Bindungslosigkeit, Einander-im-Stich-lassen. Hiergegen errichten die beiden Protagonisten mit den Bindungen, die sie zu leben beschließen, Zeichen des Nicht-Transitorischen (vgl. IV, 113). Der Roman bildet in seiner diskursiven Wirklichkeit dieses Zeichen, befestigt es damit performativ, um es dabei zugleich aber grundlegend zu negieren. Denn sein Gehalt ist entleert. Die »Bindung« ist im Falle Maries ein Wahn – sie weiß nicht, daß der gesuchte Dichter tot ist, so überantwortet sie sich einer toten Liebe –, im Falle des Ich-Erzählers wird der Preis der Zeichenbildung ausdrücklich benannt: Leere des Herzens:

---

[23] Äußere Traumata in der persönlichen und zeitgeschichtlichen Erfahrung der Autorin, die diese Krise des Schreibens veranlaßt haben mögen, lassen sich genügend aufführen: der Beginn des Krieges, Deportation und Flucht in das nicht besetzte Südfrankreich, dann über Marseille nach Mexiko; zuvor: der Hitler-Stalin-Pakt, d. h. das Bündnis des bekämpften Faschismus mit dem Sozialismus stalinistischer Prägung, der für die engagierte Kommunistin Bürge einer humaneren Welt war.

> Mein Herz, als ob es noch nicht die Leere verstanden hätte, die ihm von nun ab beschieden war, fuhr fort, zu warten. Es wartete immer noch weiter, Marie könnte zurückkehren. Nicht jene, die ich zuletzt gekannt hatte, an einen Toten geknüpft, und nur an ihn, sondern jene, die damals zum erstenmal der Mistral zu mir hereinwehte, mit einem jähen und unverständlichen Glück mein junges Leben bedrohend. (IV, 183)

Am Zeichen ist der Gehalt des Gestorben-Seins herausgearbeitet, so ist es weniger Gegenentwurf als ›Fluchtpunkt‹ (Perspektivpunkt) von ›Transit‹, der allgemeinen Bindungslosigkeit. Das Zeichen mag noch tradiert werden, aber es tradiert nichts mehr, mit einem Vers Celans zu sprechen: »Es steht das Nichts in der Mandel.«[24] Hier kommt die Semiosis der Autorschaft ›Anna Seghers'‹ Benjamins Bezug zur jüdischen Tradition als der Grundlage seiner Auffassung von Sprache und Schrift, sehr nahe: die Wahrheit preiszugeben, um an der Tradierbarkeit festzuhalten.[25] Aber Seghers' Texte öffnen sich dabei nicht einer »Antinomie des Allegorischen« im Sinne Benjamins, daß jedes der ›gleichgültig‹ gewordenen Zeichen zum Ort einer messianischen Erfüllung werden kann.[26]

Die Grundstruktur der Autorschaft ›Anna Seghers'‹, ihre Semiosis und ihr Befestigen des Verwirklichungsversprechens der geschaffenen Zeichen, ist ›zu Ende geschrieben‹. So verlangt ein Weiterschreiben einen neuen Begründungstext. Und eben dies leistet die Erzählung, die nach *Transit* geschrieben wurde: »Der Ausflug der toten Mädchen« (geschrieben 1943/44).[27] Notwendig muß die Erzählung hierfür hinter den Akt zurückgehen, da die Autorschaft ›Anna Seghers'‹ aus einem Text entstanden war. Die Ich-Erzählerin dieses neuen Begründungstextes von Autorschaft imaginiert, daß sie bei ihrem Namen gerufen werde, der Name, den sie dann nennt, mit dem sie sich mithin neu anruft, ist nun aber der reale Mädchenname der Autorin (Netty). So muß der Text autobiographisch werden; es ist der einzige autobiographische Text dieser Autorschaft:

> »Netty!« Mit diesem Namen hatte mich seit der Schulzeit niemand mehr gerufen. Ich hatte gelernt, auf alle die guten und bösen Namen zu hören, mit denen mich Freunde und Feinde zu rufen pflegten, die Namen, die man mir in vielen Jahren in Straßen, Versammlungen, Festen, nächtlichen Zimmern, Polizeiverhören, Büchertiteln, Zeitungsberichten, Protokollen und Pässen beigelegt hatte. Ich hatte sogar, als

---

[24] Paul Celan: Mandorla. In: Paul Celan: Gedichte in zwei Bänden. Frankfurt a. M.: Suhrkamp 1977, Bd 1, S. 244.
[25] Vgl. Benjamin an Scholem 12. Juni 1938. In: Benjamin über Kafka. Texte, Briefzeugnisse, Aufzeichnungen. Hg. von Hermann Schweppenhäuser, Frankfurt: Suhrkamp 1981 Suhrkamp-Taschenbuch Wissenschaft; 341), S. 61–110, hier S. 87.
[26] Vgl. Benjamin, Ursprung des deutschen Trauerspiels (Anm. 5), S. 350.
[27] Auch dieser Text ist, wie *Transit*, mit traumatischen Erfahrungen der Autorin eng verwoben: die Nachricht vom Tod der Mutter in einem KZ, ein schwerer Verkehrsunfall im Juni 1943, langsame Rückkehr des Bewußtseins aus einem viertägigen Koma, Rückkehr des Lebenswillens im Willen, zu schreiben – so die Charakterisierung von Christa Wolf: »›Der Ausflug der toten Mädchen‹ beschreibt nicht die Entscheidung, zu leben, er *ist* diese Entscheidung, er schildert nicht, sondern *ist* Genesung.« (Christa Wolf, Nachwort zur Ausgabe der Werke in 10 Bänden [Anm. 17], Bd X, S. 207–223, hier S. 216)

Re-Präsentation: Exil als Zeichenpraxis bei Anna Seghers 173

> ich krank und besinnungslos lag, manchmal auf jenen alten, frühen Namen gehofft, doch der Name blieb verloren, von dem ich in Selbsttäuschung glaubte, er könnte mich wieder gesund machen, jung, lustig, bereit zu dem alten Leben mit den alten Gefährten, das unwiederbringlich verloren war. (IX, 136)

Im fernen Mexiko als Ort der Rahmenhandlung wiederholt die Ich-Erzählerin halluzinatorisch einen Schulausflug ihrer Mädchenklasse und spiegelt die damaligen Mitschülerinnen, ihre innige Verbundenheit, mit ihren späteren Handlungen und Schicksalen (Unmenschlichkeiten, tödliche Verleugnungen und Verwünschungen, die einige der Mädchen in der faschistischen Zeit anderen ehemaligen Mitschülerinnen antun werden). Die Ich-Erzählerin ist »am äußersten westlichen Punkt« angelangt, »an den [sie] jemals auf Erden geraten war« (IX, 135), es ist das Reich des Todes. Aus ihm geschieht eine Rückkehr im Zeichen von ›Heimat‹. Auf die Bildung dieses Zeichens ist der Text ausgerichtet. Die Disposition, in der nach der semiotischen ›Regel‹ von Anna Seghers' Texten das leitende Zeichen entsteht, wird entworfen, hier als die Verbundenheit der Schulmädchen, deren Inneres erweckt worden ist in der Verbindung mit einem Repräsentanten einer humanen Welt. Als solcher fungiert hier der Geliebte einer der Schulmädchen, in dessen Gesicht die Erzählerin »die Spur von Gerechtigkeit und Rechtlichkeit« eingeschrieben erkennt:

> Er hätte wahrscheinlich dem zarten schönen Gesicht seiner Frau Marianne nach und nach einen solchen Zug von Rechtlichkeit, von gemeinsam geachteter Menschenwürde eingeprägt, der sie dann verhindert hätte, ihre Schulfreundin zu verleugnen. (IX, 144)

Die Erzählung kulminiert in der Bildung des Zeichens ›Heimat‹, das sich versinnlicht in der Umarmung der drei Schulfreundinnen, die stellvertretend steht für eine umfassende Verbundenheit:

> Marianne und Leni und ich, wir hatten alle drei unsere Arme in einander verschränkt in einer Verbundenheit, die einfach zu der großen Verbundenheit alles Irdischen unter der Sonne gehörte. Marianne hatte noch immer den Kopf an Lenis Kopf gelehnt. Wie konnte dann später ein Betrug, ein Wahn, in ihre Gedanken eindringen, daß sie und ihr Mann allein die Liebe zu diesem Land gepachtet hätten und deshalb mit gutem Recht das Mädchen, an das sie sich jetzt lehnte, verachteten und anzeigten. Nie hat uns jemand, als noch Zeit dazu war, an diese gemeinsame Fahrt erinnert. Wie viele Aufsätze auch noch geschrieben wurden über die Heimat und die Geschichte der Heimat und die Liebe zur Heimat, nie wurde erwähnt, daß vornehmlich unser Schwarm aneinandergelehnter Mädchen, stromaufwärts im schrägen Nachmittagslicht, zur Heimat gehörte. (IX, 149)

Aber das Zeichen wurde in der Zeit, in der es seine Wirkung hätte entfalten können und sollen, d. h. in der vorgestellten Welt, nicht gebildet. Die Erzählerin bildet es jetzt, im Schreibakt, in der Wirklichkeit des literarischen Prozesses, das aber heißt im Horizont eines unwiderruflichen ›zu spät‹. Der Text bildet sein Zeichen nur negativ: indem er festhält, daß es nicht gebildet worden ist. Wieder erinnert das an Benjamin, an den Schlußsatz seines *Wahlverwandtschaften*-Essays: »Nur um der Hoffnungslosen willen ist uns die Hoffnung gegeben.«[28] Die Erzählung endet mit dem Auftrag des Schreibens. Die jüdische Lehrerin trägt der Ich-Erzählerin auf, den Schulausflug sorgfältig zu beschreiben. Dieser Auftrag wird nicht in der vorgestellten Welt ausgeführt, sondern in der Wirklichkeit hier und jetzt des Schreibens der Erzählung. Kann man in dieser den Begründungstext einer neuen oder wiederhergestellten Autorschaft erkennen, so ist diese derart im Raum negativer Ästhetik situiert. Diese Negativität hat Anna Seghers – von einigen Ausnahmen abgesehen – unter dem Positivierungsdruck des Sozialistischen Realismus nicht durchgehalten.[29] Aus der Exilliteratur, aus der hier für diese geltend gemachten konstitutiven Dialektik von Vergegenwärtigung und Entzug, hat sie sich damit verabschiedet.

---

[28] Walter Benjamin: Goethes Wahlverwandtschaften. In: Benjamin, Gesammelte Schriften (Anm. 5), Bd I/1, S. 123–201, hier S. 201.
[29] Zu Anna Seghers' Konzepten des Schreibens nach der Rückkehr nach Deutschland: Bernhard Greiner: »Kolonien liebt, und tapfer Vergessen der Geist«. Anna Seghers' zyklisches Erzählen. In: Argonautenschiff. Jahrbuch der Anna-Seghers-Gesellschaft 3 (1994), S. 155–171.

Rochelle Tobias

The Homecoming of a Word: Mystical Language Philosophy in Celan's »Mit allen Gedanken«

»Weggebeizt vom / Strahlenwind deiner Sprache« (Etched away / by the searing wind of your language)[1] are the opening words of one of Celan's more famous texts in which language is compared to a wind which etches, burns and corrodes. At first glance, this searing and possibly radioactive language would appear to be German, Celan's native or mother tongue as well as the language of his mother's murderers, as is often noted in Celan scholarship.[2] And yet even in these opening lines the poem questions whether language is ever native to anyone through an indirect reference to Kabbalist philosophy, which posits that language originates in a breath of God. In this paper, I will consider Celan's poem »With all my thoughts« which alludes in several key places to Scholem's account of medieval Jewish mysticism, in particular the doctrine of the Sefiroth. The spoken word, according to this doctrine, is exiled from the start; it is ›spit out‹ – »hinausgespien« – (I,271) or exhaled by an otherwise inaccessible God. And once released, it is divided into countless other terms, a volcanic »word heap« (II,29), as Celan puts it in another poem. Even in its distance from its source, however, the spoken word is at home. It is at home in the world, because the world itself derives from God's unpronounceable name, as I will explain in what follows.

* * *

Mit allen Gedanken ging ich
hinaus aus der Welt: da warst du,
du meine Leise, du meine Offne, und –
du empfingst uns.

---

[1] Paul Celan: Weggebeizt. In: P. Celan: Gesammelte Werke in fünf Bänden. Hg. von Beda Allemann und Stefan Reichert in Zusammenarbeit mit Rolf Bücher. Frankfurt a. M: Suhrkamp 1986, Vol. II, p. 31 (my translation). All references to Celan's work are to this edition unless otherwise noted.

[2] See for instance Theo Buck's study *Muttersprache, Mördersprache* (Aachen: Rimbaud, 1993). The association between Celan's native language and the language of the Holocaust has also become one of the premises of trauma theory criticism which posit that Celan wrote poetry in an idiom in which unspeakable crimes are themselves embedded as something unspeakable, something which has yet to be consigned to the past. See in this regard Ulrich Baer: Remnants of Song. Trauma and the Experience of Modernity in Charles Baudelaire and Paul Celan. Stanford: Stanford University Press 2000.

Wer
sagt, daß uns alles erstarb,
da uns das Aug brach?
Alles erwachte, alles hob an.

Groß kam eine Sonne geschwommen, hell
standen ihr Seele und Seele entgegen, klar,
gebieterisch schwiegen sie ihr
ihre Bahn vor.

Leicht
tat sich dein Schoß auf, still
stieg ein Hauch in den Äther,
und was sich wölkte, wars nicht,
wars nicht Gestalt und von uns her,
wars nicht
so gut wie ein Name? (I,221)

(With all my thoughts I set
out from the world: there you were,
you, my quiet, my open one and –
you received us.

Who
says, that everything died for us,
when our eyes dimmed?
Everything awoke, everything started up.

Great was the sun which swam forth, bright
the souls which stood opposite it. Clear,
commanding the way they showed the sun
its path in silence.

Gently
your womb opened up, calmly
a breath rose in the ether,
and what billowed like a cloud, was it not,
was it not a shape stemming from us,
was it not
as good as a name?)

»With all my thoughts« would appear to be a love poem exclusively, were it not for its final words which introduce a self-reflexive element previously absent from the text. The feminine addressee of the poem gives birth to a cloud which is both a ›figure‹ (Gestalt) and a ›name‹, that is, an entity with shape and volume which is nonetheless a word.[3] For the medieval Kabbalists, as well as

---

[3] In three separate dedications Celan identified the addressee of the poem as his wife and the creature born in the final stanza as his son. Yet neither of these identifica-

for their Christian counterparts, there was no distinction between word and thing since the basis for all creation was God's unpronounceable name, which they considered identical with God in himself.[4] The poem invokes this tradition to create an alternative universe, a utopia in which the rift between heaven and earth is finally repaired.

In several poems in *Die Niemandsrose*, Celan alludes to Scholem's account of the Kabbala, for instance in »Hüttenfenster« which ends with a reference to the Hebrew letter *beth*, which is not only the first letter of the bible, but also the number two, which lead the Kabbalists to speculate that creation occurs in two places. The poem »Dein Hinübersein«, moreover, was originally entitled »Schechina« which is the name of the tenth of God's emanations or Sefiroth, which are arranged somewhat hierarchically.[5] Fred Lönker has argued that the addressee of »With all my thoughts« is modelled after the Shechina as well.[6] Like the Shechina she stands at the limit between two realms – the world the speaker leaves and the one he heads toward in the ether:

---

tions exhaust the significance of the feminine figure in the poem, who as the mother of something physical and linguistic must be understood not only in a biographical but also a theological context. The two dedications are printed in: Paul Celan / Gisèle Celan-Lestrange: Briefwechsel. Mit einer Auswahl von Briefen Paul Celans an seinen Sohn Eric. Hg. und kommentiert von Bertrand Badiou. Aus dem Frz. von Eugen Helmlé. 2 Vols, Frankfurt a. M.: Suhrkamp 2001, Vol. I, p. 154f.

[4] A discussion of the linguistic dimensions of the Godhead in medieval Christian mysticism exceeds the scope of what I can address here. Suffice it to say that although the unpronounceable name is not a concern of medieval scholasticism, the Neoplatonic notion of primordial forms is, and these forms like the unpronounceable name serve as the basis for all creation which begins as an expression of particular aspects of God's being. Moreover the conception of the Son as the Word points to a linguistic potential in God which the Son realizes or makes manifest.

[5] The full text for several drafts of this poem are included in Paul Celan: Werke. Tübinger Ausgabe. Hg. von Jürgen Wertheimer. Vol. I: Die Niemandsrose. Vorstufen, Textgenese, Endfassung. Bearb. von Heino Schmull. Frankfurt a. M: Suhrkamp 1996, p. 20f.

[6] Fred Lönker, Commentary on »Mit allen Gedanken«. In: Kommentar zu Paul Celans »Niemandsrose«. Hg. von Jürgen Lehmann unter Mitarb. von Christine Ivanovic. Heidelberg: Winter 1997 (Beiträge zur neueren Literaturgeschichte; 3/149), p. 94–98. Elke Günzel also notes the similarities between the addressee and the Shechina, although she cautions that in Jewish mysticism it is not man but God, who has a sexual relation with her in Günzel: Das wandernde Zitat. Paul Celan im jüdischen Kontext. Würzburg: Königshausen & Neumann 1995 (Epistemata. Reihe Literaturwissenschaft; 151), p. 174. Finally, Joachim Schulze remarks on the parallel between the addressee and the Shechina, although for him the poem is modelled after Novalis's *Hymnen an die Nacht*. The four stages of the path inward in Novalis' text are reflected in Celan's poem, which he divides as follows: a turning away from the world, an encounter with a feminine principle, a mystical death, and a face-to-face encounter with God which leads to a birth. See Joachim Schulze: Celan und die Mystiker. Motivtypologische und quellenkundliche Kommentare. Bonn: Bouvier Verlag 1976 (Abhandlungen zur Kunst-, Musik- und Literaturwissenschaft; 190), p. 69–74.

> Mit allen Gedanken ging ich
> hinaus aus der Welt: da warst du,
> du meine Leise, du meine Offene und –
> du empfingst uns.
>
> (With all my thoughts I set
> out from the world: there you were,
> you, my quiet, my open one and –
> you received us.)

At first glance, the addressee of the poem would appear to be an utterly passive figure like the Shechina, whose distinguishing feature according to Scholem is her receptivity or openness.[7] The addressee receives the speaker as he leaves the world »with all his thoughts«, that is with all that pertains to his spirit, which for the Kabbalists is divine and hence immortal. Yet the addressee does not only ›receive‹ the speaker; she also ›conceives‹ him in a play on the two meanings of the verb »empfangen« cited in the fourth line of the text. This conception would seem to occur in reverse order. The speaker returns to his beloved in the first instance only to become the child that she bears in her womb. In *Major Trends in Jewish Mysticism*, Scholem underscores that the Shechina is the mother of Israel but not its bride.[8] If she is the bride of anyone, it is God who impregnates her with the created world. Yet the disposition which the Kabbalists hail as the one most suited to an encounter with God is a »continuous attachment« to him which is erotic in nature, in Hebrew *devekuth*.[9] Humans approach God through a mystical union with the Shechina in so far as the Shechina is God's presence in the world, an angel of sorts.

The Sefiroth are not only God's emanations or aspects, as I have defined them thus far. They are also his ten names which correspond to the ten words of the first verse of the Hebrew Bible: »In the beginning God created the heaven and the earth.« Each of these names derives from God's unpronounceable name, which is identical with God in himself, whom the Kabbalists also referred to as

---

[7] Gershom Scholem: Schechina. Das passiv-weibliche Moment in der Gottheit. In: G. Scholem: Von der mystischen Gestalt der Gottheit. Studien zu Grundbegriffen der Kabbala. 4 ed., Frankfurt a. M: Suhrkamp 1995 (Suhrkamp-Taschenbuch Wissenschaft; 209), p. 135–139. Although »Mit allen Gedanken« was written in 1960, two years before the original publication of *Von der mystischen Gestalt der Gottheit*, there is good reason to believe that Celan read this essay in the *Eranos-Jahrbuch* where it first appeared in 1953 under the title »Zur Entwicklungsgeschichte der kabbalistischer Konzeption der Schechinah.«

[8] Gershom Scholem: Major Trends in Jewish Mysticism. London: Thames and Hudson 1955, p. 230. Elsewhere he notes that the one human who possibly had a sexual relation with the Shechina was Moses, whom the Kabbalists believed was the husband of God, that is his tenth Sefira, based on a particular interpretation of a passage from Midrash (see ibid., p. 226–227).

[9] Ibid., p. 233.

En-Sof, the infinite or endless.[10] In himself, God is unknowable, but to the extent that he names and knows himself he can also be known under one of these aspects, each of which proceeds from the next. For this reason the first three Sefiroth constitute an upper realm which is closest to *En-Sof*, the infinite ground of all creation. With the third Sefira, however, there is a break in the chain in so far as this Sefira contains all the remaining Sefiroth whose number is pointedly seven.

Binah, the third Sefira, gives birth to the seven lower Sefiroth in what Scholem describes as a continual process, a process in which the Sefiroth that flow from her also return to her, so that she may give birth to them again. In this manner, she becomes the mother of the seven days of creation which first unfold in God to the extent that the creation in question here is not that of the physical world, but of God's person or face. Each Sefira, according to the Kabbalists, constitutes an organ or limb of the cosmic person of God, which is the one form in which he is accessible to creatures. The other metaphor for the Sefiroth is that of a tree, which is rooted in *En-Sof*, although *En-Sof* is not himself rooted in anything. Binah's significance derives from the fact that she is the first to differentiate between the forms which are present in God, but which have yet to be realized as individual things. She receives the seven lower Sefiroth in an undivided stream which she then differentiates between as the intelligence of God, that is, as an expression of this aspect of his being.

The Shechina likewise receives a stream from above which she gives birth to in turn. But this act occurs only once to the extent that the creatures which flow from her cannot return to her, as they are not divine in substance: »God's unfiltered power flows from the Shechina back into itself. It does not proceed any further, and what comes forth from her is no longer God, but creature.«[11] It should be noted that Scholem's position on this final point is by no means consistent or clear. Elsewhere he argues that before the fall there was no distinction between body and soul, as humans had yet to acquire bodies.[12] And in his discussion of redemption, he takes up this notion again, arguing that the Kabbalists understood redemption as the restoration of an original state, in which the heavens and the earth were still connected.[13] This state was lost with the fall, when not only humans were expelled from paradise but also the Shechina, who was literally cut from the tree of the Sefiroth. The Shechina can be restored to this tree, only if humans return to her in spirit or with all that pertains to their spirit, namely ›with all their thoughts‹.

Until this happens, the Shechina accompanies Israel as an exiled part of God, that is, a branch cut from God's eternal tree or a limb severed from his cosmic person. The name the Shechina thus literally means the ›presence‹ or

---

[10] The summary of the doctrine of the Sefiroth I provide here is based on two texts by Scholem, Major Trends in Jewish Mysticism (note 8), p. 211–235 and »Schechina. Das passiv-weibliche Moment in der Gottheit« (note 7), p. 168–180.

[11] Ibid., p. 170.

[12] Scholem, Major Trends in Jewish Mysticism (note 8), p. 231f.

[13] Scholem, Von der mystischen Gestalt der Gottheit (note 7), p. 172.

›dwelling‹ of God, which is not as exalted a title as it may seem, as it says nothing about the Shechina's particular features or powers.¹⁴ And indeed she has none according to Scholem. The Shechina is nothing but a vessel for God's emanative stream which he releases in announcing his name or expressing his nature. In Celan's poem the speaker's return to the addressee is thus said to set a chain of events in motion which exceeds both him and her as individual figures. Once the speaker leaves the world, once the world dies for him, everything which until now had lay dormant in God can come to life again: »Everything awoke, everything started up.«¹⁵ In particular the speaker's departure from the world brings forth the sun, which serves as a symbol for an otherwise hidden God:

> Groß kam eine Sonne geschwommen, hell
> standen ihr Seele und Seele entgegen, klar,
> gebieterisch schwiegen sie ihr
> ihre Bahn vor.
>
> (Great was the sun which swam forth, bright
> the souls which stood opposite it. Clear,
> commanding the way they showed the sun
> its path in silence.)

The image of God as the sun is by no means an invention of this text. From the ancient Egyptian Sun-God to Louis XIV, »le roi soleil«, the sun has consistently stood as a figure for the King of the Heavens. What is, however, unique to the poem is the subordination of the sun to the souls it meets in coming forth from its concealment. These two souls direct the sun in a manner which is difficult to translate into English, as the neologism »vorschweigen« plays on the more conventional verb »vorschreiben« (to proscribe or mandate in writing).¹⁶ Through the medium of silence, rather than through writing, the souls direct the sun down a path which would seem to have been preordained for it, as it is the sun's path and none other.

This path is preordained in so far as it has been travelled once before. What the poem recounts is nothing other than the course of creation as *written* in *Genesis*. This process is explained as follows in the *Zohar*:

> In the beginning, when the will of the King began to take effect, he engraved signs into the divine aura which surrounded him. A dark flame sprang forth from the innermost recess of the Infinite, *En-Sof* […]. In the innermost center of the flame a well sprang forth […]. The well was entirely unrecognizable until under the impact of its explosion a hidden supernal point shone forth. Beyond this point nothing may be known or understood, and therefore it is called Reshith, that is ›Beginning‹, the first word of creation.¹⁷

---

¹⁴ Ibid., p. 136ff.
¹⁵ The emphasis on »alles« (everything) in the second stanza should be understood as a reference to the cosmos or »das All«.
¹⁶ Lönker, Commentary on »Mit allen Gedanken«. In: Kommentar zu Paul Celans »Niemandsrose« (note 6), p. 96.
¹⁷ Cited in Scholem, Major Trends in Jewish Mysticism (note 8), p. 218f.

According to this passage, *Reshith* or »beginning« is both a linguistic and a temporal instance. It is at once the point that bursts forth from the interior of God's flame, a point from which all creation derives, including that of God's Sefiroth or person. At the same time, it is the first word of the Torah, which the Kabbalists considered a mystical corpus, that, is a creation in its own right, divine in substance. In this respect the word ›beginning‹ not only marks the beginning of creation. It is also the beginning of the unfolding of the Torah, the mystical corpus which for the Kabbalists was identical with the Sefiroth. What enables the beginning of creation is hence ›beginning‹, the word. This first sign engraved in the ›divine aura‹ inaugurates a process which is at once spatial and linguistic. Significantly, the word ›beginning‹ is not spoken in the Bible; it is not preceded by any preamble, such as »The Lord said«. It appears out of nowhere as a solitary mark, a point beyond which »nothing may be known or understood« or *said*.[18] For ›beginning‹ is the arbitrary point from which all creation proceeds, including the creation of language which is not initially spoken, only written or engraved.

The poem likewise suggests that writing precedes speech in its variation on the motif of a light coming forth from the darkness. »Great was the sun which swam forth« we are told, in what would appear to be a mere description of the sun as a ›grand‹ or ›majestic‹ ball which illuminates the sky. But in so far as »groß« (great) is »großgeschrieben« (capitalized), it functions not only as a descriptive term but also an orthographic sign: the mark of a beginning which is always written in capital letters to distinguish it from what follows. This beginning is more precisely a renewed beginning, a return to the first word of the Bible, which can be repeated innumerable times because it is written, because it is the fixed point from which all words (and things) follow. Even the manner in which souls direct the sun assumes a kind of writing, for the invented term »vorschweigen« would have no meaning, were it not for its subtext, »vorschreiben« (to proscribe).[19] This subtext is not opposed to the silence of the souls; on the contrary it is part and parcel of it. What it is distinct from is speech which emerges at a later stage in creation, that is, at a later stage in the differentiation of God's written but unpronounceable name.

---

[18] What is not addressed in this passage is that the word ›beginning‹ is actually preceded by the letter *beth* (in this case meaning ›in the‹). Although Scholem speaks of the significance of this letter elsewhere, he does not mention it here, which raises the question if *beth* is not one of the signs engraved in the divine aura. See my discussion of the capitalization or »Großschreibung« of the adjective »groß« in Celan's text, which itself functions as a mark or point from which the sun can then emerge.

[19] It is worth noting that the 613 *Mitzvoth* (commandments or precepts) in the Torah are usually referred to as *Gebote* in German, which is the root for the adjective *gebieterisch*, which I have translated as commanding. Scholem also calls the precepts *Vorschriften*, which is based in the verb *vorschreiben*, which I am arguing is the subtext of this passage in the text, the script that makes this passage possible. See Gershom Scholem: Zur Kabbala und ihrer Symbolik. 9. ed., Frankfurt a. M: Surkamp 1998 (Suhrkamp-Taschenbuch Wissenschaft; 13), p 166–168, 172.

Speech emerges from the womb of Binah who is not only the mother of the seven lower Sefiroth, but also the soul in its purest form. In the Kabbala the order of the Sefiroth is to some extent mirrored in the soul, which is divided into three classes or categories, each of which represents a different degree of purity. In its highest form, the soul is called *neshuma* and is located in Binah as part of the undivided stream she receives from above; beneath *neshuma* stands *ruach*, spirit or wind; at the bottom of this scheme stands *nefesh* which is the breath or life force which animates all creatures.[20] This hierarchy is of significance for Celan's poem in so far as it structures the speaker's flight from the world as well as return to it. In the first stanza, he leaves the world behind to be reunited with the Shechina; in the second he begins his journey to the upper Sefiroth which are now reconnected to the Shechina; in the third both he and the addressee encounter the »hidden supernal point« as souls housed in Binah, who is the last Sefira to have direct or unmediated contact with *En-Sof*. Once the sun comes forth, creation can begin again as the migration of this single point down the Sefiroth tree. Scholem thus notes that the primordal point ›beginning‹ is also the ›divine seed‹ which is said to travel from the first to the third Sefira, where it is born as speech. In the *Zohar* this process is explained as follows:

> Until now everything was suspended in the hidden ether, which comes from the mystery of *En-Sof*. But as soon as the divine energy penetrates the supreme palace [the womb of the upper mother], whose secret name is *Elohim*, this breakthrough comes to be called speech in Scripture. ›God said‹ – […] and then the supreme palace [which is nothing but the upper Shechina] gave birth, the palace which had been impregnated with the divine seed gave birth in secret. What is born can be perceived [as it is speech]. What gave birth however gave birth in secret and is absolutely imperceptible.[21]

Binah remains ineffable even if she gives birth to speech, for only in her womb does the seed ripen which becomes the speech of *Genesis*: »And God said, Let there be light: and there was light« (Genesis I,3–4). This seed is variously described as a light, breath and word. It is each of these because for the Kabbalists the word is the basis for everything. What the poem accordingly holds secret – ›verschweigt‹ – is the name of the vessel the sun meets, not because this vessel has no name, but because its name is prior to speech. Speech emerges only through a process of differentiation in which God's unpronounceable name is articulated in ever more finite forms, such as the Lord or King.

The fourth stanza of the poem recounts the final stage in this process in which the speech of God becomes the speech of humans which Scholem calls »articulated and differentiated expression«.[22] The addressee who first received the speaker returns as a mother giving birth. In other words she delivers what she previously received from both above and below her:

---

[20] Scholem, Major Trends in Jewish Mysticism (note 8), p. 239ff.
[21] Cited in Scholem, Von der mystischen Gestalt der Gottheit (note 7), p. 174.
[22] Scholem, Major Trends in Jewish Mysticism (note 8), p. 216.

Leicht
tat sich dein Schoß auf, still
stieg ein Hauch in den Äther,
und was sich wölkte, wars nicht,
wars nicht Gestalt und von uns her,
wars nicht
so gut wie ein Name?

(Gently
your womb opened up, calmly
a breath rose in the ether,
and what billowed like a cloud, was it not,
was it not a shape stemming from us,
was it not
as good as a name?)

In this stanza, as in the previous one, the poem draws attention to distinct moments or events through the insertion of adverbs at the beginning of each clause which literally punctuate the text (great, bright, clear, commanding etc.). In this manner, the poem is able to construct a sequence of events, which resembles the chain of the Sefiroth, each of which proceeds from the next. From the ›grand‹ arrival of the sun to the ›calm‹ rising of a breath, the poem proceeds as if down a ladder to the bottom rung, which would at one level be the final line of the text. If there is a complication in this scheme, it is that the poem ends with an ascent. A breath rises from the womb of the Shechina, who represents the lowest rung of the cosmos sketched in this text.

Fred Lönker has argued that this breath must be understood in a biblical context as the spirit which hovers over the waters in the first two verses of *Genesis*: »In the beginning God created the heaven and the earth. And the earth was without form, and void; and darkness was upon the face of the deep. And the Spirit of God moved up the face of the waters.« (Genesis I,1–2)[23] Yet the word for spirit in Hebrew, *ruach*, is more a wind than a breath. Moreover – and this is crucial – the spirit or wind of God is not something spoken; it precedes the pronouncement, »Let there be light« in Genesis. As a result, this wind can scarcely serve as a model for the breath which rises from the womb of the Shechina, the mother of the created world. The allusion in this stanza, I would argue, is to the second chapter of *Genesis*, in which God is said to bring man to life by blowing breath into him: »And the Lord God formed man out of the dust of the ground and breathed into his nostril the breath of life, and man became a living soul.« (Genesis 2,7) With this breath not only does the process of creation come to completion, but also the differentiation of God's name, such that his speech can become the speech of humans, i. e., what they speak and embody simultaneously.

---

[23] Lönker, Commentary on »Mit allen Gedanken«. In: Kommentar zu Paul Celans »Niemandsrose« (note 6), p. 96.

Man is a spoken word, an instance of speech himself in so far as in Genesis he is literally spoken into being, created by means of an utterance: »And God said, Let us make man in our image, after our likeness.« (Genesis 1,26) Because this utterance is finite, it can serve as the basis as well for the language humans speak in their separation from one another as well as from their environment. In Adamic language, as is often noted, the word is identical with the thing. Only with the fall do they become related but separate entities. The poem »With all my thoughts« seeks to restore this ideal state, not for the world as a whole but for a single being which is finally the text itself. What pours into the addressee from above ›billows like a cloud‹ which is in fact the phenomenon in the Kabbala which is said to express God's presence in exile. As the Israelites left Egypt, God hid them beneath a cloud, which then settles over the tabernacle they build for him in exile. In *Exodus*, this tabernacle is identified as the dwelling of God:

> And let them make me a sanctuary, that I may dwell among them. According to all that shew thee after the pattern of the tabernacle, and the pattern of all the instruments thereof, even so shall ye make it. (Exodus 25,8–9)

But in Kabbalist interpretation, this sanctuary serves as the dwelling for the Shechina, who is finally the cloud which floats near the earth, but never touches it.[24]

The poem claims this status for its cloud as well, albeit in a manner which throws into question where this cloud is:

> und was sich wölkte, wars nicht,
> wars nicht Gestalt und von uns her,
> wars nicht
> so gut wie ein Name?
>
> (and what billowed like a cloud, was it not,
> was it not a shape come from us,
> was it not
> as good as a name?)

The precise nature of what rises from the addressee remains a question in the text. The speaker's repeated query »was it not« draws attention to the absence of a category for this phenomenon. Yet the speaker does say something positive about this phenomenon in remarking that it ›billows like a cloud.‹ He indicates that it is murky, cloudy or ambiguous which is a linguistic category. Words are murky not only when they hide their meaning, but also when they make it plain, especially if this meaning is identical with the word, if it inheres in the word's articulation. For if the meaning of a word inheres only in its

---

[24] The Shechina is often identified as God's feet by virtue of her position at the bottom of the Sefiroth hierarchy. The first Sefira by contrast is God's crown (Scholem, Von der mystischen Gestalt der Gottheit [note 7], p. 172–173).

articulation, then it can never be revealed as it is unto itself, which amounts to saying as a self-sufficient entity.

Elliot Wolfson has argued that this paradox is central to the understanding of language in the medieval Kabbala. The Sefiroth are articulations of God's unpronounceable name, which nonetheless remains unpronounceable, because it can never be named, spoken or said. Each pronouncement gives rise to another name, a veil in which God's name is revealed as something which can never be revealed, exposed or unveiled.[25] What is born in the final stanza of the poem is likewise a veil, indeed a veil for nothing other than God's unpronounceable name. For the poem as a whole is »as good as a name«, specifically the name »Bakol«, which means »with all« and is one of the names of the Shechina according to Scholem.[26] The poem »With all my thoughts« not only begins with the words »with all«. It is also »Bakol,« this figure and figuration of God's name, as the poem indicates in ending with the birth of cloud, which is the poem itself in all its murkiness. »With all my thoughts« billows like a cloud from its bottom line. It rises up from its own end in order to trace its birth after the fact, its genesis as a name for God's unpronounceable name. In this regard, »With all my thoughts« claims to be more than a poem. It claims to be a creature as well which results from the speaker's union with the Shechina, his mother and beloved simultaneously. For this reason, the birth in the final stanza of the poem is represented as an ascent. What is born is a redeemed word as well as a form, which is delivered into God's person – a breath which is embodied in the poem and which makes the poem into a bodily figure.

---

[25] Elliot R. Wolfson: Language, Eros, Being. Kabbalistic Hermeneutics and Poetic Imagination. In: Werkstatt für Philosophie und Kunst, Ha'Atelier Collegium Berlin, February 10, 2002.

[26] Scholem, Von der mystischen Gestalt der Gottheit (note 7), p. 163.

Carola Hilfrich

»The Land of Others«
Geographies of Exile in Hélène Cixous's Writings

I. Exile as Literature's Hypnotic Monstrum

Ever since her dissertation on *The Exile of James Joyce*[1] in 1969, Hélène Cixous has taken her cue from writers for whom exile is both the condition and the form of their work. Her literary criticism and her essays recall the voices of Anna Akhmatova, Ingeborg Bachmann, Karen Blixen, Paul Celan, Jean Genet, James Joyce, Franz Kafka, Clarice Lispector, Osip Mandelstam and Marina Tsvetayeva – all inhabitants of that multilingual, transnational and bisexual country of writing where exile is the key experience, even the key *for* experience, and the main metaphor of life. Cixous's readings of this modern landscape of exile illuminate what is specifically at stake here, namely *embodied* life. If we look at the different meanings of the signifier ›exile‹, we see that they all refer to either bodily actions, postures or experiences: the leap from one's home, ground or soil that is indicated by the Latin *ex solum salire*; the biblical expulsion from paradise; the exclusion from the promised land or the deportation from any land; or, simply, standing at a door that one shall not enter. In all these geopolitical, metaphysical or existential senses, exile signifies both something that is done to bodies and something that bodies do. It thematizes human beings' lives from the borders and cross-overs of their embodied existence; in an entanglement of constraint and inventive overstepping. It refers to an interaction between embodied human beings and the body of the world in which each really acts upon the surface of the other.

In Cixous's readings, the inhabitants of the global country of writing are, surprisingly, neither very tragic nor very heroic about this theme of exile. They simply use it to keep close track of embodied life. Their remarkable passion for borders, fences, gates and doors is merely a means of making these open up into scenes pulsating with linguistic, economic, political, racial or sexual disturbance.[2] Like

---

[1] Hélène Cixous: The Exile of James Joyce. Translated from the French by Sally A. J. Purcell. New York: David Lewis 1972 (L'exil de James Joyce ou l'art du remplacement. 2th ed., Paris: Grasset 1985).

[2] In her seminal work on the resistance to representation, Elaine Scarry has described embodied life in very similar terms, without explicitly referring to the theme of exile. Her analysis of embodiment, however, relies on a close reading of the representation of »door-scenes« in Hardy, Beckett, Boethius, and Thackeray, and her reading of Hardy is specifically concerned with these scenes as sites of linguistic, economic,

these writers, Cixous believes that exile is in this very precise sense »a kind of earthly condition« of life.³ It is the kind of condition that, as border and as crossing, pertains to every human body, to the body of the world, and to the practices of writing about them. And it is that kind of condition whereby each of these bodies and practices perceptibly *becomes* the scene of such linguistic, economic, political, racial or sexual disturbance.

For Hélène Cixous, this condition of exile is always both »real and imaginary«.⁴ On the face of the earth, we go where a line has been drawn and must be crossed. We do this in the name of ›more‹ life, or of survival, and on our way we keep what Cixous calls a »logbook« of exile: a *cahier du bord*⁵ as everybody's unique »book of the abyss and its shores«.⁶ Exile is both the earthly condition and the form of this *cahier du bord*, and our exilic logbooks are personal and political everyday-fictions of our reality in which we keep track of the ways in which both our embodied self and the world are being made.

I would like to argue that, in Cixous's writings, her *cahier du bord* plays the part of what Pier Paolo Pasolini has ingeniously called the »hypnotic monstrum«⁷ of every work of art: its exposure of the bodily tissue or matrix of life as something from which art is made and which, in turn, it remakes. Most works of art, however, repress this elementary condition and form of their making. Yet, there are also modes, techniques or styles of artistic practice that allow it to emerge and come to the fore. In one of his seminal film essays of the 1960s, Pasolini has described such artistic practice as »the written language of reality« (*la lingua scritta della realtà*).⁸ Pasolini's written language of real-

---

sexual, political, or racial disturbance. Cf. Elaine Scarry: Resisting Representation. New York, Oxford: Oxford University Press 1994, p. 3–11, 49–90.

³ Hélène Cixous: The Two Countries of Writing. Theater and Poetical Fiction. In: The Other Perspective in Gender and Culture. Rewriting Women and the Symbolic. Ed. by Juliet Flower Mac Cannell. New York: Columbia University Press 1990 (Irvine Studies in the Humanities), p. 191–208, here p. 196.

⁴ Hélène Cixous: Difficult Joys. In: The Body and the Text. Hélène Cixous, Reading and Teaching. Ed. by Helen Wilcox, Keith Mc Watters, Ann Thompson and Linda R. Williams. New York: Harvester Wheatsheaf 1990, p. 5–30, here p. 12.

⁵ Hélène Cixous: Preface. In: The Hélène Cixous Reader. Ed. by Susan Sellers. With a Preface by Hélène Cixous and Foreword by Jacques Derrida. New York and London: Routledge 1994, p. XV–XXIII, here p. xvi.

⁶ Ibid., p. xvi. The French term for ›logbook‹, *cahier du bord*, also signifies the ›shores‹, *les bords*.

⁷ Pier Paolo Pasolini: The Cinema of Poetry. In: P. P. Pasolini: Heretical Empiricism. Ed. by Louise K. Barnett. Translated by Ben Lawton and Louise K. Barnett. Bloomington: Indiana University Press 1988, p. 167–186, here p. 172.

⁸ Pier Paolo Pasolini: The Written Language of Reality. In: Pasolini, Heretical Empiricism (last note), p. 197–222. Pasolini's notion of art's expression of reality is highly reminiscent of Erich Auerbach's exile opus *Mimesis* (Erich Auerbach: Mimesis. The Representation of Reality in Western Literature. Translated by Willard R. Trask. Princeton: Princeton University Press 1953 [Mimesis. Bern: Francke 1946]). Evidence of Pasolini's familiarity with this text can be found in: Les dernieres pa-

ity refers to the exposure of reality's natural language – composed of behaviour, physical presence, and spoken and written language – in a mode of writing that would be poetic, political and physical.[9] This kind of writing would show us embodied life by making us see how embodied human beings and the world each act upon the surface of the other, in disturbing or disoriented ways, in unnerving scenes of linguistic, economic, racial or sexual disturbance. For Pasolini, this kind of writing ultimately even modifies how we think about reality, »transforming at least our physical relations with reality into cultural ones«.[10] Cinema is the ideal medium for such a written language of reality because, for Pasolini, »the cinematic sign is reality's own heightened articulation«.[11] Cinematographic practices allow the »hypnotic monstrum« to come to the fore while they express reality »from within: producing itself from it and reproducing it.«[12]

I have suggested reading Hélène Cixous's *cahier du bord*, her logbook of exile, as the hypnotic monstrum of her own writings. It clearly shares Pasolini's poetic-political interest in a written language of reality. And, like Pasolini, Cixous cannot confine her concern to either a purely theoretical approach or a purely textual form of expression. She scatters pieces of her logbook of exile, as well as pieces about it, across all the different genres and forms of her written expression: her poetic fictions on the mysteries of subjectivity; her autobiographical texts; her critical essays on literature and writing; and her theatrical writings on world history for the *Théâtre du Soleil*. For Hélène Cixous, however, these non-filmic forms can also express reality, in Pasolini's senses, ›from within‹. The peculiar kind of a heightened receptivity that pertains to the

---

roles d'un impie: Entretiens avec Jean Duflot. Paris: Pierre Belfond 1981, p.140–41. In a recent article on Pasolini's theology of film, Noa Steimatsky has shown how Auerbach's motif of a stylistic contamination or a heterogenous stylistics reappears in Pasolini's filmic work; Noa Steimatzky: Pasolini *on Terra Sancta*: Toward a Theology of Film. In: Yale Journal of Criticism 11 (1998), No. 1, p. 239–259, here p. 241.

[9] In an interview with the ex-exile Pablo Neruda in 1969, Clarice Lispector asked the poet »How can one best describe a human being?«, and Neruda answered: »Political, poetic. And physical«. In: Clarice Lispector: Lightning Interview with Pablo Neruda (II). In: C. Lispector: Selected Crônicas. Transl. by Giovanni Pontiero. New York: New Directions 1992, p. 65. Neruda's explicit claim for a poetic, political and physical kind of writing is shared not only by Pier Paolo Pasolini, Clarice Lispector and Hélène Cixous. For a larger number of writers who associate the ›earthly‹ condition of life with experiences and metaphors of exile, and for such different authors like Frantz Fanon, Toni Morrison, or Trinh T. Min-ha, writing means the explicit claim for a poetic, political and physical expression of reality.

[10] Pier Paolo Pasolini: Quips on the Cinema. In: Pasolini, Heretical Empiricism (note 7), p. 223–232, here p. 231.

[11] Steimatzky, Pasolini on Terra Sancta (note 8), p. 245. On Pasolini's rather unique notion of the cinematic sign and his ›heretic‹ semiotics of cinema, see also Naomi Greene: Pier Paolo Pasolini. Cinema as Heresy. Princeton: Princeton University Press 1990, p. 92–126.

[12] Pasolini, The Written Language (note 8), p. 205.

word-work of writing can articulate what she calls »non-repressed life« by »x-ray-photo-eco-graphing«[13] its reality. Cixous suggests that the written language of reality, through all the genres and forms of her logbook of exile, can serve to expose even the hidden depths of the bodily tissue or matrix of life by being attentive to its various, both human and non-human manifestations and signs.

Her *cahier du bord* suggests that we read exile as the trope for any written language of reality, as its own hypnotic monstrum. More precisely, it proposes exile as the trope for that kind of writing in which a whole set of interactions between different realms of life is exposed: between human beings and the world as they act upon the surface of the other; between the physical or natural and the cultural, the sensible and the sensitive, the real and the imaginary, the self-productive and the reproductive; and between the personal, the poetic and the political – we shall come back to these interactions later. For Hélène Cixous, the kind of writing that sustains any written language of reality serves to express reality ›from within‹ (exile) because it performs an exilic leap of its own: »Writing must out-write itself. It must go as far as possible from our limits and the limits of writing.«[14] If we listen to Cixous's native tongue,[15] the claim for a writing that »out-writes itself« is also the claim for a *s(')excrire* of writing, or writing's sexualization. In its imperative form, it asserts, along with this sexualization, writing's capacity to cross all kinds of limits, including its own; a kind of displacement of the within of writing as writing's most desirable feature.

We could call this the *exilic ethos* of writing, an ethos that claims writing's peculiar ability to respond to the earthly condition of exile. This ethos gives writing a body, one that is sexed and moving across the face of the earth, marked and re-marking (its) territories, x-ray-photo-eco-graphing non-repressed life ›from within‹. For Cixous, the exilic ethos would give us and writing, what, in her eyes, »we are lacking most: earth and flesh«.[16] It would offer us earth and

---

[13] Mireille Calle-Gruber / Hélène Cixous: We are already in the Jaws of the Book. Inter Views. In: Hélène Cixous, Rootprints. Memory and Life Writing. Hélène Cixous and Mireille Calle-Gruber. London: Routledge 1997 (Hélène Cixous. Photos de racines. Paris: Des femmes 1994), p. 48.

[14] Cixous, The Two Countries (note 3), p. 199.

[15] Cixous's lecture on »The Two Countries of Writing« was given directly in English which, as she adds in her opening note, »is not my native tongue« (ibid., p. 191). The printed version invites her readers from the very first moment to listen to more than one tongue that speaks her text.

[16] Hélène Cixous: The Place of Crime, the Place of Forgiveness. In: Qui parle. A Journal of Literary Studies, Vol. 3, No. 1 (Spring 1989), p. 120–125, here p. 121 (Le lieu du Crime, le lieu du Pardon. In: H. Cixous: L'Indiade ou L'Inde de leurs reves et quelques écrits sur le théâtre. Paris: Théâtre du Soleil 1987, p. 253). Cixous's writings suggest a feminist expression of the phenomenological mode of awareness for the earth – reminiscent of Husserl's notion of the earth as the secret depth of the life-world – and the flesh – reminiscent of Merleau-Ponty's notion of the flesh as the tissue or matrix of life, relating between human bodies and the body of the world. Like recent ecological criticism on writing, which is indebted to these phenomenological

flesh in a poetical-political way, by exposing the interactions between embodied human beings and the world, between the natural or physical and the cultural, the real and the imaginary, the self-productive and the reproductive.

Cixous's notion of writing as ›marked‹ in this way can be retraced to her influential works on feminine writing, *écriture féminine*, of the 1970s. The exilic ethos of writing is already at work in these early texts, and it finds a central metaphor; that of a birdlike »flight« as »woman's gesture in language«.[17] Faintly reminiscent of Joyce's Stephen Dedalus and the epiphany of his self-becoming, but attuned to the proliferation of meanings that runs through exilic flight in its French version, Cixous's ethos insists on the insurgent gesture of turning every propriety upside down (for Cixous, the French verb *voler*, which means both to fly and to steal, is associated with »jumbling the order of space, disorienting it, dislocating things and values, emptying structures«).[18] Woman's exilic gesture in language would be her artistic practice with the natural language of reality and embodied life, and it would tangibly expose the scenes of linguistic, sexual, economic, and political disturbance; disturbances that are so evidently already at work in Cixous's exilic *vol*-metaphor itself.

If we look at the polygeneric body of Hélène Cixous's work with and on writing, we can see how it itself is moved by this exilic ethos. The path of her writing continuously leads her back and forth from the self-occupation of

---

concerns, Cixous believes in a profound association between literary narrative and the more-than-human terrain and attempts in her own way, in David Abram's words, to »write language back into the land« (David Abram: The Spell of the Sensuous. Perception and Language in a More-Than-Human World. New York: Vintage Books 1997, p. 273). Cixous's feminist perspective, however, as well as her claim for an exilic ethos, insist on the workings of sexual, linguistic, economic and racial disturbances and resist the ecological idea of a »homecoming« that Abram quotes from the poetry of Rainer Maria Rilke (ibid., p. 261).

[17] Hélène Cixous: The Laugh of the Medusa. In: Signs 1 (1975), No. 4, p. 875–893 (here quoted from the reprint in: Feminisms. An Anthology of Literary Theory and Criticism. Ed. by Robyn R. Warhol and Diane Price Herndl. Revised Edition, New Brunswick: Rutgers University Press 1997, p. 347–362. The flight-metaphor is on p. 356–357). The French version was published in 1975 under the title *Le Rire de la Méduse* in: L'Arc 61 (1975), p. 39–54. Cixous's notion of *écriture féminine* has been extremely controversial among both Continental and Anglo-American feminists; especially its aspect of what became called »writing the body«; see f. e. Ann Rosalind Jones: Writing the Body: Toward an Understanding of l'écriture féminine. In: Feminist Studies, Vol. 7. No. 2 (Summer 1981), p. 247–263 or Susan Bordo's foucauldian critique of »the feminist celebration of the body in the 1970s« in: Susan Bordo: The Body and the Reproduction of Feminity. A Feminist Appropriation of Foucault. In: Gender / Body / Knowledge. Feminist Reconstructions of Being and Knowing. Ed. by Alison M. Jaggar and Susan Bordo. New Brunswick: Rutgers University Press 1992, p. 13–33. I would like to suggest, however, that Bordo's counter-celebratory notion of the body as a site of struggle is not only organizing Cixous's »writing of the body«, but also deeply interdependent with the theme of exile and its ethos of writing.

[18] Cixous, The Laugh of the Medusa (last note), p. 357.

much of her poetic fiction to her »self outside the self«[19] that writes world history for the theatre. For Cixous, the written language of reality is made *from* as well as *between* these two different kinds of expression. With one of her hands, her »right one«,[20] she writes in the poetic-fictional mode of an embodied self and, sometimes, of other narratable selves that inhabit the landscape of her writing. With another hand, her »right-left hand«,[21] she writes plays for the theatre; a practice that acts as an »expulsion of the self«[22] and that makes room for the histories of others and for other, non-textual practices of writing, such as staging, performing, or costume-designing.

Hélène Cixous calls these two kinds of written expression »the two countries« of her writing.[23] In both of these countries, exile is the earthly condition of the embodied human life to which she is responding. »The theme of exile«, Cixous says, »has always been with me«, as one of the things that has »prompted« her writing.[24] We shall soon see how closely this theme accompanies the poetic-fictional scenes of her own birth and life-story. No less closely, it also accompanies the theatrical scenes of world history in which Cixous's writing, as she says, »gives birth to others«[25] who are »much more and altogether other«[26] than herself; as, for example, Cambodian refugees, Indian freedom fighters, or Chinese peasants on the eve of a flood. Exile, it seems, feeds her double writing as it works with displacement and depropriation. It sustains her attempt to keep close track of an embodied human life in which »I and the world are never separate« and each »is the double of the other«.[27]

II. L'exil fait taire / L'exil fait terre

Hélène Cixous believes that »I doubtless owe this I of two scenes to my genealogy«.[28] Throughout her poetic-fictional writings, her logbook maps an extensive geography of her personal genealogical memory. It opens where every embodied life begins: with birth. In almost countless variations, the poetic I refigures her own birth as her exposure both *to* and *of* a world of exile: »I was born at / from the intersection of migrations and memories from

---

[19] Hélène Cixous: From the Scene of the Unconscious to the Scene of History. In: The Future of Literary Theory. Ed. by Ralph Cohen. New York, London: Routledge 1989, p. 1–18, here p. 9.
[20] Cixous, The Two Countries (note 3), p. 191.
[21] Ibid.
[22] Ibid., p. 204.
[23] Ibid.
[24] Ibid., p. 196.
[25] Ibid., p. 204.
[26] Cixous, The Place of Crime (note 16), p. 123.
[27] Cixous, Preface (note 5), p. xv.
[28] Ibid.

the Occident and Orient, from the North and South [...]«;[29] or: »I was born so far from my beginnings. I follow the bed of the blood. My distant blood, my foreigner, what a way we have come ...«;[30] or: »I was born in Paradise Lost. And this paradise was Algeria, a country in Africa which was a French colony«;[31] or: »I was born two hundred years ago in Spain, six hundred years ago in Palestine, a hundred years ago in Africa, and since then, once or twice here and there.«[32] In these extraordinary accounts, the moment of birth – as the exposure of the newborn – is already a poetic-political exposure of a different kind, and its theme is exile. Exile is, as Cixous says, even »the place and time«[33] of her birth: 1937 in Oran, at the western edge of colonial Algeria, to a German-Jewish mother from Osnabrück[34] and a Maroccan-Jewish father from Tangiers.

Cixous's genealogical geography shows that, from this kind of birthplace, the world is very tangibly at hand, both for the poetic I and the telling of her childhood-story:

> Geography of my genealogical memory: I stand at the edge of North Africa. On its beach. To my left, that is, to the West, my paternal family – which followed the classic trajectory of the Jews chased from Spain to Morocco. [...] My East, my right, my north: it was the landscape of my mother, [...] the landscape of a recounted Europe [in which] the border moves. It was the legend of Europe told by those who travelled it over [...] because they were searching [...].[35]

We can read Cixous's geography of her genealogical memory like an »x-ray-photo-eco-graph« of her childhood. The girl that stands so exposedly and probably barefoot at the edge of North Africa, on its beach, has world at the tips of her fingers, together with a »legend« that maps and re-maps it – the legend of her Spanish, Arab, »very German«[36] German, Czech, Slovakian and Hungarian ancestors. Hélène Cixous's genealogical geography tangibly suggests here an embodied form of what James Clifford has described as the »di-

---

[29] Ibid.
[30] Hélène Cixous: Albums and Legends. In: Hélène Cixous, Rootprints (note 13), p. 177–205, here p. 179.
[31] Cixous, The Two Countries (note 3), p. 192.
[32] Hélène Cixous: Dedans. Paris: Des femmes 1986 [¹1969], p. 149.
[33] Cixous, From the Scene (note 19), p. 2.
[34] *Osnabrueck* is the title of one of Cixous's recent works of poetic fiction (Paris: Des femmes 1999). It retraces her female genealogy in its extension over four continents; and it introduces a mode of writing that she calls »*écrire maman*« (ibid., p. 161), writing mummy / the mother. Cixous describes this writing as her »walk over the body« (ibid.) of her mother, or over the »earth that is [her] mother« (ibid., p. 16); and she describes both her mother's body and her own writing of it as scenes of a »combat« (ibid.). In these senses, we can read *Osnabrueck* as a further exploration of Cixous's figuration of the themes of exile, focusing on their relation to mothering, being mothered, motherhood.
[35] Cixous, Albums and Legends (note 30), p. 182–184.
[36] Ibid., p. 183.

asporic« attempt to account for transnational identity formations.[37] In Cixous's attempt, the theme of exile serves her to expose the transnational making of an embodied self that is made as much from known and unknown landscapes as from legends; as much from the auto-narration of memories as from its own and unique physical presence; as much from the escape routes of persecuted people as from the paths of travelling or searching ones. From the very first moment of this exilic geography of a self – »I stand at the edge of North Africa« –, the poetic I and the world each act upon the surface of the other, and in rather disorienting ways. After all, the location of the self's body also means a reversal or concomitant blending of physical, geographical, and cultural orientations: here »my left« is the West and the Orient, »my right« the East and the Occident.

In Hélène Cixous's genealogical geography, written from the edge of Algeria where, as she says, also her writing »was born«,[38] this transnational making of a self simultaneously entails an unmaking of the logic of ›home‹ and national identity. Revisiting the girl she was in Algeria, Cixous describes with exquisite simplicity her mental resistance to understanding reality in terms of this logic:

> In Algeria I never thought I was at home, nor that Algeria was my country, nor that I was French ... The French nation was colonial. How could I be from a France that colonized an Algerian country when I knew that we ourselves, German Czechoslovak Hungarian Jews, were other Arabs.[39]

Cixous's poetic I negates with the categorical wisdom of a girl »never« to think of Algeria as »her« home or country and of France as »her« nation. The reality of her exilic birthplace is shaped as much by French colonialism in North Africa as by the legend of her own genealogy. It allows her to articulate, in a both political and moral voice – »how could I«–, the extraordinary proliferation of meanings that runs through her reality and even makes it run against itself, just like the proliferation of meanings that runs through her body at the edge of North Africa; between her naked feet on the beach, her fingertips on the world and its/her legend, and her knowing mind.

Out of this simultaneously violent and subtle proliferation of meanings, the poetic I holds herself accountable for reality by »making it fly« in the senses of Cixous's feminist metaphor for exile. Here, the insurgent exilic practice refers to the moral-political work of decolonising and denationalising one's mind.[40]

---

[37] James Clifford: Diasporas. In: Cultural Anthropology, Vol. 9, No. 3 (August 1994), p. 302–338.
[38] Cixous, The Two Countries (note 3), p. 193.
[39] Cixous, Albums and Legends (note 30), p. 204.
[40] In her second critique of French feminism, Gayatri Chakravorty Spivak retraces in both metropolitan and decolonized feminisms a shared »task of decolonizing the mind through negotiating with structures of violence« (Gayatri Chakravorty Spivak: French Feminism Revisited. In: G. Ch. Spivak: Outside in the Teaching Machine. New York, London: Routledge 1993, p. 170–171). In her analysis of the metropoli-

The girl's knowledge that »we ourselves, German Czechoslovak Hungarian Jews, were other Arabs« exposes a reality in which it is impossible for herself »to be from a France that colonized an Algerian country«. The place from which the girl can articulate her reality and think herself within it, is rather like a transient site of many encounters, crossings and combats: between what I is and we are, the self and the other, France and Algeria; between Germans, Jews and Arabs and even among these themselves.

Later and elsewhere, the literary critic Hélène Cixous claims the kind of response-ability to reality that she describes in her personal genealogical geography as being a part of the »*real*« genealogy of writers. In a text concerned with the »Difficult Joys« of writing, she talks about the earthly condition of exile as »presid[ing] over the destiny of writers [...] as one of the metaphors, one of the structures of depropriation«.[41] Exile, she believes, »makes one part of it (the ›real‹ genealogy of writers), and another essential feature is *de-nationalisation*«.[42] While these features might appear somewhat too celebratory, or already faded within the fields of recent criticism,[43] they come – with difficulty and with joy – alive in Cixous's personal poetic account and its acute sense of a location that is both geopolitically and epistemologically embodied.

Cixous's geography of her genealogical memory also (re)maps those places where her exilic and denationalizing self encounters the »real« monolithic reality of national systems and institutions of identity formation. In 1955, after leaving Algeria to attend a preparatory class for the *École Normale Superieure*, she finds herself exposed to the physical torments of »real« exile for the first time:

---

tan ethics of sexual difference, from Simone de Beauvoir to Hélène Cixous and Luce Irigaray, Spivak observes »an intimation [...] of radical exile, the only other reminder of which is the mysterious anonymity of the earth as temporary dwelling place« (ibid., p. 151). Spivak's analysis suggests not only an intimate link between the ethics of sexual difference and the theme of exile, but also between an exilic mode of awareness and the ethical task of decolonizing the mind.

[41] Cixous: Difficult Joys (note 4), p. 12.
[42] Ibid., p. 13f.
[43] See f. e. Rosi Braidotti's critique of the literary trope of exile in her: Nomadic Subjects. Embodiment and Sexual Difference in Contemporary Feminist Theory. New York: Columbia University Press 1994, p. 21–28. Braidotti's critique is concerned with the ethnocentrism and the »evasive tactic« that she associates with the notion of exile and its privileged place in the writings of Hélène Cixous and Luce Irigaray. She proposes, instead, what she calls »a nomadic politics of location« as a »practice of dialogue among different female embodied genealogies« (ibid., p. 21). My reading of Cixous in this article, especially in the following section on *La Sauterelle*, suggests that Cixous's exilic ethos of writing implies just such a practice of genealogical dialogue; it is, however, not confined to »female embodied genealogies«, but rather to sexually differentiated embodied genealogies. Her insistence on an exilic politics of location can neither be read in terms of ethnocentrism nor of evasive tactics; but rather in terms of her poetic-political ethos and her understanding of borders as something that works both internal and external and has to be acknowledged as well as overstepped.

In 1955, in *khâgne* at the Lycée Lakanal – that is where I felt the true torments of exile (*les affres du véritable exil*). Not before. Neither with the Germanys, [...] nor with the Africas, I did not have such an absolute feeling of exclusion, of interdiction, of deportation (*je n'ai éprouvé un sentiment si absolu* ...). I was deported right inside the class.[44]

In the French classroom of the mid-1950s, Cixous feels the »absoluteness« of her exilic condition and its body-politics of constraint; not the difficult and joyful proliferation of national meanings (the plural Germanys and Africas) that runs through her exilic legacy and Algerian sense of embodied location. »Exclusion« prevents her from participating, »interdiction« from speaking her voice, and »deportation« from even physically being there – the living body of the Algerian girl becomes »absolutely« abject »right inside« the French classroom. The way in which she »feels« this, reveals to us an ambivalence between pleasure and displeasure and a tension between passive and active meanings: *éprouver un sentiment* simultaneously means being subjected to a feeling (pleasant or unpleasant), and verifying it, putting it to the test of a »*véritable*«, embodied reality. The girl is exposed to the body-politics of »true exile« as well as exposing them. While she is feeling the absolute denial of what would be her natural language of reality – participatory behaviour, speech, physical presence –, she is also *practising on* the reality of such denial. She is, in fact, already ›writing‹ it; verifying, showing, manifesting, articulating, expressing reality ›from within‹ (exile); between constraint and inventive overstepping (into the Germanys, the Africas ...).

And writing (exile) means putting into play the kind of heightened sensitivity that pertains to the written language of reality in Cixous's senses. In one of her works on writing, Cixous talks about the lively proliferation of meanings that writing restores to the lethal body-politics of exile. »For me, a writer in the French language, ›*l'exil fait taire / l'exil fait terre*‹ which means both that exile prevents you from speaking, makes you breathless and at the same time it makes for earth«.[45] The written language of reality hears in writing both exile's psychic-physical constraint on a human body – making you breathless[46] – and its simultaneous offer of another, non-human space to breathe in – making for earth, and making you earthbound.

In her peculiar blending of real and imaginary, natural and cultural, Hélène Cixous is also concerned with the form or kind of life that is made from the earthly condition of exile:

---

[44] Cixous, Albums and Legends (note 30), p. 204; French version: p. 206. Cixous uses the plural and literary term *affres* to talk about »true exile« as associated with both anguish and torture, or both mental and physical forms of torment. Her choice also connects between a literary or imaginary dimension of exile and this tormenting real of »true« exile.

[45] Cixous, The Two Countries (note 3), p. 196.

[46] The greek *psychein* means to breathe or to blow and refers to the cycle of breathing.

What happens when you have exile for earth? When you are a citizen of exile. What happens when you're trekking out of your Egypt [another not-home]? You go into the desert and God provides manna.⁴⁷

Manna, for Cixous, is something that is both food and word – as is evidenced in the question »what-is-that?« –; it is solid as well as liquid; »a kind of coriander seed«, but also »a kind of maternal milk«.⁴⁸ Within Cixous's written language of reality, this hybrid substance of food, words, seeds, and milk is always already the substance of her maternal city, Oran. Having the exilic privilege or »the luck to be surrounded by different tongues, by different languages«,⁴⁹ the girl

> [...] immediately realized that Oran was the signifier, though, of course I did not know that word ›signifier‹ but I knew the word Oran, [...] I had it in French and in other languages. [...] And I added, naturally, the first pronoun in French – ›je‹ – and I had an orange. I realized that by adding myself to my maternal city, I would get the fruit. [...] But a fruit was a word and the word was a fruit.⁵⁰

III. La sauterelle

The manna of this »natural« language of Cixous's own childhood reappears in the title of one of her works of poetic fiction on the life of others: *Manna, for the Mandelstams, for the Mandelas.*⁵¹ Cixous's book for Osip and Nadezhda Mandelstam and Winnie and Nelson Mandela displaces her personal response to the earthly condition of exile into an account of the lives of these two couples. It describes their shared, yet different ways of »inventing another world« and »resistance to exile«;⁵² ways of life in which the poetic epic of the Mandelstams and the political epic of the Mandelas intersect and communicate. Cixous's title suggests that her book is an attempt to both feed and articulate the various exilic terms that reverberate in and between their stories and their different-similar family names (word-fruit-names, exilic names).⁵³ Her text responds to an ethical need to add layers of reality, or to multiply them, in order to express the embodied reality of life: »And everything was written in this way by addition and multiplication: East and West, North and South, White and Black, History and Poetry, Russia and Africa, Man and Woman,

---

⁴⁷ Cixous, The Two Countries (note 3), p. 194.
⁴⁸ Ibid.
⁴⁹ Ibid., p. 193.
⁵⁰ Ibid.
⁵¹ Hélène Cixous: Manne aux Mandelstams aux Mandelas. Paris: Des femmes 1988 (Manna, for the Mandelstams, for the Mandelas. Minneapolis: University of Minnesota Press 1994).
⁵² Cixous, The Two Countries (note 3), p. 195.
⁵³ Mandelstam and Mandela do not only associate the word-fruit manna, but also, as Cixous points out, the almond, in German *Mandel*.

Heat and Ice«;[54] the geographical, cultural, economic, racial, political, poetical, historical, sexual and geological formations of embodied life.

In Hélène Cixous's work, this adding or multiplying need of the written language of reality responds to and resists its own exilic lack by »making for earth« or embodied reality in all senses. Cixous's poetic fiction thematizes elsewhere her lack of a legitimate place from which to write: »I have no place from where to write. No legitimate place«;[55] no piece of land, no homeland, language, history nor country »of her own«.[56] Even the transnational country of writing is not necessarily a country that she could call her own and from which she could write. Talking elsewhere about the »double exile« of Marina Tsvetayeva and other women writers, Cixous reminds us that

> [...] there is something of a foreignness, a feeling of not being accepted or of being unacceptable, which is particularly insistent when as a woman you suddenly get into that strange country of writing where most inhabitants are men and where the fate of women is still not settled. [...] So sometimes you are even a double exile, but I'm not going to be tragic about it [...].[57]

Instead of being tragic, Hélène Cixous responds to her own exilic lack of a legitimate place or home – »pas d'hommicile fixe«,[58] as she says – with a writing that »makes for earth« in the poetic-political sense of her book on the Mandelas and Mandelstams. She thinks that if one's writing has no legitimate language, history, sex, home or country of origin, it can always travel the surface of the earth. It can map on a global scale what is happening in the abysses and on the shores of different people's histories as they have been shaped and continue to be shaped by exilic realities.

As Hélène Cixous's writing travels the face of the earth, it walks hand in hand with the stories and histories of other people or peoples, exposing the earth as the dwelling place of both the living and the dead. Cixous talks of this kind of company as the spectral safeguards of her own writing path:

> My path is escorted by the phantoms of peoples, the whole span of my texts, they are there. At given moments I was haunted by Vietnam then by Greece then by Iran.[59]

---

[54] Cixous, The Two Countries (note 3), p. 197.
[55] Hélène Cixous: La Venue a l'Ecriture [1976]. In: Entre L'Ecriture. Paris: Des femmes 1986, p. 9–69, here p. 24.
[56] In this vein, she asks herself which history she could call her own, and her answer is indecisive: »Which History is mine? Of whose History am I the witness? How to unite History and text? I don't know which History is mine. Perhaps as a Jew it is Jewish History, but I haven't really known which one or how?« (Cixous, From the Scene [note 19], p. 11).
[57] Cixous, Difficult Joys (note 4), p. 12f.
[58] Cixous, La Venue a l'Ecriture (note 55), p. 46. Her denial of home, *pas d'hommicile fixe*, marks the domicil as masculine while teasing out the echo of man (homme) in home.
[59] Cixous, From the Scene (note 19), p. 11.

The texts that are written in such a haunted way are, as Cixous says, »composed beings«; just as we all, for her, are »composed beings, composed of many people«[60] from all sorts of places, cultures, and sexes; and composed, »at given moments«, of different histories of different peoples. As such composed beings, we resonate with »echoes that come from the whole world«,[61] from all kinds of lives and struggles for life, from all kinds of resistance to exile and reinventions of the world.

In this way, Cixous's written language of reality strives »to do away with frontiers and limits«[62] in order to express the transnational, cross-cultural and bisexual making of our embodied selves. Within this written language of reality, each single self becomes tangible as a unique »composition«. Everybody is made in a unique way from a singular blending of more or less men and/or women, heat and ice, Southern and Northern legends or Eastern and Western affiliations. Everybody resonates in different ways with the echoes of all kinds of earthly life; and everybody's life, body and work responds in unique ways to these echoes.

Hélène Cixous's unique response to the echoes and spectral companions of her narratable self, however, finds its most »immediate«[63] and intense expression not in the poetical fiction of the self nor in the poetic-political epic, but in the theatre. For her, theatre expresses reality *with* reality insofar as it is composed of all the elements of natural language itself, making it reality's own heightened articulation. She is drawing on the teachings of the Japanese 14th century nô-theoretician Zeami when she talks about theatre as the art that »is made from the art of the text, the body's art, the art of living [and] the art of the spectator«.[64] Theatre's artistic labour is attentive to all the different sites of echoes of non-repressed life: text, body, living, reception. It is a collective effort in which the desire of or for an embodied narratable self is multiplied, shared, and divided; it becomes the »desire of [and for] all the others«.[65]

Hélène Cixous calls this her desire for »Orian« – a further reinscription of her maternal city Oran as a site of difference, or »a somewhat enriched Oran«.[66] Orian even provides her with a surprising answer to the question that was put to her »a thousand times« after she staged her play on Cambodia with the *Théâtre du Soleil* in 1985: »Why did I write a play about Cambodia? Why should Cambodia be in my writing and why do I speak not of ›women‹ but of Cambodians? […] Why Asia, why the Orient?«[67] Cixous answers by saying »Orian« and suggesting an orientalized version of her own birthplace in North

---

[60] Cixous, The Two Countries (note 3), p. 197.
[61] Cixous, Albums and Legends (note 30), p. 189.
[62] Cixous, The Two Countries (note 3), p. 199.
[63] Cixous, From the Scene (note 19), p. 12.
[64] Ibid.
[65] Ibid.
[66] Ibid., p. 17.
[67] Ibid.

Africa. Her answer is given in a disturbing fashion, in the voice of both a native and a non-native speaker: »Why Asia, why the Orient? Because it is not me, because it is me, because it is the world different from myself that teaches me myself, my difference, that makes me feel my/its difference«.[68] Theatre, as »the stage, the earth, the land of others«,[69] can make us feel the kinds of difference or disturbance that are at work in each of our uniquely embodied selves and in their interaction with the world. It can make us recognize the *alterity* of the sensible world, both with regard to ourselves and with regard to the world itself.

In one of her essays on writing, Cixous recalls the voyage she made in 1984 with Ariane Mnouchkine, the director of the *Théâtre du Soleil*, to the Khmer refugee camps on the Cambodian-Thai border. Her logbook tells us of the children »who were born in the camps and have never known anything but the fences of the camp«,[70] and of the arts of resistance to exile and its menace of cultural and physical extinction that were practiced by the adults. At the end of her account, Cixous tells us of »an old man« she met there, »who for five or six years now has taken care of the Cambodians in the camps«.[71] Her logbook recalls this guardian of Cambodian life in exile, a French man named Pierre, as somebody who

> [...] resembles a grasshopper (*sauterelle*). Grasshopper in Brazilian is *Esperança*. Languages are inspired. A grasshopper is like hope or hope is like a grasshopper, these are fine things that one confuses with nature, because they are transparent and green and one sees the green of nature through them. And they are almost invisible but still very alive.[72]

For Hélène Cixous, the old French man who resembles a grasshopper embodies hope in a very concrete sense: »He gives the word hope«, she writes, which was »his word [...] the tiny bit of flesh that he has on his bones. He saves this word the way dancers save the dance. Perhaps this is another name for writing, this name Esperance. With this name, it carries us further than ourselves.«[73]

Cixous's account of the grasshopper-man in the Cambodian refugee camps offers us a further and probably her most wonderful metaphor for a written language of reality that responds to the earthly condition of exile: *la sauterelle*. The ethos of a writing that »carries us further than ourselves« in a physical, cultural, and geographic sense, is concerned with forms of life that are »almost invisible but still very alive«. It responds to these precarious forms of life by »giving them flesh« in a particular way. In her story about the grasshopper-man and his ways of safeguarding life in exile, Cixous talks about writing as an embodied word-work in which we can »save« precarious life forms »the way dancers save the dance« – with our own bodies. If we listen to the grass-

---

[68] Ibid.
[69] Cixous, The Place of Crime (note 16), p. 253.
[70] Cixous, From the Scene (note 19), p. 17.
[71] Ibid.
[72] Ibid.
[73] Ibid., p. 18.

hopper in its French expression, we can even hear how deeply this embodied word-work with life is linked to the theme of exile and the ethos of writing in Cixous's senses. In its transparency to nature, the almost invisible »*sauterelle*« composes itself of »*sauter*« (the exilic leap from one's home or ground), »*terre*« (the earth it makes for), and »*elle*« (the »she« who makes this leap); she composes herself of all the materials that make life in terms of exile.[74]

In the body of this *sauterelle* and her Brazilian sister *esperança*, the old French man in the Cambodian camps tangibly becomes a site of linguistic, political, cultural, sexual and even species-disturbance himself. His work expresses the extreme will and desire to put his own body at stake in order to safeguard all *other* forms of life that are menaced by extinction or exclusion from visibility. His embodied work of and on exile is gendered in the feminine, specified in a tiny insect's body, and metaphorizing writing. This exilic work provides »another name for writing« with which it could help us to leap by ourselves, carrying us further than ourselves and into all these other forms of life of which we are (also) composed. Writing's embodied word-work in Hélène Cixous's sense responds to the earthly condition of exile in a similar way as the man who resembles both a grasshopper and a woman responded to the refugees in the Cambodian camps: with the will and the desire to safeguard precarious, invisible or repressed forms of life, and with careful attention given to minor or almost imperceptible signs or manifestations of life.

---

[74] In Cixous's latest work of poetic fiction, a further attempt at *écrire maman* (see note 34) and an account of her mother's »tortuous and indescribable« return visit to Osnabrück, the *sauterelle* rematerializes in her mother's speech: »*la terre est une autre affaire jusqu'à la dernière minute on peut encore sauter*« (the earth is another matter until the last minute one still can leap), in: Hélène Cixous: Benjamin à Montaigne. Il ne faut pas le dire. Paris: Galilée 2001 (Collection lignes fictives), p. 136.

Frank Stern

The Two-Way Ticket to Hollywood
and the Master-Images of 20th Century Modernism

> C'est juste derrière les *De Mille's Studios*
> avec leur grand temple de Jérusalem
> qu'Iribe a abondonné,
> et qui est là, barbare et rouge, au bord du Pacifique,
> comme les temples de Nara
> ou de la Nouvelle-Guinée.
> Au loin, on voit Beverly Hill, et sur la droite
> la *Metro Goldwyn*, puis *Paramount*
> avec sa moitié de paquebot au-dessus de la ville
> qui garde du soleil dans ses soutes
> à l'heure où toute la plaine est déjà dans l'ombre.
>
> Paul Morand, *Hollywood. Poème*[1]

It seems to be a commonplace in film history and cultural studies that Hollywood was invented by Jews. However, it may also hold true that 20th century images of the Jews were invented by Hollywood, by filmmakers who had a lasting impact on cinema no matter whether they started their film careers in Europe or in America, no matter whether they were of Jewish origin or not. That many of these first-generation filmmakers were of Jewish origin definitely is a point for deliberations, however, considering firstly that in most of their films they refrained from Jewish topics, and secondly that they represent a Jewish path into visual modernism. In a documentary film based on the book by Neal Gabler, *An Empire of their Own. How the Jews Invented Hollywood*,[2] the Jewish impact on Hollywood was virtually transformed into a synonym for the movie industry. Jews were depicted as the creators of the American dream. This dream, it is suggested, was born out of the desperation, the suffering and the hopes that the emigrants from the eastern European *shtetl* and from Germany had brought to the New World. The American dream was described as an invention of European-born Jewish filmmakers and producers – as if *Yentl*

---

[1] Paul Morand: Hollywood. Poème [Excerpt]. In: USA. Album de photographies lyriques. Paris: Plaisir du bibliophile 1928. – The poem is quoted in an excellent collection of essays and documents published in *Autrement Revue* 79 (1986), edited by Michel Boujut and Jules Chancel, with the title *Europe-Hollywood et retour*. I owe the idea for the title of this essay to *Autrement*.

[2] Neal Gabler: An Empire of Their Own. How the Jews Invented Hollywood. New York: Anchor Books 1989.

had become a revised version of *Madame Dubarry, Hester Street* another name for *Boulevard Saint Germain,* and Spielberg's *The Prince of Egypt* a substitution for Griffith's *Birth of a Nation*. It is obvious that when talking about the Jewish impact on Hollywood one has to distinguish between film production, producers and film corporations on the one hand, and directors, scriptwriters, actors, composers and the like on the other. Having a producer of Jewish descent does not imply that anything Jewish will be produced; in fact, usually it even means the opposite. The American dream existed long before the first reels reproduced real history or screened historical figures, and before many filmmakers contributed to the development of the visual aesthetics of American virtues. Griffith's films *Intolerance* or *Birth of a Nation* with their strong Christian contents, values, and connotations contributed to this fact, but so did the Christianized narratives of the Old Testament. As in Europe, many Jewish artists and intellectuals were attracted by the modernist art of filmmaking, which had less to do with the American dream and more with the immense economic, social and cultural possibilities of realizing many individual and collective dreams. By the time the first talkie was seen by huge crowds of filmgoers in 1927, two things had been established. First, that talkies meant music and singing, and second that the integration of Jewish immigrants into the larger immigrant society was a topic to be represented on the screen as a mainstream event. The film The *Jazzsinger* depicted the story of a rabbi's son who becomes a singer and actor.

From the first decade of American filmmaking, it was not a small and homogeneous group of Jewish artists, intellectuals and business men with a common background that were involved but rather a diversified ensemble of Jewish individuals and collectives that had arrived from all over Europe. Different languages and cultures, social experiences, and economic aspirations lessened the impact of a common Jewish denominator. Some of these emigrants turned to the movies, to theatre and entertainment for their new livelihoods. They had Polish, Russian, Austrian, Hungarian, German, and French backgrounds. Some had left the old traditions, religions, families and social ties, some kept their traditions or adapted them to a new democratic society, and some simply freed themselves from all conventional ties in order fully to endorse the conventions of a newly evolving western society with the Pacific Ocean as its geographical limit. As much as Hollywood shaped and was shaped by their New World experience, it reflected the cultural and social changes, and, to a large extent, gave these changes the fitting images that influenced the broader audience's identification – the images of visual modernism that are much more than just images of an American dream.

In short, Hollywood has not only produced legends, but it has also become a legend, a myth, a colourful narrative of its own, a trademark that defines the habits and perceptions of millions the world over and, last but not least, one which secures the income of the American corporate film industry. When, a few years ago, Steven Spielberg, Jeffrey Katzenberg and David Geffen founded *Dreamworks*, the very name of this new corporation captured the spirit of the decades in which Hollywood had evolved, expanded, and become the synonym for world cinema. Towards the end of the 20th century, despite television, computers, digital aesthetics, and all kinds of modern entertainment industries, Hollywood has in fact reinvented itself as a global power in entertainment, as a pathfinder in the new technologies of cinematic representation, and as an enduring watershed in the long history of artistic creativity. American cinema is, of course, also an illustration of the modern success story of Jewish entrepreneurship, avant-garde innovations, and cultural playfulness. There existed only two other cities where producers and artists of Jewish origin made a similar impact on the evolving film industry: Berlin until 1933, and Vienna until 1938. From the earliest days of motion pictures, the mutual relationship between Hollywood, Vienna and Berlin, between the film communities in these three centres of the new visual medium was immense. There was a coming and going of directors, actresses and actors, cameramen and producers, most but not all of them of Jewish origin. Hollywood attracted talented »home-grown« artists and influenced their work, but in the end, it was the European impact on Hollywood in the 1920s and 1930s that transformed Hollywood into the metropolis of film, a veritable *Cinematropolis*. In short, Hollywood represents much more than Walter Benjamin's dictum implies about the image in the age of technical reproducitivity. Cinema, despite all its ups and downs, has for more than a hundred years carried the very essence of our age: the images of modernity, the visual representations of its agents and its opponents. Modernism has had the same impact on contemporary Jewish life as the enlightenment with all its consequences of acculturation had on the Jewish path into freedom, bourgeois society, and respectability. As in many other fields of modern knowledge, science, technology, conceptual thought, culture and the arts, outstanding individuals of Jewish origin not only had a lasting impact on this development but also embodied the very essence of modernism in their creativity and personal life.

The 20th century is indeed the *Century of Cinema*, as a recent BBC TV series was called. Film, and particularly American cinema, has become the mind's eye, the aesthetic narrator of collective experiences all over the world, of historical developments as well as of their traumatic recollections. American cinema, be it Hollywood or the studios on the Eastern Coast, though, is tightly interrelated with European cinema. From the very start of film, the various national cultures with their film productions and film receptions existed in a cinematographic sphere of global interaction. In the end, cinema is not synonymous with Hollywood because the glamorous impact of Californian film was always balanced by European cinema. The film road from Europe to Hollywood always was and is a two-way ticket, be it in terms of film form, narrative, technology, be it concerning producers, directors, actresses and actors, scriptwriters and composers, cameramen and technicians of all sorts. With the reels freely crossing on ocean steamers and soon on airplanes from America to Europe and back, producers had more in mind than their national audiences. The first global network in history was a film network. At the turn of the century Russian filmmakers produced films with two endings, one, usually a tragic one, for the Russian audience, the other with a happy ending for the American audience. Silent movies did not need expensive dubbing, and important filmmakers like Fritz Lang, for instance, produced silent movies in German, English, and often French as well. Based on the specific public's taste, leading actresses and actors were exchanged on the set to produce two or three foreign versions at the time. The film industry was booming when World War I interrupted the free exchange of images, reels, stars, starlets and the intriguing news and pictures about what was going on behind the scenes. But could one imagine the great Charlie Chaplin without all those films he learned from with the French actor-comedian Max Lindner in the leading role?

Western cinema represents collective memory through means that arose out of the last technical revolution of the 19th century: moving pictures that managed both to represent the evolving mass society, and to fill its unprecedented needs for entertainment. From the very start, however, cinema at its very best knew three tendencies: to acquiesce, to activate, and to enlighten through the visual and acoustic means of entertainment.

The Black Box of Modernism

Around 1910, the first group of filmmakers arrived in Hollywood after this small town had become part of Los Angeles, where filmmaking was lawful if not really respectable. In Los Angeles film production had become a real business, but the denizens of the pastoral little village disliked all those actresses and actors with their amoral attitudes. Until 1910, the sign »No trespassing for dogs and actors« was rather widespread in puritan Hollywood. This changed with the film boom as of 1910. Besides, here in California the sun was bright, clouds rarely appeared, the landscape was brilliant, the sea close, real estate and labour cheap. Culture had gone west, but it was the culture of the new age, including all the modern means of production and technology, of visual reproduction and aesthetics that transcended the theatre stage. The new technical inventions and the inter-cultural creativity that were penetrating the American film industry from all major film cultures in Europe was the best backdrop for the promotion of the right stories, plots and emotions that represented the very stuff that the dreams of millions were made of. Film, in fact, created masses and at the same time was the very medium the masses were craving for. Film brought the stage to the people, and for the first time in modern history it became apparent that the difference between high and low art or culture could fade away with the new images that all classes and ethnic groups would share.

The beginnings, however, were rather modest but characteristic for an immigrant society and culture. As of 1910, small film productions began to concentrate in Hollywood. Walter Selig had moved his movie firm to the West. The first major film company, however, was the Nestor Film Company, which was bought by Carl Laemmle (1867–1939) in 1912. Laemmle was born in the southwest of Germany, and after the death of his mother in 1883, had emigrated to the United States. He spent the years until 1910 working dozens of jobs, finally becoming a bookkeeper and a manager at a clothing firm. Upon being sacked he took his $ 2.500 savings, and in 1906 bought a movie theatre in Chicago. Soon he was also buying movies and renting them out again, the first being a Pathé film *The Pearl Fisher's Dream*. In 1909, he was the largest film distributor in the United States. By 1910, movies had become the main entertainment of the masses. They were cheap, could be found everywhere, and one didn't need a tie for admission. Laemmle imported films from Europe, but this did not satisfy all the economic and cultural needs in the New World. He began film production, and within a short time built an empire. Years before, he had added some acres to his company at Sunset Boulevard, which later became known as the first major Hollywood studio, Universal Film Manufacturing Company, later called Universal Pictures. This, in fact, was the beginning of Hollywood as a film city. That Carl Laemmle was Jewish may be of minor relevance, but it surely contributed to the myth of the Jewish beginnings of Hollywood. Laemmle soon brought over German-speaking directors, among them Erich von Stroheim, William Wyler and Paul Leni, who joined Laemmle before 1933. Others like Robert Siodmak, Edgar G. Ulmer, Douglas Sirk, Henry Koster, and Reginald LeBorg came after 1933 and became some of the most famous Hollywood directors.

These directors, particulary Ernst Lubitsch who arrived in Hollywood in the mid-twenties, but also Fritz Lang, Otto Preminger, Fred Zinnemann, and Billy Wilder who immigrated after 1933, belong to the famous group of directors with a German-Jewish background. It would be wrong, though, not to mention film architects like Richard Neutra and Rudolf Michael Schindler, composers like Friedrich Hollaender, Paul Steiner and Frederick Loewe, other directors like Josef von Sternberg, Friedrich Wilhelm Murnau, William Dieterle, or the immense number of actors, among them Marlene Dietrich, Emil Jannings, Peter Lorre, Conradt Veit, Bernd Schünzel and many others. Most of them came from Vienna and Berlin. Today we know that about 1.500 members of the German and Austrian film community left between 1933 and 1938, most of them headed for America. Their American dream was life, work and freedom of artistic expression, the American way that they already knew from those who had left for Hollywood in the 1920s.

Other producers whose studios are always mentioned as synonymous with the very word Hollywood are Adolph Zukor, born Hungarian, who build Paramount Pictures; Louis B. Mayer, born Russian, who headed Metro-Goldwyn-Mayer; William Fox, born Hungarian, who founded the Fox Film Corporation. Benjamin Warner, born in Poland, brought up four sons, who became the famous Warner Brothers. They all, and others including Marcus Loew, Harry Cohn, Jesse Lasky, had had their experiences in American business life, but had concentrated on those businesses that were not monopolized by WASP (White-Anglo-Saxon-Protestant) America. They were, as many historians later observed, not part of the traditional power elite, not New England middle class. Their craving for respectability, success and recognition had to be satisfied through other channels, in new fields of economic entrepreneurship, of daring, and with a clear view of the needs of the lower middle class and immigrant society they knew so well. This, of course, was very much similar to the success story of the integration of whole strata of people of Jewish origin in western and central Europe. *The Jazzsinger* finally had made it.

Nevertheless, he was an exception. For those producers mentioned above, Jewish topics were non-topics on the screen. An episode about Harry Cohn of Columbia »illustrates the prevalent attitude among Jewish moguls throughout the studio years. The director Richard Quine wanted to use a specific actor in a film. ›He looks too Jewish,‹ barked the irritated Cohn, adding, ›around this studio the only Jews we put into pictures play Indians!‹«[3] And Danny Kaye was asked by MGM's Louis Mayer to straighten out his nose before they could talk.[4]

Norman Zierold gives his study on *The Moguls* the subtitle *Hollywood's Merchants of Myth.*[5] These merchants of myth had their high tide in the time of the silent movies and in the period of transition to the talkies. After 1945, these heroes of the studio system and their dynasties became of less importance and made way for new forms of corporate film-making. Nevertheless, one should not forget that not all of the producers or those at the top of these companies were Jewish. Twentieth Century-Fox, established in 1933/34, was run by Darryl Francis Zanuck, who had come not from Eastern Europe but from Nebraska. Many film histories term his studio the »goy studio«. By the 1950s, the impact of those European-born Jewish producers and their rejection of Jewish topics on the screen was fading away, the studio system coming to an end, and a new generation born in America was beginning to influence the Hollywood mainstream. Films always are children of their time, reflecting shifts in public consciousness. The 1960s brought a growing awareness of ethnic diversity and problems. Sidney Lumet directed the outstanding film *The Pawnbroker* with Rod Steiger as a Jewish survivor of the Holocaust, a film that surpassed everything that the universalistic 1959 version of the *Diary of Anne Frank* could accomplish. Woody Allen with his comedies, Paul Mazursky with *Enemies a Love Story*, Mel Brooks with his humor running over the top, were all striving for new territory where a Jewish cowboy could become a reality, albeit a funny one. Barbra Streisand proudly showed her nose and sang of the rise of a female Jewish singer. Decades after it really happened, the Jewish girlfriend and later wife of *Wyatt Earp* appeared on the screen, and the father of *Cat Ballou* greeted his Indian worker with the word »Shalom«. Increasingly, the ethnic reference to Jewish American life was becoming inseparable from representations that included the Holocaust and Israel.

---

[3] David Desser / Lester D. Friedman: American-Jewish Filmmakers. Traditions and Trends. Urbana, Chicago: University of Illinois Press 1993, p. 1.
[4] Ibid.
[5] Norman Zierold: The Moguls. Hollywood's Merchants of Myth. Los Angeles: Silman James Press 1991, reprint originally published New York: Coward-McCann, 1969).

The American dream that was realized in and by Hollywood became so influential because at its very heart was the practical cooperation of Jewish and non-Jewish, American and European personalities and outstanding representatives of avant-garde business and avant-garde mass culture. The modernism of the turn of the century that was invented in Vienna and Berlin became the very essence of visual mass entertainment. Film became an industry, however, an industry that screened the aesthetics of our age. It would be wrong to reduce this to the concept of exile, or to concentrate exclusively on the merits of the European immigrants.

From Berlin's Kurfürstendamm to Hollywood's Sunset Boulevard

For decades, rumor and biographical writing assumed that Fritz Lang had escaped the grip of the Gestapo just a few days after the Nazis took over by sneaking unrecognised on a night train to Paris.[6] And all this after having been offered by Goebbels the directorship of UfA, the major German film corporation. The scenario repeated over and over in the literature is reminiscent of Lang's 1945 film *Cloak and Dagger*. Sinister powers confront the innocent hero, played by Gary Cooper, who fights evil, represented by Nazi Germany. In addition, a mysterious female spy played with a nice German accent by Lilli Palmer takes care of the necessary erotic tension. Kriemhilde of Lang's 1922 *Siegfried* saga had been exchanged for a more sophisticated heroine played by an exiled Jewish actress. Thea Harbou, Lang's former wife and scriptwriter for *Siegfried* and many other of his Weimar films, had turned Nazi and remained in Germany anyway, and so the shift of female characters in Fritz Lang's life was rather unproblematic. Yet one may ask what was real, the historical or the cinematic mise-en-scène?

Last minute escapes from the terror of Nazism were a biographical reality after January 1933. In the case of some filmmakers, however, the myth became stronger than fact. The ambiguities of real life often were transformed into a script with very much virtual truth but less reality. Even Ernst Lubitsch and Billy Wilder were sometimes put into this framework of a last-minute escape from Goebbels' endeavor to rewrite and, particularly, to recast German cinema.

Ernst Lubitsch, however, had left Germany in December 1922, and started already in 1923 to direct films in Hollywood. He was later to became one of the most successful American-Jewish directors. Like Friedrich Wilhelm Murnau he was not in exile, nor had he emigrated. After about 50 films in Germany since 1913, he had simply chosen the best opportunity to make more and better films, notwithstanding the fact that his father Simon feared for Ernst's life traveling to a world »full of Indians, mountain lions, rattlesnakes, and any number of other wild animals«.[7] Lubitsch tamed what he believed to be wild

---

[6] See Patrick MacGilligan: Fritz Lang. The Nature of the Beast. London: Faber and Faber 1997.
[7] Quoted in: Scott Eyman: Ernst Lubitsch. Laughter in Paradise. New York: Simon and Schuster 1993, p. 87.

animals, directed many more films in Hollywood, and became famous for the »Lubitsch touch«, the combination of irony, rhythm, visual narrative, comedy of manners, brilliant editing, and the sensitive reference to the mind of the spectator. His main success can be seen within the genre of elegant screen comedies. The final script, Lubitsch once advised his scriptwriter Billy Wilder, has to be written in the mind of the audience, the virtual has to contain the real. Lubitsch died in November 1947 of well-known causes, minutes before Marlene Dietrich arrived at his home to take him to a party. Friends thought for years that she never forgave him for missing this party. Lubitsch, on the other hand, had sworn long before never to come to a party if Marlene Dietrich would be there wearing her anti-Nazi Medal of Freedom. From this perspective Lubitsch' sudden death was not entirely void of the Lubitsch touch. In 1967, Billy Wilder said: »For twenty years since then we all tried to find the secret of the ›Lubitsch touch.‹ Nothing doing.«[8] And if you, the reader, cannot recall what this touch really means on the screen, just go and watch once more Lubitsch's brilliant 1943 *To Be or Not to Be*. In 1936, the French journalist and writer Blaise Cendrars interviewed Lubitsch in Hollywood and mentioned that Lubitsch had been »responsible for the 60 films that Paramount released from January 1 to December 31, 1935, an output that represents, considering that there are 125 copies of each film, 60 million feet of footage or 18,500 kilometers of finished film, therefore an expenditure, at an average of 5 million francs per film, of at least 300 million francs".[9] To talk about Lubitsch exclusively as a director may be misleading.

On January 30, 1933, Billy Wilder was skiing with his latest girlfriend in Davos. After hearing the news of the Nazi seizure of power, he returned to Berlin, began selling his Bauhaus furniture, and after the Reichstag fire left for Paris. Film biographers, however, see it differently. According to one serious source Wilder had »read *Mein Kampf* in 1932 and, finding its humor wanting, left Berlin«.[10] On April 20, when he was already in Paris, his »final German film, *Was Frauen träumen,* premiered«; his name, however, was deleted from the program material.[11] Wilder took a room at the Hotel Ansonia next to the Arc of Triomphe, and shared the lobby with the German-Jewish actor Peter Lorre, the composer Friedrich Holländer and others who would soon meet again in California. Wilder directed *Mauvaise Grain (Bad seeds)* in Paris with

---

[8] Quoted in: Herman G. Weinberg: The Lubitsch Touch. A Critical Study. 3. rev. and enl. ed., New York: Dover Publications 1977, p. 312.

[9] Blaise Cendrars: Hollywood. Mecca of the Movies. With 29 Drawings from Life by Jean Guérin. Translation and Introduction by Garrett White. Berkeley: University of California Press 1995, originally published as Hollywood. La Mecque du Cinema (Paris: Editions Bernard Grasset 1936), p. 167.

[10] Steven Bach: Marlene Dietrich. Life and Legend. New York: William Morrow 1992, p. 329.

[11] Quoted in: Kevin Lally: Wilder Times. The Life of Billy Wilder. New York: Henry Holt 1996, p. 55.

Danielle Darrieux, then seventeen years young. In December 1933 the American film company Columbia offered Wilder a ticket to Hollywood. Years later Wilder recalls: »My dream all along was to get to Hollywood, which would have happened even without Hitler.«[12]

Wilder left France on a British vessel in January 1934. Legend has it that he possessed just eleven dollars. Lotte Lenya, Brecht's artistic companion commented on their arrival in New York: »We had no first impressions, for we had all seen the movies of von Sternberg and von Stroheim."[13] When Wilder arrived in Hollywood, he met many Jewish producers, only very few Jewish directors, among them Ernst Lubitsch, even fewer Jewish actors but a lot of Jewish scriptwriters. And that was what he became. He worked for various film companies, and became Billy, with a »y«. He wrote and co-wrote many scripts, and in 1938, Ernst Lubitsch convinced his company MGM to borrow Wilder and his cowriter Charles Brackett from Paramount.[14] They were going to realize together Lubitsch's *Ninotchka*, with Greta Garbo in the title role. By 1941, Wilder had started directing, soon becoming one of the most famous Hollywood directors who always thought that *Some Like it Hot*. This brilliant comedy is about persecution and survival, among many other topics. Many European motifs reappeared in Wilder's 1948 Berlin movie *A Foreign Affair*, starring Marlene Dietrich, and in his 1961 Cold War comedy *One, Two, Three*, which was as much inspired by Lubitsch as by the Berlin films of the 1920s and early 1930s.

The literature on Hollywood and Germany, on the German-Jewish escape, or – as it is sometimes termed – the cultural exodus in 1933, the later exile, and the reestablishment in a new homeland boils down to one remarkable, and at the same time, questionable philosophy: members of the German film community, particularly those with a Jewish context in their personal files, left Germany in haste only to avoid the anti-Semitic and anti-democratic onslaught of the new regime. Most of them, we learn, emigrated to the United States, and came to represent a cultural and cinematic infusion that pushed Hollywood into the ever-expanding cinematic heaven. But, to give it the wording of a 1943 Lubitsch film produced in Hollywood – *Heaven Can Wait*.

What is the discursive logic behind this commonplace perception? First of all, it is a construction of January 1933 as a cultural divide, implying that the successes of Weimar cinema were exclusively due to the artists of Jewish origin, and that this cultural asset, now lost to Germany, became the new cinematic asset to American cinema. Second, one is to believe that contrary to tens of thousands of other German-Jewish émigrés, those artists of Jewish origin within the German film community had a remarkable political consciousness or had appeared on the lists of the Gestapo and thus had to fear especial Nazi terror. Third,

---

[12] Ibid., p. 59.
[13] Quoted in: Ed Sikov: On Sunset Boulevard. The Life and Times of Billy Wilder. New York: Hyperion 1998, p. 101.
[14] See ibid., p. 133.

this perception could help Jewish refugees to create an anti-Nazi biography that would be helpful for their new professional careers or, later on, in the McCarthy hearings. Fourth, the impact of German-Jewish filmmakers, actors and staff of all sorts could thus be reduced to their »Beitrag«, their contribution to German culture until 1933, and to their impact on Hollywood since the mid-1930s.

Let us take a critical look at this perspective. First, the modernization in style, techniques, film language and aesthetics was a common project of the cultural and cinematic avant-garde in Germany, England, France, the Scandinavian countries, and in the United States. That the Golden Twenties in Weimar Germany were particularly golden, at least from 1924 to 1930, and brought about an immense cultural integration, creativity, and productivity of German-Jewish intellectuals, artists, and filmmakers cannot be questioned. These cultural achievements, however, were fed by a German-Jewish context, and by a strong collaboration of Jewish and non-Jewish Germans, to name just Kurt Weill and Bertolt Brecht, Fritz Lang and Thea Harbou. Second, German-Jewish directors, scriptwriters, actors did not behave completely differently from the rest of those who defined themselves as Jewish or were stigmatized as Jewish by the new Aryan authorities. Third, the life stories of Lang, Lubitsch and Wilder illustrate that the impact of Weimar's Jewish filmmakers on American film is not a result of their anti-Nazi attitudes or of the antisemitic threat, although these factors were sometimes helpful when confronting political or professional authorities outside Germany. The move to Hollywood by many German artists accelerated the artistic development in Hollywood but did not create a new Hollywood. Fourth, however problematic this may sound, the achievements of Nazi filmmaking in entertainment and in propaganda as well as the achievements of German filmmaking after 1945 cannot be explained without the contextual and structural impact of Weimar cinema and its German-Jewish artists on later periods, and on other cultural spaces. As Wilder said, he would have gone to Hollywood anyhow, as did many German and German-Jewish filmmakers in the mid-twenties.

Film history has it that the imagined and the real rarely coincide. Sternberg, Murnau and Lubitsch were among those brilliant moviemakers whom American film corporations brought to Hollywood in the early 1920s, also to »regain the favor of disgruntled European moviegoers«.[15] They were followed later on by Billy Wilder, Fritz Lang, Fred Zinnemann, the director of *High Noon*, and other members of the Austrian and German film communities. The film language, the aesthetics, and the cinematic devices these German film directors had developed appealed to an American audience and guaranteed a success of their films on both continents. The mid-twenties until the mid-thirties were the high tide of an evolving international film language that was nurtured by the visual and cinematic innovations of Weimar filmmakers.

The film language, the aesthetics, the art of directing that Lang, Lubitsch, Wilder and others developed in their Weimar years became crucial for whole

---

[15] Thomas J. Saunders: Hollywood in Berlin. American Cinema and Weimar Germany. Berkeley: University of California Press 1994, p. 199.

generations of directors and script writers. This impact, however, is not a function of the Nazis' rise to power, but rather a result of the universal film language that evolved in Weimar culture, and that can only be defined as Weimar culture because it challenged the national limits of German culture by opening the unlimited screen of the cinematic imagination. Hollywood was in Berlin, but Berlin, at least a part of it, was moving to Hollywood. Given their biographical background the three directors mentioned here represent cinematic options that could be used in a modern or anti-modern way in the cultural passage into the second half of the 20th century. The Lubitsch touch is nowhere better preserved than in the films of Woody Allen, for instance. Lang's historical perspective, either in terms of collective identity, crisis-ridden fragmentation or visual enlightenment can be found in Francis Ford Coppola, for instance, in digital innovations or science fiction, but also in French film, just to mention Jean Luc Godard or Luc Besson. Billy Wilder's realism, biting satire, and cinematic quotations appeal to generations of moviegoers long after social and political circumstances have changed, and has just recently be named as the aesthetic basics of the successful movie *American Beauty*. The three directors did not alone develop Weimar's universal film language, but to this day they are its outstanding representatives because they became Hollywood directors.

Another actor and director of Jewish origin was Reinhold Schünzel. Hitler loved his movies, and Schünzel was allowed to direct until 1937, when he emigrated to the US. He could not create an anti-Nazi biography, remained rather unsuccessful in America, although he played in a number of anti-Nazi films, and returned to Germany after 1945. One of the most influential directors, although his name rarely appears on the screen, was Max Reinhardt. In Austria and Germany his name had been a legend. His 1934 open-air staging of Shakespeare's *Midsummer Nights Dream* in the Hollywood Bowl with Mickey Rooney as the Puck was a huge success, although the following movie by the same name did not turn out to be a box office hit. Reinhardt opened a Workshop for Stage, Screen and Radio that influenced many actors and directors. It is obvious that such institutions or the many composers of German-Jewish and Austrian-Jewish background who did not have any problem with language contributed to the rise of Hollywood, and, later on, again influenced European postwar cinema.

Backshadowing Images

To conclude with a backshadowing view on the past first century of film: from Lubitsch to Woody Allen, from Fritz Lang to Steven Spielberg, from Billy Wilder to Mel Brooks, from Metro-Goldwyn-Mayer to Dreamworks – is it not intriguing that a number of directors of Jewish origin summarize both one hundred years of film production and a century that shifted between Jew-hatred and Jewish success stories? The 20th century came to an end with the digitally animated story that thousands of years ago had been a Jewish narrative. Today this story belongs to everyone: it is *The Prince of Egypt*. On the screen, the 20th century concludes with the biblical Exodus, which, in real not virtual life, was exactly what was going on between Europe and America, between Berlin and Hollywood at the very start of the 20th century. In short, whether we like it or not, as a matter of fact we are all extras in this 20th century movie.

Another way of looking at the impact of people who had or have a Jewish background and who have put their imprint on cinema may be stimulated by Jean-Luc Godard. Godard was a strong admirer of Fritz Lang, and if Fritz Lang ever »returned« to Europe, it was through the enthusiasm of French filmmakers. Godard himself, in a very reflective note, once said: »Le pays du cinéma étant Hollywood et mon pays étant le cinéma, je suis le seul cinéaste américain en exil.« It was obvious that the German-Jewish exile and the virtual French exilé had much in common and that Lang's early German and later American films had a lasting influence on Godard and other French filmmakers. In 1963, Lang performed as Lang in the film of his friend, Jean-Luc Godard, *Le Mépris/Contempt*. It is at this point that any film essay begins to stumble and looks one-dimensional because one should lean back, sit in the dark and be drawn into the real world of the visual. The film is based on a novel by Alberto Moravia, showing Brigitte Bardot, Michel Piccoli, Jack Palance and Fritz Lang as »Le metteur en scène«. *Le Mépris,* we learn at the beginning through a voice from the off »est l'histoire de ce monde«.[16] The film eloquently moves between French, English, Italian, and German. Lang, in 1933, had moved from German to French and then to American cinema. The story the *metteur en scène* is supposed to realize is, in his words, »the fight against the gods, the fight of Prometheus and Ulysses«. Godard himself plays Lang's assistant which, of course, is a cinematic metaphor. After the screen has shown the gods, Lang comments: »Don't forget, the Gods have not created men, man has created Gods.« Afterwards he quotes the German poet Hölderlin. Then he is introduced to the character played by Brigitte Bardot who is informed that he, Lang, had produced a Western with Marlene Dietrich, and Lang then says »Moi, j'aime mieux *M*«, thus referring to Lang's late Weimar film about a serial killer. The character played by Bardot adds that she has seen the film on TV, and Lang, when invited to join them for a drink, departs with a famous phrase from Samuel Goldwyn: »Include me out.« The mentioning of BB, matter of factly, stands for Bertolt Brecht. This short scene, with all its invocative dialogue, its fascinating imagery and rich verbal connotations, is one of the best cinematic representations of ambivalence, universalism, and myth in the German-American-French-Jewish film context. It represents Hollywood's return to Europe. At the same time it is, as Godard ten years later wrote in *Télérama*, a film »sur les naufragés du monde moderne«.[17] By the 1960s, the images of fragmented modernism notwithstanding, the round-trip between western European filmmaking and Hollywood had become highly

---

[16] See the script and material on the movie in: L'Avant-Scène. Cinéma (May/June 1992), p. 13f.

[17] All quotes from *L'Avant-Scène*.

traveled by those who had really lived through the last decades and those, like Jean-Luc Godard, who not only kept their hopes, illusions, aesthetic achievements and their contempts, but who continued to create the extremely discursive new virtual world of European cinema. The way from Europe to Hollywood always leads back to the visual modernism of the Weimar period.

(Copy-editing by Jessica R. Nash)

Philipp Theisohn

Nach Jerusalem

... – οὐ γὰρ ὀΐω
ἥκειν εἰς Ἰθάκην εὐδείελον, ἀλλά τιν' ἄλλην
γαῖαν ἀναστρέφομαι • σὲ δὲ κερτομέουσαν ὀΐω
ταῦτ' ἀγορευέμεναι, ἵν' ἐμὰς φρένας ἠπεροπεύῃς • –
εἰπέ μοι εἰ ἐτεόν γε φίλην ἐς πατρίδ' ἱκάνω.

... denn ich kann es nicht glauben:
Ithaka fand ich nicht, das weithin man sieht; ich durchwandre
Wieder ein anderes Land und vermute, was du mir sagtest,
Sei nur ein neckender Hohn, um den Sinn mir recht zu beschwatzen.
Sag mir: Betrat ich nun wirklich das liebe Land meiner Heimat?

Odyssee, 13. Gesang, Vers 324–328

Vom Ende her betrachtet: worin besteht nun der jüdische Horizont von ›Exil-Literatur‹ und inwiefern modifiziert dieser Horizont unsere Perspektivierung des Gegenstandes? Zunächst kann festgehalten werden, daß im Rahmen der zurückliegenden Untersuchungen Zusammenhänge zwischen Exil und Poetik zutage gefördert wurden, die sowohl über die bloße Zuordnung von Texten zu historischem Kontext hinausreichen als auch nicht zwangsläufig in eine triviale Paradigmatisierung Judentum *ist* Exil *ist* Text umschlagen müssen. Es ist kein Geheimnis mehr, daß das Exil vor dem Hintergrund der ihm zugrundeliegenden kulturtheoretischen Problemstellungen spezifische textuelle Verfahrensweisen entwickelt, d. h. zu einer eigenen Poetik gelangt, die weder schlichtweg universalisiert noch über biographische Bezugsdaten rückstandslos dekodiert werden kann. Die Destabilisierung des kulturellen Kontinuums im Entzug des Kulturraumes nötigt zum Rückzug auf autoreflexive Produktions- und Rezeptionsmuster, zum Opfern der Sinnkonstitution zugunsten von ›Lesbarkeit‹, zu einer ästhetischen Negativität, in der sich nicht nur ein fortzuschreibendes Erbe der literarischen Moderne,[1] sondern auch leicht eine Anknüpfung an rabbinische Traditionen entdecken ließe. Dieses Opfer verfügt über einen doppelten Gestus, in dem die Lust und das Leiden an der exilischen Zeichenbildung sich verschränken. Die beiden sich hieraus ergebenden Narrative reflektieren dabei

---

[1] Vgl. Bettina Englmann: Poetik des Exils. Die Modernität der deutschsprachigen Exilliteratur. Tübingen: Niemeyer 2001 (Untersuchungen zur deutschen Literaturgeschichte; 109), S. 19–52.

nicht nur das Exil als poetisches Programm, sondern vor allem auch das Axiom des Exils *als Bedingung* von Poetik.

So folgt zum einen aus der Deterritorialisierung die Überantwortung des entwurzelten Subjekts an eine symbolische Ordnung, seine ›Talmudisierung‹. Mit dem Moment der ›Verkörperung‹, wie es Carola Hilfrich am Beispiel der Konzeption einer ›Schriftsprache der Wirklichkeit‹ im Werk Hélène Cixous' herausgestellt hat, hebt die Narration des Exils bereits an; diese durchquert all jene Kategorien, die kulturelle Orientierung verbürgen sollen – Nation, Rasse, Geschlecht –, um diese als Effekte, d. h. in ihrer Zeichenhaftigkeit zu bewahrheiten, dabei eine horizontal wie vertikal, diachron wie synchron verlaufende Spur, eine Schrift hinterlassend. Es ist zweifellos die Halacha Jacques Lacans, welche diese Erzählung in letzter Instanz verantwortet;[2] zweifelsohne gründet sie sich auf die Verfehlung einer dyadischen Beziehung (die in dem Maße, wie sie für Mutter und Kind veranschlagt wird, auch für das ursächliche Verhältnis von Mensch und Erde in Anspruch genommen werden kann), eine Verfehlung, mit der sich allerdings erst der Raum der Poiesis erschließt. Dementsprechend nähert sich eine derart fundierte Exilreflexion ihrem Gegenstand affirmativ; sie *muß* Zion opfern, um die Diskursivität der Symbolsysteme zu retten und sie verneint im Zuge dessen auch den Willen zur Überwindung des Exils als eines Mangelzustandes, der Tatsache eingedenk, daß die durch sie erfaßte und erschriebene Wirklichkeit sich nur einem Einbruch der Transzendenz verdankt und daß ein weiterer Einbruch diese Wirklichkeit ebenso unwiederbringlich vernichten würde.

Dem gegenüber – und gleichwohl nicht unverwandt – steht die Perspektivierung des Exils und der ihm geschuldeten Zeichenproduktion als eines radikal defizitären Vorganges, der sich nicht aus der Negativität erhebt, sondern in den sich vielmehr die Negativität selbst einschreibt. Dieser Wahrnehmung entspricht das in den Beiträgen von Bernhard Greiner und Doerte Bischoff aufgezeigte Phänomen der ›Entkörperung‹. Die Grenz-Erfahrung der Verbannung verbindet sich allzu oft mit der Vorstellung des Verlustes körperlicher Integrität, der Zerstreuung in alle Länder korrespondiert der Zerfall in leblose Einzelglieder. Das Exil entledigt das verschollene Subjekt all der Attribute, Beziehungen und Determinationen, welche den Bezugspunkt einer Identität geformt hatten, es reduziert sie auf ein Ticket, einen Paß, ein Visum. Transferiert wird damit letztendlich nur noch der Transfer selbst, die bloße Bewegung, welche in ihrem Kern immer etwas Gewaltsames an sich hat und den Tod mit sich führt. Wiewohl das Ergreifen der messianischen Option eines plötzlichen Umschlags hier offen steht und keinesfalls zwingend ist (was sich sowohl im Fall Heines wie im Fall Anna Seghers zeigen ließ), wird vor diesem Hintergrund das Ende der Verbannung, so es gedacht wird, in der Tradition von Ezechiel 37 dadurch charakterisiert werden müssen, daß die Gebeine der Toten wieder aufgesammelt und zu einem lebendigen Körper zusammengefügt werden.

---

[2] Hierzu: Susan A. Handelman: The Slayers of Moses. The Emergence of Rabbinic Interpretation in Modern Literary Theory. Albany: State University of New York Press 1982 (SUNY Series on Modern Jewish Literature), S. 153–162.

In beiden Ausfaltungen des Opfergestus haben wir es letztendlich mit einer ontologischen Schwelle zu tun, deren Überschreiten entweder euphorisch oder resignativ aufgenommen, in jedem Fall aber als ein unumkehrbarer Akt verstanden wird, in dem Sinne, daß aus der Sphäre der Literatur kein Weg zurück zur Erde mehr führt. Das eigene Schreiben als Exilierung zu begreifen, heißt immer auch, es einer Wirklichkeit entgegenzusetzen, die die Wirklichkeit des Territoriums ist, eine Wirklichkeit, aus der die Literatur vertrieben wurde, in der sie nichts ausrichten kann außer ihrer eigenen Katastrophe. Daß der Versuch, die Schrift auf das Land zu transferieren, d. h. Poetiken zu erschaffen, die nicht mehr diskursiv und partikular, sondern nur noch total gedacht werden können, in einer Feier des Todes, des ›Opferns des Opfers‹ enden muß, in der erst das ›Ganze‹, das ›Ewige Jerusalem‹ sich gegenüber den Formen des (nur im Bekenntnis zur eigenen Fragmentierung zu erreichenden) ästhetischen Ausgleichs wie der (nur in der Einsicht der Uneinholbarkeit des eigenen Ursprungs gründenden) mimetischen Vermittlung sich ins Recht zu setzen vermag – auch das macht eine israelische Gegenwart aus. Gleichwohl bleibt die poetische Wirklichkeit, wie sie die beiden skizzierten Exilnarrationen entwerfen, immer auch an die Wirklichkeit des Territoriums gebunden. Aus ihr schreibt sie sich her und gleich, ob sie in apophatischer oder kataphatischer Rede das ihnen Entzogene umschreibt, so besteht doch kein Zweifel, daß es die Sehnsucht nach dem Land ist, die sie antreibt, wie es die Furcht vor seiner Wiederkehr ist, die sie in der Literatur hält. Das Bekenntnis zu einer exilischen Existenz mag noch so pathetisch sein, niemand treibt ihm das Wissen darum aus, daß ein *Jenseits* ist, in dem dieses Bekenntnis seinen Anfang nimmt und ohne welches dieses Bekenntnis auch nicht gedacht werden kann. Umgekehrt ist auch der stärksten Bekundung eines Verlangens nach Erlösung aus der Galuth immer die in jener Erlösung sich bergende Bedrohung einer ›Versteinerung der Worte‹, der Verwandlung lebendigen Zeichenflusses in eine Ansammlung von Grabmälern eingeschrieben. Stets bleibt somit die Schrift antinomisch mit dem Land verbunden – und gerade darin bleibt es ihr verwehrt, zu totalisieren, sich selbst als unverstellter Ausdruck einer allumfassend und unbeschränkt Gültigkeit besitzenden Wirklichkeitsstruktur zu begreifen.

Der Zionismus besitzt in diesen Debatten – wie etwa die Beiträge von Adi Gordon und Sidra DeKoven Ezrahi deutlich gemacht haben – eine zentrale, da katalytische Funktion. Von Jerusalem aus betrachtet fällt es schwer, der Schrift nicht auf den Grund zu gehen und nach Strategien Ausschau zu halten, mit Hilfe derer die textuelle durch eine territoriale Repatriation suspendiert werden könnte. In der häretischen Umkehrung, die den Yishuv der Teshouvah voranstellt, d. h. das Anbrechen der messianischen Zeit von der eigenmächtigen Verlagerung des Schreibens vom Papier auf die Erde abhängig macht, sagen sich die zionistischen Galuththeoretiker und -kritiker wie Scholem, Klatzkin oder Baer los vom Bund der Simulationskultur und setzen an dessen Stelle die neuerliche Fusion der Zeichen mit den Stätten des Ursprungs, des Heiligen. Das große jüdische Projekt des 20. Jahrhunderts, die Landnahme, verschafft damit dem Gedanken der Literatur *als Exil*, als mimetischem Umweg somit überhaupt erst wieder einen Zugang zum kulturellen Gedächtnis des deutschjüdischen Diskurses – und wirft gleichzeitig die Frage auf, wozu es der Umwege bedarf, wenn es sehr wohl Abkürzungen nach Zion gibt.[3]

Was würde aber die tatsächliche Existenz einer solchen ›Abkürzung‹ nun für die Exilforschung bedeuten? Gelangen wir mit der unumkehrbaren, unmißverständlichen Setzung von ›Fremde‹ und ›Heimat‹ nicht bereits an das Ende unseres ambitionierten Vorhabens, Exil als ein strukturell distinktes Modell poetischer Produktion, als eine Verhandlung über Literatur im Raum kultureller Negativität zu lesen? Droht mit der Wiederkehr des Landes und der damit verbundenen Umkehrung der poetischen Opfergeste nicht ein epistemologischer Rückfall in die überkommenen Muster der ›Erfahrungsliteratur‹ und des Biographismus? Wie kann das uns vertraut gewordene Paradigma vom Verlust des Territoriums als Voraussetzung poetischer Prozesse im Angesicht Zions bestehen, welchen Modifikationen muß sich eine im jüdischen Horizont wähnende Exilforschung unterziehen, um mit den historischen Umwälzungen des vergangenen Jahrhunderts Schritt halten zu können, ohne die Errungenschaften diskursanalytischer, kulturwissenschaftlicher und vorrangig poetologischer Betrachtungen über Bord werfen zu müssen?

Es bedarf hierzu, so scheint es, zunächst einer »more synoptic vision that could read the mutually subversive perils and seductions of both the reterritorialized and the deterritorialized Jewish selves as elements in a larger critique«,[4] eines analytischen Blicks, der das Schreiben diesseits und jenseits der ontologischen Schwelle nicht teleologisch ordnet, sondern in seinem Nebeneinander, in seinen zahlreichen Verknüpfungen und wechselseitigen Affizierungen erfaßt. Dies gilt nun eben nicht nur für das moderne Israel, in dem beide Schriften – die Schrift des Papiers und die Schrift der Erde, die Schrift der Galuth und die Schrift des Zion, die Schrift des Diskurses und die Schrift des Absoluten – sich beständig als Widersacher gegenüberstehen, dies gilt mindestens ebenso auch für jede Betrachtung von Exilpoetik, die sich auf jüdische Traditionen berufen will. Exil als Literatur zeigt sich niemals unbeein-

---

[3] Der Talmud als Paradigma exilierten Schreibens hat sich gegenüber der eigenmächtigen Rückkehr zum Zion, mithin gegenüber der Infragestellung seiner eigenen Legitimationsgrundlage dadurch versichert, daß er den Halachoth die Kappandrija gegenüberstellte, den Durchgang durch die Synagoge, welcher für denjenigen, der die Synagoge nicht um ihrer selbst Willen aufsucht, absolut verboten ist. Vgl. die Gemara zu Megillah IV, 3: »Man benutze es [das Gebetshaus] nicht als Durchgang. Was heißt Kappandrija? Raba erwiderte: Kappandrija dem Wortlaut gemäß. – Wieso dem Wortlaut gemäß? – Wie wenn jemand sagt: Anstatt einen Umweg über Straßen zu machen, gehe ich hier durch. R. Abahu sagte: War da ein Steg von jeher, so ist es erlaubt. R. Nachman b. Jizchak sagte: Ist man eingetreten ohne die Absicht, es als Durchgang zu benutzen, so darf man es als Durchgang benutzen.«

[4] Sidra DeKoven Ezrahi: Booking Passage. Exile and Homecoming in the Modern Jewish Imagination. Berkeley, Los Angeles, London: University of California Press 2000 (Contraversions; 12), S. 236.

druckt von der territorialen Macht, bisher hat man diese Eindrücke allerdings nur als gewaltsame biographische Markierungen, also in der Vertreibung geortet. Um auf ebenjenen die tiefere Bedeutung von Exil aufschließenden Zusammenhang zu sprechen zu kommen, mußten wir bisher somit stets auf die Kategorie des ›Autors‹ rekurrieren, von der her wir die Verbannung, den Ausschluß aus einer kulturellen Gemeinschaft als Kriterium unseres Kanons, als ersten Maßstab einer Poetik des Exils veranschlagten. Der synoptische Blick wird derlei Kategorien hinter sich lassen, er wird seinerseits die Spuren des stillen Bündnisses von Land und Literatur auf der poetologischen Ebene suchen und finden, unabhängig davon, ob ihre Übermittler nun als ›Émigrés‹, ›Exilanten‹ oder ›Expatriates‹, als Nomaden, Kosmopoliten oder ›Travellers‹ klassifiziert werden. Dabei wird ihm weder das Verlangen der Erde und ihrer Sachwalter nach der ›Rückkehr von der Rückkehr‹, nach einem Übergang in die Diskursivität und nach einer Überwindung des Todes, den das Territorium den Zeichen bereithält, noch das ästhetische Ringen um die Bedeutung des Entzuges territorialer Verfügungsgewalt, um die Erzeugung einer räumlichen Präsenz und um eine Eingemeindung Zions, entgehen.

Exil erweist sich auf dieser Ebene als ein Modus, in dem Literatur auf das ihr Andere – das Land – und auf die ihr durch dieses Andere und dessen Unverfügbarkeit abgenötigten Begrenzungen reflektiert. Exil-Literatur, das besagt stets Verhandlungen ›am Limit‹, in denen das Wort, insofern es nach der Wiedervereinigung mit der Erde strebt, immer auf dem Spiel steht, »denn nur im Schweigen ist man vereint, das Wort vereinigt, aber die Vereinigten schweigen«.[5] Nach Jerusalem ist es uns aufgegeben, diese doch ganz eigene Dialogizität des Exils neu zu entdecken, ihre Selbstbehauptungsstrategien und ihre Versuchungen genauestens zu durchleuchten und sie gegenüber den Vereinnahmungstendenzen eines ›Universalexils‹ zu verteidigen. Die Wahrheit exilierten Schreibens erschließt sich keineswegs im Solipsismus, sondern nur im unablässigen Gespräch mit der Scholle; einem Gesprächspartner, der sich der Literatur weder erkenntlich zeigt, noch an dem sie teilhat, von dem aus alleine aber über ihre Verfaßtheit entschieden werden kann. Diese Entscheidung aufzusuchen, dem Urteilsspruch der Erde sich auf Gedeih und Verderb auszuliefern – darin gründet die poetische Sonderstellung des Exils.

---

[5] Franz Rosenzweig: Der Stern der Erlösung. 4. Aufl., Frankfurt a. M.: Suhrkamp 1993 (Bibliothek Suhrkamp; 973), S. 342.

Autoren des Bandes

Doerte Bischoff
studied German Literature, History, Journalism and Philosophy at the universities of Münster, Tübingen and St. Louis. 1993/94 she took a sabbatical term in Jerusalem. 1994–1997 she participated on the graduate program ›Theory of Literature and Communication‹ in Konstanz and received her doctorate 1999 in Tübingen. Since 1998 she works as an assistant lecturer in Münster. She collaborated on the research project »Female Speech – Rhetoric of Femininity« (Bochum/Münster) and is member of the research groups »Cultural Studies North Rhine-Westphalia« and »Jewish Studies North-Rhine Westphalia«. Publication: *Ausgesetzte Schöpfung. Figuren der Souveränität und Ethik der Differenz in der Prosa Else Lasker-Schülers* (2002).

Pierre Bouretz
worked as Professor for Philosophy at Paris I, Sorbonne and is teaching now at the Ecole des Hautes Etudes en Sciences Sociales, Paris. In 2002, he edited Hannah Arendt's *Les Origines du totalitarisme. Eichmann à Jérusalem*. Further publications: *Les promesses du monde. Philosophie de Max Weber* (1996), *La République et l'universel* (2002). His next book on contemporary Jewish philosophy will be published in 2003.

Sidra DeKoven Ezrahi
is Professor of Comparative Jewish Literature at the Hebrew University in Jerusalem and director of the literature section of the Institute of Contemporary Jewry. She has been visiting professor at Duke, Princeton, Yale, Dartmouth and Michigan. Ezrahi has written broadly on subjects ranging from representations of the Holocaust in the literary and performative arts, to the configurations of exile and homecoming in classical and modern Jewish literature. Her first book, *By Words Alone. The Holocaust in Literature* (1980), was a finalist for the National Jewish Book Award and her most recent book, *Booking Passage. Exile and Homecoming in the Modern Jewish Imagination* (2000), was finalist for the Koret Jewish Book Award. Booking Passage provides a fresh appreciation of the challenges of radical displacement and homecoming in our time; it identifies and defines a diasporic aesthetic, which Ezrahi poses in the context of the challenges and privileges of an aesthetics of ›return‹. The focus of this study is Jerusalem, the incompatibility between its status as nonnego-

tiable object of poetic yearning and as map for political compromise. – Ezrahi was born and educated in the United States and lives in Jerusalem, where she has raised three children and continues to write and demonstrate on behalf of justice and reconciliation between Jews and Palestinians.

Mark H. Gelber
is Professor of Comparative Literature at the Ben-Gurion-University, Beer Sheva. He has been visiting professor at the universities of Pennsylvania, Philadelphia and Graz and worked also as an Alexander-von-Humboldt research fellow in Tübingen and Berlin. Major Fields of Concentration: German-Zionist Literary History, Literary Anti-Semitism, German-Jewish Studies, and Exile Literature. Publications on Heinrich Heine, Ludwig Börne, Karl Emil Franzos, Gustav Freytag, Theodor Herzl, Max Nordau, Martin Buber, Stefan Zweig, Max Brod, Thomas Mann, T. S. Eliot, Else Lasker-Schüler, E. M. Lilien, Joseph Roth, Nelly Sachs, Erica Jong etc. Last monograph publication: *Melancholy Pride. Nation, Race, and Gender in the German Literature of Cultural Zionism* (2000).

Adi Gordon
studied History at the Hebrew University of Jerusalem, Freie Universität Berlin and University of Wisconsin, Madison. He worked at Yad VaShem since 1997 in various projects and efforts and is author and co-author of several publications on the Shoah (i. e. *Eclipse of Humanity* 1999), forthcoming a publication of his research on the journal *Orient*. Fields of research: German-Jewish history, intellectual history, Zionism and the history of Yishuv. Current research-project: the transition in Palestine of exiled Central European Jewish intellectuals.

Bernhard Greiner
is Professor of Modern German Literature at the Eberhard Karls Universität Tübingen. 2000–2002 he held the Walter Benjamin Chair for German-Jewish literature and cultural history at the Hebrew University of Jerusalem. Fields of research: Theory of Literature, Drama and Theatre, Comedy, Literature of the ›Kunstperiode‹, Literature of the 20th century, German-Jewish literary relations. Most important publications: *Die Komödie. Eine theatralische Sendung. Grundlagen und Interpretationen*, Tübingen 1992; *Kleists Dramen und Erzählungen. Experimente zum ›Fall‹ der Kunst*, Tübingen 2000; (Ed.; with Maria Moog-Grünewald), *Kontingenz und Ordo: Selbstbegründung des Erzählens in der Neuzeit*, Heidelberg 2000; (Ed.; with Christoph Schmidt), *Arche Noah. Die Idee der ›Kultur‹ im deutsch-jüdischen Diskurs*, Freiburg 2002.

Jakob Hessing
is Assistant Professor of German Literature at the Hebrew University of Jerusalem. 1992–1998 he was editor of the *Jüdischer Almanach*. Numerous publications on German-Jewish literature, among others *Else Lasker-Schüler, deutsch-*

jüdische Dichterin (1985) and *Der Fluch des Propheten. Drei Abhandlungen zu Sigmund Freud* (1989). A study of Heinrich Heine as a German-Jewish poet is in preparation.

Carola Hilfrich
is Lecturer of Comparative Literature and head of the graduate program for Cultural Studies at the Hebrew University of Jerusalem. Fields of research: Theory of representation, Theory and poetics of sexual and cultural difference, Jewish-German modernity. Publications among others: (Ed., with Stéphane Moses) *Zwischen den Kulturen. Theorie und Praxis des interkulturellen Dialogs* (1997), *Lebendige Schrift. Repräsentation und Idolatrie in Moses Mendelssohns Philosophie und Exegese des Judentums* (2000).

Christoph Schmidt
is Senior Lecturer for German Literature and Cultural Studies at the Hebrew University of Jerusalem. He mainly published articles and books on aesthetic theory, cultural theory and political theology, in particular *Der häretische Imperativ. Überlegungen zur theologischen Dialektik der Kulturwissenschaften in Deutschland* (2000). The book *Askese und Ekstase – Hugo Balls intellektuelle Biographie zwischen Dada und politischer Theologie* will be published in 2002.

Frank Stern
studied in Berlin, Jerusalem and Tel Aviv. Since 1997 he is Professor for Modern German History and Culture and Director of the centre for German Studies at the Ben-Gurion-University of Beer-Sheva, Israel, and since 2002 he holds chair of the department for the art of film and television at Sappir College, Sederot. Several publications on contemporary history, on topics of Jewish experience, on relations to Israel and on the Austrian and German movie. His book *Dann bin ich um den Schlaf gebracht. Ein Jahrtausend jüdisch-deutsche Kulturgeschichte* was published in 2002. A historico-cultural study of Jewish characters and topics in the German and Austrian movie is in preparation.

Guy Stern
is Distinguished Professor of Germanic and Slavic Languages and Literatures at Wayne State University in Detroit. He is the author of, among other works, *War, Weimar and Literature: The Story of the »Neue Merkur«, 1918–1925* (1971), *Alfred Neumann* (1979), and *Literatur im Exil* (1989). His latest book is entitled *Literarische Kultur im Exil* (Dresden University Press, 1999). He serves as Secretary of the Kurt Weill Foundation for Music and has translated two of Brecht's librettos for Kurt Weill operas and has written numerous articles on the composer. He collaborated with Lotte Lenya on a recorded anthology of German poetry. A festschrift, *Exile and Enlightenment*, was dedicated to him in 1987. He was decorated with the Große Verdienstkreuz of the Fed-

eral Republic in 1987 and with the Goethe Medal of the Goethe Institute in 1988. In 2001 he was voted outstanding German-American of the Year by the Society for German-American Studies.

Philipp Theisohn
studied Modern German Literature, Philosophy and Medieval Studies in Tübingen and Zurich. Since 2000 he is member of the graduate program ›Pragmatization/Depragmatization – Literature in the Area of Conflict between Heteronomous and Autonomous Determination‹ at the Eberhard Karls University of Tübingen. In 2001 he worked as a Visiting research fellow at the Hebrew University of Jerusalem. Several publications on German-Jewish literature and the modern epic, in particular *Totalität des Mangels. Carl Spitteler und die Geburt des modernen Epos aus der Anschauung* (2001). Current research project: The aesthetics of Zionism.

Rochelle Tobias
studied Comparative Literature in Berkeley, California. She is assistant professor of German literature at the Johns Hopkins University, Baltimore. Major fields of research: modern lyric poetry, German-Jewish literature, mysticism, ontotheology. Publications on Celan, Meister Eckhart, Rilke, Kafka and Louis-René des Forêts.

Personenregister

Abravanel, Izchak 119–120
Abram, David 191
Abulafia, Abraham 96
Achad Ha'am 100, 105
Adorno, Theodor W. 32, 65, 68, 129
Agnon, S. Y. 50, 93, 138
Akhmatova, Anna 187
Albert, Claudia 134
Allen, Woody 208, 213
Allende, Isabel 32
Alter, Robert 36
Améry, Jean 130, 140
Amichai, Yehuda 51–52
Andersch, Alfred 34
Andres, Stefan 28
Appelfeld, Aharon 33
Arendt, Hannah 135
Aristoteles 46
Arndt, Ernst Moritz 22
Arndt, Jacques 31
Ash, Scholem 108, 110
Ashton, E. B. 22–23
Auerbach, Erich 188
Augustus 34

Bach, Steven 210
Bachmann, Ingeborg 187
Baeck, Leo 115, 138
Baer, Jizchak Fritz 1, 13, 99, 115–125, 219
Baer, Ulrich 175
Baioni, Giuliano 66
Balfour, Arthur James 100
bar Chija, Abraham 120
Bardot, Brigitte 214
Barnouw, Dagmar 26–27
Barr, Alfred 32
Barron, Stephanie 27
Baudelaire, Charles 54, 58
Bauer, Felice 65, 77, 94, 161

Bauman, Zygmunt 127, 129
Bell, Robert 27
Ben Israel, Menasse 117
Ben-Chorin, Schalom 153, 158
Beneth, David 99
Benjamin, Walter 15, 36, 64, 89–94, 100, 139, 163, 172–174, 205
Benyoëtz, Elazar 34
Benzinger, Immanuel 76
Berendsohn, Walter A. 25, 28, 150–151, 159
Bergmann, Shmuel Hugo 99, 103, 138
Berthold, Werner 29, 31
Besson, Luc 213
Bialik, Chaim Nachman 93, 98, 100
Bickermann, Elias 115, 164
Bischoff, Doerte 14, 218
Blanchot, Maurice 14, 132–134
Bland, Kalman 9, 42–43
Blass, Ernst 22
Bleichrode, Isaak 95
Blixen, Karen 187
Bloom, Allan 32
Bloom, Harold 17, 66
Bodenheimer, Alfred 138
Böll, Heinrich 34
Börne, Ludwig 2
Bordo, Susan 191
Born, Jürgen 65
Bouretz, Pierre 11
Boyarin, Daniel 50
Boyarin, Jonathan 50
Brackett, Charles 211
Braidotti, Rosi 195
Brecht, Bertolt 21, 25, 29, 31, 36, 211–212, 214
Breytenbach, Breyten 32
Broch, Hermann 30
Brod, Max 92, 107
Brodsky, Joseph 130

Bronfen, Elisabeth 2, 131
Brookner, Anita 33
Brooks, Mel 208, 213
Buber, Martin 94, 105, 107–108, 145–146, 153
Buck, Theo 175
Burger, Heinz-Otto 36
Butler, Judith 85

Calle-Gruber, Mireille 190
Celan, Paul 5, 16–17, 52, 172, 175–185, 187
Cendrars, Blaise 210
Chagall, Marc 35
Chagis, Mosche 124
Chaplin, Charlie 206
Cixous, Hélène 5, 17–18, 187–201, 218
Clifford, James 193–194
Cohen, Hermann 92, 94
Cohen, Richard I. 46
Cohn, Harry 207–208
Cooper, Gary 209
Coppola, Francis Ford 213

Dahn, Felix 22
Dante Alighieri 34
Darrieux, Danielle 211
DeKoven Ezrahi, Sidra 8, 132, 136, 219–220
Deleuze, Gilles 10, 64–65, 67–68, 71, 78
Demetz, Peter 36
Derrida, Jacques 68, 132
Desai, Anita 33
Desser, David 208
Dieterle, William 207
Dietrich, Marlene 22, 207, 210–211, 214
Dinur, Benzion 99
Dische, Irene 34
Döblin, Alfred 36
Douer, Alisa 30
Duchamp, Marcel 27

Eagleton, Terry 127
Eckmann, Sabine 27
Eilert, Heide 35
Einstein, Albert 33
Eisen, Arnold M. 72
Elfe, Wolfgang 25

Englmann, Bettina 217
Epstein, Leslie 33
Ernst, Max 27
Eschelbacher, Max 95
Exner, Richard 36–37
Eyman, Scott 209

Fanon, Frantz 189
Feilchenfeldt, Konrad 27
Feinstein, Elaine 36
Feuchtwanger, Lion 22
Feuchtwanger, Marta 26
Foucault, Michel 168
Fouché, Joseph 108
Fox, William 207
Frank, Rudolf 22, 24
Frederiksen, Elke 29
Freud, Sigmund 111, 127, 140–141, 152–153
Friedländer, Moritz 10, 72–73
Friedman, Carl 33
Friedman, Lester D. 208
Frischauer, Paul 23
Frosch, Stephen 127
Frucht, Karl 22–23, 26
Fuegi, John 36
Fürnberg, Louis 152

Gabler, Neal 203
Garbo, Greta 211
Gay, Peter 36
Geffen, David 204
Gelber, Mark H. 12, 103–104, 110
Gelber, Yoav 158
Genet, Jean 187
Getter, Miriam 149
Giorgione 59
Glaeser, Ernst 28
Glatzer, Nachum Norbert 115
Glenn, Hermann 106
Godard, Jean-Luc 213–215
Goebbels, Joseph 209
Goethe, Johann Wolfgang 54, 161
Goldschmidt, Georges-Arthur 128
Goldstein, Franz 152
Goldwyn, Samuel 214
Goor, Batya 33
Gordon, Adi 14–15, 219
Grab, Walter 159
Graetz, Heinrich 10–11, 69–70, 74, 95

Personenregister

Graf, Oskar Maria 23
Grass, Günter 34
Greiner, Bernhard 16, 53, 66, 174, 218
Griffith, David Wark 204
Grosshut, Sally Friedrich 152
Grosz, George 23
Gruen, Erich S. 41
Guattari, Félix 10, 64–65, 67–68, 71, 78
Günzel, Elke 177
Guggenheim, Siegfried 24
Gurr, Andrew 127

Haan, Jakob Israel de 151
Halbertal, Moshe 42, 46, 50
Halbwachs, Maurice 50
Halevi, Yehuda 9, 46–48
Hamburger, Michael 34
Handelman, Susan 128, 218
Hanffstengel, Renata von 31
Harbou, Thea 209, 212
Hardin, James 25
Haslinger, Joseph 34
Hedgepeth, Sonja 138
Heilbut, Ivan 23
Heine, Heinrich 2, 5, 9, 53–59, 63, 218
Held, Kurt 24
Heller, Peter 27
Hermand, Jost 152–153
Herzl, Theodor 9, 99, 107, 112–113, 138
Hesse, Hermann 109
Hessing, Jakob 9
Hilfrich, Carola 17, 218
Hiller, Kurt 30
Hirschfeld, Magnus 30
Hitler, Adolf 8, 27, 31, 152, 211, 213
Hobbes, Thomas 123
Hölderlin, Friedrich 214
Hohendahl, Peter Uwe 32
Holitscher, Arthur 61, 77–78
Hollaender, Friedrich 207, 210
Holst, Gunther 25
Honigmann, Barbara 34
Horkheimer, Max 68, 129
Hughes, Robert 32
Husserl, Edmund 190
Huß-Michel, Angela 150

Ibn Virga, Shlomo 119, 121–122, 124

Irigaray, Luce 195
Iser, Wolfgang 86

Jabès, Edmond 14, 50, 61, 63, 80, 132, 136
Jahnn, Hans Henny 28
Jannings, Emil 207
Jesenská, Milena 161
Jones, Ann Rosalind 191
Joseph, Martin 95
Joyce, James 187, 191
Jungmann, Max 153

Kaasberg Wallach, Martha 29
Kafka, Franz 5, 10, 22, 61–87, 92–94, 161, 163, 187
Kant, Immanuel 7, 92
Katzenberg, Jeffrey 204
Kaufmann, Yehezkel 1
Kaye, Danny 208
Kesten, Hermann 24
Keun, Irmgard 28
King, Stephen 33
Kirstein, Lincoln 32
Kittler, Friedrich A. 80
Klatzkin, Jakob 12, 105–106, 110, 113, 219
Kleist, Heinrich 79
Klüger, Ruth 34
Kolmar, Gertrud 22
Koepke, Wulf 134
Kook, Avraham Jizchak 11, 100, 116
Korlen, Gustav 25
Koster, Henry 207
Kramer, Theodor 22
Kreutzberger, Max 26
Krishnamorthi, Kausi 30
Kristeva, Julia 14, 148
Krojanker, Gustav 155–156
Kronfeld, Chana 66
Kundera, Milan 32

Lacan, Jacques 218
Lacina, Evelyn 149
Lacoue-Labarthe, Philippe 129
Laemmle, Carl 206–207
Lafayette, Marie Joseph Marquis de 56
Lally, Kevin 210
Lang, Fritz 18, 206–207, 209, 212–214
Lasker-Schüler, Else 5, 13, 127–148

Lasky, Jesse 207
LeBorg, Reginald 207
Leftwich, Josef 110
Leni, Paul 207
Lenin, Wladimir I. 34
Lenya, Lotte 26, 211
Lerner, Motti 33
Leszynsky, Rudolf 73
Lévinas, Emmanuel 14, 74, 77, 85, 132
Lightman, Alan P. 33
Lind, Jakov 28
Lindner, Max 206
Lispector, Clarice 187, 189
Loebell, Ricardo 34
Lönker, Fred 177, 180, 183
Loew, Marcus 207
Loewe, Frederick 207
Loewy, Ernst 29, 135
Lorenz, Dagmar 29
Lorre, Peter 207, 210
Lubitsch, Ernst 18, 207, 209–213
Lubitsch, Simon 209
Lützeler, Paul Michael 30
Lumet, Sidney 208
Luria, Isaac 66, 96
Luschnat, David 25
Luzzato, Simone 117, 123

MacGilligan, Patrick 209
Magnes, Judah Leon 100
Maimonides, Moses 46, 92
Mandela, Nelson 18, 197
Mandela, Winnie 197
Mandelstam, Nadezhda 197
Mandelstam, Osip 18, 187, 197
Mann, Heinrich 23–24
Mann, Klaus 24
Mann, Thomas 21–22, 24, 29, 31, 36
Marcuse, Ludwig 24
Margalit, Avishai 46
Margulies, Heinrich 106–107
Marx, Karl 2
Masson, André 27
Matthieu, Gustave 23, 25, 27
May, Karl 22
Mayer, Conrad Ferdinand 34
Mayer, Louis B. 207–208
Mazursky, Paul 208
McCabe, Cynthia Jaffee 32
McCarthy, Joseph Raymond 212

Mecklenburg, Frank 31
Mehring, Walter 22–23, 25
Meidner, Ludwig 35
Mendelssohn, Moses 91
Merleau-Ponty, Maurice 190
Meyer, Michael A. 129
Minh-Ha, Trinh T. 189
Mintz, Alan L. 40
Miron, Guy 159
Mnouchkine, Ariane 200
Molitor, Franz Joseph 95
Moore, Erna M. 27
Moos, Alfred 159
Moravia, Alberto 214
Moritz, Karl Philipp 54, 58
Morrison, Toni 189
Mosse, George L. 91, 153, 159
Müssener, Helmut 25
Murnau, Friedrich Wilhelm 207, 209, 212
Myers, David 99

Nadav, Mordekhai 103
Nägele, Rainer 29
Nancy, Jean-Luc 129, 132
Neher, André 132
Neruda, Pablo 189
Neumann, Alfred 24
Neumann, Gerhard 83
Neutra, Richard 207
Nieraad, Jürgen 5–7, 53–54, 58
Nordau, Max 165

Ovid 2, 34, 161, 164

Palance, Jack 214
Palmbaum, Fritz Dagobert 30
Palmer, Fred 30
Palmer, Lilli 209
Parini, Jay 36
Pasolini, Pier Paolo 188–189
Pauli, Hertha 22–23
Paul-Merrit, Carol 27
Pazi, Margarita 28, 103
Peirce, Charles S. 46
Pfanner, Helmut 25
Philo 117
Piccoli, Michel 214
Pinès, Meyer Isses 64
Pinochet Ugarte, Augusto 32

Personenregister

Pinthus, Kurt 23
Platon 46
Prater, Donald 109
Preminger, Otto 207

Quine, Richard 208

Räuber, Jörg 30
Ransmayr, Christoph 34
Reichner, Herbert 104
Reinfrank, Arno 34
Reinhardt, Max 35, 213
Rilke, Rainer Maria 191
Ritchie, J. M. 30, 36
Robertson, Ritchie 66
Röder, Werner 25
Rolland, Romain 108–109
Rooney, Mickey 213
Rosenzweig, Franz 48, 100, 221
Roth, Philip 22, 35
Ruschdie, Salman 32

Sabbatai Sevi 97
Sahl, Hans 24–25
Saunders, Thomas J. 212
Scarry, Elaine 187
Schillemeit, Jost 81
Schindel, Robert 34
Schindler, Rudolf Michael 207
Schlesier, Renate 128
Schlink, Bernhard 34
Schlösser, Manfred 135
Schmidt, Christoph 1, 13
Schmidt, Rachael 35
Schmollinger, Annette 28
Schnabel, Arthur 23
Schnabel, Ulrich 23
Schönberg, Arnold 35
Scholem, Gershom 3, 5, 11–12, 16, 64, 89–101, 115–116, 124, 138, 163, 165, 175, 177–185, 219
Schorske, Carl E. 135
Schroeder, Rudolf Alexander 36
Schünzel, Bernd 207
Schünzel, Reinhold 213
Schulze, Joachim 177
Schulze, Martin 32
Schumann, Klaus 21
Schwartzberg, Idamae 21
Schwarz, Egon 27, 29

Schwerte, Hans 36
Sebald, W. G. 34
Seeber, Ursula 30
Segerens, Horst 85
Segal, Lore 34
Seghers, Anna 5, 16, 36, 161–174, 218
Selig, Walter 206
Seligmann, Kurt 27
Seligmann, Rafael 34, 106
Sevin, Dieter 25
Shakespeare, William 34, 213
Sharon, Aryeh 32
Shedletzky, Itta 145–146
Siegert, Bernhard 64
Sikov, Ed 211
Simon, Ernst 153
Simons, Leonard 26
Siodmak, Robert 207
Sirk, Douglas 207
Soboleosky, Marcos 33
Sorel, Walter 23
Spalek, John 25–27
Spiel, Hilde 29
Spielberg, Steven 204, 213
Spies, Bernhard 2, 134–135
Spinoza, Baruch de 124–125
Spivak, Gayatri Chakravorty 194
Stachel, Gideon 149
Steiger, Rod 208
Steimatzky, Noa 189
Steiner, George 50, 136
Steiner, Paul 207
Steinschneider, Moritz 92
Stephan, Alexander 25, 36
Stern, Frank 18
Stern, Guy 3, 7–8, 21, 23, 26, 28, 30–31, 134
Sternberg, Josef von 207, 211–212
Sternburg, Wilhelm von 153
Stiefel, Ernst C. 31
Stoppard, Tom 25, 34
Strauss, Leo 101, 115
Streisand, Barbra 208
Strelka, Joseph 25, 27
Stroheim, Erich von 207, 211
Susman, Margarete 129–130

Tanguy, Yves 27
Tauber, Richard 21

Tennenbaum, Sylvia 34
Tetzner, Lisa 24
Theisohn, Philipp 3, 10, 167
Thomalla, Andrea 30
Tobias, Rochelle 16
Torberg, Friedrich 36
Trietsch, David 65
Trigano, Shmuel 131–134, 136
Trommler, Frank 29
Tsvetayeva, Marina 187, 198
Tucholsky, Kurt 153
Tucker, Martin 32

Ugarte, Michael 27
Ulmer, Edgar G. 207
Usque, Samuel 120

Veit, Conradt 207

Wahrhaftig, Myra 32
Wallach, Martha 26
Walter, Hans Albert 25, 150
Warner, Benjamin 207
Wassermann, Henry 159
Wassermann, Jakob 26
Wassermann, Julia 26
Wegner, Armin T. 25
Weill, Kurt 26, 35, 212
Weinberg, Herman G. 210
Weinberger, Gabriele 29
Weiskopf, F. C. 24
Weiss, Peter 34

Weizmann, Chaim 100
Weltsch, Robert 151
Wendland, Ulrike 31
Werfel, Franz 31, 35
Werner, Renate 134
Wilder, Billy 18, 207, 209–213
Winckler, Lutz 25, 134, 136
Witte, Bernd 36
Wiznitzer, Manuel 153
Wölfflin, Heinrich 35
Wolf, Arie 158
Wolf, Christa 172
Wolfskehl, Karl 24, 26
Wolfson, Elliot R. 185
Wyler, William 207

Yerushalmi, Yosef Hayim 1, 162–163
Yourgrau, Wolfgang 14, 151–152, 154, 156–157

Zadek, Walter 152, 154, 156
Zanuck, Darryl Francis 208
Zehl Romero, Christiane 165
Ziegler, Ignaz 10, 72–74
Zierold, Norman 208
Zinnemann, Fred 207, 212
Zischler, Hanns 65
Zukor, Adolph 207
Zunz, Leopold 11
Zweig, Arnold 14–15, 151–155, 157–158
Zweig, Stefan 5, 12, 103–113